CW00796852

THE STORY
OF MYTH

THE STORY
OF MYTH

Sarah Iles Johnston

 Harvard University Press

Cambridge, Massachusetts
London, England   2018

Library of Congress Cataloging-in-Publication Data

Names: Johnston, Sarah Iles, 1957– author.
Title: The story of myth / Sarah Iles Johnston.
Description: Cambridge, Massachusetts : Harvard University Press, 2018. |
    Includes bibliographical references and index.
Identifiers: LCCN 2018007634 | ISBN 9780674185074 (alk. paper)
Subjects: LCSH: Mythology, Greek—Comparative studies. | Discourse analysis,
    Narrative. | Heroes—Mythology—Greece.
Classification: LCC BL783 .J64 2018 | DDC 292.1/3—dc23
· LC record available at https://lccn.loc.gov/2018007634

To

Alex and Damian
Wolfgang and Max
Archer and Hugo
Orion and Remy

For what good is a storyteller,
without an audience?

Contents

Note on Transliterations and Abbreviations

I HAVE USED A Latinate method of transliterating Greek names in most cases (thus, "Cronus" instead of "Kronos," for example), but in a few cases of names that are more familiar in Greek transliteration, I have stuck with that (thus, "Knossos" instead of "Cnossus," for instance). Greek festival names are usually transliterated in the Greek manner ("Synoikia"). When I occasionally transliterate short phrases from ancient authors, I use a Greek method. (In a few cases, I have presented words or phrases in the original Greek because those who read that language will find it useful to see the original Greek, but I have provided translations as well.)

In citing Greek sources, I have used the abbreviations found in Henry George Liddell, Robert T. Scott, and Henry Stuart Jones, *A Greek-English Lexicon*, 9th ed. In a few cases, I opted for a longer abbreviation in order to make my notes more user-friendly to non-Classicists (thus, I use *Bacch.* instead of *B.* for Bacchylides). I refer to the Homeric *Hymns* by the Greek names of their honorees, rather than the names of Latin divinities: *HHAphr.* instead of *h.Ven*, for example. When an abbreviation for a Greek source was not provided by Liddell, Scott, and Jones, I used those in the *Oxford Classical Dictionary*, online edition, 2012. Abbreviations of Latin authors follow those in P. G. W. Glare, *The Oxford Latin Dictionary*, 2nd ed.

In citing ancient Near Eastern sources, whenever possible I have referred my readers to a print translation, preferably one with notes, given the unpredictable longevity of online resources. When no print translation was available, I referred readers to Oxford's

Electronic Text Corpus of Sumerian Literature (ETCSL). I cite Hittite texts according to Emmanuel Laroche's *Catalogue des textes hittites (CTH)*.

The abbreviations of names of Classics journals can be found in a list in the *Oxford Classical Dictionary*.

1

The Story of Myth

THE WORD "myth" is a notoriously slippery beast. Even if we stick to scholars' attempts to define it (setting aside the ways in which "myth" is used informally to mean a misconception or a lie), we find ourselves afloat upon a sea of capacious, and therefore frustratingly vague, definitions: "a traditional story with secondary, partial reference to something of collective importance" (Walter Burkert);[1] "a narrative which is considered socially important, and is told in such a way as to allow the entire social collective to share in a sense of this importance" (William Bascom, as summarized by Eric Csapo);[2] "ideology in narrative form" (Bruce Lincoln);[3] "a basic cosmic framework . . . which indicates where cosmic power resides, what it is called, and so how it can be used" (Mary Mills).[4]

All of these scholars, and many others, are correct insofar as each of them has pinpointed some of the salient characteristics of myths as we find them in many cultures. Yet none of these characteristics can be used in an absolute way to distinguish myths from other kinds of narratives because each of them is shared by stories that we typically call by other names. The story of Sleeping Beauty, for example, is *traditional* in the sense that variations of it have been handed down for about 700 years now, and it refers to something of *collective importance* in the sense that all versions have to do with the danger faced by a girl making the transition from maiden to wife. So far, therefore,

1

the story of Sleeping Beauty meets Burkert's criteria for myths. And indeed, as with many myths, the finer points in this story can be adjusted to make the collectively important message more specific. In some versions, the prince has sex with Sleeping Beauty while she is asleep, and she gives birth to a child while still in that state; it is the child, in fact, who incidentally awakens her by nursing at her breast. This version emphasizes the subordination of the girl to her husband's desires and suggests that it is only in motherhood that she again regains an independent identity. In other versions, Sleeping Beauty is claimed by the prince only after he has awakened her with a kiss. The kiss is a far more chivalric introduction to sexuality than the first version offered, and begins to normalize what is in other senses a fantastic romance. The spinning of wool—a standard task of the mature woman—serves in all versions of the story as the danger that causes Sleeping Beauty to fall into suspended animation in the first place, suggesting that maturation carries risks.[5]

Moreover, like many myths that are periodically reworked so as to deliver timely *ideological* messages, as recently as 2014 the story of Sleeping Beauty was revamped so as to be told from the viewpoint of its traditional antagonist, the bad fairy who caused Beauty's problems (Robert Stromberg's film *Maleficent*). The new message, depending upon whom you believe, was either feminist (an initially bitter victim of violence that was similar to rape heals herself by bonding with another woman, proceeds to wreak vengeance upon her violator, and then, newly strengthened, leads her people into a happier existence) or socioeconomic ("any hierarchical rise to power inherently happens through the exploitation of others") or something else yet again.[6] Thus, the story of Sleeping Beauty would seem to fit Lincoln's definition of myth, as well.

But in spite of the fact that the story of Sleeping Beauty is *traditional*, is *of collective importance*, and carries *ideological messages* that can be changed from setting to setting and time to time, we do not usually call it a myth; we tend to categorize it, rather, as a fairy tale. One reason is that usually, the names of the characters in this story are either generic or straightforwardly descriptive ("The Prince," "The Sleeping Beauty," "The Bad Fairy") and the place and time in which the story is set are left vague.[7] What we most often call myths involve characters with specific names who are usually members of famous dynasties that include other notable people. For Greek myths, this includes Theseus, a descendant of the kings of both Athens and Troezen, for example, and Medea, who is the daughter of Aeetes, the king of Colchis, and also the niece of Circe, a goddess who plays an important role in the story of Odysseus as well as the story of Medea herself. Greek myths usually also take place within specific geographic settings—Athens, Sparta, Argos, and Troy, for instance, and somewhat more imaginatively, the Black Sea or the far western Mediterranean. Greek myths almost always unfold within a larger chronological scheme, as well. Jason is clearly an older hero than Odysseus because Odysseus is told about Jason's voyage while he is in the midst of his own.[8] Heracles, Jason's shipmate, is clearly younger than Perseus, who was his great-grandfather. Thus, we can build at least a partial timeline of mythic heroes that starts with Perseus, continues onward through Heracles and Jason, and ends in the generation of Odysseus's children and their age-mates. We cannot do the same for, say, Sleeping Beauty, Clever Hans, and Snow White.

Specificity of name, place, and time, and embeddedness within a larger network of family members and associates don't define "myth" in any absolute sense, either, however. If they did, the stories within John Galsworthy's three-volume *The Forsyte Saga* (which quickly became of "collective social importance" at the time they were published in the early twentieth century and which have stayed in print—and on the screen—ever since) could be called myths. Is the final, defining element of myths, perhaps, the presence of the divine, the supernatural, or at least the fantastic (which *The Forsyte Saga* lacks)? Greek myths and the myths of many other cultures focus closely on gods and other "Invisible Others"[9] who have special powers. What about the *Star Wars* series, then? It includes elements of the fantastic and the divine, and it has a cast of characters with specific names and well-woven connections to one another. *Star Wars*, moreover, has been socially important since its inception more than forty years ago. Characters such as Darth Vader are widely recognized and can be used as symbolic signifiers in other discourses. Phrases such as "May the Force Be with You," "Evil Empire," and "Luke, I Am Your Father" are part of our popular lexicon and have been applied figuratively to a variety of other things. The code of behavior followed by certain *Star Wars* characters has even prompted the creation of a new religion with its own particular rituals, Jediism.

Yet in spite of all of this, and in spite of the fact that George Lucas is on record as having been inspired by the myths of many cultures when he created the plots and characters of *Star Wars*,[10] we'd probably hesitate to call the stories narrated within the *Star Wars* series myths. Perhaps they still seem too young, too potentially ephemeral—not yet "traditional" in Burkert's sense? Or perhaps they (and *The Forsyte Saga*, too) are disqualified by their clearly fictional status—by the fact that we know that they were created at a specific time by an identifiable individual: must the characters in a myth have been understood to be *real* by at least some of the audience members? Does the fact that *Star Wars'* stories are set in the furthest reaches of the cosmos make them difficult to understand as myths, as well? What we call myths typically focus on the earth and its inhabitants, even if gods, demons, and other supernatural entities pay visits from other places. But speaking of the cosmos, what about Mill's definition of myth: "a basic cosmic framework . . . which indicates where cosmic power resides, what it is called, and so how it can be used"? On the one hand, theories developed by particle physicists describe cosmic power, its origins, and where it resides, yet we do not call them myths, and on the other hand, some of the stories that we do call myths have very little, if anything, to do with cosmic power. The story of Medea's attempted poisoning of Theseus, for example, has nothing to do with cosmic power other than (if we stretch this story very hard) the fact that Medea is a granddaughter of the Sun and departs in the Sun's chariot after her plot is revealed. The story has to do, rather, with Medea's determination to retain her position at the court of Theseus's father, King Aegeus of Athens.

We haven't gotten very far by empirically testing scholars' definitions of myths against other narratives that are usually understood to belong to categories that are distinct from myths; whatever criteria we use, the lines between the types are blurry. Sometimes, turning to the origin of a term and its initial connotations helps to define it—and we might particularly hope that when we're dealing with *ancient Greek* myths, at least, this technique would work, given that our word "myth" comes from the Greek word *mythos*. But *mythos* originally just meant something that was said; it could denote a word or a statement or a story of any kind, even if uttered only within one's own mind, with no implication as to whether it was fact or fiction, true or false, or something in between. In the poems of Homer, which are our earliest examples of Greek literature, a conversation about how to plan an expedition, for example, could be called a *mythos*, as could the report about unfaithful serving maids that Odysseus admonishes Eurycleia to keep to herself.[11] In the fifth century BCE, and especially in Plato, *mythos* becomes a trickier word. Plato defines it as a false story that nonetheless contains some truth— a vital tool in educating children, given that it is through such stories that the traditions of a society are handed down. For this reason, the wise founders of a state must closely control the myths that are narrated, particularly those by mothers and nursemaids but also those by poets, who are notorious for telling false tales about the gods and heroes.[12] Moreover, even if a myth is true in the sense of saying something about the gods that is correct, if it is ugly in the sense of promoting negative morals and ethics, it must not be repeated (so much, then, for the myth about what Zeus did to Cronus, which might promote parricide amongst young listeners). Better that the good philosopher / ruler make up his *own* myths—as Plato himself does, on occasion.[13] Some fifth-century poets begin to associate the word *mythos* with falsehood, too,[14] although never absolutely; *mythos* does not slide completely to the "fiction" side of a fiction / fact divide until the Hellenistic and Imperial rhetoricians push it there.

It was in the eighteenth century that *mythos* was revamped to be used more or less as we now use it—as what is nearly a technical term for a particular kind of story, especially as it developed amongst the ancient Greeks. Christian Gottlob Heyne (1729–1812), a classical philologist, wanted to understand every aspect of the ancient texts he studied, which meant understanding the remarkable stories that they told. He adopted into the German language the Neo-Latin word *mythus* to refer to them. He meant his new noun *mythus* to stand in contrast to the Latin word *fabula*, which loosely meant a tale told for entertainment. Heyne felt that *fabula* implied a certain element of both absurdity and falsehood that he wished to avoid when speaking of the Greeks' myths, which he thought contained essential truths. For Heyne, myths had arisen from early humans' awe of the gods and heroes whom they worshipped and from their awe of the natural environment; there was no frivolity about these things. Heyne's younger friend Johann Gottfried Herder (1744–1803) agreed with Heyne's views on these matters and made a contribution of his own to the developing concept of myth that was long to haunt research on the subject. He proposed that poetry arose in order to express myths, which meant that myths predated poetry. In other words, a myth could be detached from the narrative(s) that expressed it. Herder, and to some extent Heyne, was also convinced that the essential spirit of a people (*Volkgeist*) could be uncovered by studying their myths. Believing in the original *unity* of humankind, Herder went on to draw what seemed to him to be a logical conclusion: the *comparative* study of myths would eventually enable scholars to reconstruct the earliest stage of the shared human spirit. Myths, then, were beginning to take on an identity as things of deep significance—far deeper than their surface meanings might lead one to guess.[15]

What all of these tangles show us is that scholars have always been sure that myths are out there somewhere but have never been able to differentiate completely between them and other sorts of narratives by applying criteria such as social value, traditionality, cosmic focus, ideological thrust, or symbolic value. Nor was I able to completely differentiate between them on the basis of criteria that I myself introduced, such as specificity of geography, chronology, and characters' names, the intertwining of characters with one another, or the inclusion of supernatural elements. It is impossible to define "myth" in any absolute and final way from our own perspective—and as my brief review of ancient connotations of the word *mythos* showed, the Greeks as a whole had no clearly defined category of "myth" either; definitions offered by Plato and later thinkers who engaged with his ideas remained the purview of intellectuals. This left Heyne's *mythus* and all the linguistic variations that soon sprang up in its wake (*Mythus, mythe, myth, mito,* and so on) free to be used as each scholar chose to.

For these reasons, *any* definition that we assign to the word "myth" must be understood as heuristic. That is, we should use definitions as tools to better identify and understand the salient characteristics of particular groups of narratives that we decide to call myths, rather than to stake out the evanescent limits of what was an artificially created category to begin with. However salient the characteristics that we identify within a particular group of materials may be, it is unlikely that they will all be salient in all the narratives from various cultures that scholars (or the narrators themselves) choose to call "myths."[16]

This doesn't mean that myths should not be studied comparatively—across cultures, across historical periods, and even in comparison with narratives that we don't consider to be myths at all. In this book, I'll use the myths of other cultures, as well as fairy tales such as "Sleeping Beauty," early twentieth-century ghost stories, contemporary fantasy fiction, TV shows, and novels such as those that comprise *The Forsyte Saga* to help me better understand the type of story that I will call a Greek myth. Such an approach is useful because the salient characteristics of a given body of narratives never stand out as well as they do when they are placed against the contrasting backdrop that other narratives provide.

Greek Myths: A Working Definition

For most of my career, I haven't concerned myself much with thinking about the categories into which one might divide ancient sources of information. I've worked towards understanding Greek religious practices and beliefs by combining information drawn from different types of sources without feeling the need to distinguish them from one another very precisely. Epics, tragedies, lyric poetry, histories, anecdotes, parodies, funerary consolations, the remarks of ancient scholars, vase paintings, and archaeological remains, for example, have helped me put together the most complete pictures of what I was studying as I could. Thus, my work on the ancient Greek version of a worldwide phenomenon that I called the child-killing demon drew together remarks made by characters in ancient comedies, fragments of lyric poetry and tragedies, Plato's criticisms of the ways that women raise children, scholiast's comments, lexicographers' remarks, and vase paintings, amongst other things. My work on the mysteries of Dionysus combined information from inscriptions, epinician poems, Platonic dialogues, fragments of epics, remarks made by Herodotus, vase paintings, reliefs on sarcophagi, and so on.[17] Although I contextualized each piece of information according to such things as the genre of the work from which I drew it or the aims of its author, there was no need for me to think in the abstract about how those sources might be defined in any absolute sense. I think that in most cases, this is how research on religions (ancient or otherwise) should be done: we should gather information from any place that we can find it.

In this book, however, my task is different. I'll be focusing almost exclusively on a cluster of ancient Greek narratives that, ever since Heyne invented the term, have usually been called myths. These narratives, which most prominently include epics, tragedies, epinicians, and other types of poetry, were all composed to be performed aloud; many of them were composed to be performed to crowds of many people at festivals and on other occasions when people gathered together. I'll suggest that, particularly during the Archaic and Classical periods (roughly speaking, this means between approximately 800 and 300 BCE), hearing myths narrated and watching myths performed in this way contributed substantially to the Greeks' belief that gods and heroes existed and could wield significant power over humans.[18]

Before I can go any further with my plan, I need to offer my own heuristic definition of Greek myths. I've already mentioned four of its characteristics, each of which will be explored in more depth in the chapters to come. (1) Greek myths have to do with the gods and heroes—their exploits, their interactions, and the enduring implications that these had for humans. (2) Greek myths draw upon a large but limited cast of specific (rather than generic) characters, whose names are typically unique to the single character and who are always related to at least several other characters from the same or other myths. That is, Greek mythic characters belong to a network— Hesiod's *Catalogue of Women* being an early, and splendidly intentional, example of this. (3) Greek myths are set in the distant past, although the Greeks understood that past to be continuous with the time in which they themselves lived. (4) Greek myths are set in geographically specific places that are usually located within those parts of the world that at least some Greeks had visited themselves. Some Greek myths are set instead on Olympus or in Hades, and others are set in places such as Colchis, Phaeacia, or the island of the Cyclopes that we might describe as fantasy lands but that the Greeks themselves located within the real world.

So far, my heuristic definition does not differ much from those of some other recent scholars; characteristics 1 and 3 are almost always included or assumed, and characteristic 2 was mentioned by Burkert in his 1979 study of Greek myths.[19] Characteristic 4 is seldom mentioned but is usually implicit. The fifth and final characteristic of my definition is also often implicit, but I'll be emphasizing it in this book and exploring its ramifications in more detail than earlier scholars did. It is that myths are *stories*. What I mean by this is that the most influential mode by which myths were shared amongst the Greeks was through narratives that were meant to entertain and engage their listeners, rather than simply to convey information. I've already mentioned the various genres of public performance through which myths were conveyed, but there were other, less public modes of conveying much of that information, too, some of which were surely engaging in their own ways, as well.[20] We can follow Plato, for example, in assuming that mothers and nursemaids told their children tales about the gods and heroes, some of which shared plots and characters with the more polished stories told by the poets,[21] and common sense suggests that the Greeks, like most peoples, told stories informally on other occasions as well. We should remember, for instance, that Odysseus and Penelope, after making love on the first night that they had spent together in twenty years, "took delight in telling the tales [*mythoi*]" of all that had happened to them—which must have been fascinating, given the narrative skills that each of them possessed, even if the occasion was about as informal as ever one could be.[22] We cannot recover most informally told tales, however, because no one bothered to write them down. By and large, therefore, when we study Greek myths, we are studying finely wrought professional compositions, purposefully devised to enthrall as well as inform their audiences (and of course, it is within just such a composition that we hear about Odysseus's and Penelope's informal storytelling). This point, to which I'll return in the next section of this chapter, is central to everything else that I do in this book.

When I choose to make Greek myths' nature as *stories* one of the defining elements of my heuristic definition, I also mean to emphasize certain things that stories do that simpler statements cannot. Recent work in cognitive studies suggests that creating and listening to stories—a habit that grew out of the almost exclusively human ability to play and to imagine[23]—has offered us important evolutionary advantages. More than other species, humans constantly refine their skills by adjusting them to new circumstances. Stories give us the opportunity to do this vicariously in response to a wide array of conditions and in a mode that presents no actual risk to our welfare. They lure us into doing so by engaging us: they present characters and situations that arouse strong emotions within us and they keep new information flowing at a brisker, more exciting pace than we experience in normal life. And yet, because we encounter these new characters and situations at one remove, stories allow us to evaluate those characters and situations more objectively than we could if we encountered them in real life, weighing their choices and considering whether we would do the same under similar circumstances.[24]

Stories, moreover, can be infinitely tailored to suit particular tasks. They are especially good at describing events that have not been experienced by either the narrators or the listeners themselves so persuasively that those events become credible, thus enlarging the audience's sense of what *might* be possible. Stories can coax us to look beyond the witnesses of our five senses and imagine that another reality exists, in addition to the reality that we experience every day. Stories—indeed, *only* stories—can produce the *effect* of reality whether what the stories say is real or not.[25] Stories, in sum, are ideal laboratories for the refinement not only of the talents, opinions, strategies, and judgments that we need when we interact with the people whom we meet in our day-to-day lives but also of the talents, opinions, strategies, and judgments that we need when we meet Invisible Others.

What counts as a story, however? For the purposes of this book, stories are narratives that are meant to entertain and engage as well as inform us. This means that stories are not reports about such narratives, summaries of such narratives, or references to them. Consider, for example, what the historian Diodorus Siculus, in describing a festival called the Thesmophoria, says: "And it is [women's] custom during these days to indulge in coarse language as they associate with one another, the reason being that by such coarseness the goddess, grieved though she was at the rape of Kore, burst into laughter."[26] Behind the phrase "the goddess, grieved though she was at the rape of Kore, burst into laughter" lies one of the best known of all Greek myths: the story of how Kore (also called Persephone) was kidnapped by Hades and how Kore's mother, Demeter, searched for her daughter all over the earth, grieving inconsolably until she was welcomed into a group of human women who were able to make her laugh. These events were narrated vividly and evocatively by many ancient authors, our earliest extant example being the Homeric *Hymn to Demeter.* But neither Diodorus's stark reference to the story or my own, slightly fuller exposition of what Diodorus said is meant to entertain and engage you, and neither of us is likely to help you imagine what Demeter and her daughter endured and felt. Thus, by my reckoning, neither of these summaries is a story and neither of them, therefore, is a myth. Similarly, although mythographers such as Pherecydes and Apollodorus have preserved for us the basic plots and characters of some myths that we no longer have, mythographers have not preserved the myths themselves; the information they provide is typically dry in tone and scant in details. They do not *tell* stories; they *summarize* stories and leave us yearning to hear more. Although I'll use ancient reports, summaries, and references to myths from Diodorus Siculus, Pherecydes, Apollodorus, and others like them in this book to fill out our information on the stories that remain to us, it is on the stories themselves that I will concentrate, because my primary interest is in the ways that these stories that we call myths are able, through their charm and their power, to make us imagine another reality that lies beyond our daily reality, inhabited by the gods and the heroes about whom the stories talk.

The Venues of Greek Myths

That concludes my heuristic definition of Greek myths, but I need to say something more about the venues in which the myths were narrated.

To do this, I'll adapt a model developed by the folklorist Dorothy Noyes, who is interested in the varying ways in which cultural forms (under which term she includes everything from dance to oratory to parody to crafts to storytelling, and so on) enable the messages that they carry to resist entropy.[27]

Noyes chooses to categorize cultural forms not according to any literary genre or artistic medium to which they might belong, or the degree to which they are socially relevant or convey ideological messages, or their proclivity to express ideas of religious or cosmic importance, for instance, but rather according to *how people consume the forms*. Her categories emphasize, in other words, not the qualities that might be internal to a given form (which often can be found in other forms as well, as we saw in the first part of this chapter, when we looked at myths side by side with fairy tales, novels, and other narratives) but rather the *external circumstances* through which a form is experienced.

Noyes applies two principles of organization to her categories. The first concerns the sort of *attention* that a cultural form receives. By attention she means "the extent to which incoming information is processed."[28] She divides attention into two types: *focused* and *flexible*—that is, the recipients may concentrate closely on the information that the cultural form is delivering (*focused*), or they may allow their minds to wander back and forth between that and other incoming information (*flexible*). If we set aside other cultural forms for the moment and think about only narratives, we can exemplify the difference as that between consuming a story under circumstances that allow you to engage with it completely (an example would be watching a film in a darkened movie theater) and consuming a story in an environment filled with distractions (an example would be watching the same film on TV while you are at home preparing dinner).

Noyes's second principle of organization differentiates between experiences in which information is *sought* by recipients and those in which it is *unsought*. When combined with her first principle, this produces four possible ways of consuming information: (1) A *sought* experience to which one applies *focused attention*. As an illustration, we can return to the example of watching a film in a darkened movie theater. The viewer has chosen to enter the theater and thereby to immerse herself in the film as completely as possible, rather than waiting until she can stream the film at home on TV, where her environment may distract her. (2) A *sought* experience to which one applies *flexible attention*. As an illustration, we can return to the example of watching the same film on TV while at home preparing dinner. The viewer has chosen to turn on the television and stream the particular film, but she moves between paying attention to what is unfolding on the screen and paying attention to what must be done to produce a well-cooked meal. (3) An *unsought* experience to which one applies *unfocused* attention. An example would be listening to a meandering anecdote told by a loquacious person at a party. The listener's attention is likely to switch back and forth between the seemingly innumerable details of the anecdote and the barely audible (but juicy) gossip being exchanged by the couple standing a few feet away, or the music the host has selected. (4) An *unsought* experience to which one applies *focused* attention. An example would be a news bulletin that suddenly interrupts a program that one is watching on television. The viewer did not choose to watch the bulletin, but if it is sufficiently interesting (if, say, it describes a daring prison break that has just taken place near the viewer's home), then he will focus attention upon it.

Information that is important to a group of people is likely to be conveyed redundantly, manifesting itself in a variety of forms that are spread across Noyes's four categories. In ancient Greece, these would include jokes, anecdotes, figures of speech, children's games, songs sung by women as they weave, allusions made during political orations and funeral speeches, dances and songs performed at festivals, works of visual art displayed both publicly and privately, recitations of epic, theatrical performances, epinician odes, and many other things. Such coverage keeps the information, and the messages that it delivers, constantly on the collective horizon; the forms converge towards a common goal.

The forms impact their recipients in different ways, however. Forms that fall under Noyes's second and third categories (which share the quality of being "unfocused") tend to fade into the "surround"—the daily environment in which people live. This includes, for example, artistic representations of gods and heroes on

buildings that people pass by every day as they move through the
outside world; artistic representations of gods and heroes that they
see every day as they move through their own homes; the admonitory myths that they heard as children and perhaps continue, as
adults, to hear their mothers and grandmothers telling other children
(or that they repeat themselves, if they *are* the mothers and grandmothers); the anecdotes about an ancestor's participation in a famous
mythic battle that are dusted off each year as the time for a certain
festival rolls around; and so on. Repetition and familiarity may dull
recipients' awareness of such forms, but the forms nonetheless contribute to a background that continuously hums at a "low frequency"
with the messages that they carry.[29]

Other elements of the surround are more noticeable, at least at
first: a new joke about a king's mistress, who shares her name with a
mythical man-eating monster, for example;[30] or an innovative statue
group erected in the marketplace, heroizing two youths who killed
a tyrant; or the Parthenon rising upon the Acropolis to replace the
temple of Athena that was destroyed by the Persians, with new
metopes and new pediments that host new depictions of myths. Some
of these things shift from one of Noyes's categories to another as an
individual's experience with them increases. Initially, the Parthenon
must have belonged in her first category: people surely sought to see
it and they surely gave it their focused attention the first few times
that they did. But as they continued to see it, many people's experiences of the Parthenon probably moved into Noyes's second or third
category: they gave it flexible attention during the annual festivals
that brought them into its presence but they did not particularly seek
to see it. For many Athenians during most of the year, it must have
been just one of the buildings that loomed over them from atop the
Acropolis as they went about their business in the marketplace below.
The art that adorned it, and the stories that it told, initially stunned
each viewer, but eventually faded into the background hum.

The products of other cultural forms, however, particularly those
that belong in Noyes's first category, never fade into the hum. We
might call these products "punctual" in the sense that they occur
only at certain times—for example, dramatic performances presented
onstage or first-run movies showing in Imax theaters, which audi-

ence members must seek out if they wish to experience them because they won't be available at other times or in other places. We might also call them "punctual" in a sense that reflects the word's etymology: these products emphatically stand out from the surrounding cultural landscape as singular "points" of interest that engross our focused attention. Not surprisingly, those who create them typically put a good deal of effort into those acts of creation and they thereby wield a good deal of influence over their audiences. As Noyes says,

> [These forms are] consciously evaluated for their beauty and skillful execution. They are produced to be so evaluated. . . . All of this conduces to the making of concentrated "affecting presences," objects with maximal internal coherence, maximal salience in relation to their surround, and maximal indexical connections with their audience, cultivated over generations of mutual attention. Explicitly marked as art, these forms compel us both socially and sensorily, both consciously and unconsciously.[31]

In ancient Greece, the cultural forms that most pronouncedly belonged in this category were the polished public performances of professionally composed poetry, underwritten by men who could afford to guarantee that skilled poets would be hired and that the events themselves would be well produced, with all the sophisticated techniques that were then available. Tragedies, recitations of epic, poems presented at victory celebrations, and hymns and dithyrambs performed in honor of the gods all belong in this group, for example. Some of these works were subsequently re-presented in smaller, less formal venues, where attention might have been more flexible and the decision to perform the pieces more spontaneous (such as during symposia, parties that brought together groups of men who sometimes spontaneously recited poems that had originally been presented formally, or portions of those poems), but the aura surrounding any work that had once merited a specially marked public performance and then subsequently earned memorization and re-presentation guaranteed that the work would carry weight even under less focused circumstances.

The genres of public performance that I've just characterized were amongst the most prominent cultural forms through which myths were presented in ancient Greece, and myths constituted the primary subject matter for such genres (of the more than 200 tragedies that we know about, for instance, only a handful focused on recent events in human history, in contrast to the affairs of the gods and heroes).[32] Thus, in ancient Greece, myths were frequently, publicly and elaborately conveyed in a manner that guaranteed that they would become strong "affecting presences," to borrow Noyes's phrase. They constituted a *marked discourse*, and the messages that they conveyed, therefore, were highly likely to influence their audiences' opinions and beliefs. (I will talk more about some of the characteristics of mythic narration that contributed to these effects in Chapters 3–5.)

As we go through this book, however, we shouldn't forget that the environment in which these forms operated was itself replete with myths that were less formally narrated, through both words and visual images. This meant that by the time an individual encountered a myth in a polished narrative form—as a tragedy or in an epinician ode or a hymn, for example—he or she had probably already heard its story, or seen representations of it, or at least heard stories that were similar to it or that involved some of the same characters (for instance, the individual may not have previously heard the story of how Odysseus, disguised as a beggar, tested Penelope's resolve, but perhaps he or she had heard a story about Odysseus and the Cyclops or Odysseus and the Trojan Horse, and thus was familiar with Odysseus as a character who exhibited resourcefulness). Such repetition helped to inculcate at least the simpler messages of a story (to stick with Odysseus as an example, "if you want to be a hero, be clever as well as strong"), but the backdrop of familiarity that repetition provided allowed the poets to do more complicated things as well, which made myths even more effective communicators. Poets could present a well-known story with breathtakingly new dialogue and details, for instance. What woman present at a recitation of what we now call *Odyssey* 19 wouldn't have thrilled to hear Penelope tease the beggar with the declaration that there would be an archery contest, and that she herself would be the prize? How many male hearts in Aeschylus's audience curdled when they heard Clytemnestra swear that she knew no more about adultery than she knew about how to temper bronze?[33] Or, poets could confound expectations by altering a well-known myth—how could Pindar's striking revision of the story of Tantalus and Pelops have affected his audience, if they hadn't already known another, very different myth about the pair? Or yet again, poets could place a well-known figure in an unexpected role: Pindar's Chiron as an adviser to lovelorn Apollo must have come as a bit of a surprise.[34] Or, finally, poets could invent wholly new episodes or details and drop them into well-known myths: Bacchylides tells us that, in the middle of Theseus's voyage to Crete to defeat the Minotaur, he had to leap into the sea to retrieve a ring that Minos had tossed overboard.[35] In these and many other situations, new or newly revised myths manage to preserve some of what I'm arguing were the defining traits of Greek myths (for example, these stories involve well-known characters who are firmly woven into a network of other characters) and yet they also engage listeners with their novelty. By focusing on such myths in this book, I'll be looking mostly at material that belongs in Noyes's first category, but we must not forget that the poets were able to do what they did in part because the environment in which they existed was already full of the gods and heroes.

A Few Preparatory Remarks

Two planks of my methodology can be inferred from what I've already said: I engage in comparativism both across cultures and across genres of narrative, and I think that close readings of ancient myths, with special attention to the fact that they were works of literary sophistication, will enable us to understand how they helped to create and sustain belief in the gods and heroes—whether their composers purposefully aimed at that specific goal or not.

But there are a few more preparatory remarks that I should make. One thing that motivated me to write this book was noticing, over the years, the powerful effect that narratives had on my friends, my relatives, my students, and myself. The novels and comic books that we read and the television shows and movies that we watched changed our political and ethical outlooks, our ambitions, our expectations of what our family and professional lives should be, our religious and spiritual beliefs, and, cumulatively, our worldviews. The years during which I finished the book, moreover, were a time when the power of narratives to make major differences in the world—as well as in the individual—became increasingly acute to anyone observing the American and European political scenes. I became interested in how scholars of contemporary narrative tried to understand at least some of what I was observing and I eventually came to conclude that some of their approaches and methods could be applied to my ancient materials. For, although it is true that a particular culture determines the specific meanings that a narrative carries—and any comparativist must therefore take care not to export meanings across cultural and temporal borders irresponsibly—it is nonetheless also the case that, because the basic structures and mechanisms of human cognition have not changed much over the millennia, at least some of the techniques by which meanings are *conveyed* through narratives—the techniques that work to engage our attention and win our trust—tend to endure.[36] I will move forward in this book on that assumption and will use the observations and methods developed by scholars who have studied modern and contemporary narratives when they are helpful.

At the start of this chapter, I said that "myth" is a notoriously slippery beast, but "belief," which I will use a lot in the pages that follow, is at least as slippery. I define "belief in something" as the conviction that the thing really exists outside of the imagination, but behind that deceptively simple phrase lurks another problem: How do we know whether people really believe in something? What kind of proof can we adduce for a phenomenon that goes on inside their heads and hearts? The problem becomes particularly fraught when we study ancient beliefs because of the differences between pre- and post-Enlightenment assumptions about the universe, its inhabitants and how we might gain knowledge of them. Even a vigilant scholar has to work hard to avoid slipping into the assumption that ancient Greeks of average intelligence couldn't "really" have believed that Heracles slew a nine-headed water snake or that Zeus might see—and punish—bad behavior towards a guest. The folklorist David Hufford has astutely observed that there are modern "traditions of disbelief," that is, dismissive ascriptions of any belief that cannot be proven by modern scientific methods to various kinds of errors on the part of the believers—hallucinations, illusions, or gullibility, for example.[37] In other words, we tend to reject not only the possibility that the anomalous phenomena that others believe in could actually exist but also the idea that healthy, reasonable people would really believe in them in the first place. We are schooled to assume that such beliefs are either marks of insanity, transient reactions to psychotropic pharmaceuticals, tainted food, extreme physical stress, or third-party hoaxes.

In the end, I think, the best we can do to determine what people "really believe" is simply to accept what they say about the topic themselves. There are relatively few formal statements about ancient Greek belief in the gods and heroes, outside of philosophic discussions, but we do have numerous testimonies of entreaties to the gods and heroes for their help or thanks for their having given it, such as those inscribed and displayed at the great healing sanctuary of Asclepius at Epidaurus; the small representations of body parts left as votives at Epidaurus and other healing shrines; the many inscriptions that credit gods and heroes for success in conceiving and bearing a child, for support in battles, for turning away plagues, and for other things; the small gold tablets found in graves, expressing the expectation that the gods of the afterlife will aid the individuals who were buried with the tablets; and sometimes statements that simply ask for help or express thanks without any indication of what the specific situations involved. We also have copious evidence for the Greeks' participation in a huge number of rituals that were directed towards honoring the gods and heroes and motivating them to help humans (prayers, sacrifices, libations, votive offerings, and so on). Whatever else scholars have argued that these rituals accomplished (social cohesion or ideological formation or reduction of anxiety or displacement of authority onto abstractions, and so on), we must assume that a majority of those who participated in them were doing so because they believed that the recipients of the rituals existed and were paying attention. This book attempts to understand one of the factors that created and sustained such beliefs, namely, the public performance of myths.

Having raised the topic of belief, I should pause on Claude Calame's recent discussion of *feintise ludique*, which might be translated as "playful pretense" or "making believe."[38] Calame derives the concept from the philosopher Jean-Marie Schaeffer, who developed it in connection with a broad range of fictional forms—video games, traditional children's games, opera, and films, as well as the forms of fiction that we typically think of when we use the word: novels, for instance.[39] Schaeffer stresses that the boundary between the real world and fiction, even in adulthood, is far more porous than has previously been recognized. The habit of playful pretense endures far beyond childhood games of playing house or cops and robbers, becoming subtler and more sophisticated as the individual grows up and engages with role-playing games such as Dungeons and Dragons and with literary creations that range from openly fictional novels to works that purport to present truths, such as *The Protocols of the Elders of Zion*. Schaeffer stresses how easy it is for the creators of fiction (much like Hesiod's Muses) to mislead consumers with lies that are so well narrated that they seem like truths. Under Schaeffer's model, then, any person's span of experiences with fiction is likely to include both situations in which that person participates in a "playful pretense" that a given book, game, or online experience is true, knowing full well that it has actually been created out of whole cloth by its author(s); and situations in which the person is convinced that a work that has been constructed out of whole cloth is actually truthful—situations in which, we would say, the person has been *deceived* by what the author(s) created. We could exemplify the latter situation by someone who is convinced that *The Protocols of the Elders of Zion* is genuinely ancient and must be acted upon, and we could exemplify playful pretense by someone engaging with the online role-playing game "Hogwarts Extreme: The Interactive Harry Potter Experience," well knowing that Harry Potter and his friends were invented by J. K. Rowling and that the game itself was developed by a group of individuals represented by a company called HEXRPG, LLC.[40]

Yet there is a third way of engaging with works that look like fiction (at least to us), which I take up in depth in Chapters 3–5 of this book. A work that presents situations unlike those experienced in everyday life might be understood by some or all of its audience members as truthful without its author having intended any deceit. Perhaps even the author him- or herself understands it to be truthful. After all, the Greeks thought that the Muses might whisper stories to a poet and then leave it up to the poet to shape those whispers into entrancing poetry.[41] A myth might be understood to be true, in other words, even if it were acknowledged that the way that the characters in the myth were represented and the details of the plot had been devised by a particular human at a particular time for a particular purpose. Audiences might engage with the myth, therefore, neither in a spirit of "playful pretense" nor in a state of delusion, but rather in a state of sincere belief.

Calame remarks upon this possibility as well; he is especially interested, here as well as in some of his earlier work, in the fact that when a performed myth was received by its audience as true, its pragmatic effect—its ability to persuade people to apply the ideas that they encountered in the myth to situations that they encountered in their lives—was strengthened. But in Calame's formulation, the pragmatic effect of a performed myth concentrates on the specific, and typically immediate, aftermath of that performance. The royal audience of Pindar's fourth Pythian ode, for instance, might be moved to pardon the exiled man who had hired Pindar to compose the ode. I agree with Calame on this point, but my interest in this book goes further. I will be arguing that engagingly performed myths that were regarded as true *cumulatively* helped to create and sustain belief in the gods and heroes more generally.

This is not to say that every person left every performance of a myth with newly confirmed beliefs. I take it as a given that each performance of a myth affected different people in different ways. Some people remained unchanged; the narrative entertained them, and perhaps even pragmatically moved them to change their opinions or behavior, but it did not affect their level of belief in the gods and heroes. Other people present at the performance became newly confirmed in what they already believed. And some people were so affected by the performance that they came to believe—or at least started to believe—things that they hadn't believed before. This breadth of effect is another quality that characterizes stories: stories, including myths, offer a latitude of ambiguity that opens doors but does not compel people to walk through them.

The Chapters of This Book

So far, I have offered a general description of what I intend to do and how I intend to do it; a sketch of the remaining chapters may help to orient readers further.

Chapter 2, "Ritual's Handmaid," looks at the primary ways in which Greek myths have been studied and lays out some of the standing assumptions that I challenge in the rest of the book. Most importantly, this chapter tells the story of how scholars followed Herder's lead in essentializing Greek myths—that is, studying them only after they had severed what they considered to be the "real myths" from the poetic compositions that they viewed as merely the myths' narrative vehicles. In telling this story, the chapter also explores the far-reaching, and deleterious, effects that essentialization has had on our understanding of Greek myths.

In particular, I focus in this chapter on the ritualist approach, which was pioneered by the Semiticist W. Robertson Smith in 1888 but made famous by the slightly younger Cambridge classicists James Frazer and Jane Ellen Harrison—and then was energetically revived, decades later, by Walter Burkert and his students. At the heart of the ritualist approach lay the assumption that ancient myths had emerged in order to *support* rituals. A myth may have done so by verbally articulating a ritual's goals, by justifying the ritual's existence through telling the story of its creation, or (if the myth is understood as a performative speech act) by helping, literally, to bring the ritual to fruition. Particularly central to the ritualist approach have been *aitia* (myths that tell about the origin of a ritual or some other aspect of a cult) because these have often been interpreted to perform at least two of these functions—or even all three—at once. I show that the assumption that *aitia* were regularly narrated in connection with Greek rituals is wrong. Although myths in general were very frequently narrated in connection with rituals, *aitia* themselves seldom were.

I also note that the essentialization of Greek myths was further encouraged by two other approaches to the study of myths that developed later in the twentieth century: the psychological and the structuralist. I end the chapter by emphasizing that because, for the Greeks, the "vehicle" *was* the myth, the only way in which we will fully understand what Greek myths did and how they did it is to look more closely at the effect that these polished narratives had on their audiences.

Chapter 3, "Narrating Myths," begins by showing that, in contrast to myths found in many other ancient Mediterranean cultures that served as performative utterances (that is, as recitations that ensured that rituals they accompanied would succeed), Greek myths found their power in metaphorical, figurative language, which the Greek poets used to subtly bring the world in which the myths took place closer to the world in which the myths were being performed.

Building upon this idea, I show in more detail how Greek myths, precisely in the poetic versions in which they have come down to us, could help to create and sustain beliefs concerning the gods, the heroes, and the ways in which the divine world operated. I start by looking at two recent explorations of how certain kinds of fiction, when consumed under particular conditions, can alter people's beliefs. The first is Joshua Landy's study of "formative" fiction—fiction that inculcates its audience not with facts but with new modes of thinking and experiencing the world. Formative fiction, Landy demonstrates, has the potential to change audience members' understanding of the nature of reality and their place within it. His case studies range from Plato's dialogues and the Gospel of Mark to Jean Eugène Robert-Houdin's nineteenth-century stage magic and Samuel Beckett's novels.[42] The second exploration is Tanya Luhrmann's work on an Evangelical church called the Vineyard. Vineyard congregants condition themselves to feel the presence of God through techniques that hone their ability to perceive what cannot be perceived by the corporeal senses alone—techniques that include the reading of fiction.[43] Although Luhrmann's work is firmly anchored in twenty-first-century America, her insights as to how fiction affects human emotions and cognition are broadly applicable to experiences across time and place.

I finish this part of Chapter 3 by looking at another phenomenon that attests to the power of well-wrought fiction: the parasocial relationship (PSR). PSRs are established when an individual forms an attachment to another person who is not even aware that the individual exists (a fan sending letters to a movie star, which only the star's staff members ever read, is an example). Recently, psychologists have shown that virtually everyone forms at least a few PSRs in the course of life—and also that PSRs with vividly drawn *fictional* characters not only are common (Sherlock Holmes is an enduring case) but also elicit the same cognitive and emotional responses as do PSRs with real people.[44] Psychologists suggest that the only significant experiential difference between PSRs directed towards real people and those directed towards fictional characters is that an individual who has formed a PSR with a real person is told by his or her society that the person really exists (even if he or she is out of reach) but that an individual who has formed a PSR with a fictional person is told by his or her society that the person does *not* exist. I draw on this idea to propose not only that the vividly drawn characters of Greek myths elicited the same cognitive and emotional responses as engaging fictional characters do nowadays but also that, in a society that promoted the idea that those characters *did* exist and *could* affect the lives of humans, what we might view as PSRs (imaginary unilateral relationships) would be experienced by worshippers as vibrant, fully reciprocal social relationships with gods and heroes to whom they paid cult.

The effective narration of well-composed fiction, in short, disposes its audience members to embrace entities and even whole worlds for which everyday logic and experience provide no support. In the remaining sections of this chapter, I look at some of the specific features of Greek mythic narration that made it particularly good at doing this. First, I review some recent work showing that narrating a story *episodically* (that is, narrating only a portion of a larger story at one time, as was the practice with Greek myths) encourages audience members to think about and talk about the story's characters in between episodes, which gives the characters additional depth and reality and strengthens the audience members' attachment to them. Then, I review the work of folklorists who have studied the ways in which ordinary people narrate supernatural experiences in contemporary Western communities. These scholars have isolated the types of speech and speech patterns that best convince listeners to believe such stories. I note that these real-life techniques have been mimicked by authors of fictional ghost stories since the nineteenth century and then look at the ways in which the techniques are used in Greek myths about the gods and heroes, as well. I suggest that, consciously or not, Greek poets adapted techniques of narration that they had observed to be effective in convincing listeners that a remarkable story was true.

Chapter 4, "The Greek Mythic Story World," shows how the nature of Greek myth-*ology* (i.e., a structure that was above and beyond individual Greek myths) meant that each contribution that the narration of a myth made to belief in a given hero or god simultaneously contributed to belief in a larger divine world more generally. In particular, I suggest that an essential element that enabled this to happen was the story world that was cumulatively being created, on a continual basis, by the myths themselves. Because, for example, a skillfully narrated myth about Heracles was embedded within this story world, it had the power to sustain and enhance belief not only in Heracles himself but also in the entire *cadre* of gods and heroes to which the story world linked him.

I begin with a discussion of what makes story worlds coherent and credible in general, with particular attention to recent theoretical work by scholars who have studied fantasy worlds such as Middle-Earth and Oz—worlds that are often assumed to be similar to those of myths.[45] I go on to show that the story world constructed by Greek myths possesses relatively few of the characteristics that the story worlds of fantasy do. Rather, I suggest, the credibility and coherence of the Greek mythic story world was anchored in the fact that the myths drew on a pool of characters who were each closely entwined with the others, creating a dense network of relationships.

I then discuss some of the other benefits that accrue from embedding myths in such a story world, drawing on novels and television shows for my comparative material. For example, the subtlest of allusions, when made within such a system, potentially evokes the history of not only a single character but also an entire dynasty or a complex of companions who are associated with that character. And, a well-known character may be "crossed over" into a new myth that a poet is creating and used to endorse the new myth by his or her mere presence. Thus, for instance, the fact that Persephone became Dionysus's mother in the myth that poets developed to anchor the Bacchic mysteries in the late Archaic Age secured the new myth within longer-standing myths about Persephone and *her* mother, and thereby lent weight and credibility to the new mystery cult that the myth of Dionysus and Persephone underpinned.

The final part of this chapter takes up the question of whether the story world of Greek myths is truly a "Secondary" world (to use J. R. R. Tolkien's influential term).[46] That is, was it significantly different from the "Primary" (that is, the everyday) world in which the Greeks really existed? I conclude that it was not, and suggest that this situation served Greek religion well, given that the gods and heroes of the myths were presumed to still exist and intervene in the lives of mortals at the time that the myths were being narrated. The world of the myths was understood to be distant in *time* from the real world but not overwhelmingly distant in *nature*.

Chapter 5, "Characters," falls into four parts. The first draws on the work of analytical philosophers and narratologists to explore the question of what makes a fictional character "real"—and, in some cases, develop a life that is independent of the work(s) in which the character appears.

I begin by proposing that there are four types of characters that are familiar to twenty-first-century people: (1) The fictional character who is the work of only one author or artist. (2) The fictional character who has been presented by more than one—perhaps many—authors and artists. These characters develop composite identities and in some cases take on existences that transcend the works that described them (Sherlock Holmes is a well-known example). (3) Real people who are familiar to us through news reports or history books but who have also been represented in fictionalizing works (Queen Elizabeth II is an example). As with the second type of character, these characters develop a composite identity. (4) Entities who are the subject of belief and who are described by both canonical and noncanonical narratives (for example, the Christian God as he is known in the modern Western world). The composite identities of these entities is constructed along the same lines as those of the third type.

I then propose that the gods and heroes of Greek myth were different from all four of these familiar types. The gods and heroes were not strictly bound by any canonical narratives. Therefore, there was no "Real Hermes" who could be clearly distinguished from "fictionalizing" portrayals of Hermes; different portraits of Hermes simply sat alongside each other, none of them claiming to be true in an absolute sense. For centuries, therefore, Greek authors, artists, and their audiences implicitly participated in an ongoing conversation about exactly who the gods were and what they had done during the early epochs of the cosmos' existence. The material that fed this conversation came almost completely from what we in the twenty-first century understand to be fictional sources—sources that the Greeks themselves understood to be, if not *fully* fictional in the sense of having no basis in fact, then at least fictional in the sense of being *ficta*, that is, as having been presented in forms that had been generated by human individuals who adapted their material to suit the occasions on which the stories were performed, their own ideas, or their patrons' desires. Characters such as these—characters for whom there is no clear original and whose existences are anchored instead within the drifting overlaps of traits shared by different portrayals—can be adapted in bolder ways than can other types of characters. Indeed, the disagreement amongst poets about exactly who they were and what they had done gave them an air of verisimilitude like that of famous "real" people.

In the second part of the chapter, I look at two related concepts, *plurimediality* and *accretive characters*. When characters are presented through more than one narrative and perhaps more than one medium, each narrative offers a different instantiation of that character— sometimes a strikingly different instantiation. Such characters are *plurimedial*. A single person's experience of a plurimedial character is *accretive* insofar as when he or she encounters the character in different instantiations, his or her concept of the character gradually *accrues* traits from some or all of those instantiations. This process

requires an investment of cognitive and emotional energy that encourages each person to form an unusually close bond with the
character.

I go on to look at how plurimediality and accretive characters
worked in antiquity, focusing on Theseus as an example. I suggest
that the many different types of works—verbal, visual, and cultic—
through which a god or hero was presented offered rich resources
from which an accretive character could be built over time. I also
suggest that in a society where people were told that these characters really existed, the close emotional and cognitive relationship that
an individual might have forged with Theseus (for instance) would
be even stronger. I also look at the way in which richly plurimedial
characters elude the confines of any particular narrative that portrays
them and come to live in the "margins" between works.

The third part of the chapter looks at the ways in which gods are
presented in Greek myths, drawing on the work of the anthropologist Pascal Boyer and the psychologist Justin Barrett, who note that
Invisible Others are described in different ways on different occasions. In some cases, the "theologically correct" view of an Invisible
Other is emphasized: a god, for example, may be said to be omniscient, omnipotent, and omnipresent. In other cases, the same god
is portrayed as being closer to humans in nature: the god is prone to
being deceived by other gods or even by humans, for example.

A "human" god is easier to believe in, but a "theologically correct"
god can better be used to explain certain aspects of the way the world
works and to elicit thought about how, if at all, humans can hope to
improve the circumstances of their existence. I look at the ways that
the Greek gods were portrayed in myths, demonstrating that each
of these modes was adopted by certain types of narratives: epics and
the Homeric *Hymns* tended towards "human" gods, and tragedy and
epinician tended towards theological correctness. I suggest that together, these modes provided gods who were usefully flexible; either
the "human" or the "theologically correct" god could be pondered
as a situation demanded.

Chapter 5 finishes with a look at names. The many different instantiations of plurimedial, accretive characters are held together by
the stability of a name—however each of us might conceive of the

king of the gods, he is always called "Zeus." Correspondingly, this means that behind each name, each time it is used, there shimmers a rich reserve of significance and associations with other characters within the mythic network that I examine in Chapter 4. Poets could play with these significances and associations simply by mentioning a name. "Medea" was likely to evoke infanticide, however subtly, even when that part of her story was not being narrated. Evocative names are one of the salient features that set myths apart from other types of stories, in fact. Novels, for instance, must spend a great deal of time developing their characters because those characters are new to the readers; their names mean little or nothing when the novel begins. Fairy tales are populated by characters whose names are typically generic and who carry no individualized personalities or histories. The closest analogy for what myth accomplishes through its specifically named characters probably comes from contemporary fan fiction, whose characters already possess well-developed personalities and histories that they bring forward into the new narratives that fans write and share with one another.

An important backdrop to my project as a whole, as I present it in Chapters 3–5, is the fact that the places and times in which Greek myths were publicly performed were in themselves conducive to creating and sustaining belief—that is, the myths were frequently performed in sanctuaries dedicated to the gods and heroes, during festivals dedicated to the gods and heroes. The audiences were primed by these conditions to open their minds to the ideas that the myths conveyed. Festivals and myths, thus, mutually supported each other.

Chapters 6 and 7 focus on the two subjects that I suggest are most distinctively characteristic of Greek myths and of their particular ways of engaging audiences: the frequency with which myths tell of metamorphosis (a person being changed into an animal, plant, or mineral) and the prominence of heroes (humans with extraordinary traits or abilities). Each of these chapters is underpinned by the methodology and conclusions of Chapters 3–5 (that is, they look for the particular ways in which the narrative vividness inherent to each type of myth enabled it to help create and sustain belief in certain aspects of the divine world and its inhabitants), but in order to do this, each delves into its topic in other ways as well. These two chapters also share an increased emphasis on comparison. Because I want to argue that these two types of myths are characteristically *Greek*, I discuss how they do, and do not, share certain aspects with myths taken from other cultures and sometimes with stories from other cultures that are typically called legends or fairy tales. Comparison brings the qualities of the Greek myths into sharper focus and thus enables us better to understand *why* Greek myths are different from, or similar to, other myths.

Chapter 6, "Metamorphoses," begins by noting just how remarkable the Greek penchant for stories about metamorphosis is; other cultures fall far behind in this respect. (I distinguish between *metamorphosis*, in which an outside power permanently changes a human into something else, and *shape-shifting*, in which a human has the ability to turn him- or herself into something else temporarily. Stories of shape-shifting are fairly common in other cultures but very rare in Greece.)

In the next section, I look at hybrids (e.g., the Chimaera, Pegasus, the Hydra), a category of creature that is often discussed alongside myths of metamorphosis but which, I argue, should be kept distinct. I show that mythmakers put considerable effort into anchoring hybrids within the network of Greek mythic characters that is discussed in Chapter 4. The hybrids have mothers and fathers, children, and friends amongst the gods and heroes; they are, in that sense, a normal part of the divine world. Story details flesh out those relationships: Callirhoe and Pasiphae suckle their monstrous babies (Geryon and the Minotaur) and Circe tells Odysseus that Crataeis, the mother of Scylla, will be able to restrain her daughter from making a second attack on Odysseus's ship, if Odysseus asks Crataeis to do so. For hybrids, family relations determine the experiences of a character just as much as they do for anyone else in the divine world, in other words.

The chapter then shifts to its main focus, metamorphosis. I argue that the long history of scholarly attempts to find a system of specific meanings hidden behind metamorphic myths has been misguided. Although a myth about a woman turning into a dog might *secondarily* say something about the male view of women, for example, or a myth about a cannibalistic king turning into a wolf might *secondarily* say something about human dietary prohibitions, no single interpretative key (or even set of keys) has ever been found that convincingly decodes metamorphic myths as a whole. The individual stories themselves changed quite a bit in antiquity, moreover; the details behind Hecabe's transformation into a dog are staggeringly varied, for instance.

After having presented case studies that test several modes of interpretation, I suggest two things. The first is that the most successful approach to understanding metamorphic myths will combine aspects of work pioneered by Maurizio Bettini[47] that centers on affordances (characteristics of a person, animal, or object that are open to multiple interpretations) and aspects of work by John Scheid and Jesper Svenbro[48] that emphasizes the fluidity of myths, each of which is a concatenation of various ideas that uniquely suits the circumstances of its narration. I use a myth about Arachne as a case study to show this. The second is that the primary characteristic of metamorphic myths, collectively, is their ability induce wonder—to grab and hold attention.

In this sense, the metamorphic myths fall into line alongside sightings of the Dioscuri atop the masts of ships, reports of the gods appearing on battlefields to shore up their favorite side, and Asclepius appearing to cure patients in their dreams—all of which are alleged to have happened in the "real life" of historical Greece. The metamorphic myths included—indeed, they fervently embraced—the negative side of the gods' power and how it affected humans, however. Metamorphic myths, then, were a place where the Greeks could think about an aspect of the gods' nature, and its potential to explode at any moment into mortal life that they did not care to confront in other venues, such as public inscriptions and prayers.

Chapter 7, "Heroes," begins by emphasizing the enormous popularity of myths about heroes in ancient Greece. A survey of Archaic and Classical literature demonstrates that, although gods are found to some degree in almost every kind of mythic narrative, heroes are far more often the *main* characters, around whom the narratives revolve. For comparison, I look at myths from ancient Near Eastern cultures. Although scholars agree that Greek cosmogonic and theogonic myths were strongly influenced by ancient Near Eastern myths, the situation is different when it comes to myths about heroes. In ancient Near Eastern myths, gods most often took center stage. The hero, then, as the Greeks developed him, was a distinctive feature of their myths and cults.

The chapter goes on to look at the hero as a narrative character, developing some of the ideas on episodic narration that were presented in Chapter 3. There are two distinct types of episodic narration: *serials*, in which narratives told across episodes have an overall arc; and *series*, in which there is no overall narrative arc. In *serials*, characters undergo changes and develop; in *series*, they change very little, remaining stable in episode after episode, existing eternally in a sort of "golden age." Whereas gods in Greek myths are series-type characters, heroes partake of both sorts of episodic narration. Because every hero is born and dies, there is necessarily a narrative arc to his overall story (which audience members knew very well and which poets sometimes emphasized), but because poets could almost infinitely invent new adventures for the heroes, or insert new side episodes into existing adventures, heroes also went on forever, eternally unchanged. This dual mode of presenting heroes kept them in a balanced tension between the human and divine.

I next discuss the hero as monster killer. I begin again from ancient Near Eastern myths, in which the norm is for *gods* to kill monsters and in which monster killing usually has cosmogonic associations. In contrast, Greek gods seldom kill monsters. Instead, there are many Greek myths about *heroes* killing monsters; this is, indeed, one of the defining characteristics of the Greek hero. A close reading of some passages from Hesiod and the Homeric *Hymn to Apollo* suggests that originally, Greek gods, like their Near Eastern counterparts, did kill monsters but that, as the Greeks developed the figure of the hero during the Archaic Age, the heroes gradually took over this task. The heroes—figures poised halfway between gods and humans—thus assumed a significant part of the responsibility for creating a world in which normal humans could live and thrive.

The chapter finishes with a look at the end of heroes. Once again developing a new twist on some Near Eastern stories, the epic poets sang of a moment in cosmic history when the gods had come to feel that the flourishing human race was a burden. Zeus decided that war was the best means of trimming the population and instigated first the Theban War and then the Trojan War. Many heroes died on these battlefields or while returning home from them.

These wars gave the last of the heroes ample opportunities to display their skills in combat, but after the carnage had cleared, the humans who were left behind could only pray for their heroic ancestors' help from beyond the grave and reiterate what had made those ancestors great by telling myths about their exploits. Those stories, and the stories about the gods that were intertwined with the heroes' stories, are what the pages that follow will discuss.

2

Ritual's Handmaid

AT THE TURN of the last century—a time when classicists still ruled the academic roost and every educated man and woman knew their Greek and Roman myths—there arose an idea that circled out into the wider world, changing the way that the myths and literatures of many cultures were understood, and then circled back again into classics like an aboriginal boomerang. I want to begin the work that I'll do in the rest of this book with a history of that idea—for, until we examine its ancestry and the effects that it has had, we won't understand how the study of Greek myths ended up where it did and why we now need to take a different path.

By "idea," I mean what is commonly known as the "ritualist approach"—that is, the idea that myths are somehow connected to rituals. In its strongest version (the one offered by its founding father), this meant that myths were created in order to explain or justify the existence of rituals. As time went on, some scholars argued the opposite—that rituals enacted myths—or conceded that myths and rituals might arise hand in hand, yet even in these versions of the theory, myths were implicitly the weaker partners: rituals were what people *did* and myths were only what people *said*.[1] Whichever version of the theory one embraced, myths had to be adjusted in some way before they neatly matched up with the rituals in question. Typically, this meant stripping away or altering what was taken to be

34

the extraneous narrative material through which myths were conveyed—the characters' names or details of the plot, for example—in order to get at what was understood to be a myth's true core and its real, essential meaning. Having been thus extracted from any real, lived experience, myths ended up seeming more like equations to be solved by clever scholars than tales that had once engaged and entertained ordinary people—a situation that set the study of myth on a misguided track for more than a hundred years.

The King That Wouldn't Die

In a series of lectures delivered at the University of Aberdeen between 1888 and 1891, William Robertson Smith, a biblical critic and Semiticist,[2] proposed that whereas the heart of any modern religion lay in its system of beliefs, "primitive" religions focused instead on rituals.[3] Rather than beliefs, these religions had myths, and the myths were intended to explain not the nature of the universe and all it contained (as E. B. Tylor had proposed two decades earlier in his magnum opus, *Primitive Religion*) but the existence of the rituals themselves, whose real origins had been long forgotten. In other words, as props for religious systems, myths were doubly derivative and doubly defective: they existed only because rituals did, and those who performed the rituals could not even remember why they did so in the first place. "Primitive," a word that Smith used more or less interchangeably with "ancient," included the religions of Greece, where

> certain things were done at a temple, and people were agreed that it would be impious not to do them. But if you had asked why they were done, you would probably have had several mutually exclusive explanations from different persons, and no one would have thought it a matter of the least religious importance which of these you chose to adopt.[4]

Smith's book drew considerable attention within the scholarly community, but it was his younger (and much longer-lived) friend James Frazer who carried the link between myth and ritual out into the wider world with *The Golden Bough*, a work that, in its third edition, filled twelve volumes with myths and rituals that Frazer had patiently gathered from "primitive" cultures throughout the world and across historical periods.[5] He used this material to promote two ideas that interest us here. The first was that cultures pass through three evolutionary stages. During the earliest and most primitive stage, people trust in magic and therefore focus their energies on the performance of rituals. During the second, people trust in religion and focus upon dogma or creed, which is expressed through myths. During the last and most highly developed stage, into which the industrialized Western world had already moved, according to Frazer, people trust in science and need neither myth nor ritual. Cultures that are stalled between the first and second stages—cultures hanging halfway between magic and religion—tend to bind together rituals and myths, Frazer proposed. More specifically, in these stalled cultures, myths are used to lend meaning to rituals, and rituals reenact myths in such a way as to ensure that the action narrated by the myth will recur in the real world.

Frazer's second idea was that many myths and rituals center on a figure who sometimes appears as a god and sometimes as a king but who always represents the vegetation, and thus the vitality of the world. Like the vegetation, this figure has to periodically die and be "reborn" in order to renew the world's vitality; many rituals enact this death and rebirth either metaphorically or in reality. Frazer proposed that Adonis, Attis, Osiris, Balder, and Dionysus were instantiations of this dying-and-reviving god, which doesn't stretch credibility too far, but he also proposed that many, far less obvious candidates belonged in the group as well: Jupiter and the entire mythical dynasties of Boeotia and Thessaly, for example.

The paradigm of the dying-and-reviving god caught the imaginations not only of other scholars, who used it to interpret the myths and literatures of the cultures they studied but also of literary authors, who helped to bring it to wider public attention—T. S. Eliot evokes it in *The Waste Land* and William Butler Yeats in *Sailing to Byzantium*, for example. This, in turn, gave the accompanying idea that myths and rituals were mutually dependent a remarkable tenaciousness. The paradigm also helped to revive an older and more general paradigm: the idea that, even in the absence of a central god or king, many myths and rituals were at heart about the annual growth, death, and regeneration of plants, however deeply buried this agenda might be beneath what were dismissed as superficial features. Versions of this paradigm had been around in various forms since the time of the ancient allegorists, but by focusing it upon the figure of a god or king who dies and is resurrected, Frazer gave it new élan and, within the largely Christian West, a new relevance.

This gave new life to an idea that had been around since the early nineteenth century, when comparative mythology had become popular: namely, that there were a limited number of "Ur-myths"— myths that had been shared by all or most cultures since the beginning of time, however varied the forms of expression they took. The identification of these Ur-myths and their underlying meanings was, in fact, amongst the most pressing tasks of a comparativist such as Frazer. The search for Ur-myths (and the Ur-figures who populated them, such as Max Müller's solar deity or Frazer's dying-and-reviving god) had led to the scholarly habit of reducing any given myth to what one had decided was its true essence—which in turn meant disengaging the myth from its narratives, which were understood to be merely its vehicles. Thus, for Frazer, who provided fifty-two pages of parallels for the story of Odysseus and Polyphemus in his commentary to Apollodorus's *Library of Mythology*, what seems to have mattered most was not how Apollodorus or Homer or anyone else had told the tale but rather the fact that certain episodes within it were echoed by episodes in similar stories from around the world. For example, Frazer proposed that Odysseus's taunting of the blinded Polyphemus, which led Polyphemus to throw rocks at Odysseus's ship, echoes stories in which a hero has a ring or some other magical object stuck to his body that cries out to a blinded foe as the hero tries to escape. Frazer concluded that behind all of these stories there must be "a common original, whether that original was the narrative in the *Odyssey*, or, more probably, a still older folktale which Homer incorporated in his epic."[6]

Frazer was by no means consistent in his presentation of this idea (how could he be, over the span of a continuously evolving, twelve-volume work, to say nothing of his other publications on the topic?), but generally speaking, at least for the cultures on which he focused his attention—the cultures stranded between the first and second evolutionary stages, including ancient Greece—he suggested, in contrast to Smith, that myths were chronologically prior to the rituals with which they were paired. Rituals enacted what myths had already described; without the preexisting tale of a god of vegetation who dies and is revived there could be no ritual in which a human king, standing in for the god, was killed and revived in order to ensure the return of that god and the vegetation that accompanies him.

The next important figure in this story—and probably the most important figure in this story, period—returned to Smith's prioritization of ritual. Jane Ellen Harrison, who like Frazer was associated with the University of Cambridge off and on throughout her career, was at the center of a group of scholars who later came to be called the Cambridge Ritualists. The label is not entirely correct: they were never a formal group, as the capitalization of "Ritualists" might imply, and "Cambridge" is too limited a geographic tag, given that one of them, Gilbert Murray, taught at Oxford and that the theories of (the German) Friedrich Nietzsche and (the French) Émile Durkheim were at least as important to their version of the ritualist paradigm as were Frazer's. The fact that the label has nonetheless stuck tells us something about how deeply later generations were invested in the theory that the group was understood to promote; situating its birth within a collective of scholars working at one of the fonts of European learning gave it additional legitimacy.

The word "collective" also stretches a point. Murray and Francis Cornford, who are always included amongst the "Cambridge Ritualists," as well as A. B. Cook, who is sometimes included, certainly had important and influential careers as classicists and made contributions to the theory and its popularization. Murray's widely read *Four Stages of Greek Religion*, revised as *Five Stages of Greek Religion*, was particularly significant in underscoring the primitive stage of Greek religion (a world ruled by "Giants and Gorgons") that had preceded the time of "quiet splendour" overseen by the Olympians.[7] It was Harrison, however, who put a distinctive stamp, as well as a dark glamour, upon it. One of the first female scholars to make an international name for herself, she knew how to play to her audience: her flamboyant mode of dress and her use of the magic lantern (a proto-version of PowerPoint and at the time the latest thing in technology), in combination with the intrinsic excitement of her material and interpretations, gave her lectures a drama seldom found in the rhetorical desert of academia and helped to carry her ideas well beyond Cambridge.[8]

Harrison took up Frazer's dying-and-reviving god and gave him a different name, Eniautos-Daimon, a Greek term of her own invention that meant "Year-Spirit."[9] Her introduction of this figure rested on an ancient hymn that had been recently discovered in a sanctuary of Zeus on Crete. She proposed that the hymn was the libretto of a ritual performed annually to welcome home Zeus in the guise of a young man (*kouros*). The advent of this god reawakened the vitality not only of the fields and flocks but also of the social order itself. And with the involvement of the social order, things took a new turn. In a development that cast a very long shadow over the study of Greek religion, Harrison proposed that the ritual celebrating the return of the divine *kouros* simultaneously functioned as an "initiation" ritual like those that anthropologists were discovering amongst primitive tribes of her own day. That is, the hymn was composed to accompany a ritual in which adult status was conferred on local youths, and Zeus, as the *kouros* of the hymn, represented those youths.[10] Durkheim's sociological approach to religion is clearly evident here, but Frazer himself provided the most valuable example for Harrison's initiation paradigm, which he found amongst the Wiradthuri, aborigines of New South Wales.[11] Here again, we see comparativism at work and, in its wake, the idea that, if primitive cultures elsewhere had initiation rituals and myths, then ancient Greece must have had them as well, and in approximately the same forms, which we would be able to discover if only we could prevent ourselves from being distracted by extraneous particulars that disguised them.

In this case, those extraneous particulars included the fact that whereas initiation myths and rituals typically narrate or dramatize the advent, death, and resurrection of their central characters, the Cretan hymn tells about only the advent of the *kouros*—not his death and resurrection. To help fill the gap, Harrison drew on myths in which Zeus, Dionysus, and an enigmatic god known as Zagreus appeared as babies or young children who were guarded by divinities known as Kouretes; in some of these myths, the young god was killed in spite of the Kouretes' care and then was resurrected. With what Harrison assumed was the full myth behind the Cretan hymn now in hand, she reconstructed what must have had happened in the Cretan ceremony, closely following along the lines of Frazer's example from New South Wales and concluding that "with the Cretan ritual in our minds it is clear that the Wiradthuri rites present more than an analogy; *mutato nomine*, the account could have been written of Zagreus."[12]

In spite of Harrison's precarious mode of argumentation (the myth behind the hymn is reconstructed from other myths, and the reconstructed myth is paired with selected aboriginal *comparanda* to reconstruct the ritual, which then matches up nicely with the reconstructed myth), she was more or less right as far as subsequent scholarship has concluded: at some point, what we can call an initiation-type ritual probably was performed for young men on Crete, and the myths of Zeus, Dionysus, and Zagreus probably reflect that ritual (although as we see them in our existing sources, these myths are being put to other uses).[13] Not content to stop with the Cretan material, however, Harrison strove to prove that her own version of the initiation paradigm, centering on the Eniautos-Daimon, was more widely established in ancient Greece. She claimed that it lurked behind the myths of Heracles, Achilles, and Neoptolemus and, more distantly, the fates of mythic sinners condemned to suffer punishment in the Underworld, for example. Francis Cornford contributed a chapter to her book in which he argued that it underlay the myth of Pelops, as well; Gilbert Murray contributed a chapter in which he suggested that aspects of Theseus, Hippolytus, and other heroes could also be explained by this paradigm.[14] The fact that some of these characters were killed but never resurrected didn't seem to pose a problem. Nor did the fact that some of them underwent their deaths and "resurrections" when they were fully grown. Myths, in the opinion of the Cambridge Ritualists, were notoriously unreliable, forever drifting away from representing rituals accurately until a scholar yanked them back into line. A statement about this issue that Harrison made early in her career became emblematic not only of her own work but also of the ritualist approach more generally: "*ritual practice misunderstood* explains the elaboration of myth."[15]

This is not to say that for Harrison, strictly speaking, rituals had to exist before myths, as they had for Smith. At one point, she conjectured that the two could have arisen *pari passu*, with the first myths (*muthoi*) being nothing other than the emotionally charged, barely articulate outcries ("*mu!*") made by participants when they performed the rituals. Slowly, she suggested, these cries evolved into stories that narrated what the ritual enacted and then, much later, became *aitia* that justified a ritual's existence in much the way that Smith had imagined.[16] But her conjecture that myths and rituals had arisen simultaneously at the dawn of human existence in no way changed her opinion that the myths we inherited from classical authors were secondary growths, aggravatingly distorted by the niceties of the narrative vehicles that carried them forward in time. These myths would always be only handmaids to rituals, in the sense of justifying their actions, and handmaids to scholars in the sense of helping them reconstruct those rituals, which was the real prize after which the scholars quested. Like handmaids, in other words, the myths that scholars had inherited needed to be properly disciplined if they were to be of any use. By their nature, they tended to dissemble, hiding their true meanings behind the loveliness of their expression. They were, for Harrison, "shifting," "manifold," "unsatisfactory," and even "absurd."[17]

This is where Nietzsche's influence on Harrison becomes especially interesting.[18] Harrison turned the schematic opposition between what Nietzsche called the Apollonian and Dionysian forces in Greek culture into her own evolutionary (or rather devolutionary) theory of Greek religion. In the earliest stages of Greek culture, she suggests, the Greeks were Dionysian; they practiced genuine rituals that were full of excitement, enacting raw, primal instincts. Their "gods" were not really gods at all but rather daimonic projections of Durkheimian collective effervescence. As these *daimones* began to be anthropomorphized, they became "ghosts, sprites and bogeys,"[19] to whom one dedicated rituals that had been previously performed without any thought of a recipient. These bogeys then developed into more clearly differentiated entities such as the Erinyes, and from them, in turn, there developed goddesses concerned with ethics and morals, such as Athena. Eventually, the bogeys were altogether displaced by the family of Olympian gods, and Greek religion entered its fully rational "Apollonian" period—that is, it moved to the other end of the schematic spectrum. For Harrison, this period was characterized by the subordination of genuinely religious rituals to a religion dominated by myths that were intended primarily to showcase Olympian splendor.[20]

This was not the sort of religion for which Harrison felt any affinity: "Great things in literature, Greek plays for example, I most enjoy when behind their splendours I see moving darker and older shapes,"[21] she wrote in her autobiography of 1925. The sentiment echoes the broader mood of the time, a period when an irrational, and even savage, side of human nature seemed to lurk just beneath its civilized shell, ready to burst through at any moment. The fifteen years preceding Harrison's *Prolegomena* saw the publication of Robert Louis Stevenson's *Dr. Jekyll and Mr. Hyde* (1896), Oscar Wilde's *The Picture of Dorian Gray* (1890), H. G. Wells's *The Island of Dr. Moreau* (1896), and Bram Stoker's *Dracula* (1897), to mention just the high points of a literary trend towards tales of "the savage within."[22] Hand in hand with a desire of the time to peer into the dark recesses of the soul went a desire to peer at the soul beyond the curtain of death, as well. Interest in spiritualism soared, and classicists were not exempt: Gilbert Murray was a "sensitive" (that is, a medium); A. B. Cook had a strong interest in uncanny phenomena; Margaret Verrall— the old friend of Harrison's with whom she coauthored *Mythology and Monuments of Athens* and who, along with her husband, the classicist Arthur Verrall, sat on the fringes of the Cambridge Ritualist group—was a psychic investigator.[23] Somewhat earlier (1882), the Society for Psychical Research had been cofounded by Frederic Myers, a Cambridge-trained classicist and former fellow and lecturer at Trinity College; Murray served as its president twice.[24] Yet another marker of the mood of the time was the emergence in England of modern pagan witchcraft—a movement that sought to recover earlier, more genuine religious impulses (read: "rituals"), which was nourished by the widely popular writings of Frazer and Harrison.[25]

Late in life, Harrison turned away from classics and embarked on the study of Russian literature. Nonetheless, during this period she produced two books that explicitly focused on ancient myth: *Mythology* (1924) and *The Myths of Greece and Rome* (1928). Of the latter there isn't much one can say. It is tiny in size, which suits the series in which it appeared—"Little Books of Modern Knowledge"—and it concentrates on "The Gods of Homer's Olympus," as a section heading proclaims. It was published in the year of Harrison's death and was probably written at some point during the three preceding years, while she and her friend Hope Mirrlees shared a flat in London, working together on translations of Russian novels.[26] One wonders whether Harrison wrote it because money was tight.

The other book, *Mythology*, is more interesting. It must have been written while Harrison and Mirrlees were living in Paris, shortly after Harrison departed from Cambridge and the life of a classicist. Like *The Myths of Greece and Rome*, it was written for the average reader: it was the twenty-sixth volume in a series published by the Marshall Jones Company under the rubric "Our Debt to Greece and Rome" (in the postwar era, the public was eager to be reminded of the more admirable aspects of European civilization). Nevertheless, even in this venue, Harrison manages to make it clear that "real" Greek religion had to be excavated from beneath the bright surfaces laid on by myths. She begins by reasserting her familiar distinction between ritual ("what a man *does* in relation to his religion") and myth ("what he *thinks* and *imagines*") and then throughout the book continually reminds her readers that myths as we know them were created by poets and artists, who were at heart shapers and makers—that is to say (as anyone who has read Plato knows quite well) dissemblers: "The Greeks were not priest-ridden, they were poet-ridden, a people, as the word 'poet' implies, of *makers, shapers, artists*."[27] Or again, "From religion Greek mythology banished fear, fear which poisons and paralyzes man's life. . . . Some *rites* of fear and repulsion they kept, for ritual is always conservative, but their mythology and theology, their *representations* of the gods, was informed throughout by reason, lighted by beauty."[28]

After Harrison

Harrison's *Mythology* was the last time, for a long time, that a classicist invoked the ritualist approach.[29] Amongst Semiticists, however, it was just then gathering speed—and so, too, was the comparativism that always seems to accompany it. Its main proponent after Smith, Samuel Henry Hooke, was a generation younger than Harrison. He started his academic career late in life and spent a good part of it away from British academia—he returned to England with a professorship in Old Testament Studies at University College London only in 1927, at the age of fifty-three. His first major publication on the topic, an edited volume entitled *Myth and Ritual*, appeared in 1933, twelve years after Harrison's *Epilegomena*, and his first monograph on the topic, *The Origins of Early Semitic Ritual*, appeared in 1938.[30]

Like Harrison in her later years, Hooke understood a myth to narrate the actions of a ritual as it was being performed, and therefore he understood the two to be of virtually simultaneous origin (for this reason, the approach as it was developed by Semiticists is formally called the "myth-and-ritual approach" rather than the "ritualist approach"). Hooke also embraced the paradigm of the dying-and-reviving god/king and gave pride of place within it to the ancient Babylonian Akitu festival, a New Year's celebration during which the human king was first deprived of office and then reinstalled while a priest recited the *Enuma Elish*, a cosmogonic poem that culminates in the installation of Marduk as king of the gods.[31] Hooke argued that it was with this particular myth-and-ritual pairing that the paradigm of the dying-and-reviving god/king had originated and then traveled wide and far, expressing itself through many other myth-and-ritual pairings. In other words, Hooke presented the story of Marduk as the Ur-myth par excellence, from which all others had descended and then been diffused around the world. As Hooke's work spread, it fanned not only the flames of the myth-and-ritual approach and of comparativism but also the flames of essentialization: scholars felt newly encouraged to purge away any inconvenient details in a given myth or ritual, in order to show that its structure was parallel to what Hooke had described.

It wasn't only Semiticists who continued to use and develop the models that the classicists had pioneered, however. At midcentury, the literary critic Stanley Hyman, for example, pushed Harrison's ideas so far as to argue that ritual underlay not only all myths but also all literature. In his view, literature had sprung from myths whose connections to rituals had been weakened. Hyman was enthused about Gilbert Murray's 1914 attempt to trace *Hamlet* to the same ritual origins as the story of Orestes, and he also admired Jessie Weston's 1920 use of the theory to illuminate Arthurian legend.[32] The ritualist approach to myth was also taken up by Lord Raglan. In his 1936 *The Hero: A Study in Tradition, Myth and Drama*, Raglan extended the thesis of the dying-and-reviving god into hero tales (Oedipus, Heracles, Moses, and Robin Hood were amongst his examples). One of Raglan's most enduring contributions is his observation that twenty-two traits frequently appear in hero stories throughout the world (although almost no story includes all of them). For instance, the circumstances of a hero's conception are often unusual and he often meets a mysterious death. Raglan's neatly enumerated formulation makes it clear not only that ritualists are almost always comparativists, too, but also that the sort of comparison they prefer focuses on *similarity*—that is, on collecting as many instantiations as possible of a given "type" but paying relatively little attention to their differences. This, again, encourages the essentialization of any single myth so as to make it fit whatever pattern a scholar is championing.

The ritualist approach was taken up by anthropologists, as well, although hesitantly at first. Bronislaw Malinowski and Clyde Kluckhohn agreed that there was a tendency for myths and rituals to depend upon each other, but Kluckhohn warned that the variety of ways in which they might do so made monolithic theories about how and why it had happened dangerous. He also rejected the idea that there could be any all-encompassing thesis as to which had come first. In a 1942 essay that presaged some aspects of Walter Burkert's work, Kluckhohn universalized only so far as to say that myth and ritual "both are symbolic processes for coping" with the anxieties that life presents and that they are a "cultural storehouse of adjustive responses for individuals" that "supply fixed points in a world of bewildering change and disappointment."[33] In 1954, nonetheless, Edmund Leach confidently asserted that "myth implies ritual, ritual implies myth, they are one and the same,"[34] and it was his voice that carried the day: the paradigm was firmly implanted amongst anthropologists for a long time to come.

The Classicists Return to the Fray

In 1959, the classicist Joseph Fontenrose criticized the version of the ritualist approach that literary scholars had developed. In his *Python: A Study of Delphic Myth and Its Origins*, Fontenrose argued that although myths were "traditional stories that accompany rituals,"[35] myths did not necessarily *originate* in rituals but might instead become "attached" to rituals at a later stage, in one way or another. He also took up the diffusionist banner of the myth-and-ritual school, but with a new emphasis: he assumed that once a myth had begun to spread from its place of origin, it might join forces with a variety of different rituals that it encountered and itself be changed in the process. Much of the book is spent demonstrating that what Fontenrose called the "combat myth"—that is, the tale of a hero defeating a monster—enjoyed just this sort of diffusion, linking itself now to the Babylonian New Year's ritual, then to certain Egyptian rituals and myths, and then again to the Delphic Septerion festival, for example. "It is simpler to suppose," he wrote, "that a well-known type of story was introduced in many places to serve as the primeval precedent of the rituals than to believe in so many places the rituals spontaneously generated a uniform pattern of myth."[36] Like others, then, Fontenrose assumed that there were Ur-myths (or at least Ur-types of myths), but the way in which he understood them to have spread throughout the world meant granting them much more independence and flexibility than earlier scholars had been willing to. His version of comparativism left room for differences, as well as similarities.

Stanley Hyman reviewed *Python* in 1960, in the first issue of a magazine called the *Carleton Miscellany*. It's worth pausing on the venue of this review: during its twenty years of publication, the slender and highly selective volumes of the *Miscellany* brought to-gether essays, poems, and works of criticism that were contributed not only by academics but also by poets laureate and winners of the Pulitzer Prize: the *Miscellany* aimed to please and stimulate the broadly educated, intellectually inclined person. In other words, the myth-and-ritual question was once again perceived as something central to the life of the mind.

Hyman's review marshaled the ghosts of Smith, Frazer, Harrison, Murray, and Cornford (who collectively, he said, had definitively established the real, ritual origins of myth) to support his contention that every aspect of Fontenrose's approach was utterly wrong. What was under threat for Hyman and for many other people as well, we might guess, was the treasured idea that "if myths arise out of ritual, [then] they are an expression of deepest human needs, of leaping for crops and flocks and goodly *themis*, and [they] have a profound sociological and psychological truth, whatever the literal unreality of their stories."[37] If one took away the direct link between myths and rituals, then perhaps the whole assumption that myths *meant* something—something primal and genuine about our deepest selves—might collapse. For Hyman and others like him, this turn of events threatened to pull the rug out from under a lot of literature, too.

Fontenrose gave as good as he got in the next issue of the *Miscellany*, concluding his response to Hyman, with:

> I know of no competent anthropologist, folklorist or classicist (or none at all, in fact, unless you call Lord Raglan an anthropologist) who accepts the view that Mr. Hyman considers to be well established. But it does seem to be the rage at present among literary critics, none of whom has done any of the spade work in mythological study.[38]

More importantly, earlier in his response Fontenrose brought out an underlying assumption of *Python* more effectively than he had in the book itself: "once you have myths," Fontenrose asks, "why can't they suggest new myths?"[39] In his next book, *The Ritual Theory of Myth* (1966), Fontenrose renewed his attack against the ritualist approach by further emphasizing the *imaginative* contribution that narrators make to myth. Myths do not exist in some abstract form, he insisted, but rather are promulgated through literary and artistic narrations, and in the process they are continually and productively re-created to suit their audiences. In other words, when one essentializes a myth—when one simply boils it down to the Ur-myth from which it supposedly emerged and leaves it at that—one loses a great deal of what actually constituted the myth as it was received by people. This is a crucial point, as is a related plea that Fontenrose made for studying myths "not in a vacuum, but in their institutional settings."[40] For the Greeks, this meant studying myths as they were performed at festivals, first and foremost. Even as he rejected the *ritualist approach* to myths, in other words, Fontenrose returned myths to their ritualized settings.

Shortly after Fontenrose's *The Ritual Theory of Myth* appeared, Geoffrey Kirk published his Sather Lectures on myth, in the course of which he briefly addressed the myth-and-ritual question (*Myth: Its Meaning and Functions in Ancient and Other Cultures*, 1970). Kirk's return to the topic in 1974, in chapter 10 of *The Nature of Greek Myths*, presents a more developed version of his ideas. Like Fontenrose, Kirk thought that the connection between myth and ritual had been exaggerated, at least for the Greeks, and therefore argued strenuously against its use by classicists. He pointed out that in both ancient Greece and other cultures, there were stories that anyone would be apt to call myths that had no apparent connection to ritual at all. His prime example was the Greek theogonic myth: "the ancient Greeks did not carry out actions designed to imitate or reproduce the separation of sky and earth."[41] He also distinguished between "significant" myths and "insignificant," "trivial," "feeble," or "half-baked" myths. For Kirk, the first category included myths that either had been associated with a given ritual over a long period of time (which for him meant *aitia* that were hoary with age) or were well-known through important literary sources (the theogonic succession myth being a good example, as it comes to us through Hesiod). The second category constituted myths that, in Kirk's opinion, had neither literary importance nor a long-standing attachment to ritual, such as an *aition* for the Anthesteria that tells of Orestes's arrival in Athens on the day of the *choēs*. Kirk judged this to be a late addition to the festival and "a feeble affair."[42]

This mode of categorization meant, in turn, that for Kirk there were "significant" links between myths and rituals (although the only two Greek instances to which he granted this designation were those connected with the Lemnian women and those connected with the daughters of Cecrops), and there were "insignificant" links (into which category fell the vast majority of links that scholars had proposed in the past). Regarding the myth of Orestes that purported to explain the ritual performed during the Anthesteria, Kirk concluded that in this and many other cases, "pre-existing myths, or faintly plausible details from them, are dragged in as *aitia* [for rituals], which is a very different process from solid mythical invention."[43] In a similar vein, the fact that there were several different *aitia* for the Buphonia disqualified all of them, in his view: in this case, the "degree of myth involved was minimal and the generation of real narrative extremely slight."[44] The story of Orestes biting off his finger and then establishing cult to the Eumenides was similarly judged "a superficial aetiology."[45] The myth of Demeter and Persephone was labeled a "crude *aition* for seasonal agriculture [that in adapted form] was applied to a particular fertility cult that had been known in Eleusis at least from the Mycenaean period," and the story of Neoptolemus's death at Delphi was judged a "minor invention that drew on the ritual use of knives there in an unimportant way."[46] More generally, in Kirk's opinion, what rituals frequently had done was to "encourage half-baked *aitia* in the form of loosely applied or ill-chosen details from other and obviously independent tales."[47]

In other words, Kirk rejected the ritualist approach to myth not so much because he had a problem with the approach itself as because he saw little evidence of its relevance to the analysis of *Greek* myths. In making this call, ironically, Kirk presented *aitia* as being more central to the ritualist approach than some other scholars had (recall that Harrison, in fact, found the aitiological link between myths and rituals to be relatively late and secondary). Kirk also seems to have thought that he knew better than any ancient author what made for an appropriate myth-and-ritual combination.[48]

Myths, Rituals, and Programs of Action

To some extent, Fontenrose and Kirk were flogging a dead horse— or at least a horse that most classicists had stopped riding a long time ago. Fontenrose initially revived discussion of the approach because his own topic of interest (the combat myth) had motivated him to develop a new variation of it. Subsequently, he critiqued the approach as it was traditionally applied because he had come to realize how deeply it was still influencing literary studies. Kirk dissected the approach as part of a broader criticism of monolithic approaches to myth during the twentieth century (although he seems to have taken particular delight in attacking this one).

At about the same time that Fontenrose and Kirk were speaking out against the ritualist approach, it was finding its way back into classics by an unexpected route. In 1972, Walter Burkert published *Homo Necans* and then, in 1979, *Structure and History in Greek Myth and Ritual*. One of the most important ideas that Burkert explored in these two books, as well as in a series of articles,[49] was the premise that both myths and rituals are symbolic expressions of "programs of action" that have deep roots in biologically determined events such as puberty and the seeking of a mate or in social realities such as the hunt. Given this, he suggests, myths and rituals usually arise independently of each other, although they sometimes end up functioning in tandem. Like Fontenrose's insights, this laid the groundwork (as Burkert himself signals several times)[50] for better appreciating the contributions made by specific narrations of myths, and yet the two greatest effects of Burkert's work were to spur onward again the search for myth-and-ritual pairings and, correspondingly, to encourage further still the essentialization of myths.

The revival of the search for pairings can be traced to two aspects of Burkert's work.[51] First, Burkert used programs of action to offer a particularly captivating revival of Jane Harrison's argument that the initiation paradigm underlay many Greek myths and rituals—which inevitably revived her ritualist approach to myth as well.[52] Renewed attention had already been brought to initiation in the ancient world by Henri Jeanmaire in 1939, and then again by Louis Gernet and Angelo Brelich in the 1960s, but by combining initiation with ideas borrowed from ethologists such as Konrad Lorenz and with the idea (shocking at the time) that violence lay at the heart of many religions, Burkert galvanized the topic like no one else had before.[53] His timing was right, moreover; the younger classicists who took their cues from Burkert, such as Hendrik Versnel, Fritz Graf, Jan Bremmer, and Christiane Sourvinou-Inwood, had come of age during the 1960s, a period when the Western world developed a heightened awareness of society's power to enforce normative expectations of behavior during adolescence.[54]

Second, while endorsing the idea that myths and rituals could operate independently, Burkert nonetheless confirmed that they were more effective when working together and offered attractive interpretations of myths that relied on their partnership with rituals. Odysseus's sufferings in Polyphemus's cave could be shown to echo a werewolf story pattern—which in turn reflected initiatory rituals. The tale of Proetus's maddened daughters and their gruesome sacrifice of a child could be linked to a festival that marked the temporary dissolution of society and suspension of its rules. The story of Demeter's angry withdrawal and mollified return could be paired with widespread rituals in which images of deities were ceremoniously taken away and then retrieved.[55] Although Burkert had already reminded his readers of an important point regarding Greek myths in an earlier publication that laid some of the groundwork for his books: "[In ancient Greece] we are not dealing with myths that perform *a direct ritual function*. In [the present] case, nothing suggests that the myth of Kekrops' daughters was *officially recited* during the festival of the Arrhephoria, as the creation epic would have been at a given time and place during the Babylonian new year festival,"[56] this and other cautionary statements paled in the light of his exciting analyses. In the more than forty years since Burkert first published on the topic, numerous scholars, following what they take to be his lead, have proposed further myth-and-ritual pairings that pay relatively little attention to the issue of how, exactly, the myths were narrated or enacted in their particular ancient settings.[57]

The second effect of Burkert's work was to further encourage the tendency towards essentializing myths and rituals. Scholars who embraced the ritualist approach were already liable to do this—in part because they also tended to be comparativists, as we have seen, and in part for another reason that I will discuss shortly—but Burkert's ideas added fuel to their fires for an additional reason. Building on the work of Vladimir Propp, who had proposed that a limited sequence of thirty-one actions (or "functions") underlay each of the 100 Russian wonder tales he had examined and that a limited pool of actors ("hero," "villain," "donor," and so on) populated those tales,[58] Burkert developed his own sequences, which he suggested reflect "the reality of life"—that is, they narrate or enact biologically driven programs of action. For example, Burkert proposed that there was a connection between a program of action experienced by virtually all women in premodern societies (puberty/loss of virginity/pregnancy/birth) and a sequence of story motifemes that he called "the girl's tragedy": (1) a girl leaves home, (2) she is secluded from others, (3) she is raped and impregnated, (4) she is severely punished by her parents or other relatives, and (5) she is rescued, sometimes by the son to whom she gave birth. Given the universality of this program of action, Burkert reasoned, we should not be surprised to discover that "the girl's tragedy" is a nearly universal type of tale.[59]

Burkert is careful to remind his readers that such sequences cannot tell us, on their own, what a myth "means." Early on in *Structure and History in Greek Myth and Ritual*, he offers the following definition: "myth is a traditional tale *with secondary, partial reference to something of collective importance*,"[60] and he reminds us several times that a significant part of any myth's relevance stems from its application in a specific place, at a specific time, in response to specific circumstances. He rejects the search for "origins" in the traditional sense, and in the course of the book (which, after all, includes the word "history" in its title), he demonstrates several times how a myth can "crystallize" in a certain form that includes particular details and then "re-crystallize" with new details under new circumstances.[61] For Burkert, tracing a myth to a more general type or to a program of action is only a first step in understanding it.

And yet it was Burkert's programs of action—the primal modes of behavior hiding behind the niceties of history, the hermeneutically alluring "structures" that provided the first word in the book's title—that grabbed his readers' attention and inspired a new flurry of publications on myth. One of these is especially interesting for our purposes. In 1993, in a detailed review of the ritualist approach, Hendrik Versnel demonstrated that its advocates had long been fix- ated on two paradigms, each of which was believed by its backers to be the interpretive key that could reveal the true meaning of most, if not all, myths and rituals. The first was the New Year's paradigm, which included Frazer's dying-and-reviving god, for example, and the second was the initiation paradigm, as explored most famously by Harrison and then again by Burkert. The fervor to apply these paradigms had tempted scholars into jettisoning inconvenient de- tails, adjusting plotlines and tailoring myths and rituals in various other ways in order to streamline them into one paradigm or the other and thus reveal their real, core "meaning."[62]

Versnel tried to avoid doing this by looking beyond the two para- digms. He noted that they each shared structural affinities with a third pattern that he called the "primordial crisis"—that is, a se- quence in which a character leaves familiar territory, confronts dan- gers in a landscape marked by marginality (in some cases to the point of death), and triumphantly returns in a state of renewal. The *Od- yssey*, which advocates of both the New Year's paradigm and the ini- tiation paradigm claimed to be able to decipher, provided Versnel with a perfect example of the primordial crisis in action and an op- portunity to bring the warring factions together. Perhaps, he sug- gested, the *Odyssey* was able to be read as *both* a New Year's tale *and* an initiation story because at heart it was really a tale of primordial crisis. Many other contested myths and rituals could be similarly understood in this way, he claimed—and one needn't stop there: the plot is also behind numerous fairy tales, other kinds of stories and even the dreams of individuals. The pattern is widespread, he concluded, because its roots are planted in Burkert's programs of action—that is, the pattern reflects biological and social drives of an exceedingly old and elementary nature.

Thus, in order to avoid the two paradigms that ritualists had em- braced for decades, Versnel introduced another paradigm that essen- tialized myths in a different way—for what is left of a myth once it has been condensed to a three-part primordial crisis? Versnel was well aware of this problem; on the penultimate page of his essay, he

said, "Of course, whoever thinks all this much too vague and prefers to sit down and reread the *Odyssey* itself is right, too"—a nod to
the importance of the well-wrought tale itself.[63]

Meanwhile . . .

Over the past twenty pages or so, I've sketched the effects that the
ritualist approach has had on scholars of ancient Greek myths. Born
out of the comparative method, the ritualist approach was suscep-
tible to essentializing the myths it treated, since comparison itself
had a long history of stripping myths down to what was perceived to
be their cores and either ignoring or explaining away inconvenient
details. Hand in hand with this sort of comparison went the assumption that there were Ur-myths, from which other myths had
evolved. To reconstruct an Ur-myth, one had to cut away the extraneous matter that had accumulated around its descendants in their
different cultural contexts. For a comparativist, this meant that Greek
myths, like all other myths, needed to be pruned before they were
useful.

The ritualists' own agenda further encouraged the essentialization
of Greek myths for two reasons. First, because the ritualists thought
of myths as ancillary phenomena, created to serve as librettos for the
rituals that constituted "true" religion, they were willing to refashion
myths to fit whatever patterns they saw in the rituals. Second, because
they assumed that poetry and art had embellished Greek myths to
the point of disguising any genuine religious feeling that they might
have once expressed, the ritualists were willing to extricate what they
decided the myth really was from what they claimed were merely its
artistic or literary vehicles.

In the 1960s and 1970s, Burkert tried to put myths and rituals on
an equal footing by suggesting that they both had emerged from biological programs of action. In doing so, he endorsed Fontenrose's
suggestion that myths could develop and operate independently of
rituals, even if they sometimes joined forces, and Fontenrose's emphasis on the imaginative contribution that individual narrators
could make to myths. This should have pushed scholars of ancient
religion to reconsider the narratives through which myths were ex-

pressed in ancient Greece, but Burkert's work instead inspired a new spate of myth-and-ritual pairings that, just as in earlier times, tended to focus on finding the "true essence" or the "original meaning" of a myth. This quest, once again, led to treating what was understood to be the "myth" separately from what were understood to be its narrative "vehicles."

For scholars whose training and interests lay primarily in ancient religions, the ritualist approach has long been the most popular way of studying Greek myths. Other approaches to myth emerged during the twentieth century as well, however, including, most prominently, the psychoanalytical and structuralist approaches. The psychoanalytical approach assumes that myths reflect universal concerns of the human psyche; it follows that myths are bound to share a universally valid system of symbols, too, which can be recovered from individual myths if one looks beneath their surfaces. This, in turn, means discarding or reinterpreting details in the ancient narratives.

The structuralist approach requires one to discard, or at least to disregard, surface details, too. According to Propp's brand of structuralism, everything except the plot and some basic character roles is disposable; one can change, for instance, the name of the hero, the destination to which he travels, or the very goal of his quest without changing the core meaning of the story. According to Claude Lévi-Strauss's version of structuralism, in contrast, plot is irrelevant; what matters are the smaller units of a story that he called "mythemes" and how they articulate a culturally embedded system of binary oppositions.[64] What Propp and Lévi-Strauss had in common was that each thought that the particular narrative through which a story was told was of little importance; each of them worked from a simplified version of whatever story they chose to treat. Lévi-Strauss created his simplified version by homogenizing as many possible variants of the story as he could find into a sort of abstract. Propp implicitly did the same, deriving a model from the 100 exemplars that he studied, against which every individual exemplar could then be measured.

Most scholars who adopted a structuralist approach tended to treat the myths that they dealt with in one of these two ways. Jean-Pierre

Vernant was an exception. Rather than working from abstracts of myths, Vernant started from individual narratives. He paid close attention to the authors' choices of words, to the ways in which the stories unfolded in narrative time, and to the chains of causality that the authors chose to emphasize. In other words, for the first time in the modern study of myth, Vernant was interpreting myths in the specific forms through which they had been conveyed to ancient audiences. Furthermore (under the influence of his teacher, the sociologist Louis Gernet), Vernant contextualized narrations of myths within their historical and social settings, so that he might more fully recover the codes of meaning through which characters, objects, and actions were used to convey a narrator's ideas. This required Vernant to do close readings not only of the myths themselves but also, alongside them, close readings of a variety of other ancient texts and artistic representations. This enabled him to show, for example, that Hesiod's description of Pandora having a "mind like a bitch" drew its force from a much broader Greek collocation of female lust, dogs, hungry stomachs, and the burning heat that the Dog-star Sirius brought at the height of summer, when women were most wanton.[65]

Vernant's method was carried forward by other scholars; I will be drawing on some of their work in later chapters. Vernant's student Marcel Detienne needs to be mentioned now, however. Detienne turned away from Vernant's practice of interpreting a single, specific mythic narration and back towards Lévi-Strauss's approach, constructing each of his objects of study as an "ensemble of its variants disposed in a series to form a group of 'permutations.'"[66] His particular rationale for doing this was that, throughout the history of ancient Greece, myths had been continually remade to suit their immediate environments. There were no canonical versions, and in his opinion, one would get at what he called a myth's "hidden system" only by standing back and taking a panoptic view of all the variants. Indeed, "the more numerous the variants, the better structural analysis works."[67] For Detienne, then, a myth was both constituted by, and disappeared into, its own multiformity.

It was perhaps Detienne's fascination with multiformity that led him, a few years later, to dismantle the very concept of myth as a unity, as scholars had understood it. In *L'invention de la mythologie* (1981), he argued that the category of myth as a distinctive form of discourse had been invented during the fifth century BCE, by men such as Plato, Herodotus, and Thucydides, who needed something to set in opposition to their newly conceptualized category of "reason." The modern study of myth, he asserted, starting with figures such as Bernard le Bouvier de Fontenelle in the eighteenth century, had replicated this move. In the Western world, then, both "myth" and "reason" (or "science" or whatever else one chose to set in opposition to myth) had never been more than cultural constructs. Greek myth per se could not be isolated as a definable phenomenon, much less studied as such.

Detienne's book was just the first shot in what quickly became a larger assault on the integrity of myth as a category. A year later, Luc Brisson published *Platon, les mots et les mythes*, which looked more closely at Plato's innovative use of the word *mythos* to characterize stories that were not true, and the year after that saw both Paul Veyne's *Les Grecs ont-ils cru à leurs mythes?*, which argued against the assumption that the Greeks had understood "myth" as an essential mode of thought, and Fritz Graf's *Griechische Mythologie*, the first two chapters of which went even further than Detienne had in tracing the development of the modern European conception of myth as a particular *type* of story. For the next fifteen years or so, attention shifted away from what had long been assumed to *be* Greek myths (that is, all those stories in which Zeus, Athena, Heracles, and their ilk were characters) and towards the very question of whether, or how, one could genuinely isolate, much less define, any such thing.[68] Although the study of individual myths did not completely stop, methodological innovation slowed down; the default approach continued to be that of looking for myth-and-ritual pairings, even if with more flexibility.[69]

There was one important exception. Claude Calame had been amongst those who came to the conclusion that "there simply is no ontology of myth,"[70] but he took things further. In his 1990 *Thésée et l'imaginaire athénien*,[71] and even more so in his 1996 *Mythe et histoire dans l'antiquité grecque: La création symbolique d'une colonie*, Calame insisted that, far from being a mode of thought, discrete or otherwise, for the Greeks myth was a *process of symbolic production* that came to exist *only* in the course of narrative production itself (for this reason, he called his approach "semionarrative"). In other words, Calame insisted that scholars should neither neatly excise "a myth" from its assorted "versions" nor magically reconstitute it by agglomerating those versions into a homogenized whole. Each "version" was in effect its own myth, arising in a particular form in response to particular needs on particular occasions.[72] Moreover, rejecting the traditional relationship between myth and ritual, Calame argued that myths themselves could have a pragmatic effect upon their audiences and become instruments for change—affecting the emotions of the audience and thereby shifting public opinion, for example. I'll return to these ideas in Chapter 3, where I'll be asking *how* myths affect emotions and to what sorts of ends they do so.

Aitia

In ending this chapter, however, I first need to return briefly to the ritualist approach and look more closely at one of its most persistent features: the tendency to emphasize myths' aitiological functions. That there were plenty of Greek myths that undertook to explain why this or that ritual existed is not in doubt. The issue, rather, is that scholars have seldom stopped to ask *when* and *why* these aitiological myths were narrated or performed. Typically, there has simply been a vague understanding that a given *aition* was linked to its partner ritual in some way—perhaps it was performed during the ritual, for instance. Occasionally, this presumption led a scholar to "recover" an underlying structure that a myth shared with other myths that were more straightforwardly aitiological. Sometimes, it led to the hypothetical reconstruction of rituals that no longer existed in historical Greece but that scholars perceived as aligning both with the recovered myths and with ritual paradigms that were borrowed from other cultures. In the end, these sorts of operations required a good deal of imaginative re-creation of both myths and rituals and a good deal of circular argumentation.

In more recent decades, scholars have also paired myths and rituals by looking for thematic resonances between the two (thus, for example, my own proposal that the Homeric *Hymn to Hermes* was performed at boys' athletic festivals, which relies on understanding both the myth and the festival as articulations of male social maturation)[73] or by looking for contextual motivations that would have prompted a poet to narrate a particular myth at a particular festival or at a particular time (thus, for example, the various interpretations of Pindar's second *Olympian* that rely on assuming that its recipient, Theron of Acragas, belonged to a particular religious cult).[74] Certainly, both of these approaches have their virtues, but they still leave us with a large number of myths that have no obvious aitiological, thematic, contextual or other sort of connection to the occasions on which they were narrated. Why tell the story of Deianira's accidental murder of Heracles during a dithyramb performed in Delphi, as Bacchylides did, for example?[75]

Certain genres of poetry do seem to have had a tendency to take *aitia* as their topics, the paean being a prime instance. Several paeans composed for performance at Delphi tell us about how the Oracle was established there (as does the Homeric *Hymn to Apollo*, which includes, towards its end, a paean-like refrain).[76] Alcaeus's paean narrates Apollo's first trip to Hyperborea, after which he traveled to Delphi and assumed his duties there as an oracular god. The story reflects cultic reality insofar as Apollo was understood to leave Delphi in Dionysus's care for three months each winter while he enjoyed an annual vacation amongst the Hyperboreans. Pindar's sixth paean explains that Neoptolemus has a tomb in Apollo's Delphic precinct because he had been killed there in a fight over how the priests were distributing sacrificial meat. Apollo's conception and birth were also appropriate subjects for paeans.[77]

But as a group, these paeans raise two questions that can also be asked of many other myths that were narrated or performed in cultic settings. First, what are we going to count as an *aition*? Broadly speaking, a poem that narrates the foundation of the cult site probably qualifies, given that it explains how the site became sacred—but such stories do not fit the ritualist paradigm in the stricter sense insofar as they do not tell us how a particular *ritual* that was performed at the site had been established. Similarly, divine birth stories are aitiological insofar as they tell us how, where, and sometimes why a god came into existence, but they do not usually explain why specific rituals were performed for that god: the closest we typically get is some indication of the god's future talents or responsibilities, as when the newly born Hermes stole cattle.[78] Both birth stories and site-foundation stories fit into a broader category that we might call "exaltation of the god and his or her deeds," which is common in ancient Greek poetry of many types.

Second, even when we get something that looks like an *aition* in the stricter sense of the term, how often can we link it to a specific ritual setting in the manner that the ritualist approach demands? We have no evidence for a formal festival celebrating Apollo's annual return to Delphi, for which Alcaeus's paean might have been composed, for example.[79] That paean, moreover, portrays Apollo as arriving in Delphi at midsummer and brings cicadas, swallows, and nightingales onstage to sing their distinctively seasonal tunes—whereas Delphic tradition said that Apollo arrived each year in early spring. If the paean were performed at a festival celebrating Apollo's return, this discrepancy would have jarred, as would have the poem's meter, which is more suited to a symposiastic setting.[80] We know that Pindar's sixth paean was composed for performance at a Delphic *theoxenia* ("feast for the gods"). Ian Rutherford is surely right that this paean's story of a disrupted sacrifice that led to Neoptolemus's death was thematically appropriate for such an occasion, but in no sense does it provide an *aition* for the *theoxenia*.[81]

When poets *do* narrate what looks like an appropriate *aition* (that is, one suited to the ritual at hand), they seem to do it out of sheer choice, with no indication that they are following a tradition and no expectation that other poets will follow their lead. For example, we might point to Pindar's first *Olympian* as an aitiologically satisfying poem. It narrates Pelops's chariot race against Oenomaus, which according to one strand of tradition led to the establishment of the Olympic games, at which the victor honored by Pindar's poem (the Sicilian tyrant Hieron) had just won a crown in the single-horse race. Thus, in this case, an Olympic *aition* was used to celebrate an Olympic victor and, more generally, to glorify the Olympic games themselves. But Bacchylides was also commissioned to celebrate Hieron's victory that year, and he did so with an ode that told the story of

Heracles's descent to Hades—which has nothing to do with the Olympic games as far as we can see. And Pindar himself, in two Olympian odes written during that same year for the winner in the four-horse chariot race (Theron, another Sicilian tyrant and a rival of Hieron), told a different story associated with the foundation of the Olympic precinct in one of them—how Heracles had provided shade for the first competitors by fetching olive trees from Hyperborea—but in the other one offered complex ruminations on the afterlife, which, again, had nothing to do with the foundation of the Olympic games. The poet of the Homeric *Hymn to Apollo*, who tells the story of the Delphic Oracle's foundation, prominently expresses his uncertainty about what he should sing about—he toys with the idea of singing about Apollo's love affairs instead of the Oracle's foundation, for example. Whatever the authorial intention behind that statement may have been (I will return to that question in Chapter 7), it shows that the poet's audience could imagine hearing non-aitiological stories at the same event where they would hear aitiological stories.[82]

These examples could be multiplied, but my point is probably clear by now: even if poets sometimes chose to narrate *aitia* that were more or less appropriate for the occasions on which their compositions would be performed, they felt no obligation to do so or to stick to any other aitiological guidelines that would have satisfied Jane Ellen Harrison. Geoffrey Kirk was right then, even if for the wrong reasons: there were more "significant" aitiological myths in ancient Greece than he was willing to grant, but their significance did not necessarily mean that they would be narrated in connection with rituals, as the ritualist paradigm expected.

How else, then, did Greek *aitia* get passed down, if not in poetry composed for performance alongside the rituals? As in most societies, oral transmission must have been important, not only for *aitia* but also for other kinds of myths: the stories told by grandmothers and nursemaids that Plato disparaged, the tales with which women wiled away time in front of their looms, those told by men at symposia, and others that were passed along in all kinds of conversational situations, such as when Socrates, strolling along the river close to an altar to the wind god Boreas, told Phaedrus that they were nearing

the spot where the Boreas had once snatched away the Athenian princess Oreithyia.[83] *Aitia* were also repeated in more formal situations.
Isocrates mentioned the *aition* for the Proerosia as part of his praise
for Athens, for example,[84] and the tragedians incorporated *aitia* as
well, if it suited their programmatic purposes. The ending of Euripides's *Medea*, for instance, tells of the foundation of Hera's cult in
Perachora, and the ending of his *Iphigenia in Tauris* gives us *aitia* both
for a ritual bloodletting performed in the Attic *demos* of Halae Ara-
phanides and for the practice of dedicating the clothes of women who
died in childbirth to Iphigenia at Brauron.[85]

And then there were what we would call the writers of history
(even if the ancients would not have divided "history" from "myth"
in the same hard and fast way that we would). Starting by at least
the fifth century, a great number of myths, including *aitia*, were incorporated into historians' chronicles. From Hellanicus, we get the
story of how the court of the Areopagus was established, for example.
From Androtion, we get the *aition* for the Buphonia.[86] Thucydides
mentions the origin of the Synoikia during his discussion of how
Theseus had reorganized Athens. The Hellenistic poets, particularly
those who, like Callimachus, worked at the Alexandrian library
where the historians' writings were collected, found in these *aitia*
ample material for a new form of learnéd poetry. Callimachus, in his
Aitia, an elegiac poem in four books, narratively traversed a wide
swath of Greek cities, explaining the origins of their more puz-
zling rituals along the way: why, for example, is it customary for
maidens in Elis to be visited before their marriages by armed warriors? The practice looks back, Callimachus tells us, to an occasion
when Heracles and his soldiers sired new children upon the Elean
women, whose husbands they had just killed.[87]

All of this aitiological material was passed further along in each
generation by other historians, poets, travel writers, mythographers, scholiasts, and lexicographers. In other words, there were numerous ways in which cultic *aitia* could be transmitted in ancient
Greece that lay outside of performance during the cults themselves,
and there are no indications that performing *aitia* in close association with rituals was obligatory, or even standard. The transmission
of Greek *aitia* in no way depended on their narration during rituals,

and the successful performance of Greek rituals in no way depended on the recitation of their *aitia* in the same way as, for example, the successful performance of the Sumerian Akitu festival depended upon the annual recitation of the *Enuma Elish*, or as the successful performance of the Catholic mass depends on the priest reciting the Words of Institution, which repeat what Christ said at the Last Supper. The Greeks just didn't understand the relationship between myths and rituals to be like that which the ritualists proposed two and a half millennia later.

In fact, the Greeks were remarkably silent about this relationship. To the best of my knowledge, no ancient author tells us why myths are narrated in connection with rituals or what types of myths they should be. The closest we come to an answer to the first question are the statements that we find at the end of some hymns and dithyrambs when a poet hopes that his narration has pleased the god. Or in other words, the professed reason that myths were narrated at festivals was to entertain and honor the gods whose festivals they were. Of course, we can be sure that human audiences were on the poets' minds as well: entertaining them was the way to accrue fame and commissions.

As for the other question—what types of myths were suitable—the closest we come to an answer is found in Aristotle's *Poetics*. He doesn't really tell us which *types* of myths were appropriate, however, in the sense of what relationship, if any, they should have with the festival at which they were performed or with any other outside factor. Rather, he tells us that their plots should include reversals of fortune, changes from ignorance to knowledge, and suffering—all of which should arouse strong pity and fear in the audience. He also tells us how the narrator should present these elements: preferably, as arising from unexpected events that will surprise the audience. He notes, as well, that tales of certain old mythic families (the House of Atreus, the House of Laius, and so on) are best suited to fulfilling these criteria.

Aristotle, in other words, stresses the idea that the myths narrated by poets should engage the audience, emotionally and cognitively, as deeply as possible, and should be about well-known, favorite characters. These may seem like desiderata too obvious to need mentioning, but the point I am trying to make is just that: rather than looking for *other* explanations of why the Greeks narrated myths in connection with festivals, we need to accept that the Greeks understood their myths, first and foremost, as a means of entertaining both themselves and the gods. With this in mind, we can step back and ask ourselves what other effects such engaging narrations might have had—on their mortal audiences, at least. Chapters 3–5 will do just that.

3

Narrating Myths

diffusion?

IN CHAPTER 2 we saw how, under the long shadow of Sir James Frazer, the study of Greek myths has tended to start from the assumption that a myth must be extracted from the narrative vehicles that conveyed it before a scholar can do anything with the myth qua myth. For Frazer, this assumption grew naturally out of his zeal for comparative work: until he had set aside what he perceived as the ornaments in which an Aeschylus or a Homer had draped a myth, he could not demonstrate how the myth was similar to other myths that he had gathered from the four corners of the globe and how they were all, as he believed, derived from a single original myth. Although many of Frazer's other ideas have been discarded by later generations, his tendency to essentialize myths has survived—not only amongst those who, like Frazer, focus on the connections between myths and rituals, but also by those who embrace structuralist or psychoanalytical approaches to myth. If myths are to reveal the lost rationales behind mysterious rituals, the universal concerns of the human psyche or the basic structures of the human mind, it has seemed necessary first to pare away their surface details, however enchanting those details might be (indeed, the more enchanting the details, the more they threaten to obscure the "real" myth underneath).

I do not reject these approaches completely—each of them has enhanced our understanding of what myths can do in significant ways. But I do want to suggest that, having fallen into the habit of excising Greek myths from their narratives, most scholars have long overlooked one of the most salient and significant features of mythic narratives: their ability to engage their audiences emotionally and cognitively. I argue that this habit not only has prevented us from understanding some of the most important reasons that myths were able to help create and sustain ancient Greek beliefs in the gods, the heroes and the divine world more generally (and, thus, one of the reasons that it was appropriate to narrate myths in connection with rituals) but also has excluded Greek myths from a larger contemporary dialogue on the power of narratives. Wendy Doniger, an insightfully comparative scholar of myth, once described the stories told by the Greeks as "mythological zombies"— that is, she felt that the Greeks had killed anything that was really alive in the myths in the course of polishing them into the beautiful literary and visual forms that still survive today. This isn't true, as I will show, but I can understand how Doniger came to such a conclusion: scholars of Greek myths have done almost nothing along the lines of what Doniger has done so well for Hindu myths: demonstrate the vibrant way in which they permeated their audiences' daily experiences, thereby keeping the characters and their stories vigorously alive.[1]

In this chapter, I'll try to capture some sense of those ancient Greek experiences. I'll begin by laying down some context that will help us understand how Greek myths were different from those of many other cultures. First, I'll look at the *historiola*, a type of myth that was very common in the ancient Mediterranean. *Historiolae* are performative utterances in the sense that what happens in them is expected to start happening in the real world as well, if the *historiola* is properly narrated. Next, I'll take up the fact that the Greeks, in contrast to their neighbors, do not seem to have adopted the habit of using *historiolae*. This suggests that the idea of narrating a myth in order to cause something directly to happen in the real world did not align well with what the Greeks thought myths were and what myths could do. I'll also show that in the single, seemingly experimental *historiola* that they did create, the Greeks shifted away from the genre's typical reliance on performative utterance towards what George Lakoff and Mark Johnson have called the "conceptual metaphor"—or, in other words, that the Greeks expected that the myth comprising this *historiola* would affect the real world through the *figurative* force of its language. I'll suggest that such an expectation is characteristic of Greek mythic narration more generally: it relied on figurative language and other rhetorical techniques such as *deixis* to draw connections between events in a story and events in the world outside the story. This quality contributed to what Claude Calame has called the "pragmatic effect" of Greek mythic narration—that is, the potential of mythic narratives to bring about changes in the outlook and behavior of its audience members. Such changes were less directly tied to the specific actions of the myth and less focused on a specific goal than were the changes expected when a *historiola* was narrated, but I suggest that, by the same token, Greek mythic narratives carried a greater potential for more broadly making the audience feel as if their world and the world portrayed by the myth were one and the same and as if they lived on a continuum with the events that the myths narrated.

After this preliminary discussion of how Greek narratives merged the world of the myths with the world of their audiences, I'll move on to the topic that occupies the rest of this chapter: how recent work on the specific effects that engaging narratives can have on emotion and cognition will help us better to understand how the narration of myths in ancient Greece conditioned listeners to open themselves to realities that could not be perceived by normal means—to the idea that gods and heroes were present amongst them, listening, watching and affecting the course of mortal lives. I'll begin by expanding upon Joshua Landy's study of how narratives can change not only *what* audience members think, but more importantly the *ways in which* they think, priming their minds to accept as truths what might otherwise be dismissed as fiction. Then I'll look at Tanya Luhrmann's recent work on the ways in which narratives are used in contemporary American religion to prepare worshippers to experience divine presence more regularly and more intensively than they otherwise would, thus creating and sustaining belief. More generally, I'll also review work by social scientists showing that there is a widespread human propensity to develop emotionally and cognitively rich relationships with characters encountered in fictional venues. Throughout these discussions, I'll pause to reflect on how the insights gained from these studies can be applied to the narration of myths in Greece.

Following that, I'll borrow from recent work by media scholars and look at one particular characteristic of Greek myths that conditioned audience members to believe in the gods and heroes who populated them: the fact that Greek myths were narrated in an episodic fashion. Finally, I'll look at the styles of narration used in myths and make some suggestions about how they would have contributed to belief in the gods and heroes, as well. I'll take my general inspiration here from the recent turn in narrative theory towards rhetorical poetics—the attention given to how narrators selectively use the resources of storytelling to affect their audiences in particular ways. I will have two specific models, however. The first is the informal stories that people of our own times tell one another about encounters with the supernatural. The second is the literary ghost story as it was developed beginning at the turn of the last century. In applying what we can learn from these two models to my ancient Greek materials, I will draw on what contemporary folklorists have discovered about the ways in which such stories help to create and sustain belief in the phenomena that the stories describe.

Historiolae

Historiolae are brief myths that are recited in order to solve an immediate problem—most commonly, illness.[2] Typically, at least some of the characters in a *historiola* are gods, heroes or other supernatural agents. These characters have names that are familiar to their audiences; in and of themselves, therefore, such names already evoke histories, actions, and personal characteristics that are relevant for the work that a *historiola* will do. Thus, for example, Isis, a goddess whom myths portrayed as healing her son Horus, is a central character in many *historiolae* that are intended to heal humans.[3] The characters in *historiolae*, moreover, inhabit a realm (I will call it the "mythic realm") that is rife with powers greater than those available in the "quotidian realm"—the realm of everyday people and their everyday abilities. Therefore, although *historiolae* are narratively compact, they are potentially tales of great power.

The actions that are performed by the supernatural agents in a *historiola* are understood to affect the world directly, at the very moment that the words of the *historiola* are recited. That is, narrating a *historiola* constitutes a performative utterance. The following is an example from an Egyptian papyrus dating to about 1325 BCE. A mother whose child has a fever is told to say:

> Isis came out of the spinning house [at the hour] when she loosened her thread. "Come, my sister Nephthys! See, my deafness has overtaken me! My thread has entangled me! Show me my way that I may do what I know [how to do], so that I may extinguish him with my milk, with the salutary liquids from within my breasts. It will be applied to your body, Horus, so that your vessels become sound. I will make the fire recede that has attacked you!"

While the mother recites these words, she applies her own milk to her child just as Isis applied hers to Horus. The child's fever is expected to break, just as Horus's fever broke.[4]

But *historiolae* are not performative utterances in quite the same sense that the words "I now pronounce you husband and wife" or "we find the defendant guilty as charged" are performative utterances. The main point of a *historiola*, rather, is to establish a *paradigm* to which the situation confronted in the quotidian realm is expected to adjust itself: when the *historiola* about Isis's milk is recited, the mortal child is expected to follow the paradigm that the *historiola* established and recover just as Horus recovered.[5] *Historiolae* are performative utterances that work by means of *persuasive analogy*, in other words. To take another example, if a baby has a headache, then its mother might invoke the paradigm of "banished headache" by telling of how Christ pushed the Evil Eye off a rock to stop it from giving headaches to another baby, thus "persuading" her own child's headache to go away as well.[6] The relationship between the paradigm and its application in all of these *historiolae* can be represented this way:

$$A : B \ :: \ a : b$$

Isis's actions : Horus's fever :: narration of Isis's actions : present child's fever

Christ's actions : mythical headache :: narration of Christ's actions : present headache

mythic power : mythic crisis :: narration of mythic power : present crisis

Historiolae built on this analogical principle were common in most ancient Mediterranean cultures, and in many other cultures as well.[7] Frequently, the effectiveness of the *historiola* itself is enhanced by narrating it under various "felicity conditions"—that is, it is narrated at certain times of day when its power will be greatest, it is narrated by a certain type of person (midwives, healers, ritual practitioners), or its narration is accompanied by the application of a salve, an amulet or some other material (such as breast milk), whose discovery, invention or use by a supernatural agent is sometimes described within the *historiola*.[8]

Historiolae from many different cultures share another feature, too: an emphasis on the *place* where the action occurs. Here are just the first lines of two:

Isis comes down from the mountain at midday, in summer, the dusty maiden; her eyes are full of tears and her heart is full of sighs.[9]

Saint Lazarus and Our Lord were going for a walk in our town.[10]

In the first example, Isis is crying at the base of a mountain, and in the second, Lazarus and Christ are walking in "our town." My earlier example was similarly set in a spinning house where Isis and Nephthys were working, and many other *historiolae* are set in specific places as well—places that are virtually always terrestrial in nature and sometimes even places in the speaker's immediate environment. Such *em-placement* of the paradigm narrated by the *historiola* subtly reiterates one of the genre's underlying principles: what is described as happening in the mythic realm will also happen within our own, quotidian realm. Indeed, the terms "mythic *realm*" and "quotidian *realm*"—heuristically useful though they may be for discussing what *historiolae* do—have the unfortunate side effect of suggesting that the actions narrated by the myths occur in places that are completely separate from our own world.[11] This is contradicted not only by the insistently familiar settings of *historiolae* but also by the ontological underpinnings of the cultures that produce them: gods, heroes, saints and other supernatural entities may be understood to make their homes in a place that is geographically distant (higher or lower than where humans make their homes, beyond the western ocean, and so on), yet that place is not understood to be cut off from our places; sacrificial smoke can rise from our altars to their nostrils, prayers uttered by our mouths can reach their ears, and when they choose to visit us for whatever reason, they find it quite easy to do so. Setting the paradigmatic action of a *historiola* within familiar, everyday geography in effect *conjoins* the mythic and quotidian realms; each time the *historiola* is spoken, the distance between the two is narratively erased so as to momentarily create a *shared* realm and thus to bring the paradigm into immediate contiguity with the situation that is meant to replicate it.

The Getty *Historiola*

Remarkably, the ancient Greeks have left us almost no *historiolae* of their own design, and we do not find mention of anything like them in Greek authors, in spite of the fact that we hear a lot about other ritual behaviors that make use of persuasive analogy and performative utterances—for example, *katadesmoi* ("curse tablets"). The Greeks used the basic concepts that underlay *historiolae*, in other words, and were undoubtedly exposed to *historiolae* during their interaction with other Mediterranean cultures, but they don't seem to have themselves adopted the idea that by narrating a myth they could directly cause something to happen in the real world.[12]

There is an exception to that statement, however, from which we can begin to learn more about the Greek view of what myths *can* do. It is the so-called Getty Hexameters, which were inscribed on a lead tablet dating to the fourth century BCE (the tablet is now owned by the J. Paul Getty Museum in Malibu). The tablet was found at the site of the ancient city of Selinus, on Sicily—an island through which we suspect that ritual techniques from foreign lands often entered the Greek world. Both the Getty Hexameters and several abbreviated copies of them (three from Sicily and five from other places) were derived from an older archetype that probably goes back to the late sixth century BCE.[13]

The *historiola* on the Getty tablet is set within a double frame.[14] The innermost of these presents the god Paean (well-known for healing illnesses and for saving people in other dire circumstances) as the original narrator of the *historiola;* in the outer one, an unidentified speaker tells us that the "sacred words" that Paean is about to speak (that is, the *historiola*) will guarantee protection from a broad variety of ills on land and at sea. Later in the text, after the *historiola* has been concluded, additional lines, apparently narrated by the unidentified speaker, specify that these ills include war, sickness, and dangerous animals. What the Getty *historiola* offers, then, is wholesale safety and well-being (lines 4–6, 23–32, 46–50).

The latter part of the *historiola* itself survives only in fragments, but the first part, which seems to constitute the heart of the matter, is almost intact:

> As down the shady mountains in a dark-and-glittering land,
> a child leads out of Persephone's garden, by necessity for milking,
> that four-footed holy attendant of Demeter,
> a she-goat with an untiring stream of rich milk
> laden; and she follows, trusting in goddesses, bright
> with torches . . . [15]

As I've shown elsewhere, the story here is borrowed from Egypt, where we find many myths about both Isis and also the goddess Hathor using either their own milk or the milk of a gazelle (a bovid closely related to the goat and similar in appearance) to do remarkable things—including curing Horus of fever, as in the example of a *historiola* that I provided in the preceding section, and curing Horus of blindness.[16] So, on the one hand, we could say that the Getty *historiola* is Greek in language, but otherwise Egyptian. On the other hand, from earliest times, milk had been independently associated in Greek culture with blessedness and security: "falling" or "jumping" into milk meant to arrive at a state of the highest possible happiness, rivers of milk were common features of paradisiacal times or places and milk was an important healing agent in a wide range of cures discussed by Greek and Roman medical writers.[17] Therefore, the agent of efficacy that is central to the Getty *historiola* would have made the story instantly resonant for Greek audiences, as would the presence of the Greek goddesses Demeter and Persephone.

But there is an important quality that sets the Getty *historiola* apart from those that we looked at in the preceding section—a quality that, I suggest, was introduced by the Greeks themselves when they adapted what was a foreign technique to their own use. Remember that the analogical relationship in *historiolae* is typically like this:

$$A : B \ :: \ a : b$$

mythic power : mythic crisis :: narration of mythic power : present crisis

In the Getty text, instead, we have something like what the linguists George Lakoff and Mark Johnson have called a "conceptual metaphor." In a conceptual metaphor, an abstract concept, such as "love," is compared to a concrete image, such as "journey," producing, in this case, the familiar expression "love is a journey," as well as other expressions that draw on the journey metaphor, such as "we've come too far together to give up on our marriage now."[18] As in the case of all metaphors, in conceptual metaphors the two things that are compared must share one or more salient characteristics but must stop short of being identical or even close to identical—otherwise, the descriptive power of the metaphor would be nil (it is hardly metaphorical to compare mandarin oranges to tangerines, for example). In the Getty text, we have an abstract concept ("wholesale protection and prosperity") and a concrete image ("abundant milk") that together constitute an implicit conceptual metaphor that we might express as "prosperity is milk"—a metaphor that was already familiar to the text's Greek audience. Situating the power of a *historiola* within a metaphor (conceptual or otherwise) rather than within an analogical paradigm is unparalleled as far as I know, which makes a certain sense: the aim of a traditional *historiola*, after all, is to cause something in the quotidian realm to pattern itself after something in the mythic realm not in only one or two salient ways, but rather *as closely as possible*.

The Getty text complicates things yet further. The outermost frame of the *historiola* includes lines that describe the "felicity conditions" under which it should be narrated—that is, the ritual that will help to activate its power:

> Whoever hides in his house of stone the notable letters
> of these sacred words [of the *historiola*] inscribed on tin,
> As many things as the broad Earth nourishes shall not
>   harm him
> nor as many things as much-groaning Amphitrite rears
>   in the sea.

The felicity conditions for using traditional *historiolae* frequently include manipulating materials that are cognate to those manipulated in the *historiola* itself: the mortal mother's milk in our first example, which is cognate to Isis's milk, is an instance of this. In the Getty example, however, the goat milk described by the *historiola* does not seem to have any cognate in the quotidian realm. Instead, the *story* of the goat's milk becomes efficacious when it is inscribed on tin and "hidden in a house of stone" (whatever "house of stone" means).[19] In other words, the Getty *historiola* operates on a strictly *figurative* plane; it requires the manipulation of a semantic substitute for the efficacious agent rather than the manipulation of a quotidian cognate. Perhaps such a change was inevitable, given another way in which the Getty text runs counter to traditional *historiolae*. Namely, when compared to the goals of other *historiolae*—to cure a fever, a scorpion sting, a headache or another immediate problem—the wholesale protection from a broad variety of ills that the Getty text promises constitutes an enormous, rather vague and ongoing aim. Even if one wanted to apply real goat's milk to something in the quotidian realm as the Getty *historiola* was being recited, what would that something be?

On the single occasion when we catch the Greeks experimenting with a *historiola*, then, they change the basic rules by which the technique worked. Instead of adopting the idea that the narration of a myth could directly cause something similar to happen in the everyday world, they employ a myth as a figurative discourse: the provision of abundant milk described in the Getty text was a *metaphor* for the provision of protection and prosperity.

Leaving aside the Getty Hexameters, the closest that Greek mythic narration ever comes to a mode of operation like that which we see in *historiolae* is in the *pars epica* of certain Greek prayers. There, a god might be reminded of what he or she did in the past in order to persuade him or her to do something similar in the present. Yet the words of such prayers are not understood to be directly efficacious in the performative sense; we are still far away from the ideology that underlies *historiolae*.

How to Do Things with Metaphors

This observation shouldn't come as a complete surprise; it aligns well with the norms of Greek myth telling as we know them already in the Archaic and Classical periods, when metaphor and other forms of figuration played important roles in linking a myth to the occasion or purpose for which it was performed. The story of Persephone's annual return from the world of the dead, for example, when narrated in connection with the Eleusinian mysteries, was not meant to suggest that initiates into the mysteries would similarly return to the upper world for a portion of each year after they had died, but rather reminded them that initiation ensured them happier existences in the Underworld, once they had gotten there. Persephone's experiences were a *metaphor* for those of the initiates, in other words; the two shared the salient characteristic of being partial triumphs over death but differed insofar as Persephone annually returned to the world of the living and the dead initiates did not. When narrated in connection with the Thesmophoria, the same story *metaphorically* expressed the celebrants' hopes that crops would once again rise from the dark earth into which seeds were cast. The two situations shared the salient characteristic of anticipating the annual return of something desirable but differed insofar as Persephone returned each year in her own right and the crops "returned" only in the sense that their seeds generated new plants to replace those that were dead and gone (an idea that, in turn, served as a metaphor for the Thesmophoria's other focus, the successful conception and birth of new children). The fact that some stories, such as this one, could serve as meaningful accompaniments for two different festivals with different primary goals underscores myth's metaphorical nature. Had the relationship between the myth and the two rituals I just described been one of straightforward analogy, such double service would not have worked very well.[20]

Epinician odes, and especially those composed by Pindar, relied heavily on the metaphorical uses of myths as well. It was unusual for an ode to narrate a myth that was directly connected to the victor or the athletic event at which he had won. Rather, the myths narrated in epinicians typically evoked the nature of the victors' accomplishments and the effects that their attendant glory would have upon the victors, their families and their cities by telling stories about heroes and gods. A victor could not hope to gain actual immortality, but victory—especially when celebrated publicly by a poem in which a hero's or god's story was embedded—could bring an everlasting fame that was as close to immortality as any ordinary human could get.[21] Pindar's fourth *Isthmian*, for example, encourages us to compare the young victor, Melissus, to Heracles (Pindar goes so far as to point out that both were small in build; lines 49–53), but leaves it up to us to choose exactly how we read Heracles's story into that of Melissus. When skillfully done, the narration of myth plays a crucial role in bringing about the social benefits that athletic victory could garner, but it does so without drawing explicit, one-to-one equations between the circumstances of the myth and the victor's own circumstances. These myths are not *historiolae*, in other words, but rather *extended metaphors* that invite us to consider the salient characteristics shared by two individuals or situations.

Epinicians bring us to Claude Calame's observation that mythic narratives could have a *pragmatic effect* upon their audiences, for his explorations of this idea frequently draw on Pindar's epinicians for their examples. (In fact, Calame suggests that because they were performed in ritualized community settings, epinicians and other forms of melic poetry—e.g., paeans, dithyrambs, maiden songs, wedding songs, and funeral laments—provided particularly good contexts for myths that were meant to have a pragmatic effect).[22] In the case of an epinician ode, this change usually meant elevating the victor's status within his community, but it might also include, for instance, persuading a king to let an exile come home.[23] In the case of a tragedy, the change might mean altering the audience's opinions about a war, politics, or other current events. In other situations, the change might affect just a single person: Achilles's narration of the story of Niobe in *Iliad* 24 causes the grieving Priam to finally break his fast.[24]

Calame's realization that narrating myths can have a pragmatic effect is important, as is his observation that this effect is bound to be more powerful when a myth is narrated within a ritualized, communal setting. But two issues remain. First, exactly how does the narration of a myth bring about this pragmatic effect? In the case of *historiolae*, explicit, one-to-one analogies are expected to bring the quotidian world sharply into line with the mythic world; a *historiola* is essentially a speech act that relies on the principle of performative utterance. In the case of the Getty Hexameters, the myth works metaphorically, building on milk's salient characteristic of being able to cure, protect, and bring blessings to everything it touched. Yet there is still a strong element of *ritual efficacy* present in the Getty Hexameters, as there is in traditional *historiolae:* the words of the myth have to be carved on a particular type of metal and then deposited in a particular place in a particular way for the words of the myth to take their metaphorical effect. This is not the mode in which we see the majority of other Greek mythic narratives being composed and narrated.[25] What happens in those cases, then? What qualities make them potent enough to have pragmatic effects?

Second, Calame's pragmatic model of mythic narration works best in cases where the similarities between the two things being compared are fairly obvious, even to us—modern readers who are far removed from the social and cultural contexts in which the myths were first presented. We can guess from the start that Euripides's

Erechtheus, a play narrating the tale of a war waged during Athens's earliest days, was likely to provoke thought amongst its audience members about the Peloponnesian War in which Athens was engaged at the time of its production. The examples I offered of using Persephone's experiences as a metaphorical expression of hopes for a better afterlife or abundant crops are less straightforward than the linkage between the *Erechtheus* and the Peloponnesian War, but they are not obscure, and the idea that athletic victors were understood as the heroes of their day makes intrinsic sense.[26]

I don't mean to diminish the importance of Calame's insight that mythic narratives could have pragmatic effects (or to ignore his close readings of some mythic narratives whose metaphorical frameworks are less readily apparent), but I do want to raise the question of how we are supposed to understand the many mythic narratives for which we can discern no pragmatic goal other than the general one of praising a god and thus winning his or her favor (I think here of the Homeric *Hymn to Aphrodite*, for example, and of one of Bacchylides's dithyrambs, which tells a gripping story of Theseus's plunge to the bottom of the sea and then closes with the hope that Apollo has enjoyed the story and will reward those who performed it).[27] It's not that entertaining gods (and mortals) was unimportant, but in theory there were other ways of doing that than by narrating *myths*. We know that it was possible to use a non-mythic story as the kernel of a tragedy, for instance: Aeschylus's *Persians* proves that, although the fact that it floats almost alone amongst a vast ocean of tragedies that *do* use mythic stories suggests that such subject matter was an exception. Indeed, the comic poet Antiphanes complained that tragic poets had a big advantage over comic poets: the audience already knows the basic plot of a tragedy the moment the central character's name is mentioned, he charges, because tragedies are always based on well-known myths.[28] All of the epics that remain to us (which were re-performed at festivals for centuries after their composition) take myths as their subject matter, too. Shorter hymns and melic compositions sometimes abstain from narrating anything at all, offering only praise and entreaty, yet by and large, when they do narrate something, it's a myth. In sum, narratives performed in honor of the gods and heroes almost always took myths as their subject matter—even if

those myths had little or nothing to do with the specific gods, heroes
or rituals with which their performances were connected. Again, we
must wonder, how and why did the habit of narrating myths at festivals become so engrained that a wide variety of subjects were judged
appropriate, as long as they were myths? What desires did narrating
myths fulfill? What purposes (conscious or unconscious) did it serve?

For the moment, I want to put this bigger issue on hold (we will
come back to it later in this chapter) and return briefly to the first
question I raised, which will help to prepare the way: how, exactly,
does the narration of myth sustain a metaphorical connection between the mythic and quotidian worlds? For Calame and others who
have worked on the topic, the metaphorical connection between (for
example) a victor and a hero in an epinician myth is activated by a
number of consciously deployed narrative techniques that bring the
two worlds together. The place where the myth is being narrated or
performed may be mentioned in the narrative itself—perhaps the
events of the myth are even set in the very place where the narrative
is delivered. The action of Euripides's *Erechtheus*, as I mentioned earlier, takes place on the Athenian Acropolis that loomed above the
theater in which it was first performed. One of the goals towards
which the Argonauts strove, in Pindar's fourth *Pythian*, was the establishment of Cyrene, where the poem itself was presented many
generations after the actions that the myth describes.[29] A mythic narrative might also be delivered in, and perhaps indeed composed for, a
setting that visually cued its events: Pindar's *Isthmian* 4, which tells the
story of Heracles and Antaeus, was performed in front of a Theban
temple of Heracles that included a pedimental relief showing the two
characters wrestling.[30] Verbal, and perhaps physical, gestures on the
part of the poet (*deixis ad oculos* or *deixis ad phantasm* or some blend
of the two) could bring the two worlds together, as well.[31] Lines
362–363 of the Homeric *Hymn to Apollo*, for example, suggest that
its performer, standing in Delphi, directed the audience's eyes to the
very spot where Apollo had once left the body of Python to rot, as
the performer repeated what Apollo had said on that occasion—
"Now rot *here!*" Such an emphatic statement suggested, even if only
for a split second, that the snake was rotting there, still. Apostrophe
worked similarly: when, in *Olympian* 1, Pindar directly addresses

Pelops in the second person, it is as if the poet, and also we, his audience, are suddenly in the hero's presence.[32]

The two worlds may also be presented as sharing the same values, limitations, and advantages: Calame suggests, for example, that in both the (mythical) Athens of Erechtheus's day and the Athens in which the *Erechtheus* was performed, citizen culture was construed as being rooted in maternal nature.[33] The poet may express such shared conditions by applying to each the same metaphorical figures (what Calame calls isotopies, adopting the term from A. J. Greimas). In *Pythian* 4, the isotopies of matrimonial union and agricultural cultivation are used to explore both the experiences of the Argonauts and those of Cyrene's later colonists.[34] In *Isthmian* 4, Heracles and the victor's family are described as undertaking travels (either real or metaphorical), to "the west," a place that Pindar associates, disquietingly, with both darkness and achievement.[35] Sometimes, a narrative may leap back and forth across generations so rapidly and repeatedly as to conflate them, blurring any chronological distinction between the mythic and the contemporary worlds. An extreme case is *Pythian* 4, which jumps back and forth amongst seventeen generations of the Battiad dynasty and its ancestors that stretch from the Argonaut Euphemus to his descendant Arcesilas, the victor whom Pindar celebrates.[36]

All of the techniques I have mentioned so far help to draw together a specific figure or event from the mythic realm and a specific figure or event in the quotidian world. Kennings (circumlocutions whose sense depends on the listeners' knowledge of myths) work to momentarily immerse listeners in the mythic world more generally. When Pindar says that a victor won a crown at "Nisus's hill with its lovely glens" (i.e., in the city of Megara), we perceive the victor, if only for a moment, against the backdrop of the remarkable story of King Nisus, his treacherous daughter, and his fatal lock of purple hair.[37] To a certain degree, then, kennings work like *historiolae* insofar as they use narrative elements, and particularly names, to temporarily collapse the distance between the mythic and the everyday realm. But there is an important difference. In contrast to *historiolae*, neither kennings nor any of the other techniques that I have just surveyed are performative utterances—that is, they are not expected to *cause* to happen in the everyday realm what once had happened in the mythic realm. (Indeed, one probably would not *wish* to cause to happen again what had happened to Nisus.)[38] By using kennings and other techniques, the poet is able to *merge* worlds without ever promising—or threatening— to make anything in the quotidian world align *precisely* with a particular paradigm that has been set in the mythic world. In fact, all of the techniques that I've been discussing for the past few paragraphs might be said to help merge the two worlds not only spatially (as in the case of the *historiolae*, where, for example, Saint Lazarus and Our Lord take a walk in our town) but also temporally: the Acropolis under whose shadow a tragedy is presented morphs into the Acropolis where Poseidon once struck the earth with his trident and Medea once offered Theseus a poisoned cup of wine. In this way of thinking, there was no moment at which the mythic world decisively changed into the world that we know today; the deeds described by the myths existed on a continuum that flowed uninterruptedly into the time of the listeners. A well-narrated Greek myth would leave those listeners feeling not that they were *repeating* paradigmatic actions of the gods and heroes that had been performed eons ago (as is the case with *historiolae*), but rather that they were *living* amongst the gods and heroes, even if as lesser partners.

Narrating Fictions

It did take some preparation to feel that way, however. I don't mean only the preparation of crafting a narrative that included deictic references, complex chronologies, kennings and the other devices I have just reviewed, if you were a poet, or the preparation of going to the festival where the narrative was to be recited, if you were an audience member. That was important, of course; situating yourself in a time and place given over to worship and celebration of the gods and heroes, amongst other people who were there for the same reason, was certainly conducive to putting you in the right frame of mind.

What I'm interested in here, rather, and what will eventually bring us back to the second issue that I raised earlier (why myths were so persistently narrated at religious festivals), are the ways in which Greek mythic narratives *cumulatively* prepared their audiences to feel as if they were living amongst the gods and heroes. Recent work by scholars of narratology, anthropology, social psychology and cognitive science has shown that some types of fictional narratives, when they are well designed and well executed, not only teach their audiences certain facts (in the case of Hilary Mantel's *Wolf Hall*, this might include details about life at court in Cromwellian England) or certain values (in the case of *The Wonderful Wizard of Oz*, this might include the idea that collaboration with friends will get you further than you would have gotten alone) but also teach them new modes of thinking or new ways of looking at the world, which they subsequently apply, consciously or unconsciously, to other narratives they consume and to situations in real life.

Joshua Landy has called such narratives "formative" fictions—to stress the distinction he wants to make between their role in "forming" or "fine-tuning" our mental capacities and habits and the emphasis that traditional approaches to literary criticism have tended to put upon fiction's "informative" role (its role in conveying facts to its audience).[39] Amongst Landy's test cases are the parables of Jesus, as recorded in the Gospel of Mark. Landy suggests (as have scholars of early Christianity such as David Brakke)[40] that these were not meant to be interpreted in ways that *decoded* their metaphors once and for all (the long history of varied interpretations of most of the parables in itself argues against this idea), but rather to give followers practice in reading the physical world metaphorically until, eventually, they came to view everything that they experienced here and now as nothing *but* a metaphor for the higher plane of existence to which all Christians were expected to aspire. In other words, reading parables trains people to engage in a form of abstract, figurative thought that enhances faith in an idea that is central to Christianity.[41] Another of Landy's test cases focuses jointly on the illusions of the stage magician Jean Eugène Robert-Houdin and the works of the Symbolist poet Stéphane Mallarmé, each of whom sought to re-enchant the secular world of nineteenth-century Europe by training his audiences in the skills of detached credulity—a state of mind in which distrust of what their senses perceived, and yet conviction that those perceptions must be true, were able to coexist. By helping them hone this capacity for "lucid self-delusion," Robert-Houdin and Mallarmé taught their audiences to generate fictions that made their lives more interesting and restored a touch of the miraculous to a world that science had threatened to disenchant completely.

Well-constructed narratives that are effectively delivered, then, can change the way in which people decide what is real and unreal—and more importantly, change the way in which people decide whether, and when, to accept the evidence of their senses as the *only* guides to distinguishing between the two, or rather to admit into consideration another model of the world, in which parts of reality are understood to lie outside the reach of the conventional senses. With regular exposure to such types of fiction, it becomes easier and easier to slip into the new mode of thinking that those fictions encourage. It may become an individual's dominant mode of thinking, as in the case of (idealized) Christian parabolic thinking, or an alternative mode into which an individual slips when prompted to do so by the right circumstances—by opening a book of poems, for instance, or entering a theater where an illusionist is performing. In either case, the effects are cumulative: as Mark's Jesus said about the difference between those who understood his parables and those who did not, "to him who has, more will be given." Or in other words, those whom fictions have begun to train in a new mode of thinking will enter into what Landy calls a "formative circle," in which their proficiency in the new mode of thinking continues to increase, making it easier and easier to enter into that mode of thought again.[42] Christopher Partridge, a scholar of contemporary religions, and Michael Barkun, a political scientist who studies contemporary apocalyptic Christianity, have made similar observations about how the products of popular culture (films, television shows, novels, music) give people new perspectives on theological and metaphysical issues and "provide resources for the construction of religious and paranormal worldviews"—which then fuel the further production of popular narratives on these topics, eventually leading to what Barkun calls "fact-fiction reversals" (a situation in which something understood by its creator to be fiction is eventually moved by its audience into the realm of fact). Jeff Kripal similarly has studied the important contributions that are made to contemporary Western belief systems by science fiction, superhero comics and other popular representations of the paranormal. He stresses the crucial role that "fiction" plays: "It is almost as if the left brain will not let the right brain speak . . . so the right brain turns to image and story to say what it has to say (without saying it)."[43]

Fictional narratives—as opposed to ostensibly fact-based narratives such as news reports or documentary films—offer an ideal venue for formative training and other types of cognitive adjustment such as Partridge, Barkun, and Kripal describe, for several reasons. Whether a fictional work is the creation of single mind (a novel, a poem, a stage illusion) or drawn from common cultural property (a fable, an urban legend), it can be tailored almost infinitely to suit the tasks that its narrator intends it to serve.[44] And when it is tailored and narrated skillfully, a fictional work can present something that we have never experienced before so convincingly that our minds accept it—thus enlarging our sense of what might be possible.[45] Therein lies, at least partially, the popular success of any number of fantasy authors—J. R. R. Tolkien, Ursula K. LeGuin, Madeleine L'Engle, Neil Gaiman, and so on. Or to switch to a darker genre and some startlingly concrete results, *The Exorcist* enlarged our sense of what might be possible so effectively as not only to cause some readers to throw the book away unfinished and some moviegoers to faint and vomit, but also to "stimulat[e] an unprecedented demand for Catholic exorcisms" for decades to come.[46] William Peter Blatty's novel and William Friedkin's film were able to make even doubting minds believe in demonic possession at least temporarily, and in some cases much longer. (As a friend of mine once said about *The Exorcist*, "I don't believe in possession, but if I did, I know that's what it'd be like.")

Moreover, by definition, as audience members we leave our day-to-day expectations at the door when we enter a narrative and tacitly agree to be pulled along by the story without continually comparing it to what happens in our everyday lives. This means that we temporarily dismantle the cognitive barriers that are patrolled by mundane logic, the five senses, and our customary value systems in order to open ourselves up to scenarios that may differ significantly from what we encounter outside the narrative. Consumers of vampire fiction enter a universe where some of the most basic postulates of normal life (such as death being final) are no longer valid. Less alarmingly (perhaps), as twenty-first-century readers of Jane Austen, we must immerse ourselves in a world that lacks telephones and the right of females to inherit. Still other fictions depart from our normal experiences in only the mildest of ways—most viewers of American TV sitcoms can empathize with their main characters by doing little more than imagining that they live in a different part of the country, have a different family structure or are employed in a different profession. Yet even these minor departures from our personal reality require us to drop our cognitive guard and open ourselves to the realm of what a good narrator has made *plausible* rather than sticking to what is *provable*.[47] And from that point on, we become putty in the hands of that narrator, until we put down the book, leave the theater, or turn off the TV.

Narrating God

But what if you can't turn off the TV because you don't even think it's there? What if the materials that train the mind to think in certain ways and to accept alternative realities are not understood by the audience—and perhaps not by the authors, either—to be fictions, at least in the usual sense of that word?

Tanya Luhrmann spent four years with members of the Vineyard Church (an Evangelical church with congregations throughout the United States), observing how they train themselves to feel the presence of God in their daily lives—how a form of cognitive self-training enables them to cultivate God as a daily reality that is as vivid as their friends and family.[48] One of the first major hurdles they face in doing so is overriding a basic feature of human psychology in the modern West: the assumption that our minds are private. Once congregants come to accept that the barriers between their individual minds and God are porous (once they have adopted what Luhrmann calls a "participatory theory of mind"), they practice specific techniques to enhance their ability to experience the presence of God.

One of these techniques is kataphatic prayer, which is also called "Ignatian" prayer, after the sixteenth-century saint who developed it. Kataphatic prayer encourages worshippers to fill their minds with vivid images, symbols, and ideas while praying. By doing this, they gradually condition their minds to perceive things that are not present to the ordinary senses. During prayer, they feel that they are able to experience events described in the Bible with remarkable detail—down to the "dust motes in the sunlight when Mary heard the news from Gabriel." A study conducted by Luhrmann, in which non–church members were trained in kataphatic practices for thirty minutes a day during a four-week period, showed that, even over this relatively short period of time, participants could significantly enhance their minds' abilities to generate sensory experiences that were similar to their memories of real events.[49] Another technique practiced by Vineyard congregants involves treating God like a flesh-and-blood friend—setting out a coffee cup for God once a week, for example, or an extra dinner plate and chair. Behaving as if God is present (although Vineyard members would not use the phrase "as if") encourages congregants to view God not as a "packet of rules and propositions," but as someone directly involved with their lives, just as a friend or family member would be.[50] Through these and other activities, congregants practice suspending disbelief and learn to trust that what is ordinarily judged by the senses to be "unreal" is actually more real than the physical world around them. Consuming fiction—the right kind of fiction, at least—is understood to help with this precisely because fiction also requires the mind to suspend disbelief and (like kataphatic prayer) gives a vivid reality to things that might otherwise be hard to conceptualize. The *Chronicles of Narnia* by C. S. Lewis are popular amongst Vineyard congregants for this reason. Lewis's portrayal of God in the form of the lion Aslan takes its cue from certain metaphors in the Bible, but it gives those metaphors a palpable reality that sustains readers as they school themselves in more sophisticated ways of conceptualizing God. For readers of *Narnia*, God becomes a vivid presence whose roar you can hear and whose fur you can touch.[51]

What are the rewards of all this? The title of Luhrmann's book is *When God Talks Back*, and that is exactly what he does, eventually, according to those who have diligently followed the path I've just described. Sometimes God helps them decide important issues in their lives—and sometimes he answers such workaday questions as what to wear.[52] From an outsider's point of view, it looks as if members of the Vineyard Church have learned to interpret some of the experiences of their minds and bodies as being not their own, but God's—a remarkable demonstration of how reading fiction, talking to others about suprahuman entities and engaging in cognitive practices that stimulate the sensory and social regions of the brain can reinforce the belief that those suprahuman entities are present and paying attention to us.[53] Like Robert-Houdin's audiences, members of the Vineyard Church have learned how re-enchant their world, but without any intention of "leaving the theater."

Parasocial Interaction

Those of us outside the Vineyard Church could choose to interpret the congregants' experiences as self-conditioned instances of what psychologists call *parasocial interaction* (PSI). *Parasocial* interaction— as opposed to *social* interaction—occurs when one person thinks about another person, perhaps even communicates with another person, unilaterally, without receiving a response. An everyday example of PSI would be someone noticing an attractive colleague, imagining in some detail how to strike up a conversation and what that conversation would be about, but never taking the next step towards actually starting a social relationship. If parasocial interaction is more than transitory—if it continues over a sustained period of time—then a *parasocial relationship* (PSR) is established. A good example of a PSR would be a fan idolizing a rock star, attending concerts, and writing fan letters for years, while the star remains oblivious to the fan's existence.[54]

Recent research has shown that all of us engage in PSI to some degree—with both celebrities and people in our immediate environments—and that most people develop one or more PSRs in the course of their lives. Research has also shown that it is very common for psychologically normal people to develop PSRs with fictional characters—feeling grief, for example, at a character's death that is not measurably different in quality from the grief felt at the death of a real person.[55] A famous instance involves Dickens's serialized novel *The Old Curiosity Shop* (first published in 1840–1841). When readers realized that Dickens was about to kill off a character named Little Nell, Dickens was inundated with letters begging him to spare her. Dickens did not relent, however, and after the fatal episode was published, his audience went into mourning. A member of Parliament, Daniel O'Connell, began to cry while reading the episode on a train and threw his copy of the journal out the window. Ships arriving in New York from England carrying copies of the serial were met with shouts of "Is Little Nell dead?"[56] A similar, although more intense, outcry arose following Arthur Conan Doyle's extermination of Sherlock Holmes in 1893. Doyle, however, unlike Dickens, eventually capitulated, resurrecting Holmes ten years later. Even today, people still write to Holmes at 221B Baker Street, asking for help.[57] More recently, J. K. Rowling's characters have inspired a flurry of PSRs amongst both children and adults. Online chat rooms and blogs discuss questions such as whether Severus Snape was actually fond of Harry Potter or only protected the boy because of the love he had once borne for Harry's mother. Fans offer arguments on either side that extend well beyond anything that the books actually say. The case of Snape, incidentally, demonstrates that PSI is not restricted to fictional characters whom we love or admire. Indeed, actors and actresses who play villains on screen are chastised and sometimes even physically attacked by viewers who have grown to detest their characters. (Fans of *Breaking Bad* expressed vitriolic hatred for the character of Skylar White that occasionally spiraled into homicidal rage directed at Anna Gunn, the actress who portrayed Skylar.)[58]

And yet, even if a few people forget themselves long enough to accost an actress, the vast majority of people who experience PSI or develop PSRs with fictional characters, when asked about their existential status, immediately concur that the characters do not really exist. As David Giles, a scholar of media psychology, puts it, "PSI takes place because the figures are encountered in a narrative context that makes a 'humane' response a logical one."[59] In other words, we engage parasocially with fictional characters because their creators have made them so convincing that they prompt the same emotional and cognitive reactions in us as real people do.[60]

It is probably clear by now why I think that we could choose to call the relationship that the Vineyard congregants develop with God a self-conditioned form of PSR: the congregants train themselves to experience sustained and personal interaction with an individual who, as far as an *outside* observer can tell, never responds and perhaps does not exist. Such a relationship looks just as unilateral as a fan's relationship with a rock star or a reader's relationship with Little Nell. But it is probably also clear why this characterization is a problematic one: as I have just emphasized, ordinarily, people engaging in PSIs and PSRs understand that the subject of their fantasies is not responding and in some cases is not even real. In contrast, for Vineyard congregants, and for that matter for many other Christians and members of other faiths as well, God or the gods are decidedly *not* fictional and are expected to interact with their worshippers occasionally—through prophecies, lightning strikes, miraculous cures and a variety of other means. Which opinion really matters, anyway, when it comes to distinguishing between social and parasocial interaction—our scholarly opinion or their experiential opinion? If *we* can't see, hear or feel the god with whom someone is communicating, does this automatically make the relationship *para*social, whatever the recipient says? This is a very basic question, which deserves much more research and discussion than it has been given by scholars (oddly, the similarities between PSRs and religious beliefs have barely been acknowledged by either psychologists or scholars of religion).[61] I cannot entertain it adequately here, but I do want to emphasize the necessity of not allowing our own lack of belief in particular suprahuman entities to prevent us from accepting that they can be vividly real to others and from understanding the variety of means through which that reality might be constructed. This is particularly important for—but also a challenge to—scholars of antiquity, due both to the distance that separates us from those we study and to the fact that ancient gods have had long careers as subjects of Western art, which has imposed additional layers of fictionality upon them.

There is, then, a widespread human capacity to form strong emotional and cognitive attachments to figures with whom there can be no social relationship in the normal sense of that term (that is, no relationship that is reciprocal in the eyes of outside observers). I am suggesting that we should extend this observation to figures of belief whom we usually call "gods," "heroes," "angels," "saints," and so on, and that we try to use some of what researchers have learned about this capacity to understand the ways in which vivid narrations of myths, centering on vibrant characters, might have enhanced the ancient Greeks' relationships with their gods and heroes. The more skillfully developed are the narratives through which such figures are presented, the higher are the chances that people will experience PSIs and PSRs with them.

Under the term "narratives," I would include a wide variety of things—not only traditional media such as books, theater, films, and TV programs, but also worship (during which the figure's history, attributes, and activities may be presented, celebrated, or discussed), the viewing of artistic representations of the figures,[62] and personal conversations (in the Vineyard Church, congregants' stories of their own encounters with God are important factors in other congregants' development of a capacity to envision and experience God; a similar situation must exist in any other community where people talk about the Invisible Others that they have experienced).[63]

Under "skillfully developed," I would include not only traditional narrative skills such as those needed to write a gripping novel, direct an exciting film, create a captivating statue or give a stunning performance as an actor, but also a variety of contextual considerations such as where the narrative is performed and anything else that might accompany it—costumes, music, scenery, and the like. As I have already mentioned, simply entering a space that one knows to be given over to encounters with supernatural entities (a sanctuary, a temple, a mosque, a church—even a theater, in ancient Greece) helps one to enter into a new state of mind that entertains the possibility that those entities exist. "Props" (fonts of lustral water, saints' or heroes' relics, lamps in the dark interior of a sacred building, divine images, bells-and-smells) can help, too. As Landy notes in his account of nineteenth-century theatrical re-enchantments, the suggestive use that Robert-Houdin made of what he told the audience were bottles of ether (at that time, a new wonder drug) lent both a touch of reality and an aura of mystery to his illusions.

I am *not* suggesting, however, that the ancient Greeks purposefully sought to train themselves, cognitively or emotionally, to encounter the gods and heroes in the way that the Vineyard congregants train themselves to encounter God (or at least the vast majority of the Greeks didn't do that—we might entertain the possibility that something more or less like kataphatic prayer was used by figures such as Aristeas or Abaris, for example, who claimed that their souls journeyed while their bodies slept and then returned to report on what they had seen). Nor am I suggesting that ancient Greek sanctuaries were frequented by figures such as Robert-Houdin, who sought to "re-enchant" the populace by suggestive sleights of hand (some of the itinerant ritual specialists whom we hear about already in the early fifth century were probably skilled in what we now call stage magic, but I can't imagine them choreographing illusions to accompany public narrations of myths—nor can I imagine the sponsoring institutions allowing such things). Rather, my aim has been to offer examples of the human capacity—indeed, I would say the human *desire*—to open the mind and the heart to being transported by well-crafted and well-delivered narratives into a state in which figures who are not part of the ordinary world seem real, and in which one's view of how the cosmos works is altered. Some people, ancient or modern, walk away from such narratives with nothing more than a temporary uplift of the spirits. Others walk away with their existing belief in an alternative reality newly confirmed. Others yet again find themselves changed to some degree—perhaps so affected by a narrator's vision that they are more inclined than they were before to start believing, or to believe in a deeper sense, what they had been hearing about all their lives—from priests, ritual experts, parents or friends. During the moment of engagement itself, I suspect, very few remain unaffected altogether.[64] In fact, this power to affect an audience lay at the root of the objections that Plato and later philosophers made to tragedy.

Episodic Narratives

Good narratives, then, when well delivered, can be powerful stuff—indeed, a good narrative leads to at least a temporary, and sometimes a longer-term, erasure of the line between fiction and reality. We can begin to see how the very fact that Greek myths were often delivered as polished narratives lent credibility to the worlds that they constructed—worlds in which mortals and immortals interacted freely—and therefore made those narratives fitting partners for rituals that were intended to elicit divine response.

In this and the next section, I want to look more closely at some specific features of Greek myths that encouraged such an erasure of the line and that therefore helped to sustain belief even after a festival was over. Some features, such as *deixis* and the other techniques I mentioned earlier, were wielded intentionally by skillful narrators—even if not with the specific intention of effecting such results as those I've just been describing. Others, I suspect, evolved alongside Greek mythic narration itself and became standard features (although good narrators, of course, might learn to deploy them in particularly effective ways). Overall, I want to suggest, Greek myths can be distinguished from many other sorts of narratives by the fact that their characters became known to the audience in a particularly vivid and intimate way, which forged an especially strong bond between those characters and the audience members and nurtured the idea that the characters could have a real effect on audience members' lives.

To talk about some of these features, I'll borrow insights from scholars who work on narratology and, in particular, those who seek to understand how episodic narratives work—that is, narratives that extend their story arcs across installments that are temporally separated from one another. Thus, for example, if we had read Dickens's *Old Curiosity Shop* as it was originally published, we would have had to read eighty-eight installments, each of them appearing a week apart, to learn how Little Nell's story turned out. If we had read George Eliot's *Middlemarch* as it was originally published, we would have had to read eight installments, each of them appearing two months apart, to learn how Dorothea Brooke's story turned out. If we watched the first season of *Homeland* when it was originally broadcast in 2011, it took us twelve weeks to discover whether Nicholas Brody was a hero or traitor (which is not to say that this question wasn't reopened in the second and third seasons and episodically treated again).[65] Following the fates of *Downton Abbey's* characters required us to view fifty-two episodes, stretched out over six years.

One of the most interesting effects of cutting up a story into episodes is that audience members continue to think about the story in between installments. During these periods, they look forward to meeting the characters again and begin to contemplate the finer points of character development and plot. They might speculate about what a favorite character is going to do in the next installment, or even about what the character would do in a situation unrelated to the story. Such engagement between episodes gives characters a life that is independent of the narrative and its creator and thus increases the chances that the characters will become the objects of PSIs and PSRs.[66] Particularly since the advent of broadcast serials that simultaneously reach a large number of people through radio or TV, discussion and speculation about characters have often taken place within groups as well as in the minds of individuals. Colleagues at the copy machine ruminate about what will happen to Lady Mary in the next episode of *Downton Abbey* or what Eleven will see in the next episode of *Stranger Things*. But even before broadcast technologies arose, the characters in episodic stories were objects of public discussion, as the stories I told about the death of Little Nell attest. Such group involvement heightens the effects of any single individual's PSI with a character. If we are all "believing" in Little Nell together, our grief at her death is more intensely experienced.[67]

Many episodic narratives are "series," in which each episode presents a self-contained story that has few connections to other stories in the series, although the characters continue from episode to episode (most situation comedies work this way—for example, *Modern Family*). Other narratives are "episodic serials": that is, although the main story arc extends across a number of installments or episodes, each installment or episode includes a smaller story arc that is resolved within it.[68] Within an episode of *Mad Men* that was first broadcast in 2012, for example, the character Betty was told by her doctor that she might have cancer, but by the end of the episode Betty knew that she was healthy after all. The larger, ongoing narrative arc in which Betty took part—the ups and downs of her relationship with her ex-husband, Don—scarcely got any closer to resolution than before, however. Ancient bardic and rhapsodic recitations fit this model well. On a given occasion, a rhapsode might narrate the story of Odysseus and Polyphemus, for instance—but this would have been recognized by most members of the audience as being just a part of the longer story arc constituting Odysseus's return to Ithaca. Indeed, many episodic narratives, both ancient and modern, characteristically remain incompletely resolved even when they are formally "complete" (Odysseus will set out again from Ithaca soon after landing there, as we learn from Tiresias in book 11 of the *Odyssey*, before that epic itself is even half over). Other stories are revisited by new authors, who offer other endings that may (or may not) be more satisfying than the earlier ones. (Must Antigone and Haemon always die instead of wed? Must Electra remain unmarried?)[69] The mixture of satisfaction and dissatisfaction with which many "completed" serials leave their audiences, as Sean O'Sullivan notes, is an extended manifestation of the very hunger that episodic narratives cultivate on a weekly (or monthly, or some less regularly articulated) basis: we yearn to hear more about the characters who have roused our interests, to whom we have become attached, and with whom the serial has provoked us to form bonds.[70]

The difference between ancient mythic narratives and the modern episodic narratives I have mentioned would seem to be one of chronological control. An ancient listener might have heard the story of Odysseus and Polyphemus only after he had known for some time that Odysseus eventually made it back to Ithaca—and thus he knew, before the rhapsode even began to narrate *Odyssey* 9, that Odysseus would escape from Polyphemus's cave and make it back to his ship. When viewers watched a *new* season of *Downton Abbey* or read a *new* serialized novel, they consumed its episodes in a predetermined order, over the span of which the larger story arc developed in exactly the way that its creator intended. The difference is not as extreme as we might initially think, however. As twenty-first-century showrunners know quite well, not all viewers are "ideal viewers"— that is, some viewers haven't faithfully followed the stories as the episodes unfolded over the course of a season.[71] Moreover, once a season is over, viewers may consume episodes in a different order by watching reruns or downloading episodes from the Internet. Under these circumstances, some elements of the larger story arc and the rewards of watching it unfold are suppressed, just as they would be in the case of a rhapsodic recitation heard out of sequence—most obviously, the element of suspense as to how the larger story will turn out will be gone. Audience members can nonetheless enjoy each episode as part of a longer story through the practice of habits that are deeply engrained in most of us, of which I will mention just two that are especially common. The first might be called "willful forgetfulness." That is, we suspend our knowledge of what will happen in order to experience it again—we jump with fright every time that Margaret Hamilton makes her initial appearance as the Wicked Witch of the West even though we know that she will later end up as a puddle. Moreover, as Alfred Hitchcock once observed, the effect of what we commonly call suspense comes at least as much from knowing what is about to happen and being unable to intervene as it does from *not* knowing what is about to happen—a sentiment that any member of a Greek tragic chorus would endorse. It is the *way* that the story is told that generates emotional response in both "spoiled" and "unspoiled" audience members, as much as the story itself.[72] The second habit involves treating an episode that one consumes out of sequence as a backstory that explains how the characters ended up where they did or that offers new insights to their natures. The original readers of serialized novels such as *Middlemarch* sometimes missed an installment that they could read only later, in the home of a friend who had been scrapbooking the serial or in the completed novel itself, once it had been bound between covers. Such a person might read chapter 21 only after she already knew that Dorothea Brooke had married Will Ladislaw at some undescribed moment between chapters 84 and 85, but chapter 21's narration of an unexpected meeting between Dorothea and Will in Rome, years earlier, adds interesting insights as to *why* their marriage eventually took place.

Consuming episodes of a novel or a television show out of sequence is a good analogy for the way that Greek audiences experienced mythic narratives. People who listened to *Odyssey* 9, to Bacchylides's dithyramb about Theseus's trip to Crete, to Pindar's tale of Jason's adventures,[73] to Sophocles's *Philoctetes* and to many other mythic narratives were thrown into each hero's story in medias res (perhaps into a part of the story they hadn't heard before or even into a part of the story that didn't exist until the poet invented it), but most of the listeners brought to those performances a basic knowledge of the heroes' larger histories. And in fact, particularly if we think about the body of Greek mythic narratives as a whole—a body to which many different authors independently contributed episodes of gods' and heroes' stories—we can more fully appreciate that this mode of consumption brings its own rewards: if the single episode is imaginatively composed, then it inevitably exists in a productive tension with the larger story arc as the audience knows it. Good narrators play with this fact. Later poets often presented the smaller story they were narrating in a way that challenged the larger arc that had been provided by epic, for example. Helen as we meet her in Euripides's *Helen* is quite a different woman, who has had different experiences, from the Helen we meet in the *Iliad.*[74] Hesiod states outright something that Homer never mentioned: Odysseus had three sons by Circe and another by Calypso.[75]

But to return to the main point I've been making, Greek mythic characters, like Dorothea Brooke, Little Nell, Nicholas Brody, Lady Mary Crawley, Eleven, and other serialized characters, were served up to their audiences in small doses, a circumstance that (if the narratives were effective) whetted listeners' appetites to hear more about them and encouraged them to think about those characters—even to develop PSRs with those characters—during the intervals in between. The fact that, in contrast to all of the modern characters I have just named, Greek mythic characters endured through the centuries enhanced this effect: almost everyone knew at least parts of their stories from an early age.

Narrating Belief

In the preceding section, I looked at what happens when a narrative is delivered episodically, as ancient Greek myths were: audiences tend to become more personally engaged with the characters and their story lines. In the section before that, I discussed an aspect of human psychology that makes it easy for audiences to form strong attachments with characters, including the characters of myths, with whom they cannot interact in the ways that they do with people in their everyday lives.

In this section, I look at certain features of narratives themselves that make them good at persuading their listeners to believe in phenomena that are not accessible to our everyday senses. Generally speaking, in doing so I align myself with a recent emphasis on rhetorical poetics in literary criticism, as represented by the work of James Phelan, for example. Phelan has urged us to pay more attention to literary narratives' affective, ethical, and aesthetic effects and to the way that narrators use "the resources of narrative in order to accomplish certain purposes in relation to certain audiences."[76]

To date, however, rhetorical poetics has not been interested in unpacking the ways in which literary narratives affect *beliefs*. To get at that, I begin from two folklorists' studies of how people in contemporary cultures *informally* narrate experiences with the supernatural. One is Gillian Bennett, who studied beliefs in visitations (that is, visits from dead relatives and friends) experienced by women in 1980s Manchester, England. The other is Kirsi Hänninen, who studied beliefs in supernatural encounters experienced by Finnish people in the early 2000s. Bennett and Hänninen have identified a number of techniques that people telling stories about such experiences—with ghosts, with God and with other entities—employ to help persuade listeners that the stories are true.[77] Folklorists usually call this type of narrative a "memorate," to distinguish it from "literary" ghost stories. The term springs from the assumption that the narrators of memorates believe that the stories they are narrating are genuinely drawn from their *memories*, whereas the authors of literary stories acknowledge them to be their own "fictional" creations. A criterion that so sharply divides "fiction" from "truth" is problematic for the materials that this book addresses, but the terms "memorate" and "literary ghost story" are conveniently concise and so I will use them here.[78]

In the majority of Bennett's and Hänninen's cases, the techniques used by those who narrate memorates are employed unconsciously; the narrators have internalized the characteristics of persuasive narratives about the supernatural that they have heard and then replicated them themselves. The circumstances of presentation are usually informal; although by definition, the subjects in Bennett's and Hänninen's studies have been prompted to narrate their stories, memorates typically are told amongst groups of friends and relatives, with little or no preparation beforehand on the part of either the narrator or the audience. With memorates, then, we seem to be moving from Noyes's first category of cultural forms, which are sought out and receive focused attention, into her fourth category of forms, which also receive focused attention but which are unsought. These modes of creation and presentation are so different from the very conscious polishing that Greek poets put into their narratives about the gods and heroes as to make comparison between the two seem impossible, perhaps. However, some of the most successful authors of literary ghost stories from the turn of the last century—the period during which ghost stories were developing as a genre and being purposefully honed to what is considered to be their peak of excellence—employed some of the same techniques as do the narrators of memorates. These techniques persuade us to believe that the stories they are telling are true, at least during the time that we are reading them, and perhaps longer. This should encourage us to look within ancient literary narratives about the gods and heroes for variations of these techniques as well and to try to gauge what effect they had on ancient audiences.

In the next part of this section, I'll describe some of the techniques that Bennett and Hänninen have discussed and sketch how M. R. James (1862–1936), a master of the literary ghost story, employed them. I'll then turn to passages from Greek narratives that I suggest worked similarly.

The X/Y Format

Many of the techniques used by the narrators of memorates contribute to what the sociologist Robin Wooffitt has dubbed the "X/Y format" of narration.[79] These narrators need to persuade audiences not only that the extraordinary experiences they relate really happened (what Wooffitt calls the "Y" factor) but also that the narrators themselves are sane, normal people who function successfully within the familiar world (Wooffitt's "X" factor). Therefore, memorates frequently begin with statements that describe the familiar world and the protagonist's ordinary life within in it (the X factor), such as this one, taken from Bennett's work:

> Ned was working at the time of the story for a local farmer, Sam Black, at the Manor Farm at Dell, and he used to have to go to

market with these cart horses, and he was going to Bradbury market one terrible frosty day.

The story continues with Ned's lead horse slipping on the ice and dragging the other horse down as well; Ned finds himself in a fix on a lonely country road. Then the supernatural element (the Y factor) enters the narrative, as Ned's dead father speaks to him:

> [Ned] said that Dad's voice CAME TO HIM QUITE CLEARLY,[80] said "Cut the girth cord, Ned! Cut the girth cord!"[81]

X factors needn't come at the beginning of a story, however, and they needn't focus only on the normalcy of the *outside* world. Narrators' descriptions of their own thoughts and intentions can help to establish their credentials as normal, sensible people, as well. One Finnish woman in Hänninen's study described an attack by a threatening supernatural entity in detail, and then concluded with:

> I woke up and shivered in horror for several hours. My husband and I went to the emergency room and I got sedatives. We decided that if this event happened again, we would move to another apartment, but it didn't.[82]

The narrator emphasizes the real-world, goal-oriented logic that she used to respond to her experience: her visit to the hospital, her taking of sedatives, her plans for relocation. By doing so, she establishes that she did what any ordinary, sensible person would do in any emergency.[83] In addition, the reference to her husband is a subtle *call to witness* that endorses the narrator's story by suggesting that another person took it seriously.

At times, the X factor in a memorate can be developed to a high degree, including such things as banal descriptions of the weather at the time the incident occurred or what the people involved were planning to have for dinner that evening. This is what Bennett calls "evidential scene-setting." Some of the best turn-of-the-century ghost stories do this to a luxurious extent—which, given that they were destined for publication over many pages of a book or feuilleton,

was possible in a way that it isn't for the narrator of a briefer memorate. Characters in these stories engage in conversations about train
timetables and upcoming charity bazaars; they are described going
about their daily business as clerks, curators of museums, head-
masters on holiday, and so forth, when the supernatural bursts
upon them. As M. R. James himself said,

> If [a ghost story] is to be effective, I think that as a rule the set-
> ting should be fairly familiar and the majority of the characters
> and their talk such as you may meet or hear any day. A ghost
> story of which the scene is laid in the twelfth or thirteenth
> century may succeed in being romantic or poetical: it will never
> put the reader into the position of saying to himself, "If I'm not
> very careful, something of this kind may happen to me!"[84]

In a variation of the X/Y strategy, the narrator may express *ambiguity* about what he or she is describing, insisting first (for example), "I
was fully awake" and "[the uncanny visitor] stood in front of me," but
then declaring, "I don't know whether I was dreaming or not," before
returning to the assertion, "and he [the uncanny visitor] was there"—all
within a short narrative space. Bennett suggests that this strategy
is adopted in order to save face—narrators try to distance themselves
from their remarkable declarations even as they make them, so as
to align themselves with sensible people[85]—but the strategy simultaneously serves to reassure listeners that the narrator strives to
operate under the same "commonsense" principles as they do and
strives to understand his or her experience in that way.

Interjections and the Dialectical Relationship
There are several types of interjections that a narrator might make
while telling a memorate. *Endorsements* and *justifications* are amongst
the most frequent used by Bennett's and Hänninen's subjects. Most
common is endorsement by personal assertion ("I know I experienced
this!") or emphasis ("Oh yes, yes, yes. Oh, yes. I do [believe], yes"),
but some narrators have recourse to religious principles, adding jus-
tificatory remarks such as "God wouldn't allow it" or "It was Saint
Paul, wasn't it, said we're encompassed with a great cloud of wit-

nesses?"[86] And so it is in literary ghost stories as well. Near the end of James's "Canon Alberic's Scrapbook," the narrator, a friend of the man who suffered the supernatural experience, says,

> I never quite understood Dennistoun's view of the events I have narrated. He quoted to me once a text from Ecclesiasticus: "Some spirits there be that are created for vengeance, and in their fury lay on sore strokes." On another occasion he said "Isaiah was a very sensible man; doesn't he say something about night monsters living in the ruins of Babylon? These things are rather beyond us at present."[87]

Interjections play another important role, in addition to endorsing, justifying or doing whatever they individually do. When a narrator interrupts a story, he or she also interrupts the integrity of the diegetic[88] world that the story has been creating. Such interruptions remind listeners that there is a difference between the "Narrating I" (the person relating the memorate, who exists in the "Story-Realm," that is, the time and place in which the story is being told) and the "Experiencing I" (the person who lived through the experience that the memorate describes, who exists in the "Tale-World," that is, the time and place in which the events took place).[89] Anything that asserts the difference between these two "I's" helps to establish that the person telling the story has distanced him- or herself sufficiently from the extraordinary experience as to be able to carefully consider whether it really happened. In a sense, this works towards the same result as does the X/Y format; it helps to show that the narrator is trustworthy while nonetheless allowing the narrator free rein to tell a remarkable tale.

Moreover, those who narrate memorates in the X/Y format or with interjected comments are implicitly inviting audience members into a dialectical relationship, using the story not simply to persuade listeners to believe in what they describe but also to explore the nature of that experience along with the narrator—questioning it, doubting it, trying to understand it, and eventually, if the narrative is successful, believing it. The introduction of ambiguity, which I mentioned earlier as a means of establishing the X/Y format, helps to set up this dialectical relationship, as well, given that it compels listeners to make a choice between (or amongst) the different possible messages that the narrator is sending.

As Bennett says, traditions of both belief and disbelief are transmitted through interactive processes such as face-to-face communication, the sharing of information and the telling of stories.[90] Storytelling is particularly crucial here for a reason that I discussed in Chapter 1: a story can describe events that have not been experienced by the listeners themselves so persuasively that the events come to seem credible, thus enlarging the sense of what *might* be possible beyond the quotidian witnesses of the usual five senses. It is no surprise therefore that, as Bennett says, "people customarily respond to questions of belief with *narrative* answers. The more controversial the topic, the likelier it is that the conversation will include a lot of narrative."[91]

Ancient Narrations of Remarkable Incidents

From antiquity, we have no true memorates—there were no folklorists to record them. We do have a few first-person narratives of supernatural encounters within formal literary works, however: Hesiod's encounter with the Muses on Mount Helicon, for example.

We also have some "vicarious memorates"[92]—that is, secondhand accounts of someone else's experience. (We have already seen two vicarious accounts from the twentieth century: the story about Ned and his father's voice, told by a relative and recorded by Bennett, and the end of "Canon Alberic's Scrapbook," a literary ghost story that is narrated by the friend of the person to whom the supernatural experience happened.) From antiquity, we have, for example, Herodotus's report that the runner Phidippides met the god Pan on Mount Parthenium. The god told Phidippides to instruct the Athenians to pay more attention to him; if they did so, he promised to help them. Phidippides must have been a persuasive narrator, for the Athenians duly built a shrine to Pan and instituted an annual festival in his honor.[93] Herodotus doesn't give us the kind of details we'd like to have about this incident, however; he is more interested in telling us about interaction between the Spartans and Athenians on the eve of the Battle of Marathon, in which Phidippides played a role—Phidippides's encounter with Pan is just a side story. Ideally, we would like to know what Phidippides saw, heard and felt when he met Pan and what words and techniques he used to tell his story to the Athenians so convincingly.

We also find vicarious memorates tersely preserved in inscriptions that were displayed in sanctuaries, recording miraculous things that the indwelling god had done. The Epidaurian *iamata* ("cure stories") are the best known of these. Patients who slept in the *abaton* (a special inner room of the sanctuary) at Asclepius's sanctuary in Epidaurus would be visited by the god or one of his divine children in their dreams and wake up healed. Some of the most remarkable of these cures were recorded by the priests and engraved on tablets that were erected in the sanctuary.[94] Patients would read these (or have them read aloud) before they entered the *abaton* themselves, which, hopefully, would bolster their belief that the god would help them, too. Some of the *iamata* include vivid details—one patient dreamt that Asclepius ordered some servants to bind him tightly to a door knocker to keep him from moving while Asclepius cut his abdomen open to remove an abscess, for instance. Afterwards, when the patient woke up, cured, he found that the floor of the *abaton* was covered in blood.

These cure stories are short and have been stylized to fit particular narrative formulas.[95] As a result, the patient's voice has been lost almost completely. It is interesting to note, however, that the priests who configured the stories before they were inscribed often included physical proofs that what the patient said happened had really happened: the door knocker to which one patient had been bound, for instance, or the blood on the floor of the *abaton*, the kidney stone that Asclepius handed to a patient after removing it from the man's urinary tract, the arrow pulled out of another patient's lung and the statement that before the arrow was pulled out the patient's wound had filled sixty-seven basins with pus.[96] Although the X of the X/Y format in these stories was implicitly established by the fact that the miraculous cures happened in a building that was within sight of where tablets were erected, details such as these must have contributed to establishing veracity as well—to a sort of *evidential scene setting*.

One can imagine a priest, reading aloud these stories, gesturing towards the door knocker to which the patient had been bound or showing his audience the arrow pulled from a lung. Many of the *iamata* include another element that evokes Bennett's work, as well. The omniscient narrator of the story often says, "*it seemed* to so-and-so that Asclepius appeared in a dream and did such-and-such."[97] The phrase "it seemed to" subtly distances the narrator from the event, thus helping to establish that the narrator is trustworthy before the rest of the remarkable tale unfolds.

The *iamata* and the story of Phidippides are set in what was, for the Greeks, contemporary time—that is, these stories involved individuals who lived at the same time that their audiences did or in the very recent past. Some of the people who heard or read these stories knew the individuals to whom the experiences had happened or had parents or grandparents who knew them. The stories that most interest me in this book—the myths composed by poets—are different in two ways. First, they are set during an earlier age when, it was thought, heroic humans were still walking the earth and encountering gods firsthand. The poets needed to show that at least some of the people in that world were like their audience members in order for the audience to feel a connection to them, but the poets also had to show that the heroes were exceptional figures—figures who did remarkable things that helped or hurt other humans while they were alive and who, now dead, could continue to do remarkable things that would either help or hurt humans. This sometimes required breaking the guidelines that M. R. James set for himself, as expressed in the earlier quotation, as we'll see. Sometimes, effective poetic narratives needed to convince the audiences that such things *had* been possible in a world that operated somewhat differently from the way that theirs did.

Second, the poets' stories have been very consciously shaped to affect their audiences—in this sense, they are a lot like James's ghost stories. We will never know, however, whether a given poet purposefully adopted narrative techniques that he or she recognized as being conducive to belief, unconsciously replicated what he or she had heard other convincing storytellers doing, or something in between, because the poets (unlike James) have not left us any comments about how they thought such stories should be shaped. My presumption, moving forwards, is that the poets were probably aware that certain modes of telling a story and certain features within a story had greater effects on their audiences than others did, and so used those modes and features when it was appropriate. They probably would not have articulated this in anything like the terms that James did, however. In other words, I assume that although they were consciously crafting effective narratives, usually the poets were not consciously setting out to induce belief per se in the same *direct* sense that the priests who composed the *iamata* were.

To pursue these ideas further, I'll take as my representative samples the beginning of Hesiod's *Theogony*, portions of the longer Homeric *Hymns*, some portions of the *Odyssey*, some selections from poems by Bacchylides and Pindar and the messenger's speech from Euripides's *Hippolytus*.

Hesiod's Theogony

At the beginning of *Theogony*, Hesiod informs us that he was tending sheep at the foot of Mount Helicon when the Muses burst upon him, spoke to him, taught him how to sing beautiful songs, and handed him a branch of flowering laurel as a token of his new skills and responsibilities.[98] Before they did all of this, however, they berated him and the class of shepherds as a whole: "Field-dwelling shepherds! Ignoble disgraces! Mere bellies! We know how to say many false things similar to genuine ones, but we also know, when we wish, how to proclaim true things."[99]

Suggestions as to how we are to understand this encounter have run the gamut.[100] Was it a dream? A waking vision? Is there even a significant difference between the two? Or is the scene, when all is said and done, just a literary topos, anyway? Tilting the scale towards the latter assumption are all the other cases from the ancient Mediterranean world in which a poet or a lawgiver receives instructions during an encounter with a god on or near the mountain where the god dwells (for instance, Moses) and all the other cases in which a future poet or holy man is caring for animals when the Muses or some other extraordinary experience descends on him (for instance, Archilochus, Epimenides, and Moses).

But as M. L. West said, "the presence of these and other typical elements in Hesiod's vision need not mean that it was not genuine."[101] Or, to shift the viewpoint slightly, the presence of typical elements in Hesiod's account need not mean that those elements were simply rote. Indeed, if they continued to be included in such stories, and especially in Hesiod's poem, which was much admired already in antiquity, then they must have had some effect on their audiences. Carolina López-Ruiz has urged that "rather than assessing the experiential nature of Hesiod's self-representation (which we shall never know), we need to be aware of how, as a narrator, he presents himself in a way that predisposes his audience to take his account seriously and that elevates its contents to those of exceptional revelations."[102]

Interestingly, the lines provide a setting that nicely fills out the X part of an X/Y format. "There I was, just minding my own business on Mount Helicon, tending my sheep as I did every day (X), when suddenly the Muses appeared and gave me an incredible gift and their divine advice! (Y)." The Muses' description of the class of shepherds—and thereby Hesiod—as "mere bellies" heightens the effect, given that it accentuates the difference between the human and the divine that have just come together so precipitously.[103]

The coda to these lines is important, too: "But what is this to me, about an oak or a rock?" asks Hesiod rhetorically, before he launches into the poem proper, leaving his personal experience with the supernatural behind. The expression, proverbial in ancient Greece, meant something such as "Why have I bothered to talk about all of this?[104] What he is saying, of course, matters a great deal—most of his poem will constitute a saga of the gods' early days, how they battled to bring the cosmos into its final state and eventually produced the generation of heroes. Therefore, how and from where Hesiod got the information that he tells us also matters a great deal. By inviting us into an implicit dialogue about how to assess the supernatural experience that he has described, Hesiod makes us pay close attention to what is to come, therefore; we will bear some of the responsibility for deciding whether it is trustworthy, which will make our commitment to its truth all the stronger if we choose to accept it.[105]

The Homeric Hymns

The longer Homeric *Hymns* give us stories in which divinities invade the human world unexpectedly, with terrifying ramifications for the humans whom they visit. Demeter comes to Eleusis in disguise, Apollo kidnaps a boatload of Cretans, Aphrodite seduces Anchises and Dionysus terrorizes some pirates who kidnapped him.[106] In each of these cases, the poet shows us not only how humans react to the presence of a god (the Y factor) but also something of what normal life in the everyday world was like before the god arrived (the X factor).

This is done most extensively in the *Hymns* to Demeter and Apollo. In the *Hymn to Demeter*, daughters of the Eleusinian king's household are going about their daily business, fetching water from a well, when they encounter the goddess Demeter, who at this point in the narrative has disguised herself as an old woman. The girls take Demeter home to their mother, Metanira, who has recently given birth to a son and is therefore in need of a nursemaid—a post that the disguised Demeter has told the girls is ideally suited to a woman of her age.

Metanira is sitting in the palace amongst her serving women when Demeter steps onto the threshold, filling the doorway with divine radiance as her head touches the lintel. In spite of the fact that Demeter is still disguised as an old woman, Metanira is seized by "awe, reverence and sallow fear." Some time later, after Demeter has been working in the household for a while, Metanira peers out from her bedchamber one night to see Demeter placing her infant charge in the hearth fire. Metanira "slaps her thighs and cries out in alarm and lament." Angered by this, Demeter casts off her disguise, which fills the house with "a brilliance like lightning." Metanira gives way at the knees, is struck speechless and fails to notice that her beloved son lies crying on the floor, where Demeter has dropped him. Trembling, the other women spend the rest of the night trying to propitiate Demeter.[107]

In the *Hymn to Apollo*, a boatful of Cretan sailors—"fine men" who are going about their daily affairs, "sailing on business towards sandy Pylos and Pylos' people"—are struck "silent in terror" when Apollo manifests himself on board ship as a huge dolphin, an "enormous and terrible beast." Whenever anyone tries to touch the dolphin, it "tosses him off in any old which-way, shaking the whole ship down to its timbers." When the sailors try to steer the ship, it will not obey the rudder. When Apollo subsequently goes ashore and enters his temple, filling it with radiance, the wives and daughters of the local town "scream under [Apollo's] force, for the god has filled everyone with terror."[108]

In the *Hymn to Aphrodite*, Anchises, a cowherd on Mount Ida, is playing his lyre in his hut when he is approached by Aphrodite, disguised as a human maiden. She convinces him to make love to her in his own humble bed, strewn with animal skins. When, upon waking from his postcoital nap, he sees her in her true form and learns that he has slept with a goddess, he is afraid, and covers his face with a blanket.[109]

In the *Hymn to Dionysus*, Dionysus, disguised as a handsome, well-dressed young man, is spotted by some Tuscan pirates who happen to be sailing past, "speeding over the wine-dark sea," as pirates are wont to do. They stop, leap from their ship, grab the boy and drag him aboard, presuming that he comes from a wealthy family. As the pirates are tightening the sheets, Dionysus causes grapevines and ivy to climb all over the ship, a sight that "seizes the pirates with astonishment." When the god changes himself into a lion and causes a bear to appear on deck, as well, the pirates flee to the stern, where they halt in terror. When the lion eats the captain, the other pirates jump into the sea, where they are transformed into dolphins.[110]

The juxtaposition of the everyday lives of these humans with the terrifying advent of the gods creates X/Y formats. The effect in these cases, however, is not so much to establish that the narrator is a normal, reliable person whose remarkable story must therefore be true (as in the cases studied by Bennett and Hänninen) but rather to establish that the humans in the story are very much like those in the audience, in spite of the fact that at least some of them (Anchises and the Eleusinian royal family) formally qualify as heroes (as entities who deserved worship) from the audience's point of view. The time in which the myths are set and the time in which the poet is narrating them are telescoped by the details of familiar life that the poet includes, making it easier for the audience to imagine themselves in these circumstances and to vicariously experience a god's presence. If scholars are correct that some of these hymns were composed to be performed at cult sites that had connections to the stories being told, then the settings would have helped to accomplish that elision.

Before we leave the encounters narrated by these *Hymns*, I want to underscore how unpleasant most of them are. It's true that Anchises is "seized by desire" when first he sees the disguised Aphrodite and that the Eleusinian infant, Demophon, grows "like a divine being" while under Demeter's care.[111] It's also true that Demeter establishes the Eleusinian mysteries and Apollo the Delphic Oracle, both of which are of great benefit to humanity. But in the *Hymns*, we hear most often about "fear," "alarm," "terror," "screaming," "astonishment," and the necessity of hiding under bedclothes even when the gods in question intend no actual harm. For the audiences who listened to these hymns, the gifts that the gods had bestowed upon mortals were valuable assets, but the conditions under which they were bestowed were reminders of the fact that gods were very different from mortals, that a face-to-face encounter with one was likely to be terrifying—and that at any moment gods might be walking through the human world in disguise.

The Odyssey

Most of the *Odyssey* is narrated by the poet, who omnisciently describes what is happening to the characters, but books 9 through 12 are narrated by Odysseus himself, as he tells the Phaeacians about his amazing adventures, and part of book 4 is narrated by Menelaus, who had an amazing adventure of his own with Proteus, the Old Man of the Sea. This presents us with two different kinds of reports about extraordinary experiences. In the first, we should look for the ways in which the poet presents Odysseus, his companions, and his family members reacting to such experiences. The other kind of reports come close to being memorates (although, like the rest of the *Odyssey*, they are delivered in a formally determined meter, diction, and style). We should be alert within these reports for the ways in which Odysseus and Menelaus use something like the techniques described by Wooffitt, Bennett, and Hänninen to persuade their listeners of what they are saying—particularly Odysseus, who had quite a reputation as a raconteur.

Prime examples of the first kind of report are episodes such as those that Richard Buxton has recently discussed: scenes in which a god, typically Athena, changes into an animal, typically a bird.[112] I will take as an example the incident with which Buxton opens his own discussion, a passage from *Odyssey* 3 that is set in Nestor's palace in Pylos. Telemachus and Athena, who is disguised as Mentor, are visiting Nestor, and "Mentor" has just finished advising Nestor about what he should do to help Telemachus. Having finished this task, Athena decides to depart for Olympus: "So saying, green-eyed Athena went away, likening herself to a vulture, and astonishment [*thambos*] took hold of all those who were looking, and the old man was amazed [*thaumazen*], as he saw it with his eyes."[113]

Interpreters have sometimes tried to wriggle out of what the text so clearly says—that Athena turned herself into a vulture—by arguing that, for example, the poet is speaking only metaphorically: Athena is merely "as swift as a vulture." After Buxton has rehearsed these arguments (which he suggests are anchored in the discomfort of thinking about an anthropomorphic divinity lowering herself to such a disguise), he concludes that "such a move, like other attempts to rescue the poem from fantasy and render it more 'real,' is not only unsustainable but also unnecessary."[114] I agree with him, but what interests me most at the moment is a topic that is more broadly taken up in his book: the amazement with which this remarkable occurrence is greeted. Indeed, in this brief passage, the amazement is signaled twice: once through the noun *thambos* and again through the cognate verb *thaumazen*.

Up until this point in the story, the visit of "Mentor" and Telemachus has been pleasant and productive but completely as one would expect: they have been entertained, they have been present at a sacrifice that is narrated in familiar detail, they have talked, and Nestor is preparing to make his visitors comfortable for the night. The X of Wooffitt's X/Y format has been generously laid out, in other words. And then the astonishing thing happens—our Y factor!—as "Mentor" transmogrifies himself before their very eyes. Telemachus, Nestor, and the other people who see this are understandably surprised, and their surprise serves to stress the remarkability of what has just happened for the people listening to the poem, disposing them to be amazed as well. The final phrase in the passage, "as he saw it with his eyes," is a variation of Bennett's *call to witness*, as it insists that Nestor, whom the *Odyssey* and other epics have firmly established to be a reasonable person, was not dreaming or half asleep but fully awake and in control of his senses when he saw what he claims to have seen.

There are several examples of the second kind of extraordinary experience in books 9 through 12 of the *Odyssey*, as Odysseus and his crew encounter various monsters, an enchantress and the ghosts of the dead and then, finally, witness the weird portent of the skins of the slaughtered oxen of the Sun crawling across the sand, while their flesh bellows and moos as it rotates on spits over a fire. The descriptions of remarkable experiences in these books run contrary to the typically terse way that epic poetry describes such things; in the *Iliad*, descriptions of the Chimaera, Cerberus, and Typhon are all dispensed in just a few words, for instance.[115] Two of the reasons for this difference seem obvious: Odysseus is narrating his own story and wants to make himself look as good as possible—the greater the foe, the greater the hero. And, given that he is a hero known particularly for his way with words, we would be surprised if he didn't linger over extraordinary events.[116]

Some of Odysseus's more extended descriptions include a feature for which Wooffitt, Bennett, and Hänninen have not prepared us: Odysseus knows in advance exactly what awaits him, for Circe has told him about what he will encounter and has advised him about how to deal with it. We, his listeners, therefore know all of this in advance, as well. There is little or no element of surprise when the encounter actually takes place, therefore, either for the internal audience (the Phaeacians) or for us. This stands in contrast to the amazement when Athena turns into a vulture and the amazement or horror evoked by the events described in modern memorates and literary ghost stories. But even as Circe's words dull surprise, they create a proleptic *call to witness:* however fantastic the experience may be about which Odysseus tells us, it has already been confirmed by a goddess who knows about everything that is going on in her particular section of the world, a goddess for whom the Sirens, Scylla, and Charybdis are normal parts of life.

The case of Scylla and Charybdis is especially interesting in this regard. Circe's preview of Scylla's physique and modus operandi is extensive—a bit longer, in fact, even than Hesiod's description of the great monster Typhon[117] and longer by far than any other description of a monster in Archaic or Classical literature. Scylla is an "evil monster" who "howls terribly," although her voice itself is like that of a new puppy. She has twelve feet that wave about in the air and six gangly necks, each topped with a horrible head that has three rows of close-set teeth that are "full of black death." From the waist down, her body is hidden by the cavern in which she lurks, but she pokes her heads out the door in order to fish over the cliff, looking for dolphins, dogfish or one of the sea monsters that Amphitrite tends. If she spots a ship passing by, all six heads dart out at once, gobbling up six sailors at the same time. Later, when Circe and Odysseus discuss the best strategy for getting through the strait where Scylla and Charybdis lurk, Circe adds that Scylla "is no mortal thing, but an immortal evil—dread, dire, ferocious, unfightable, against whom there is no defense." Circe's description of Charybdis is much shorter but still terrifying: three times a day, Charybdis sucks down the black water and three times a day she vomits it up again. Not even the Earth-shaker himself could rescue a ship caught in that whirlpool, she warns.

The next day, after a close encounter with the Sirens, the men in Odysseus's ship are almost immediately "struck with terror" again because they already see smoke and heavy surf ahead and hear a thundering sound—indications that Charybdis is near at hand. In fear, they let their oars drop. The blades dangle free in the oarlocks, drifting about and banging up against the side of the ship—a bit of *evidential scene setting*. The vessel is now dead in the water, dangerously stranded. Odysseus walks back and forth between the lines of rowers, giving them a pep talk, reminding them of the dangers they've already survived, telling them to move forward, and instructing the helmsman about how to handle the steering as they get nearer to Charybdis—a sensible, real-life response to the danger they are about to confront and very characteristic of what we already know of Odysseus.

And then Odysseus tells his audience what he was thinking at the time that all of this was happening and how he had prepared for it. He reveals that he had told the men in advance only about Charybdis and not Scylla, "a problem that could not be dealt with," lest they leave their benches and cower fearfully in the belly of the ship. In other words, Odysseus testifies to the fact that, even under extraordinary circumstances, he operated in the same way as he always did, in a rational, goal-oriented manner. Less rationally perhaps (although just as characteristically), in spite of Circe's admonition to stay under cover himself, Odysseus puts on his armor, takes up two spears and stands at the ship's prow—preparing to confront Scylla.

The X that precedes the Y in this episode is somewhat less developed than in the examples we have looked at from Hesiod and the *Hymns* and less developed than in some of Odysseus's own adventures.[118] This is mostly because Odysseus has moved straight from one extraordinary encounter (the Sirens) to the next; the dangling oars banging against the ship provide a touch of everyday reality, however, as do Odysseus's practical instructions to the men and his own interior considerations. And so they draw nearer to the strait on either side of which Scylla and Charybdis lurk, and Odysseus describes what he saw next:

> Charybdis churns up the water around her, vomiting it forth like a cauldron over a strong fire, the whole sea boiling up turbulently and the sea-foam spattering the tops of the surrounding rocks. When Charybdis sucked down the salty sea-water, the turbulence revealed what lay beneath the sea, and the rocks all around her groaned terribly, and you could see the ground at the bottom of the sea, black with sand. Green fear took hold of the men. In terror of destruction, we kept our eyes on Charybdis.[119]

But while they are staring at Charybdis, Scylla darts from her cave. Odysseus says,

> [She] snatched up six of my men, the strongest and most able of them, and when I turned round to look at my ship and my other crew, I saw their feet and hands from below, already lifted high

above me, and they cried out to me and called me by name, the last time ever they did so, in heart's sorrow.[120]

This is a graphic, evocative description, more than enough to paint a horrifying picture in our minds. But Odysseus adds an extended metaphor that pulls us back, for a moment, both to Circe's earlier description of Scylla (thus tacitly confirming its evidential value) and into the normal world that offers such a contrast to the scene he is witnessing. By doing so, he reminds us that even in the midst of this extraordinary experience he is capable of a certain calm reflection that allows him to draw on his everyday experiences—and that, therefore, he is a man whose description of events can be trusted:

> And as a fisherman with a very long rod, on a jutting rock, will cast his treacherous bait for the little fishes, and sinks the horn of a field-dwelling cow into the water, then hauls them up and throws them on the dry ground, gasping and struggling, so did my men gasp and struggle as they were drawn up the cliff. Right in her doorway Scylla devoured them. They were screaming and reaching out their hands to me in this sickening struggle. That was the most pitiful thing I have ever seen during my sufferings as I travelled the seas.[121]

The metaphor also serves in somewhat the same way as do the shorter *interjections* that Bennett studied, moving us away from an extraordinary scene for a moment, giving us some room to decide whether we will accept the story that Odysseus is telling us.

Odysseus's immediate audience, the Phaeacians, reacted to this and the other strange tales that he told them by sitting in silence, spellbound by his narrative but believing it; the king, Alcinous, promises to take Odysseus home, at last, in order to escape from all of his *many earlier sufferings*.[122] An audience listening to a rhapsode recite this tale in historical Greece would not, perhaps, have been able to experience what Odysseus did, even vicariously, with quite the same depth of verisimilitude as I have suggested they experienced what the Homeric *Hymns* described, but the features that I have stressed in my reading of the episode involving Scylla—the proleptic *call to witness*, the *evidential scene setting* and the extended metaphor that drew on normal life—helped to persuade them that these things had happened once in an earlier time, in a faraway place, to a man who was not so different from themselves.

Bacchylides and Pindar

The characters in Bacchylides's and Pindar's myths do not live the lives of normal people in historical Greece, either.[123] These characters—the heroes—travel to Hyperborea, Crete, and Hades; capture animals such as the Cerynitian Hind, Pegasus, and Cerberus; kill monsters; fight in the greatest wars of all time; and marry minor goddesses—or clouds. The two poets, however, have a habit of breaking into the diegetic worlds of the myths that they are narrating with interjections similar to those employed by the narrators of memorates and modern ghost stories, in order to endorse the stories they are telling and their own interpretations of what happened.

Often, they have what Bennett calls "recourse to religious principles" for their endorsements. Thus, Bacchylides interrupts his story of Theseus's return from a thrilling visit to the undersea palace of his father with the exclamation, "Nothing that the gods wish is beyond the belief of sane mortals!" He cuts into the story of Croesus, who is rescued from certain death on a pyre by a timely rainstorm sent by Zeus and then carried off by Apollo to live amongst the Hyperboreans, with the affirmation, "Nothing that the planning of the gods brings about is past belief!"[124] Pindar introduces the story of Bellerophon's capture of Pegasus and his triumph over the Chimaera and the Solymoi with the declaration, "The gods' power easily brings into being even what one would swear to be impossible and beyond hope"; he concludes the story of Ixion's intercourse with a cloud (which eventually leads to the birth of the centaurs) with "The god accomplishes every purpose just as he wishes, the god who overtakes the winged eagle and surpasses the seagoing dolphin, and bows down many a haughty mortal, while to others he grants ageless glory"; he follows the story of Perseus's beheading of Medusa and his use of that head to petrify his enemies by insisting, "but to me no marvel, if the gods bring it about, ever seems beyond belief"; and he interjects into the story of Coronis's infidelity and Apollo's revenge, "The anger of

Zeus' children is no vain thing."[125] Pindar is fond, as well, of endorsement by emphasis, using such interjections as τοι or καί τοι or ἦρα καί (meaning something such as "indeed!" "and surely!" or "verily!") to assert the truth of a tale.[126]

At the same time as such interjections endorse these myths as accurate accounts of the gods' and heroes' power, they remind us, by breaking into the diegetic worlds of their stories, that the poets are inevitably standing at a distance from what they are narrating. The same effect comes from many of Pindar's gnomic statements and from comments such as "Wonders are many, but then, too, I think, in mortals' talk stories are embellished beyond the true account and deceive by means of elaborate lies. For Charis, who fashions all things pleasant for mortals, by bestowing honor makes even what is unbelievable often believed; yet days to come are the wisest witnesses,"[127] which is virtually a programmatic statement of Pindar's view of myths and their narrators. Even as these statements support Pindar's version of events and more generally his operational mode as a poet who deals in myths, they remind us that he is *mediating* the myth for us. Inspired or not, neither he nor any other poet can claim to have been an eyewitness to the events they describe. And inspired or not (as Pindar concedes in the lines that follow those I just quoted), a poet might choose to speak well of the gods to escape divine blame and its concomitant retribution, even if speaking well meant speaking less than the truth.[128] Recognizing this invites us to enter into a dialectical relationship with the poet and the story he tells, to explore the nature of the experience that it describes, to try to understand why and how it happened, what that might tell us about the gods and eventually to decide to what degree we think the poet has portrayed the experience accurately. If we do believe the poet's story (or even only portions of it), our commitment to believing it will be more strongly held than it would have been, precisely because we have reached it on our own.

Pindar's transitions are especially interesting in this respect. Pindar has a habit of gliding seamlessly from the world of the victorious athlete whom he has been hired to celebrate and into the world of the hero whose myth he will narrate by using a single, seemingly inconsequential word such as a particle or relative pronoun to pivot between the two. In his first *Olympian*, for instance (from which the lines that I quoted in the previous paragraph were taken), Pindar uses the relative pronoun τοῦ to move from a mention of the Peloponnesus, where the athletic victory that he is celebrating had taken place and which he characterizes as the "colony of Pelops," into the myth of the hero Pelops that will consume most of his poem's remaining lines.[129] These pivoting transitions work well to collapse the distance between the here-and-now of the victor's achievement and the there-and-then of the mythic hero's accomplishments, which makes the hero seem more like one of us, potentially, or at least more like the victor being celebrated. Yet the line between the two worlds that is dissolved by such devices is soon reestablished by an interjection or gnomic statement, reminding us of our distance from the heroes and the fragility of our knowledge about them.

The Messenger Speech from Euripides's Hippolytus

Messenger speeches in Greek tragedies are a venue through which remarkable things can be narrated—things that couldn't, or shouldn't, be shown on the stage itself: the miraculous rejuvenation of Iolaus in Euripides's *Heracleidae*, or Heracles wrestling with Death in Euripides's *Alcestis*, or the mysterious disappearance of Oedipus into the grove of the Semnai Theai in Sophocles's *Oedipus at Colonus*.[130] These speeches must describe extraordinary eruptions of the divine into the human world in a manner that makes them thrillingly real but also in such a way as to make them credible for at least their internal audiences, the other characters in these plays. About the external audience, sitting in the theater, I will say something shortly.

I take as an example here the messenger speech from Euripides's *Hippolytus*, which describes the sudden appearance of a gigantic bull that comes out of the sea, scaring Hippolytus's horses so badly that they wreck his chariot and gravely injure Hippolytus himself.[131] The internal audience of this speech is the members of the chorus and Hippolytus's father, Theseus.

The speech does a good deal of *evidential scene setting* through its description of quotidian activities and local geography: the messenger tells us about how he and other servants were combing their horses' manes on the shore when they were joined by Hippolytus, who had just been banished from Athens by Theseus. Theseus had additionally called down a curse upon his son, asking his own father, Poseidon, to kill Hippolytus.[132]

When Hippolytus arrived on the shore, the servants readied a chariot for him and he mounted it: he put his feet into the driver's rings, took the reins from the rail into his hands, picked up the goad and touched the horses with it. With the servants following on foot, he left town by a road that ran along the shore of the Saronic Gulf, leading first to Argos and then to Epidaurus—a road that would have been familiar to many of the men in Euripides's audience. The X of the X/Y format is set firmly in place, in other words.[133]

And then comes the Y: a terrible rumble was heard, deep within the earth, which caused the horses to prick up their ears. "Violent fear came upon all of us," says the messenger. Looking towards the water, they saw an enormous, uncanny wave blotting out the sight of Sciron's coast, the Isthmus and Asclepius's Rock (once again, points of local geography that would have been familiar both to the internal audience and to Euripides's audience). When the wave broke on the shore, it cast up a monstrous, savage bull, whose bellowing filled the land. The horses panicked, and Hippolytus tried to control them by pulling back on the reins, but they refused to be steered by him, paying no heed to either their harnesses or the chariot itself. Maddened with frenzy, they crashed, taking their driver along with them. And then, all was utter confusion. Axles and linchpins flew into the air, and Hippolytus, tangled in the horses' reins, was dragged along the road, his head bouncing on the rocks.[134]

This is a vivid scene that works to firmly anchor the extraordinary within the ordinary; the detail of axles and linchpins flying through the air in the very midst of the supernatural crisis is especially effective in this regard. By the standards laid out by Wooffitt, Bennett, and Hänninen, the messenger would have had a high chance of persuading his immediate listeners that what he described had really happened (and, in any case, the arrival of the dying Hippolytus soon after the messenger finished speaking, carried on a litter, would have been an extraordinarily effective instance of Bennett's *call to witness*). But what about the other listeners, sitting in the theater, just across the gulf from where Hippolytus's accident occurred? They probably did not worry that *exactly* such a thing could happen to them—they were not the sons or grandsons of gods after all, as Theseus and Hippolytus were—but the scene would have been a formidable representation of an incident that was accepted as part of Athenian history.[135] This *had* happened to their ancestors. This *was* what the gods, and the heroes, were capable of. Powerful forces had once been at play in the cosmos, and there was no reason to doubt that they still were. To adapt M. R. James's formula, if they weren't very careful, something awful (albeit less spectacular) might also happen to them.

A Final Question

All in all, then, myths as they were publicly disseminated in Greece, through the skillful performance of highly engaging narratives, were ideal partners for festivals because the myths helped to sustain the basic premises on which the festivals depended: that the gods and heroes existed and that they might choose to interact with mortals, for better or for worse. Myths were particularly able to do this, I have suggested, because, amongst other things, they were narrated episodically, which encouraged individuals in the myths' audiences to develop closer, more personal engagements with their characters, and because the poets used techniques that were conducive to belief, such as Wooffitt's X/Y format and the call to witness, evidential scene setting, ambiguity, endorsements and justifications that were described by Bennett and Hänninen. These features, as well as some that are more familiar from literary studies of Greek literature, such as *deixis* and apostrophe, and the habit of performing the narratives at ritually important times and places, imbued the myths with what Landy would call a formative effect. They conditioned the audience members to experience the gods and heroes as a daily reality and to forge enduring relationships with them.

There is one more issue that is central to our understanding of how Greek myths worked in concert with festivals, which I have left dangling up till now. Granted that well-narrated myths about Theseus, for example, helped to sustain belief in *his* existence and *his* availability to respond to worshippers, how does that help us to understand the contribution that such a myth made when it was narrated, for instance, at a Delian festival in honor of *Apollo* (as was Bacchylides's seventeenth ode)? Traditionally, such questions have been answered contextually or thematically when they could not be answered aitiologically: narrating a story about Theseus in honor of Delian Apollo, for example, has been said to make sense because Delos, the home of the god, was presented in myth as one of the places where Theseus and his friends stopped on their victorious way home from Crete and because Apollo was generally regarded as the divine protector of young men. This is certainly a valid approach, but it risks a potential circularity. Bacchylides's eighteenth ode, which describes Theseus's journey from Troezen to Athens from the point of view of his father, Aegeus, is assumed by scholars to have been written for performance by Athenians simply because it concerns the royal family of their own city. What if our manuscripts did not tell us that the seventeenth ode was composed for the Ceans to perform on Delos? Would we invent a different way for it to "make sense," perhaps assuming that it, too, was meant for the Athenians, and for performance in Athens, simply because it concerned Theseus and a group of other young Athenians? Or what about cases where even our most imaginative scholarly logic can't contrive a connection, such as the brief dithyramb that Bacchylides composed to be sung at Delphi during the winter months when Dionysus, not Apollo, was in charge there?[136] How does the story that Bacchylides tells us, about Heracles's accidental murder at Deianira's hands, help sustain belief in anyone other than Heracles himself? And how (famously) could so many tragedies get away with having nothing to do with Dionysus, the god at whose festivals they were originally performed?[137]

Context and theme (as well as the personal tastes of the poets and their patrons) certainly could matter when a poet chose a myth to narrate, but they cannot answer the question of why, seemingly, a wide variety of myths were appropriate for narration at a wide variety of festivals. For this, we have to think about myths not in the individual sense but as a whole—as a corpus. This is what I will take up in Chapter 4.

4

The Greek Mythic Story World

IN CHAPTER 3, I took up the question of how the highly polished nature of Greek mythic narratives—the vivacity and expressive power that earned so many of them an enduring place in the *pleroma* of world literature and art—contributed to the creation and sustenance of belief in the gods, the heroes, and a divine world more generally. I focused particularly on how Greek myths evoked emotional and cognitive responses from their audiences that were virtually indistinguishable from those evoked by real-life people and situations and on how the ancient modes of narrating myths helped to keep the stories and their characters alive in an audience member's mind and heart long after a narration was over, thus further sustaining the beliefs that the stories had nurtured.

One question that I temporarily set aside was why the narration of almost any myth, focusing on almost any character, was appropriate for recitation at almost any festival dedicated to almost any god—even when there was no obvious aitiological, thematic or contextual link between the myth and the festival. The general answer must be that the Greeks cared less about always making tightly "logical" connections between festivals and myths than we have imagined—or, to put it otherwise, that the contributions that mythic narratives made to creating and sustaining belief in the gods and heroes must have been more broadly based than we have previously acknowledged. More specifically, I want to suggest that an important element enabling this breadth of applicability was the tightly woven story world that was cumulatively created, on a continuous basis, by the myths that were narrated. This story world validated not only each individual myth that was part of it, but also *ta palaia* more generally—all the stories about what had happened in the mythic past, the characters who had lived then and the entire worldview on which the stories rested. Because a myth told about Heracles, for example, was deeply embedded in this story world, it had the power to sustain and enhance belief not only in Heracles himself but also in the entire cadre of the divine world and the possibility of their interaction with mortals, if it were well narrated.

I'll begin with a discussion of what makes story worlds in general coherent and credible and will then move on to ask whether the story world created by Greek myths fulfilled those criteria or operated in a different manner. Along the way, I'll discuss some characteristics that Greek mythic narratives share with narratives that are familiar from our own times, which will further heighten our appreciation of the way that the Greek mythic story world created and sustained belief. Of course, an important backdrop to my project as a whole, as sketched in this chapter and the preceding one, is the fact that the *places* and *times* in which Greek mythic narrations were frequently performed were in themselves conducive to creating and sustaining belief—that is, the narrations were performed in *sanctuaries* dedicated to the gods and heroes, during *festivals* dedicated to the gods and heroes. The audiences were primed by these conditions to open their minds to the ideas that the myths conveyed.

Story Worlds

One of the first scholars to theorize about how story worlds are created was himself the creator of a very famous story world: J. R. R. Tolkien. In an essay titled "On Fairy-Stories," which was delivered in 1939 as the annual Andrew Lang Lecture at the University of St. Andrews and then published in 1947 in a Festschrift for the fantasy writer Charles Williams that was edited by C. S. Lewis, Tolkien introduced the term "Secondary World," which he contrasted with

"Primary World," the world in which we live. The virtue of these terms, he suggested, is that they allow us to avoid the terms "real world" and "fantasy world," which obstructed an idea that Tolkien and a number of other authors and scholars wanted to emphasize (including Lewis, in his own essay in that collection),[1] namely, that a well-constructed fictional world elicits responses from us that are almost indistinguishable from the ways in which the real world affects us, even if that fictional world has fantastic elements. Samuel Taylor Coleridge's well-worn phrase "willing suspension of disbelief," which he invented in 1817 to discuss poems that included elements of the fantastic, such as his own *Rime of the Ancient Mariner*,[2] misses the mark completely as far as what well-constructed fiction does to readers, according to Tolkien. What really happens, he says, is that an author makes

> a Secondary World which your mind can enter. Inside it, what he relates is "true": it accords with the laws of that world. You therefore believe it while you are, as it were, inside. The moment disbelief arises, the spell is broken; the magic, or rather art, has failed. You are then out in the Primary World again, looking at the abortive little Secondary World from outside. . . . [T]*hen* disbelief must be suspended. But this suspension of disbelief is a substitute for the genuine thing.[3]

The media scholar Michael Saler has recently coined the term "willing activation of pretense" to describe this process that Tolkien discussed,[4] but I think that Tolkien meant something more than that: a truly well-constructed story world requires no *conscious* decision at all on the part of audience members who participate in it—neither the suspension of disbelief nor the activation of pretense. It immerses readers or viewers so completely and yet so subtly that they pass into it without even noticing that they are doing so.

In addition to credibility, a Secondary World requires something else. As the media scholar Mark Wolf puts it, what it needs is a

> distinct border partitioning it from the Primary World, even when it is said to exist somewhere in the Primary World, or

when the Primary World is said to be part of it, as in the case of the Star Trek universe containing earth. It is connected to the Primary World in some way but also set apart enough to be a world unto itself.[5]

"Partitioning with a distinct border" can refer to devices such as wardrobe doors, rabbit holes, deadly deserts over which cyclones carry houses and distances that only warp-speed vehicles can traverse, but it also refers to giving the Secondary World a sufficient number of sufficiently striking features—geographical, botanical, zoological, technological, and so on—that make it different from the Primary World. For example, the world in which the Oz stories are set has Munchkins, flying monkeys, kalidahs, talking trees, mangaboos, and a queen who can change her head as easily other women change their hats (to name just a few of its oddities).[6] Wolf argues, in fact, that one can't really be said to have created a truly Secondary World if one simply introduces a single element—vampires or space aliens, for example—into a world that in all other respects aligns with our Primary World.[7] One might nonetheless have created a gripping story—after all, Bram Stoker's *Dracula* essentially does what I just described: it introduces vampires into a world that is otherwise identical to that of late nineteenth-century Europe. One might even make such a story coherent and credible—Stoker did this particularly through the introduction of diary entries, letters written by one character to another and newspaper clippings, for example. But it is doubtful that the original readers of *Dracula*, who were, after all, the same sorts of Victorian folk who populated the novel, felt that they had entered a wholly new story world in the same way that readers of the Oz books or the viewers of the *Star Wars* movies do.

That takes care of the word "Secondary" in Tolkien's term: a Secondary World must be different enough from the Primary World to merit the adjective. But what about the word "World"? When we talk about a story world, we typically mean something that goes beyond the narratively constructed space in which a *single* story is set, something that constitutes a space where *many* stories, whether they be directly connected to each other or not, can be set and that is perceived by its audience as consistent and coherent. The story world of

Oz, which slowly developed over the course of sixty-plus volumes, is again a good example: it includes not only the country of Oz itself but also some neighboring lands, such as Ev and Ix, which were explored both in some of the later Oz books and also in books that formally lay outside the Oz corpus. Characters transfer from one book to others, sometimes traveling from one country within the Oz world to another.[8] Tolkien's story world, including the land called Middle-Earth, is the setting not only for *The Hobbit* and *The Lord of the Rings* but also for stories narrated in the *Silmarillion*, which take place in lands contingent to Middle-Earth, all of which are contained in a world called Arda, which is itself part of a cosmos called Eä. Some of these stories, especially those from the final section of the *Silmarillion*, serve as prequels to *The Lord of the Rings*. There are story worlds outside of fantasy and science fiction, too. William Faulkner's Yoknapatawpha County, in which twenty-two of his novels are set, qualifies as one, for example, as does Garrison Keillor's Lake Woebegone. These latter two worlds are not distinctively *secondary*—that is, they don't differ significantly from the Primary World in their geographic, botanical, zoological, and technological features—but they are well enough described to hold together as discrete places over the span of the different stories. You can even map them, as Faulkner himself did.[9] (In fact, the creation of maps and other paratextual materials to accompany a series of stories—lexicons of invented languages, timelines, genealogies, bestiaries, and other guides to its infrastructure[10]—is a sure indication that a story world has taken on an existence of its own.)

With these two sets of guidelines in place—what it takes to make a story world a *world* and what it takes to make it *secondary*—let us turn now to Greek myths and consider what kind of story world underlies them.

The Greek Story World

My first question is whether we find strong characteristics of a *Secondary* World in Greek myths. Are there an adequate number of sufficiently odd geographic, botanical, zoological, and technological features and the like to qualify? Let us take stock—trying to be

representatively inclusive without becoming pedantically exhaus-
tive. In our bestiary, we have some remarkable creatures: Gorgons,
griffins, harpies, sphinxes, centaurs, Cyclopes, Sirens, Typhon, the
Hydra, Scylla, Pegasus, the Chimaera, the Minotaur, a couple of
dragons and Cerberus. But many of the other creatures who appear
in myths are just larger or more vicious versions of creatures found
in the Primary World: the Nemean Lion, the Erythmanthian and
Calydonian Boars, the Crommyonian Sow, the Mares of Diomedes,
the Teumessian Vixen, the Cretan and Marathonian Bulls, Python,
and Sciron's giant turtle.[11]

Botanically, there is very little: from the *Odyssey*, we get *moly* and
lotuses, and Epimenides mentions a plant called *alimos* ("banishing
hunger") that kept Heracles from starving while in the desert,[12] but
I can't think of other examples. Technologically, we have the various
automata built by Hephaestus, Perseus's (or rather Hermes's) winged
shoes and Hades's cap of invisibility. As for unusual geographic features, I can offer only the Symplegades and Charybdis.

Aside from the zoological catalogue, this is not a particularly
strong record of weirdness. And we must remember, moreover, that
the catalogue I just presented is a pasticcio, gathered together from
many different works. In single episodes, Greek myths usually introduce only one remarkable feature—a monster, most often. This
amounts to the same thing as a seriatim introduction of vampires
and aliens into an otherwise Primary World. Usually, moreover, ancient authors seem relatively uninterested in a monster's remarkable
features, describing them only briefly. Consider this passage from
the *Iliad*, for example, in which the story of Bellerophon and the
Chimaera is told:

> So off went Bellerophon to Lycia, under the excellent escort of
> the gods. And when he reached the river Xanthus, the king wel-
> comed him and honored him with entertainment for nine solid
> days, killing an ox each day. But when the tenth dawn spread
> her rosy light, the king questioned him and asked to see the to-
> kens that his son-in-law Proetus had sent. And when he saw the
> evil tokens, he ordered Bellerophon to kill the furious Chimaera,
> a creature that was not human but divine; a lion in front, a ser-

pent in the rear and a goat in the middle, and breathing fire. Bellerophon killed her, trusting in signs from the gods.[13]

Homer doesn't fail to mention the Chimaera's triple physiognomy and fiery breath, but he does not choose to take full advantage of their narrative possibilities (nor does Pindar, for example, who allots to her a single adjectival phrase, "fire-breathing").[14] Similarly, in Sophocles's *Trachiniae*, Deianira, quoting the centaur Nessus, describes the Hydra only as "the monstrous beast of Lerna"—no mention even of the Hydra's nine heads, much less their ability to duplicate themselves when cut off. The chorus of Aeschylus's *Agamemnon* refers to Scylla simply as "dwelling in the rocks, a harmful thing for mariners," and Euripides's Medea describes her as just "a dweller on the Tuscan cliff."[15] This is not to say that Greek authors could not focus more closely on the wondrous or the horrible when they wished to: Aeschylus's portrait of the unnamed goddesses who invade Apollo's Delphic Oracle, for example, is detailed and chilling: black and utterly abominable, they snore forth repulsive breath and foul ooze drips from their eyes. But that is the point, after all: the epiphany of these disgusting goddesses is meant to be understood as a sudden irruption of maddened rot into a space of reasoned light; the contrast has to be striking. Similarly, if for different reasons, Odysseus's own narrations of the monsters he encountered and their dreadful modes of attack are hair-raising—but what else would we expect from such a talented, self-aggrandizing storyteller?[16] Hesiod's description of Typhon, the king of all monsters and the greatest threat to Zeus's world order, which constitutes the topic of Hesiod's poem, also goes on at some length: from Typhon's shoulders sprang a hundred serpents' heads, all licking with their dark tongues; fire shot forth from his eyes and terrifying voices echoed from his many mouths, mimicking gods, bull, lions, puppies, and horrible hissings. The battle between the two is prodigious and vividly described.[17]

But generally, the monstrous and the marvelous are treated with restraint by ancient authors; the one big exception is metamorphosis (the transformation of a person into an animal, plant or mineral), which happens frequently in Greek myths and which I'll treat in Chapter 6.[18] Overall, the effect of introducing the monstrous and the marvelous into Greek myths is much like that produced in the modern genre of magic realism, where elements that, in isolation from their narratives, might stand out as magical or fantastic—ghosts conversing with the living, telepathy, and extraordinary longevity, for instance—are integrated into the everyday world in such a way as to be accepted by audience members. This does not rob them of their marvelousness; rather, it enables them to contribute to an expansion of the narrative world's possibilities.[19] We should note the contrast between this way of narrating the marvelous and that found in many examples of fantasy writing, in which remarkable elements are accentuated by vivid description, such as this passage from Neil Gaiman's *Neverwhere:*

> Upon [Hunter's] arrival, it comes through the underbrush, a fury of brown and of white, undulating gently, like a wet-furred snake, its red eyes bright and peering through the darkness, its teeth like needles, a carnivore and a killer. The creature is extinct in the world above. It weighs almost three hundred pounds and is a little over fifteen feet long, from the tip of its nose to the tip of its tail. As it passes her, it hisses like a snake and, momentarily, old instincts kicking in, it freezes. And then it leaps at her, nothing but hate and sharp teeth.[20]

This giant weasel creature enhances the strangeness of a subterranean world that Gaiman has already painted as being weird, dangerous and utterly disconnected with "normal" existence above ground.

My initial conclusions, then, are that the story world of Greek myths is not a strongly secondary one, that the secondary qualities that it does possess focus upon single events or single characters, and that those events or characters are often integrated into descriptions of the Primary World in such a way as to expand the possibilities of the latter, rather than to highlight the extraordinariness of the former. This isn't because the Greeks weren't able to envision or create what we would call more truly Secondary Worlds, according to Tolkien's standards: some examples that prove they could are Lucian's *True History,* the latter parts of the *Alexander Romance,* those portions of the old *Argonautica* that are set in Colchis or on the journeys to and from Colchis, and books 9 through 12 of the *Odyssey*.

The latter two instances are particularly interesting because their reception histories once again demonstrate the Greek preference for keeping their story world closer in nature to the Primary World than to a Secondary World. Over time, the fantastical lands that Jason and Odysseus visited began to be pulled back into the category of the unremarkable, as the Greeks repeatedly tried to map them onto the world that they knew. Phaeacia became Corcyra, for example, the Symplegades became the straits of the Bosphorus, and the island of the Cyclopes became Posillipo. We should note as well that, leaving aside these travels of Odysseus and Jason, when Greek heroes came from or journeyed to exotic places, they typically were places that nonetheless had a firm location in the world as the Greeks knew it: Cadmus and Europa came from Phoenicia, Theseus went to Crete, Bellerophon journeyed to Lycia and Iphigenia ended up amongst the Taurians in Scythia, for example. Perseus and Heracles traveled to more fantastical lands for some of their labors—each of them went to the Garden of the Hesperides, for example (see Figure 4.1 for Heracles's trip there)[21]—but "Hesperides," after all, is nonetheless a firmly geographic name: even if no one who told or listened to these myths had themselves been there, the very word "Hesperides" (Westworld) insisted that the heroes had gone west, and thereby kept them within a world articulated by familiar cardinal points. The name of the longest-running fantasy land that the Greeks invented— Hyperborea (Beyond-the-North)—reveals a similar determination to keep exotic realms tethered to the known world, even if on a longer leash. Perhaps, as Pindar once said, you couldn't get to Hyperborea by ordinary means such as walking or sailing, but you could pin Hyperborea to a spatial relationship that was essentially no different from that to which you would pin Oropus if you lived in Athens. If you found the right mode of transportation and just kept going north, you'd eventually arrive there. Perseus and Heracles each managed to do so, after all.[22]

Greek myths, then, clung to familiar geographic templates, familiar botany and familiar technology, and they limited the degree of strangeness to which their monsters could aspire. They do not

4.1 Heracles approaches the Garden of the Hesperides in the cup of Helios. Atlas and one of the Hesperides look on; Athena and Hermes flank the scene (further on the image, see Chapter 4, note 21). Attic red-figure bell krater by the Nikias Painter, dated to between 420 and 400 BCE (detail). Now in a private collection. Photo credit: Christie's Images / Bridgeman Images.

constitute a clearly Secondary World by Tolkien's terms. Nonetheless, I suspect that many of us feel it in our bones that Greek myths do, collectively, have a distinct story world. One reason for this is that we grew up surrounded by books that corral individual myths into anthologies. Translated or renarrated by the voice of a single author, illustrated by the pen or brush of a single artist and then bound between two covers, the myths are perforce given cohesiveness. The practice has a long history: Ovid and Apollodorus were already doing it, as were predecessors such as Pherecydes and Hellanicus. Centuries of European art cemented the idea, not only insofar as artists took particular pleasure in illustrating Ovid, the greatest of all unifiers, but also insofar as there was an implicit agreement that Greek myths—virtually any Greek myths, whether they came through Ovid or not—were, along with stories from the Bible, amongst the few appropriate subjects for upper-class décor. Walking today through a museum gallery within which such works have been gathered together is like strolling through a mythographic handbook.[23]

The Mythic Network

But another, and more important, reason that the Greeks seem to have a mythic story world is that the gods, heroes and monsters whom we meet in the individual stories are always part of a network.[24] There is no such thing as a Greek mythic character who stands completely on his or her own; he or she is always related to characters from other myths, and the narrators take some pains to tell us that (and, one assumes, to invent such relationships when they need to). Python may have been a new monster to some people when they heard the Homeric *Hymn to Apollo*, but the poet ties her into the larger family of mythic monsters by mentioning that she had been the nursemaid of Typhon, a dreadful creature about whom Hesiod had a lot to say. And the poet makes Apollo himself tell us, a few lines later, that Python was a pal of the Chimaera—who first appeared in the *Iliad* and whom Hesiod said was the *child* of Typhon (as were Cerberus and the Hydra).[25]

The branches of heroic family trees are at least as entangled as those of the creatures that they kill or subdue: Heracles was the descendant of Perseus; by killing a Gorgon, Perseus played midwife to the marvelous horse Pegasus upon which Bellerophon rode to kill the Chimaera; and Bellerophon was the ancestor of the Trojan ally Glaucus—who was the first to narrate the story of Bellerophon and the Chimaera.[26] Cadmus, meanwhile, searched for his sister Europa, who had been kidnapped by Zeus to start a dynasty on Crete—which eventually led to the birth of the Minotaur, whom Theseus killed.[27] Theseus journeyed to the Underworld to help his friend Pirithous kidnap Persephone—a favor in return for Pirithous having helped Theseus to kidnap Helen (who was later kidnapped again by Paris, thus starting the Trojan War, in which Glaucus fought). Failing in this quest and trapped in the Underworld, Theseus was rescued by Heracles, who while he was down below also met the ghost of Meleager, whose sister Heracles later married . . . by whom he subsequently was murdered, with the result that Odysseus met *Heracles*'s ghost in the Underworld.[28] To get back to Cadmus: teeth from a dragon that he had slain while looking for his sister were carried to Colchis, where they later caused problems for Jason, who was aided by Medea, who later tried to kill Theseus and subsequently married Achilles after they both were sent to the paradisiacal White Island, where the elite of the heroic race hung around after their lives were over.[29]

Gods were notoriously intertwined with one another, too, not only in the sense that, during those early epochs of creation, there was no one else with whom they could dally and reproduce but in other ways as well: Aphrodite fought with Persephone over Adonis, who had been killed by a boar sent by Artemis, who was angry with Aphrodite for having contrived the death of Hippolytus, the son of Theseus.[30] Hera wheedled Aphrodite into lending her a magic charm under the pretense that she wanted to settle a quarrel between their grandparents, Tethys and Oceanus, and then used that charm to seduce Zeus, so that Poseidon could cause trouble on the battlefield while Zeus was taking a postcoital nap. Hermes stole his big brother Apollo's cattle and then won forgiveness by singing a song about how the whole family of gods had come into existence in the first place.[31] Gods were intertwined with monsters and heroes as well—as their parents and lovers, impeders and helpers. Athena helped Bellerophon put a bridle on Pegasus so that he could kill the Chimaera. Zeus made love to Io (thus becoming the great-great-grandfather of Cadmus and Europa, to the latter of whom he eventually also made love), and as a favor to Zeus, Hermes killed the one-hundred-eyed herdsman Argus, whom Hera had sent to guard Io.[32]

Those last three paragraphs were far easier for me to compose than anything else I have written in my scholarly career. As a child, I read almost nothing except Greek mythology books, and by the time I was ten, I was an expert at my own private version of "Six Degrees of Kevin Bacon": if you gave me two figures from myth, I could find a way to link them together (and in fewer than six steps, usually). Such mental gymnastics have a long and respectable pedigree: starting already in late antiquity, scholiasts and mythographers reported fully on the loves, hates, and other connections amongst gods, heroes, and monsters. Earlier still, Ovid sewed his *Metamorphoses* together with the threads of such relationships, some of which he may have invented, but still, they *sounded* real. He said, for example, that Arachne was a girlhood friend of Niobe—and if readers are mythically well informed, they get frissons when they read that line, knowing that the two girls are also linked by a shared hubris that leads them to sorry ends.[33] The Hellenistic poets played such complex versions of this game that even my precocious talents were at times confounded. Whom did the poet Lycophron mean when he referred to the "five-times-married frenzied descendant of Pleuron?" Helen, of course, as A. W. Mair's footnotes to the Loeb edition so kindly informed me: the great-great-granddaughter of Pleuron, Helen was carried off by a smitten Theseus when she was a girl, was properly married to Menelaus when she was a bit older, was kidnapped again by Paris and lived as his wife for more than nine years, was married to Deiphobus after Paris's death and then, finally, after the end of her earthly life, was married to Achilles, on the White Island. (But wait—didn't I just say that Achilles married *Medea* on the White Island? Well, Lycophron mentions that, eventually, too.)[34]

But the weaving of the net with which these later poets played their games began much earlier, and it was not meant exclusively for the erudite. The Hesiodic *Catalogue of Women* includes such morsels of information as the fact that the daughters of Pelops and Hippodamia married the sons of Perseus and Andromeda. It's from one of Bacchylides's epinician odes that we first learn about Heracles meeting Meleager in the Underworld, and it's from the end of Euripides's *Hippolytus* that we first learn about the tangled web of relationships amongst Artemis, Aphrodite, Adonis, and Hippolytus.[35] Those who wished to create new myths, moreover, understood the importance of tying their threads securely into the existing tapestry. When the ritual *bricoleurs* behind the new mysteries of Dionysus decided, at some point in the late Archaic period, that they needed an *aition* for their cult, they created what was essentially a sequel to the well-known story of Demeter and Persephone, turning the famously kidnapped daughter into the grieving mother of a kidnapped child herself.[36] Theseus, who seems to have been a fairly low-key hero until the sixth century,[37] was groomed for the big time by being linked to such stars as Medea (who became his evil stepmother) and Heracles (who became his rescuer), as we have seen.[38] Even Orpheus, a character who in most ways stood aloof from the great mythic families and from the mythological network itself (and properly so; singers are by nature marginal figures in Greek society), was drawn into service as an Argonaut.[39] Indeed, the voyage of the *Argo* more generally is a perfect example of a story that grew through a type of agglomeration encouraged by the mythic network: over time, almost every hero of the generation that lived before the Trojan War (including one woman), ended up on that ship. The Calydonian boar hunt is a similar case (and it recruited the same woman—but then, there weren't more than handful of heroic women to choose from).[40]

Studying this network for its own sake is pretty boring. Few people read Timothy Gantz's *Early Greek Myth* straight through from page 1 to page 743, valuable though it be as a reference work, and few, I suspect, actually study those schematized wall charts that trace every mythic character back to Chaos in exquisite detail. Until we hear or see the stories behind the relationships and meet the personalities connected with the names, the relationships themselves just aren't very interesting. Yet when embedded in myths, the relationships not only come to life but also help to create a coherent story world that in turn serves to anchor and validate each individual myth, in an infinitely reciprocal way. That is, effective narration of Theseus's adventure with the Minotaur also lends credibility to Perseus's defeat of snaky-haired Medusa or to the birth of Erichthonius as a creature half snake and half human, because all of these hybrid figures are presented as inhabiting the same realm—a realm that is thickly crisscrossed by the relationships that I've been talking about. Each story stands as a guarantor of the existential rules underlying the others and is in turn guaranteed by them. Each of them contributes to a completely furnished world, from which audience members may subsequently break off pieces to use as a situation demands—pieces that still refract the authority and allure of the whole.[41] This is one reason that figures and incidents from myths are so powerful as symbols: even when we regard them singly, they are never actually alone.

In a sense, what I am describing is a sort of hyperseriality: that is, an extended version of the seriality common to Greek myths that I began to describe in Chapter 3 and will discuss again in Chapter 7. In simple seriality, the tale of Odysseus and Polyphemus, for instance, is but one episode in a closely linked set of tales narrating Odysseus's travels home, but in hyperseriality, any individual's cumulative story is also, implicitly, an episode within a far larger story that stretches "vertically" from the very first gods (Gaea and her shadowy siblings, if you believe Hesiod; Phanes or Protogonos, if you believe Orpheus) through to the children of the heroes who fought at Troy, and stretches "horizontally" to connect each individual to characters in other mythic families or groups (thus, Odysseus, for example, is connected vertically to Hermes, through his grandfather Autolycus,[42] and horizontally to other warriors who fought at Troy and to the strange people he met on his way home). This sort of hyperseriality is very familiar from soap operas (how many generations of Quartermaines have marched through the corridors of *General Hospital* and with how many generations of Spencers have they fought and made love?), but we find it in plenty of "higher" cultural products as well: John Galsworthy's *The Forsyte Chronicles* is an example, as is C. P. Snow's *Strangers and Brothers* series. Then there are the hyperserials whose position between high and low depends on whom you ask: Stephen King's popular *Dark Tower* series of novels and the other novels and stories with which King intertwines it, for example, and Robert Graves's *I, Claudius* and *Claudius the God* (the fact that the Julio-Claudians really existed does not exempt them from being prime fodder for the sort of hyperseriality that I am talking about). Within such a hyperserial, an individual's story can be enjoyed on its own, but it is more resonant, credible and just plain interesting as part of the bigger picture that is always shimmering behind it. Our knowledge that Fleur Forsyte's father had once been married to Jon Forsyte's mother—which Fleur and Jon do *not* know when they fall in love with each other in the third book of the *Forsyte Chronicles*—gives their relationship a pathos it would not otherwise have. Similarly, knowing that Deianira will later murder Heracles gives the scene at the end of Bacchylides's fifth ode, where Meleager's ghost promises Heracles her hand in marriage, an extra pathos, too.

Some hyperserials come into existence when someone (it may be the original author) gloms on to a good thing and expands it by creating sequels, prequels, midquels (previously unnarrated episodes from the middles of established stories), and paraquels (previously unnarrated stories that take place at the same time as an established story but that focus on different characters, some of whom may have already appeared in more minor roles in the established story).[43]

These -quels are not necessarily poor relations to the "original." *The Horse and His Boy* (a paraquel to C. S. Lewis's *The Lion, the Witch and the Wardrobe*) can stand completely on its own as an adventure story. Each of the eleven novels in Snow's *Strangers and Brothers* (which span five decades in the life of their narrator, Lewis Eliot) stands as a paraquel to some or all of the ten other books (confounding the very idea that there is an "original" story amongst them) and draws from a common cast of characters. And yet *The Light and the Dark* (which falls fourth in the series's internal chronology) immerses us so completely in Roy Calvert's development into one of the first scholars of Manichaeism that we may be surprised, in chapter 4, to be reminded of how Calvert's irresponsibly homoerotic behavior (an episode for which he is brought briefly on stage near the start of the second book in the series) once wreaked havoc in the lives of a number of Lewis Eliot's other friends. In fact, this kind of movement of a character back and forth between prominence and unimportance (in one novel, Calvert is merely the match that lights the fuse of a story from which he then departs; in another, he stays at the story's heart) is essential to hyperseriality as I understand it here: characters fade in and out of one another's stories in a manner that begins to dissolve any single story into something much larger ("Lewis Eliot's recollections of how interactions amongst his friends affected the course of academia, politics, and science in twentieth-century Britain"). Sometimes it can be difficult to decide whom a given story is even "about." Is *To Let*, the third book of *The Forsyte Chronicles*, still about Soames Forsyte, on whom the first two books centered, but more specifically about Soames's problems with his daughter, Fleur? Or is *To Let* about Fleur and her problems with Soames? Or to return now to Greek myths, is the tale of a certain love affair about *Jason*, who according to the tale's internal chronology already had begun his career as a hero, or is it really about *Medea*, whose career as an enchantress and all-around "bad woman" would continue well beyond the demise of her relationship with Jason? Does Pegasus really "belong" to the story of Medusa, only being "borrowed" by the story of Bellerophon—or vice versa? Is a certain story set in the Caucasus about *Heracles* releasing Prometheus, or is it about *Prometheus* being released by Heracles? Who is incidental to whom?

Crossovers

The answers to these questions (which depend in part on who is telling the stories and who is hearing them) are irrelevant for my purposes, and in the abstract, they matter very little anyway, except to people such as Apollodorus, who strove to organize the stories he told according to a single, coherent plan that avoided repetition. Apollodorus abruptly truncated the story of Prometheus, for example, at the point where the fettered god had been bound to a peak in the Caucasus mountains, wrapping up that part of his mythology with the words, "This was the penalty Prometheus paid for stealing fire until Heracles later released him—as we shall show in the chapters concerning Heracles."

In contrast to Apollodorus, I want to highlight the dense *intertwining* of characters and their stories in ancient narratives and the concomitant difficulty of completely disengaging any single character from the larger network of which he or she is a part. Although my description of the mythic network in the previous section was necessarily linear—verbal communication is always linear—the Greek mythic hyperserial, like all hyperserials, stretched in many directions at once, entangling each of its participants with many others. Chart One (shown in Figure 4.2), which diagrams all the relationships that I mentioned in the three paragraphs with which the last section began, illustrates what I mean: the lines connecting one character to another cross thickly. Chart Two (shown in Figure 4.3), which adds lines that represent relationships amongst those characters that I could not easily insert into my linear narrative, demonstrates this point even better. Popular characters, such as Zeus and Heracles, have links to many other characters, but even Pegasus has several links. A few paragraphs ago, I proposed that such intertwining lends credibility to the stories in which these characters participate simply because they all are understood to inhabit the same expansive and yet bounded story world—each story guarantees and in turn is guaranteed by the others—but I am further proposing now that it is precisely this intertwining of characters and their stories that cumulatively constitutes the story world of Greek myth.

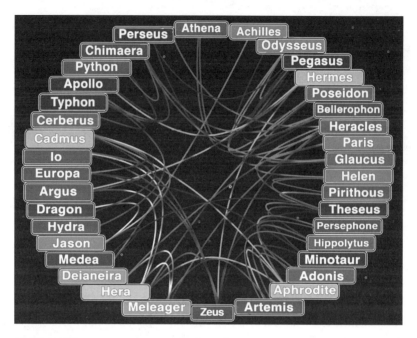

4.2 Chart One.

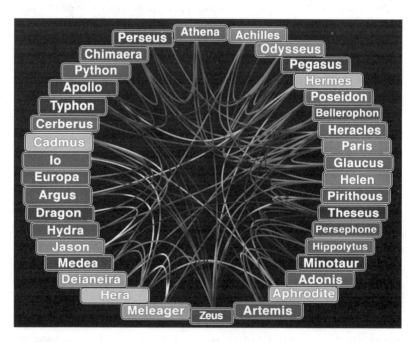

4.3 Chart Two.

Intertwining brings us to another, more specific, and often deliberately deployed, technique to which I want to draw attention as well, namely the "crossover," that is, the appearance of a character who is familiar from one context in the middle of another.[44] A character may be crossed into a new context by his or her own creator: twenty-nine years after introducing Father Donald Callahan as a main character in 'Salem's Lot, Stephen King crossed him over into the final three books of The Dark Tower, where the priest's deep knowledge of evil and the shakiness of his Catholic faith played out well against different monsters in a different universe. Crossovers also occur when a narrator borrows someone else's character and plants him or her in a new context: Sherlock Holmes, not surprisingly, is one of the most frequently borrowed (or, as the Doyle estate insists, "stolen") characters of all. And then there is a mode of crossing over that works on the all-star principle, bringing many established characters together into a single new venue. Alan Moore and Kevin O'Neill's League of Extraordinary Gentlemen is probably the best-known all-star example from recent years. I am not the first to suggest that the Argonautica is the grandfather of them all. The Calydonian boar hunt is another.[45]

The line between crossovers and what I have been calling hyperseriality can be exceedingly slender, but I would like to pause on one difference that is important for my purposes. As I emphasized, hyperserials, either by authorial intention or through evolution, tend to obscure the priority of any "original" or "dominant" narrative and its characters (and in fact, the last type of crossover I just described, the all-star gathering, may better be understood as a special form of hyperseriality for this very reason, given that all of the borrowed characters typically meet on narrative ground that is new to some or all of them). The use of crossovers, in contrast, thrives, at least initially, on the unexpected introduction of someone from outside. The surprise of meeting a familiar character where we don't expect to generates an additional level of interest in the story. If we are right in guessing (along with Pausanias)[46] that it was Sophocles who pioneered the story of Oedipus's death and burial at Athens,[47] then this is a perfect example; the ancient audience of the Oedipus in Colonus would have been intrigued to discover the hero wandering in an

Athenian suburb. Crossovers may also reward audience members with a sense of having special knowledge, which makes them feel complicit with the narrator and thus further encourages them to buy into the narrative—somewhat like the "Easter Eggs" that contemporary viewers spot in movies and television shows. A good example is Heracles's meeting Meleager's ghost in the Underworld. The unexpected encounter between the two in and of itself rewarded listeners who were familiar with mythological genealogies: they could pride themselves on knowing that Deianira, who later became Heracles's wife, was Meleager's sister. But the final lines of the myth as Bacchylides narrated it—in which Heracles asks Meleager whether he has an unmarried sister at home and Meleager says that he does—must have sent a chill down their spines.

Crossovers almost always serve another important purpose as well: by evoking a story world that is already familiar and accepted, a crossover character is a powerful way of giving verisimilitude to a new tale and its characters. The most familiar application of this principle is probably the television spin-off, in which a character from a well-established show is sent out to start a new show, transporting parts of the old, familiar story world into the new one so as to give it instant credibility. The sci-fi story world of the British series *Torchwood* (2006–2011), for example, had already been well limned by the older series *Doctor Who* before the character of Jack Harkness crossed from the latter into the former. This meant that some of the more fantastic aspects of *Torchwood* (the need to defend the planet against aliens; the existence of a covert agency in charge of doing so; rifts in the time-space continuum) were simply accepted by the new show's audience as givens. I've already mentioned the way in which the *bricoleurs* behind the mysteries of Dionysus did something similar by incorporating Persephone into the story that underpinned their cult; she carried with her, from her existing role in the Eleusinian mysteries and their myths, a stamp of eschatological authority. Sometimes, a crossover validates or revivifies a story by bringing its central character into contact with one or more characters who are already well established. For example, a revision of the Athenian myth of Erigone wove characters from the House of Atreus into her story, giving that Attic heroine panhellenic potential.[48]

There are subtler uses of the crossover as well. The opening lines of C. S. Lewis's *The Magician's Nephew* (the sixth entry in *The Chronicles of Narnia*) read,

> This is a story about something that happened long ago when your grandfather was a child. It is a very important story because it shows how all the comings and goings between our own world and that of Narnia first began.
>
> In those days Mr. Sherlock Holmes was still living in Baker Street and the Bastables were looking for treasure in the Lewisham Road.

Lewis first anchors his story with an explicit reference to the preceding five *Chronicles* (the word "Narnia"), but given that this new installment will be set two generations before the others—meaning two generations before the lives of the readers for whom he was writing in the 1950s—he additionally anchors it with crossovers from Victorian fiction with which his readers were sure to be familiar: Sherlock Holmes (of course) and the Bastable children, whose adventures, narrated in three books by E. Nesbit at the turn of the century, were still popular in the 1950s. These crossovers will not appear again in Lewis's story, but they create a *climate* in which it will unfold. Notably, it is a climate that is decidedly rational (Holmes) and quotidian: although Nesbit had also written many successful books about children who have magical adventures,[49] Lewis chose to refer to those about the Bastables, which take place in a London that is firmly realistic. In other words, Lewis used these opening crossovers to lay down a solidly rational and believable outer story world in which he could then locate the magical story world that begins to appear in chapter 2—by extension helping to make that second story world believable as well. The trick is an old one. Thucydides similarly predisposed his audience to accept his report on the earliest days of the Greeks by backing it with what was, for them, indisputably real and authoritative: the witness of Homer.[50] Similarly, by renaming local Athenian goddesses "Erinyes," Aeschylus and Sophocles gave epic authority to the local cults whose foundation stories they were refashioning in the *Eumenides* and the *Oedipus in Colonus*.[51]

Sometimes a crossover character lingers longer in a story in order to set the mood. Formally, Pindar brings Chiron into the tale of Apollo's love affair with Cyrene as an adviser and a prophet of what will result from the tryst, should Apollo pursue it. Thematically, Chiron instantiates a balance between the wild and the civilized that the rest of the poem explores as well. Compositionally, his speech breaks the linearity of the poem.[52] But as a figure who had been associated with the nurture and training of young heroes since the earliest stages of mythic narration, Chiron (like Holmes and the Bastable children, but at greater length) also establishes an atmosphere within the myth. This is no longer just one of many stories about Apollo's pursuit of nubile virgins or just one of Pindar's many tales about a colony's foundation; Chiron's presence subtly helps to make this a narrative about maturation, which in turn helps to set the proper ambience for an epinician ode in honor of a young victor who is poised on the verge of adulthood himself.[53]

Crossovers, in sum, can do a number of things very efficiently: establish the existential, ethical, and operational rules of a new story; lend it credibility and authority by their mere presence; and establish a particular climate or mood by gesturing towards other stories. Sometimes, they do one more thing, as well. By inventing the conversation between Apollo and Chiron about Cyrene, Pindar not only creates an opportunity to forecast the entire span of Apollo and Cyrene's courtship, the birth of their son and the foundation of her eponymous Libyan colony but also tells us how the god and the nymph crossed paths in the first place. By inventing the conversation between Heracles and the ghost of Meleager, Bacchylides tells us how the seeds for Heracles's marriage and death were planted. Both stories, in other words, claim to reveal "how it all came about"—a perennial object of human curiosity. Filling such holes can do more than just satisfy curiosity; by borrowing characters, information and episodes from other established narrations in order to fill those holes, backstories become yet another way of weaving a particular tale more tightly into the mythic network. How did it happen that both Cadmus and Jason had to fight armed men who sprang from dragon's teeth sown in the soil? Because (Pherecydes answers) after Cadmus slew the dragon, Athena and Ares collected its teeth, giving half to Cadmus to sow immediately and half to Aeetes, who used them to cause trouble for Jason many years later. And thus, events from the Theban cycle were woven into the story of Jason. How did Apollo manage to convince the Moirai to trade Admetus's life for that of another? By getting them drunk (answers Aeschylus's chorus in the *Eumenides*). And thus, events from a Thessalian saga were woven into a newly emerging Athenian myth. How did Creusa end up possessing Gorgon's blood with which she could try to kill Ion? Because (Euripides tells us) Athena gave it to Creusa's ancestor Erichthonius, who passed it down through the royal line.[54] And thus, a parade of kingly Athenian ancestors glimmers behind Creusa, further legitimating the son she is about to reclaim as an heir to the throne. Everything can be made to fit together, everything can be understood as part of a single, bigger picture and thus ratified, if only you know where to look for the missing pieces—or how to fashion them yourself. As H. P. Lovecraft put it when responding, once, to the question of how he felt about fans using materials of their own construction to caulk the gaps in his Cthulhu universe, even *artificial* mythology (his term) can be given an air of verisimilitude if it is widely enough cited—or if it is provided with enough citations to other works.[55]

The Story World of Greek Myth

Earlier, I concluded that the story world of Greek myth is relatively short on the sorts of oddities that typically set a Secondary World apart from the Primary World, but if I am right that its identity, coherence, and credibility rests on the thickly crisscrossing network of gods, heroes, and monsters that I have been describing in the preceding two sections, don't I need to revise that conclusion? Aren't gods and monsters (leaving aside heroes for the moment) by definition things that don't belong in the Primary World?

This is where we most clearly begin to see the difference between a story world created by myths and story worlds created by genres such as fantasy and science fiction—or, to put it differently, between story worlds inhabited by characters in which a society encourages its members to believe and story worlds inhabited by characters who are not intentionally created to be objects of belief (even if they later become such objects). I suggest it was precisely myths' representation of the gods and heroes as existing in a world that looked much like the Primary World that helped to make it possible for the Greeks to believe that those gods and heroes still existed at the time the myths were being told (even if they no longer manifested themselves so grandly and so frequently as they once had). For the Greeks, the things, people, and events of what they called the old days and what we would call the mythic period were understood to have melted into those of the present age without an abrupt change. They characterized an *earlier* age but not a time and place that was *disconnected* from the present age.[56]

Greek historians attest to this. Herodotus begins his history of the Persian Wars by reporting a tradition about a tit-for-tat series of abductions of Greek women by Eastern men and of Eastern women by Greek men—Io, Europa, Medea, and Helen, all of whom we now are accustomed to think of as characters in myths. Eventually, the enmity begun by the abductions brought about invasions into Greece by very real Easterners, the dire effects of which Herodotus's audience knew quite well. Or so said many people—Herodotus himself declines to weigh in on whether this tradition is accurate or not.[57] Thucydides opens his history of the Peloponnesian War by suggesting that it was the necessity of attacking Troy that finally welded small, independent kingdoms together into a unified Hellas and then goes on to note that such a war would never have been possible without Minos's development of the first navy. He posits that Agamemnon was able to muster the Greek troops more because he was the strongest of the Greek chieftains than because of the romantic oath that they all had sworn to defend Helen's honor, but he does not call the existence of that oath into question.[58]

Behind Herodotus's and Thucydides's remarks, we glimpse a widespread assumption that the time in which Io, Europa, Minos, and Agamemnon had lived was continuous with the time in which these historians were writing, even if there were some qualitative differences between those two times and even if one might niggle about the accuracy of certain details (as Herodotus and Thucydides certainly did in some cases). The Greeks did not assume that there had been an *illud tempus* (as Mircea Eliade would have it) that was categorically different from *hoc tempus*.[59]

Later authorities were more explicit about this continuity. The Parian Chronicle, a lengthy inscription recording Athenian history from 1582 BCE to 299 BCE, starts with matters such as the rule of Cecrops (an early king who was half snake and half human), the dispute between Ares and Poseidon on the Areopagus, the kingship of Minos and the institution of agriculture by Demeter. Moving forward, it slowly wends its way through events such as the institution of the Eleusinian gymnastic games and the tyranny of Pisistratus towards events in what was then quite recent history: the ascension of Ptolemy I to the Egyptian throne and Philocles's archonship in Athens. The Chronicle, as Peter Green nicely formulates it, "uses chronological specificity as a guarantee of truth."[60] The Lindian Chronicle, inscribed in 99 BCE, recorded gifts made to Athena by Cadmus, Minos, Heracles, and Helen right next to those made by Phalaris, Darius, Alexander, and Ptolemy.[61]

This continuity of time is evoked by Demosthenes when he praises fallen Athenians by placing them within a long line of glorious ancestors that goes back to those who expelled the invading Amazons and Eleusinians and who saved the sons of Heracles. It is also evoked when he praises Athenians of his own day for standing up against northern forces as staunchly as their ancestresses Procne and Philomela once had.[62] And it is also evoked by off-hand remarks such as those made by Socrates and Phaedrus as they strolled along the Ilissus river: "Isn't this the place where they say that Boreas snatched away the princess Oreithyia?" asked Phaedrus. "No, I think it was about a quarter-mile further along, where you cross to the sanctuary of Agra," replied Socrates. "There is, I believe, an altar dedicated to Boreas close by."[63] Walking through an ancient city, especially if you were a native, meant being constantly reminded by the monuments and landmarks that surrounded you of what was said to have happened there before; they were part of the surround of Noyes's second and third categories, as discussed in Chapter 1. If you weren't a native, there were always natives from whom you could learn the local lore as you strolled. Pausanias's many descriptions of places that evoke myths—here is the well where Demeter sat disguised as an old woman; there is the chasm through which Heracles dragged Cerberus up from Hades; this is the city founded by Lycaon, who later turned into a wolf—are particularly meticulous examples.[64]

According to such a view, although it might not be reasonable to expect to encounter more nine-headed snakes in Lerna or three-bodied giants in Spain (the passage of time was understood to have changed *some* things, after all; while Heracles and the other heroes still dwelled on earth, they had cleared the world of such creatures) or to expect gods to transmogrify people into new animals and plants (the natural world had been holding steady for some centuries), it *would* be reasonable to expect the heroes and the gods to remain an active part of the contemporary world. And so it was: Heracles warded off evil from houses that displayed his image and watched over young men at the gymnasium; Asclepius and Amphiaraus worked cures in their sanctuaries while their clients slept; Pan spoke to Phidippides in the mountains; and Apollo fought alongside his worshippers against the barbarian Gauls in 279 BCE, helped by local heroes and perhaps his sisters Artemis and Athena.[65] Athena manifested herself to her worshippers several times in Lindus, as her temple's chronicle recorded; in 490 BCE, she brought rain to the thirsty people when they were besieged by the Persians. Other gods and heroes, on many other occasions, were seen, heard or felt by their worshippers.[66]

Greek myths provided templates against which such manifestations of gods and heroes could be shaped, measured, and confirmed. The myths also, as I have suggested in this chapter, provided a story world that bound their protagonists—divine, heroic, and human—into a larger network. Each bond of this network was tight enough to secure the others; each story could thereby accredit, and be accredited by, the others. Yet the bonds were supple, as well, allowing the sort of revision that kept Greek myths in step with changing beliefs about the gods and changing practices in their honor. They were supple enough, too, that interesting new details and episodes could emerge, keeping the stories and their characters vigorously alive. The story world of Greek myth was the ideal companion for a religious system whose conceptions of divinity were anchored not by sacred texts or canons of doctrine, but rather by shared beliefs.

5

Characters

CHAPTER 3 was about how narratives, including myths, could be constructed and delivered in ways that helped to create and sustain belief in Invisible Others, including the Greek gods and heroes. Chapter 4 was about what made the world that Greek myths portrayed seem like a single, cohesive whole and how that, in turn, also helped to sustain belief. This chapter will look more closely at the characters who populated that world.

I'll start with a basic question: what is the ontological status of the gods and heroes whom we hear about in myths? Believers (or at least the intellectuals amongst them) were interested in one angle of this issue insofar as they sometimes attempted to categorize gods and heroes, to establish the *sorts* of creatures they were. What qualities set a god apart from a human? Immortality? Omniscience? Omnipotence? Something else? And what about the heroes? Did they constitute a separate group that lay between gods and humans, sharing qualities of each? Later on in this chapter, I'll return to a variation of these questions, when I look at how the special qualities of the gods were presented in narratives.

But first I want to pursue some other ontological questions, which are better asked from our own vantage point, standing outside of ancient Greek culture. Can we say that the gods and heroes existed independently from the stories in which they appeared as characters?

And if so, what was the relationship between those characters and the "real" things? Or to put it otherwise: to what extent, if at all, did the Greeks distinguish between the gods and heroes as they appeared in narratives and the gods and heroes whom they worshipped? In recent years, analytical philosophers and narratologists have argued that some fictional characters (such as Juliet Capulet, Sherlock Holmes, and James Bond) have achieved existences that transcend the individual narratives in which they appear, and thus can be said to exist independently of those narratives.[1] Did the Greek gods and heroes similarly achieve transcendence beyond the words and images that portrayed them, and if so, how might that have enhanced belief in those characters?

The Ontology of Fictional Characters

In one way, these issues may not matter much. As I noted in Chapter 3, the distinction that an individual perceives between reality and fiction and therefore between real and fictional characters, is conditioned to a large extent by what sources of authority tell him or her is real and fictional (religious authorities, civic authorities, scientific authorities, parental authorities, educational authorities, and so on). As long as the particular reality offered by one of these authorities does not significantly contradict an individual's own experiences, it constitutes a viable alternative, and so the individual might adopt it as his or her reality. When more than one viable reality is on offer, the relative importance of the authorities who promote each one will influence the choice. Thus, to take a contemporary example: Darwin's theory of evolution tends to be endorsed by those who have been raised in a home and an educational system that prioritize scientific authority, but it tends to be rejected by those raised in a home and an educational system that prioritize what the Bible is understood to say in a literal sense. Those who accept either of these endorsements live in a different reality from those who accept the other, at least as far as their view of how the physical world and its creatures were generated, which in turn has ramifications for their assumptions about humanity's place in the larger scheme of things, what humanity's responsibilities are of the natural environment and what role, if any, god(s) play in such matters.

Not all societies generate and promulgate a range of views, however; in ancient Greece, what we might call "scientific" models of how the cosmos came to exist and what made it work were available almost exclusively to intellectual elites; by default, most non-elites accepted the reality that was articulated by poets and endorsed by religious and civic officials, which assumed that the gods existed and wielded a lot of power. In other words, Zeus, Athena, Heracles, and all the other gods and heroes whom most of us living in the twenty-first century have been conditioned to call fictional characters were treated as real by the authorities whose opinions mattered most to ordinary Greeks, and because they did not encounter significant evidence to the contrary, most of them probably also took the gods to be real. This does not mean that every single person accepted every single thing that every poet told them about the gods, but the existence of the gods as the poets had cumulatively portrayed them constituted a framework of belief.

But to return now to philosophers' and narratologists' discussions about the ontology of fictional characters. In spite of what I've just said, it's worth testing some of the approaches that these scholars have developed for understanding fictional characters against the Greek gods and heroes, in order better to understand how the Greeks' perception of the gods and heroes differed from our own perception of fictional characters.

Central to all such discussions is recognition of the fact that there are different types of fictional characters; I am going to propose that there are five. Characters of the first type exist only in a single instantiation, and therefore always appear to us exactly as their creator fashioned them. At the moment that I write this, for example, the characters in Alexander McCall Smith's popular *44 Scotland St.* series have never appeared outside of Smith's narratives, and thus Bertie, Angus, Dominica, and the rest have been presented to us only as Smith (and his illustrator, Iain Mcintosh) conceives of them. Of course, we each add our own elements to these characters while reading the books—we invent details of their physiques and clothing, the timbre of the voices, and so on, without even realizing that we

are doing so—but we unconsciously rein in our imaginations as we
do so, keeping the characters within the parameters that Smith established. Bertie and the others therefore retain stable identities and
we will instantly recognize them in the next book of the series that
Smith writes—unless he contrarily decides to change them in significant ways. By the same token, however, it is difficult for these
characters to exist independently of Smith's narratives; they live only
within the specifically envisioned, semi-fictional version of Edinburgh that he has created.

(2) Characters of my second type are portrayed by more than one author or artist and yet can still be recognized as that character in
each portrayal, even if details differ. The philosopher Maria Reicher
suggests that we approach these situations by thinking in terms of
"maximal characters" and "submaximal characters." The maximal
character (who is only a heuristic convenience and is not actually
manifested in any narrative) possesses *all* the properties that any instantiation of the character ever exhibits.[2] Some of those properties
may be mutually exclusive. The maximal James Bond has both dark
hair (as in Sean Connery's portrayal of him) and blond hair (as in
Daniel Craig's portrayal), for instance, even though no single instantiation of Bond is both naturally dark-haired and naturally blond.
Submaximal characters, which are those we encounter in actual
narratives, manifest only some of the properties possessed by the
maximal character, but enough to be recognized: whatever James
Bond's hair color may be in one of these submaximal instantiations,
he is always a secret agent working for Britain, always dresses well,
and always prefers his martinis shaken, not stirred.[3] Characters like
these have more fluid identities than the first type I looked at, but
they nonetheless retain a core stability.

The most popular amongst these fluid characters are likely, eventually, to make a leap into the collective imagination that enables
them to stand completely *outside of* all the various narratives in which
they have appeared, recognizable as a coherent individual even by
those who have never read or viewed their stories. Thus, for instance,
a person who has never consumed a single narrative in which Sherlock
Holmes appears might see a drawing of a man wearing a deerstalker
hat and smoking a meerschaum pipe in an advertisement, infer

that the man is Holmes because this type of hat and pipe are closely associated with him, and know enough about Holmes to be able to guess that the business being advertised has something to do with tracking down information. It is this type of character who most interests the narratologists and philosophers who have worked on the ontology of fictional characters, because it is this type that comes closest to breaking free not only of the original narrative in which he or she appeared, but also of all narratives altogether, becoming an independently existing entity.

Characters of my first type, for which I used Smith's Bertie, Angus and Dominica as examples, are fully fictional, so closely circumscribed by the narratives in which they appear as to be unlikely to dissociate themselves from those narratives. Characters of the second type usually remain fictional as well: even if many audience members cannot state who it was that first created Bond and Juliet, most of them realize that Bond and Juliet were created by someone, at some point, ex nihilo. A few characters of the second type, however, begin to cross the line into nonfictional status: a business that installed its headquarters at 221 Baker Street in 1932 soon had to hire a full-time secretary to handle all the mail addressed to Holmes and continued to keep a secretary on staff for that purpose until the company closed in 2005 (all the mail addressed to Holmes is now redirected to the Sherlock Holmes Museum, a few steps up the street).[4] In other words, some people believed, and still believe, that Holmes is real; he has transcended the narratives that present him.

A third type of character appears in fictionalizing narratives but is based on a real person (living or dead). This type develops in ways that are similar to the second type I discussed, with one important difference. I will take Queen Elizabeth II as my example. The fictionalized character of Elizabeth II as portrayed by Helen Mirren in Stephen Frear's *The Queen* (2006) and the fictionalized character of Elizabeth II as portrayed by Claire Foy in Netflix's series *The Crown* (2016–2017), for instance, participate in the larger character concept "Elizabeth II" in the same way that Ian Fleming's novels and Daniel Craig's portrayal of Bond participate in the larger character concept "James Bond." But in contrast to Bond, for Elizabeth II, we see and hear the real Elizabeth herself, in addition to seeing and hearing Mirren's and Foy's fictionalizing portrayals.

This "Real Elizabeth" provides fodder for the construction of a single, maximal "Elizabeth" character in more or less the same way as Mirren's and Foy's Elizabeths do. These three Elizabeths (and others) converge in the minds of those who have experienced them towards a single Elizabeth concept. The fodder provided by Real Elizabeth, however, tends to carry extra weight because we have been repeatedly told by numerous authoritative sources that Real Elizabeth is authentic in a way that Mirren's and Foy's Elizabeths are not. This doesn't drown out the contributions made by Mirren's and Foy's Elizabeths—after all, they come to us in narratives that have been carefully orchestrated to hold audience attention and to imbue their Elizabeths with charisma. Indeed, particularly if we watch Mirren's and Foy's performances *before* we have seen or heard Real Elizabeth, our cumulative concept of Elizabeth II might be so significantly shifted in the direction of those performances as to forever inflect what we subsequently learn about Real Elizabeth.[5] And yet, I suggest, the overwhelming agreement amongst authorities that Real Elizabeth genuinely exists means that at least some aspects of Elizabeth's cumulative character—her hair color, date of birth, marital history, number of children, favorite breed of dog, typical mode of dress and moral outlook, for instance—are inevitably governed by the ways they are expressed by Real Elizabeth.

Notably, it seems that few people are uncomfortable with the co-existence of Mirren's and Foy's Elizabeths alongside Real Elizabeth, even if they notice that some things that Mirren's or Foy's Elizabeths say and do are inaccurate or unsubstantiated. We are used to the fact that real people and real events must be altered in the course of being dramatized, either because the narrator has little idea of what the real words and details were or because the real words and details are inadequate to express what the narrator aims to convey. The ancients were also familiar with, and comfortable with, this situation, as Thucydides makes clear: "my method has been, while keeping as closely as possible to the general sense of the words that were actually used, to make the speakers say what, in my opinion, was called for by each situation."[6] In other words, people have long understood, and accepted, the idea that their impression of a real character is gleaned, in part, from sources that are written with the aim of providing entertainment or instruction as much as or more than providing a factual portrait. The fact that a representation has been scripted doesn't mean that the subject it represents must be understood as an invention. These scripted versions of real people, moreover, have an advantage over what we know of the real versions: those who create them can give us as much access to their characters' thoughts, desires, fears and motivations as they wish. Even the most intimate sibling or friend of a real person is unlikely to possess that. In other words, these scripted versions have a narrative advantage; they make for characters with whom we can interact more fully.[7]

A fourth type of character—Invisible Others who are anchored by canonical narratives—offers a twist on the issue of combining "real" characters with fictionalized versions. Just as there is a Real Elizabeth, for believers there is a "Real God" (or "gods"), for example, and what those believers think they know about Real God is combined with portrayals of God in fictionalizing narratives to make up a cumulative God concept. For most contemporary Western Christians, Real God is the one described in the Old and New Testaments. Fictionalizing portrayals include the God of Milton's *Paradise Lost* (1667), the God whose voice (provided by Charlton Heston) is heard talking to Moses in Cecil B. DeMille's *The Ten Commandments* (1956), God as portrayed in a stained-glass window that one sees every Sunday while at church, God as portrayed by the singer Alanis Morissette in Kevin Smith's film *Dogma* (1999), and so on. The main difference between Real Elizabeth and Real God (as is typically the case for Invisible Others) is that information about Real God is less readily accessible than information about Real Elizabeth. Such things as Real God's physical appearance and his favorite breed of dogs remain mysterious, and God therefore remains what narratologists call a less "complete" character than Elizabeth—and less complete even than Holmes, about whose personal history and tastes we learn a great deal by reading Doyle's stories—to say nothing of the hundreds of Holmes stories that have been generated since Doyle's death.

We can make two observations about the four types of characters I have sketched. First, that characters of my second type, who are portrayed in more than one narrative, are likelier than characters of my first type to eventually develop into characters of the collective imagination and may even break free of narratives altogether to win an independent existence that eventually dwarfs those narratives; second, that characters of my third and fourth types, who are based on real individuals—not only real humans but also real Invisible Others who are anchored by canonical narratives—develop in much the same way as characters of the second type, although the real individual usually exerts a more powerful force over the cumulative character concept than do other (fictionalized) instantiations of the character. Of course, the other difference between my second type and my third and fourth types is that some or all of a society's authorities agree that types 3 and 4 are real but not that type 2 is.

Things are different when it comes to Invisible Others in cultures such as ancient Greece, where there were no dogmas concerning the nature of the gods and heroes and no canonical texts that wielded authority like that of the Bible. Because of this, there were no widely agreed-upon sources of knowledge for "Real Hermes," for instance, that could be clearly distinguished from "fictionalizing" portrayals of Hermes; different portrayals of Hermes simply had to sit alongside each other, none of them irrefutably able to claim to be true. In epic, Hermes is a helpful, lighthearted god, who, as Zeus puts it in the *Iliad*, "greatly enjoys having humans as companions."[8] And yet the *Prometheus Bound* presents Hermes as a ruthless tool of Zeus, willing to inflict cruel punishments on Prometheus, humanity's greatest advocate. Each of these portraits of Hermes, and others, were understood by their recipients to be "true" in the sense of expressing something about the nature of Hermes, even if they jarred against one another. If anything in ancient Greece approached canonicity, it was the narratives attributed to Homer and Hesiod and yet even their information could be challenged—in fact, the two poets famously contradicted each other on some points. Homer says that Aphrodite's parents are Zeus and Dione, but Hesiod says that she was born from the foam that arose when Cronus threw Ouranos's castrated genitals into the sea.[9]

For centuries, then, Greek authors, artists, and their audiences implicitly participated in an ongoing conversation about exactly who the gods were and what they had done during the early epochs of the cosmos's existence. The material that fed this conversation came almost completely from what we in the twenty-first century understand to be fictional sources that the Greeks themselves understood to be, if not *fully* fictional in the sense of having no basis in fact, then at least fictional in the sense of being *ficta*—in the sense of being articulated in forms that had been generated by human individuals.

There are important differences between this type of character and the other types that I discussed earlier. As long as the work that first created a fully fictional character continues to be read, viewed or in other ways present in the audience's consciousness, it exerts an influence over subsequent portrayals. James Bond has not yet escaped from Fleming, and Sherlock Holmes has not yet escaped from Doyle. Similarly, in the case of fictionalized characters based on real people, such as Queen Elizabeth, or Invisible Others for whom there are canonical portrayals, such as the Christian God, our knowledge of the real characters prevents fictional portrayals from going too far astray. Audiences are unlikely to accept a portrayal of Elizabeth in which she has an extramarital affair as anything but a parodic inversion of Real Elizabeth's well-known adherence to traditional moral codes,[10] and it is unlikely that many people's concepts of God were significantly affected by *Dogma*'s casting of Alanis Morissette in the role.

In contrast, characters for whom there is no clear original—whose existences are anchored instead within the drifting overlaps of traits shared by different portrayals—can be adapted in bolder ways. To be sure, as with the other types of characters, some elements may never be changed: an impotent Zeus or an ugly Helen could be understood only as figures of satire, Heracles must always travel to distant lands and Theseus must always be an Athenian. But Heracles can be portrayed either as a symbol of virtuous self-control and abstention or as a gluttonous, drunken lecher, without either portrayal being understood as satire. Theseus's faces are manifold (see later in this chapter). Helen can be either a slut who ran off with a handsome young visitor, a virtuous wife who was kidnapped by that visitor, or an unsullied woman who never slept with the visitor at all.

One reason that the existence of such varying portrayals is tolerated is the very fact that their subjects are assumed to have really existed—and still to exist, even if on a higher existential level than
before in the case of mortals who have become heroes. Because of
this, it is thought possible to discover new information about them
or a new slant on old information. Most fictional characters—even
those who have been instantiated in different ways a number of
times—are not like this. We do not expect that new information
might become available about Madame Bovary that would change
our evaluation of her choices and actions. We do not expect that new
information about Don Quixote's childhood might someday help us
understand why he undertook his misguided chivalric quests. Indeed,
if anything argues for the *mythic* status into which Sherlock Holmes
is sometimes said to have moved, it is the constant generation of new
representations of him and his associates by authors such as Michael
Chabon, Caleb Carr, and Karem Abdul-Jabar, which delve into
Holmes's childhood, his old age, his relationships with women (or
with Dr. Watson), his brother Mycroft's personality, and so on. In
doing so, these narratives sometimes offer us a Holmes who departs
significantly from the character whom Doyle created without becoming parody.[11]

Plurimediality and Accretive Characters

I suggest, then, that rather than bemoaning the fact that the Greeks'
ideas about the gods and heroes come to us mostly through fictionalizing art and literature, we should acknowledge that those portraits,
cumulatively, *were* the gods and heroes—that is, that the nature of
our own experience of these gods and heroes at least approximates
that of the Greeks themselves. From there, we can begin better to
understand the contributions that the characters in narratives made
to the creation and sustenance of belief.

This brings me to two interrelated concepts, *plurimediality* and *accretive characters*.[12] When characters are presented through more
than one narrative (as are the characters of types 2, 3, 4, and 5, described earlier), each narrative offers a different instantiation of that
character from the others—sometimes a strikingly different instan-

tiation. Such characters are *plurimedial* insofar as many different media, and sometimes many different manifestations within a single medium, represent that character. Sherlock Holmes, for example, has been represented through printed stories written by several different authors (accompanied by drawings produced by many different illustrators), through stage plays, movies, and television shows starring different actors, through comic books, on advertising logos, and so on.

But if "plurimedial" describes the nature of the sources from which a single person's concept of a particular character may be drawn, "accretive" better describes the state of the character, as it is taking form in the mind of a particular individual. As the individual encounters the character in different instantiations, the individual's concept of who the character is slowly *accrues* traits from some or all of those instantiations. In what follows, I will use "accretive" and "plurimedial" as appropriate.

When experiencing plurimedial characters, each of us must repeatedly choose, even if unconsciously, to engage more deeply with some instantiations than with others, and with some aspects of our preferred instantiations more deeply than with others. Each of us therefore ends up creating our *own* accretive character, no two of which are likely to be exactly the same. It is a process that may continue over the course of many years. Because, as a child, I always engaged with instantiations of Sherlock Holmes that wore the distinctive deerstalker hat, I found it difficult, later on, to accept one who wore a fedora, as Jeremy Brett sometimes did when portraying Holmes for the BBC. And yet Brett's portrayal was so appealing to me in other ways that my image of Holmes began to incorporate the fedora. Similarly, once I began, as a teenager, to read Doyle's own work rather than the expurgated versions of it that are offered to children, the element of cocaine addiction became important to my concept of Holmes, which predisposed me to accept portrayals of Holmes that emphasize his drug abuse, such as those provided by Jonny Lee Harris in the CBS series *Elementary* and by Benedict Cumberbatch in the BBC series *Sherlock*. Harris's and Cumberbatch's portrayals of Holmes brought his intellectual arrogance to the fore, and therefore that arrogance also became central for my concept of

Holmes, which made it harder (although not impossible) for me to accept the older, kinder Holmes that Ian McKellen portrayed in the film *Mr. Holmes* (2015).

Plurimedial characters continually compel audience members to make decisions such as the ones I made for Holmes, even if only unconsciously. The cognitive and emotional energy that each person invests in doing this forges an especially close bond between that person and the character. Or in other words, because my vision of Holmes really is *my* vision, it opens me up to being affected by Holmes more strongly than I would be if I had adopted a single instantiation directly from a single source. And this situation, in turn, is conducive to my believing that Holmes really exists—if the authorities in my society endorse that belief.

I want to stress a few more things about plurimediality before I continue. First, although I have associated plurimediality with the existence of multiple portrayals of a single character by different authors or artists, plurimedial characters are not themselves the creation of authors or artists. Rather, plurimediality is something that accumulates around a character as a by-product of the work that different authors and artists collectively do.[13] A plurimedial character, then, is a product of its own popularity—popularity that its plurimedial status in turn continues to promote.

Second, an individual's experience of a plurimedial character is normally confined to the imagination of that individual alone. If it moves out onto the screen, the stage or the page, this is a secondary development, at the hands of an author or artist who uses his or her perception of the character to create something new or to make a point. For example, Shane Denson has demonstrated how a representation of Frankenstein's monster in a graphic novel of the 1960s skillfully evokes elements of both Mary Shelley's literary portrayal and Boris Karloff's cinematic portrayal in order to ponder the nature of the monstrous.[14]

Third, understanding a character as plurimedial frees us from the constraints of another approach to which it may seem to bear a resemblance, namely, intertextuality. By definition, a plurimedial character shimmers at the nexus of several, perhaps even many, different instantiations of that character, taken from different texts, none of which has absolute authority over that character and any one of which may therefore dominate the others in the mind of the individual who creates it. Plurimediality, in other words, foregrounds, and indeed thrives upon, the somewhat messy and constantly metamorphic state in which popular characters exist. It encourages us to embrace a dynamic view of characters' development and of personal engagement with characters, according to which frequent transformation is not only tolerable, but even fruitful. It releases us from the deadening pursuit of *Quellenforschung*, given that the point is not to trace particular traits of a character back to an earlier source or sources (with which a given audience member may or may not be familiar), but rather to understand how new figurations emerge and reemerge against the background of a *range* of earlier treatments, never fully obligated to any of them.[15]

Plurimedial Characters in Antiquity

Although the examples I have given so far focus on the nineteenth and twentieth centuries, plurimediality and its ramifications have always been around, as earlier parts of this chapter have already begun to suggest. Ancient literary and artistic sources provided many portrayals of the gods and heroes, from which each individual would have had to form his or her own personal versions. We meet quite a different Odysseus in Homer from the one we meet in Sophocles's *Philoctetes* and yet again a different one in the final book of Plato's *Republic*—and then there is the burlesque Odysseus whom we see on a black-figure vase from the Theban Kabeirion: squat and grotesque, his eyes and mouth wide with terror at the approach of Circe. Or take Theseus as an example. An Athenian man of the late fifth century might have encountered Theseus as a somewhat foolhardy young leader-in-the-making, leaping into the sea to settle a bet about his paternity (in symposiastic re-performances of Bacchylides's seventeenth ode) or as a paradigmatic hero conquering paradigmatic monsters (in the same poet's eighteenth ode); as a noble, magnanimous defender of the downtrodden (in Sophocles's *Oedipus in Colonus*) or as the cruel betrayer of a woman who saved him (in the Hesiodic *Catalogue of Women*); as a democratizing king embracing civic virtues (in Euripides's *Suppliant Women* and Thucydides's "archaeology"), or as the careless cause of his own father's death (in Simonides fr. 550); as the founder of rituals for young men in Athens and on Delos (popular traditions that made their way into the Atthidographers and thence into Plutarch), or as a short-tempered and suspicious father (in Euripides's *Hippolytus*); as a middle-aged man traveling to Hades to back up his best friend (in recitations of the epic *Minyas*), or as a dead king whose bones Cimon had retrieved from the island on which Theseus spent his last days in exile. And of course, that Athenian man also would have met Theseus in vase paintings, on coins, on the metopes of the Hephaestion and in many other works of art, which sometimes showed the hero with his signature weapon, the primitive club, and at other times with the hoplite's sword or spear, sometimes as a youthful slayer of the Minotaur and at other times at an older age, conquering the centaurs. Like Frankenstein's monster or Sherlock Holmes, in other words, Theseus was a dynamic character, of whom each Athenian would have had a somewhat different conception but to whom, by the same token, each would have felt an intimate and lively connection as a result.

But in contrast to Holmes and the monster, Theseus was worshipped in cult; that is, not only did the Athenians *think* about him as if he really existed, but the great majority of Athenians also *treated* him as if he could have a significant effect on the contemporary mortal world—indeed, inscriptions tells us that the Athenian Council decreed that he should so be treated. At the Theseion near the agora, for example, the Athenians stored the bones of Theseus that Cimon had retrieved, on the understanding that those bones would protect Athens against its enemies. The annual Theseia was celebrated at the Theseion, and all year round the site provided asylum for runaway slaves and anyone else "who is poor and downtrodden and fears the strong."[16] In Phaleron, near the western harbor of Athens, the sons of Theseus (and probably also Theseus himself) were paid cult. The Oschophoria that was celebrated there, in which two young men of noble birth dressed up as girls, was said to have been founded by Theseus at the time of his youthful journey to Crete—an occasion on which, according to myths, he had disguised Athenian youths as maidens so as to smuggle more manpower aboard Minos's ship. At the Pyanepsia, which was celebrated on the same day as the Oscho-phoria and which was also said to have been founded by Theseus, younger boys took center stage (although we don't know exactly what they did). The annual Synoikia celebrated Theseus's unification of Attica.[17]

The fact that Theseus was paid cult at these and other festivals leads to two complementary observations. On the one hand, the cults' activities—sacrifices to Theseus, prayers to Theseus, and so on—can be understood as yet further media through which the Greeks encountered Theseus, and therefore as yet further factors contributing to his plurimediality and to the dynamic nature of his reception amongst Athenians. Activities at the Theseion and the celebration of the Synoikia, for example, seem to evoke his reputa-tion as good and kindly king, whereas the atmosphere in Phaleron has a transgressive accent. But on the other hand, and for my im-mediate purposes more importantly, the accretive nature of any single person's concept of Theseus and the intimate connection to Theseus that this fostered helped to create and sustain the very as-sumption that Theseus existed, which in turn sustained the practice of his cults. The same can be said for other heroes and gods.

Life in the Margins

The absence of any strict canon governing how the gods and heroes were supposed to be imagined left room not only for the rise of plu-rimedial characters but also for the continual revision of old stories. Frequent revision was virtually a necessity, in fact, given that poetic narration of myths served as one of the main forms of public enter-tainment. Because there were intrinsic limitations as to whom nar-rators could use as the protagonists of their stories (the family of gods didn't grow much larger during the historical period, and few new additions to the roster of heroes were widely enough known to merit big-time poetic attention), narrators who wished to please their au-diences with something new had to find ways to inject novelty into material that was already familiar. In addition to offering new slants on established characters, authors could innovate by tucking new myths inside of old ones (thus, for instance, fifth-century audiences heard, for the first time, about Heracles acquiring olive trees for the new Olympic precinct from the Hyperboreans—trees that he had first seen while completing his well-known third labor—and also heard about Theseus plunging into the sea to retrieve Minos's ring).[18] Yet another way was to invite audience members to consider new readings of the truth behind an old tale. Pindar asserts that Tantalus was punished not for killing his son Pelops and trying to serve the child's flesh to the gods, as the familiar story said, but rather because he stole nectar and ambrosia from the gods and distributed them amongst his friends. Pindar also offered an explanation for why the wrong story became popular: he said that Tantalus was accused of killing and cooking Pelops by envious neighbors after Pelops had been stolen away by a lovesick Poseidon.[19] The poets Acusilaus, Pherecydes, and Bacchylides challenged Hesiod's story about the daughters of Proetus by claiming that it had been Hera, not Dionysus, who drove the girls mad. Bacchylides challenged *all* of the other sources by saying that the girls were cured not by the famous seer Melampus but by Hera herself, after Artemis interceded with her on their behalf, which Artemis was motivated to do by the twenty red cows that Proetus sacrificed to her.[20] In the religious system of ancient Greece, famous figures and their myths were malleable materials, through which new speculations about the nature of the gods and heroes could be explored.

In a narrative environment filled with such protean characters and shifting stories, audience members were bound to notice that there were varying—sometimes strikingly varying—reports about the gods and heroes. Under these circumstances, even the oldest and most appealing stories had to be accepted as just single reports about someone whose real nature might never be fully captured by human words. And yet the very fact that so many voices had independently arisen to tell tales about a particular character helped to confirm that someone real stood behind them all, somewhere. Pindar's interjection, "surely you all know about Ajax's blood-stained valor? . . . Homer has made him honored amongst humans by setting straight his entire achievement,"[21] implies that Ajax's story has been transmitted by particular humans who had particular opinions about him, some of which were closer to the truth than others, but it also confirms that there is a real Ajax who can be recovered. Herodotus's efforts to discover who the real Heracles was, by visiting Egypt, Tyre, and Thasos and interviewing local people in each of those places, was, perhaps, an extreme reaction to the diversity of stories that circulated about Heracles, but it reflects Herodotus's confidence that a real man stood behind the various legends.[22] Plutarch articulates exactly the same problem at the start of his biography of Theseus: "Let us hope, then, that I shall succeed in purifying what is mythic [*mythodes*], and make it submit to reason and take on the appearance of history."[23] Of course, Stesichorus's palinode to Helen demonstrates that if a narrative fell egregiously short of truth, the divine figure behind the story might be expected to intervene and compel a poet to set the record straight.[24]

This state of affairs—this general tolerance for a swirling cloud of opinions about the strengths and peccadillos of the gods and heroes—resembles that around figures who are undeniably real: was there just one opinion about the accomplishments of Pisistratus or the morals of Alcibiades? Was there agreement about whether Pythagoras had really experienced metempsychosis? It is a character about whose traits and actions there is unanimity, in fact, who risks looking fictional. Another reason that the gods and heroes whom the narrators described seemed real, then, was precisely the fact that they could *not* be contained within any single diegetic[25] world; they seeped beyond the boundaries of the individual myths that the poets told about them and flourished in the margins, nourished *by* particular narrators but never becoming the *property* of particular narrators.

Divine Ontology

I want to switch to a different ontological question from those that I started with. I want to think about the *ways* in which—and the *degree* to which—Greek gods were different from humans, and why (I'll discuss the heroes in more depth in Chapter 7).

In one sense, Greek gods *were* human: they emerged from a collective consciousness that couldn't imagine gods in any other manner—a tendency shared by many cultures. Most of the Greek gods had arms, legs, eyes, a nose, a mouth, genitals, and so on that looked exactly like ours—except that they were more beautiful, more impressive. These gods slept, ate, made love, became pregnant and gave birth, participated in athletic contests, fought wars, were wounded, sweated, urinated, farted, shat (at least in comedies), took baths, and ornamented themselves with clothing, jewelry, and perfumes.

But if this had been all that there was to them, they wouldn't have been gods. What set them apart from humans, first and foremost, was their immortality, as a common term for them, "those without death" (*hoi a-thanatoi*), makes very clear. In this respect, they were as different from humans, "those who die" (*hoi thnētoi*), as they could possibly be. They also had powers far beyond those possessed by humans: they could travel across great distances rapidly, fly through the air, move heavy objects with ease and shift their shapes to mimic anything or anyone they chose. They knew what people were doing even when people thought that they were alone, as Lycaon and Croesus each discovered.[26]

This is an impressive list that makes it tempting to add omnipotence and omniscience to the traits that set the gods apart from humans. And yet, myths narrate plenty of incidents that suggest that the gods were neither omnipotent nor omniscient. Gods could be deceived by other gods or remain ignorant of what other gods (and even humans) had done until those deeds were called to their attention, for instance. Zeus didn't realize until too late that Hera had an ulterior motive for seducing him in *Iliad* 14. Poseidon was ignorant of the other gods' decision to bring Odysseus home because Poseidon was far away in Ethiopia when they made it. Poseidon was also ignorant of how Odysseus had injured his son Polyphemus until Polyphemus told him.[27] Zeus knew that he could sleep with a certain goddess only at his own peril, but Prometheus alone could tell him which goddess that was; in spite of all Zeus's power, he could not learn the answer on his own.[28] Hades was able to lure Persephone away to her doom by an attractive flower. Although Hecate heard Persephone cry out when Hades snatched her, she did not know who had done the snatching until Helios told her, and Helios knew this only because he saw the whole thing happen as he was driving his chariot through the skies, just as we might see something in our immediate environment. None of the other gods even heard Persephone call out, and Zeus, who had masterminded the kidnapping, was able to spare himself the painful sound of his daughter's cries by removing himself to one of his temples and listening to people's prayers. (Apparently, unlike Superman, the gods couldn't hear what was happening far away any better than we can.) Persephone was tricked yet again by Hades when he convinced her to eat something in the Underworld.[29] Eileithyia didn't know that Leto was in labor, in spite of Leto's agonized prayers to Eileithyia, because Hera had isolated Eileithyia within a cloud. Apollo didn't know that Telphousa was lying to him about the best place to build a temple;[30] nor did he know, on another occasion, why his cows had disappeared until he had put in the same sort of investigative legwork as any victim of a cattle theft would.[31] Demeter, distracted by grief, ate a bite of Pelops's shoulder without realizing what it was. The children of Helios forgot to carry fire with them when they set out to honor the newly born Athena. Eos forgot to ask that Tithonus be made eternally young, instead of just eternal.[32] And so on, and so on. I could extend this list of the gods' instances of ignorance and error to a considerable length.

Gods were not able to prevent their favorite mortals from dying at the time that the Fates had decreed, as several instances in the *Iliad* demonstrate—most spectacularly, the case of Sarpedon, whose father, Zeus, wanted to snatch Sarpedon off of the battlefield and out of harm's way but had to settle, instead, for ensuring his son's honorable burial and shedding tears of blood upon the earth.[33] Apollo did a little better for his friend Admetus, convincing the Fates to accept another human life in place of Admetus's own when his death came due (although time showed that this was less of a bargain than Apollo had hoped). Zeus similarly tried to bargain for Castor's life, but the Fates relented only on the condition that Castor's immortal twin, Polydeuces, agree to take on half of the debt and thereby spend half of the time in Hades, himself. Although gods were immortal themselves, they could be physically wounded by mortal warriors: Heracles wounded Hera and Hades; Diomedes wounded Aphrodite and Ares and made Apollo cry out in fear.[34]

And in spite of all the other remarkable abilities of the gods, they apparently need tools to accomplish at least some of their tasks.

Hermes uses special sandals to travel from place to place.[35] Hades owns a cap of invisibility—which Athena borrows in order to help Diomedes wound Ares, so that Ares won't see her.[36] Why does a god need such a thing in order to become invisible? Why does Athena need an aegis to shake fear into mortal hearts, for that matter? Why does Hermes need to wear special shoes to cover his tracks after he steals Apollo's cows—why can't he just fly over the ground? And why does he throw those shoes into the Alpheus River to get rid of them after he's committed his crime? Why can't a god who is able to "twist sideways and slip through the latch-hole" of his mother's door simply cause those shoes to disappear?[37] Instances like these once again show that narratives evolved to portray gods who were subject to at least some of the same physical limitations as humans, at least some of the time.

Of course, fallible gods like these make for better stories. If Apollo, in the Homeric *Hymn to Hermes*, had known that Hermes had stolen his cows as soon as it happened, and if he had been able to recover those cows with just a snap of his fingers, then the rest of the tale would have disappeared. We would never hear about Hermes's charming pretense of being "just a baby" when Apollo confronted him in his cradle, his comic fart when Apollo manhandled him, his skillful use of his newly invented lyre to soothe Apollo and the brothers' eventual friendship. And if Poseidon had been omniscient and omnipotent, Odysseus never would have gotten as far as Phaeacia, much less Ithaca—and we would have no *Odyssey* to entertain us now.

Templates and Their Violation

But there is more behind the gods' fallibility than just the yen for good stories. The anthropologist Pascal Boyer and the psychologist Justin Barrett have studied the ways that people tend to think about Invisible Others differently on different occasions. On some occasions, people engage in what Barrett calls "theological correctness."[38] That is, they are careful to talk about Invisible Others—who they are, what they can do, how they interact with humans—according to what their society officially thinks.[39] On other occasions, when people are thinking and speaking more casually, they reveal their underlying, and probably unconscious, assumption that Invisible Others are bound by at least some of the same rules of biology and physics as humans are. Barrett, whose work focuses on American Christians, ran an experiment in which his subjects read a story about God saving a man's life and *at the same time* helping a woman find her lost purse. When the subjects were asked to tell the story in their own words later on, many of them said that God *first* had helped either the man or the woman *and then later* had helped the other one. When thinking "officially," Barrett's subjects accepted the idea that God could be in more than one place at once, doing more than one thing, but when telling a story about what God actually did, many slipped into imposing upon God the same rules of time and space as the narrators themselves experienced every day.[40]

One reason that there are dual sets of expectations for Invisible Others is that people think in terms of what Boyer has called "ontological templates." These templates are blueprints for the basic ontological categories that exist in the world.[41] Boyer proposes that there are very few of these; in his work, he mentions only five: *person, animal, plant, natural object, tool.*

As children mature, Boyer suggests, they intuitively learn which characteristics define each template and apply that knowledge to new things that they encounter. Thus, if a child has learned that cats and dogs must eat and sleep, that they give birth to creatures that grow up to look like themselves and that they are members of a group called "animals," then the next time that the child encounters something that he or she is told is an "animal"—say, a walrus at the zoo—the child will infer that the walrus must also eat and sleep and that it will give birth to little walruses. Eventually, the child will automatically assume that *all* animals eat, sleep, give birth to creatures that look like them, and so on.

Supernatural concepts are ontological templates that have been altered by either the subtraction or the addition of salient characteristics. A ghost, for instance, is a *person* from whom has been *subtracted* physical substance. A statue that can hear your prayers is a *tool* to which has been *added* cognitive functions. In the majority of religious systems, Boyer observes, gods can similarly be understood as *persons* to whom have been added special cognitive powers (omniscience), physical powers (omnipresence, flight, and so on) or both, and from whom characteristics such as mortality have been subtracted.

Barrett and Boyer have shown that such violations are more easily remembered than what they call "violations of expectations" or "mere oddities"—things that are possible within the everyday world but highly uncommon, such as a table made out of chocolate, a man who has six fingers or a woman who has given birth to thirty-seven children. This is probably both because the counter-ontological violations constitute more extreme departures from what we encounter in everyday life than mere oddities do, but also because many of the counter-ontological violations are capable of creating situations that are highly significant to our lives. Or in other words: the chocolate table is something we can consume and the six-fingered man or the amazingly fecund woman are people whom we can marvel at, but a person who knows everything and can do anything (i.e., a god) effectively holds the power of life and death over us.

A delicate balancing act is constantly going on in the imagining of a counter-ontological entity, however. If too many violations are added to a template, people stop believing in the resultant entity because too much cognitive energy is required to override so many of the deeply engrained inferences that are associated with that template. The entity becomes, quite literally, "incredible." If an author described the ghosts in a story as lacking physical substance *and* lacking cognitive functions *and* having the power of bilocation *and* sustaining themselves exclusively on the bones of salamanders *and* being active only during months with an *r* in their names, the ghosts would become too cognitively expensive for anyone to maintain interest in them even while reading the story, much less as a serious belief.

Successful counter-ontological entities avoid this problem in either of two ways. The entity may include only a few violations of the template upon which it is built, leaving people to infer that in all other ways it operates just like normal examples of that template. Thus, we accept that a ghost has no physical body and can therefore go through walls, for instance, but when a ghost manifests itself in a story, we expect it to be able to see, hear, and understand what is happening in its surroundings because other members of the *person* template can do so. Or the entity can be said, officially, to include more than a few violations, but any given narrative about that entity evokes only some of those violations—other "official" violations are ignored or even contradicted in the course of the narrative. This is effectively the mode of control to which the people interviewed by Barrett subjected God when they rewrote the story of Him saving a man's life and *at the same time* helping a woman find her lost purse.

This brings us back to the instances of slippage in the stories about the Greek gods that I collected a few paragraphs earlier—Zeus's failure to perceive what Hera was up to when she seduced him, Apollo's lack of knowledge about his stolen cows, and so on. These are excellent examples of the second way of dealing with multiple ontological violations. Interestingly, almost all of them come from the *Iliad*, the *Odyssey*, and the Homeric *Hymns*. Other genres were more insistent about the expansiveness of the gods' powers. Tragedy, for example, includes statements such as this one from the end of the *Bacchae:* "The gods have many shapes. The gods bring many unexpected things to pass. Things that seem likely are not accomplished, while a god finds a way to accomplish unlikely things. And thus has the present matter been concluded as well."[42] Epinicians reject and correct well-known stories of the gods' shortcomings. Instead of the familiar story of a raven informing Apollo of Coronis's infidelity, for instance, Pindar gives us this: "But she did not escape the watching god, for although he was in flock-receiving Pytho as lord of his temple, [Apollo] perceived it, persuaded by the surest confidant, his all-knowing mind."[43]

Greek mythic narratives, then, served two complementary roles in the construction and maintenance of belief. It was easier to believe that gods such as those described in the epics and the Homeric *Hymns* existed because they aligned with the *person* template fairly closely. They had counter-ontological features but not so many of them, or of such severity, as to require a great deal of cognitive energy to maintain belief. In contrast, the gods presented in tragedy and in epinicians tended to be significantly different from humans. As such, they could better be used to explain certain aspects of the way the world worked and to elicit thought about how, if at all, humans could hope to improve the circumstances of their existence.

(The distinction I am drawing here is heuristic; I do not mean to imply that epic and the *Hymns* never prompted questions about the limits of human existence, or that tragedy and epinician never showed gods who fail in knowledge or power. Rather, I want to point out that the Greeks found ways to think differently about the gods on different occasions.) The strength of a religion depends, I suggest, on the availability of such a variety of narratives—on not only having vivid, engaging narratives that create cognitive and emotional bonds between audience members and the Invisible Others whose stories are told in those narratives, but also on having different *kinds* of engaging narratives.

Names

In arguing that fictional characters had unified existences outside of their narratives, Maria Reicher suggests that the only thing that was genuinely vague or nonspecific about them were their names. Thus, Reicher says, "Faust is not a vague object. If anything is vague at all, then it is the meaning of the name 'Faust.' It is vague in the sense that different users (or the same users on different occasions) use the name to refer to distinct characters."[44]

Implicitly, this suggests that it is a name, first and foremost, that holds together the different—perhaps the very many, very different—instantiations of a character. This is what makes a plurimedial, accretive character work: the name corrals a large and varied collection of ideas and opinions about that character, and the continuing use of the name steadfastly insists that there is a single figure behind them all somewhere, even if opinions differ as to who exactly that figure is. This suggests that the continuing use of a name is particularly important for sustaining belief in an Invisible Other who can never be completely known and about whose actions and experiences there is no complete agreement. Indeed, the more varied the opinions about that Invisible Other, the more important the name is likely to be.

But by the same token, names are extraordinarily rich reserves of significance. From behind a character's name shimmer forth not only bits of the different portrayals of that character that any single person has consumed, but also those aspects of the character's history upon which everyone agrees. The name "Orestes" will always evoke the act of matricide, however else his story may be changed, and "Antigone" will always evoke the defiant burial of a brother. The name "Hera" is likely always to evoke her marriage to Zeus,[45] and "Demeter" a mother's grief, whatever other roles these gods explicitly play in a narrative. These associations intone, however subtly, every appearance of that character. A name also evokes, however subtly, the familial line to which the hero or god belongs and the other gods and heroes of the larger network to whom he or she is connected. This power of names to evoke whole histories is the reason that alternative names for certain gods are sometimes used in cult worship, as opposed to myths. Both the name Kore (literally, "Girl") and a variety of names for Hades (such as Clymenus, "The Famous One," or Plouton, "The Wealthy One") are used in cult much more frequently than are the names "Persephone" and "Hades," for example. "Persephone" and "Hades" were so fraught with meaning, so powerfully evocative of the most famous story about these two gods—the rape of Persephone by Hades—as to be ill omened in ritual settings. The names "Kore," "Clymenus," and "Plouton" did not *erase* the interpersonal history and the characteristics implied by the names "Persephone" and "Hades," but they emphasized the gods' kinder sides.[46]

The memories of a character's history that a name can subtly induce usually fly below the audience's conscious radar, but skillful narrators know how to bring them forward to good effect when they choose. In the first line of the *Iliad*, for example, the patronymic "son of Peleus" suffices to fleetingly evoke, for a mythically embedded listener, the entire story of how Achilles was sired upon a goddess by a mortal man and the tale of how the gods' self-interested machinations led to that liaison— both of which underlie the problems that drive the rest of the poem. Had the poet chosen one of the other formulaic epithets that were frequently applied to Achilles—"swift-footed" or "lion-hearted," for instance—the effect would have been quite different. Poets could also play *against* the resonance that a mythic name carried. Pindar introduced Medea into his narrative of how Cyrene had been founded without mentioning the famous episode during which Medea killed her children and ruined her husband's life. Yet the audience's knowledge of it problematized Pindar's portrayal of Medea as a sort of epinician Muse—and thereby lent greater stature to Pindar's claim, within his poem, to have conquered her and utilized her gifts.[47]

Perhaps Roland Barthes was right that there are no objects that are inevitably and eternally sources of suggestiveness, but within the culture that possesses them, the names of gods and other Invisible Others are, in fact, enormously suggestive.[48] In contrast, novels, to take up another form of narrative, must spend a great deal of time developing their characters because those characters are new to readers; the names mean little or nothing when the novel begins (unless the novel is one in a series). In contrast yet again, most folktales and fairy tales rely on generic characters (the hero, the princess, the stepmother) from whom one expects certain generic qualities (bravery, beauty, cruelty) but who typically have no real names, and therefore no individualized personalities or histories.[49] If they have names at all, they are usually descriptive of their most salient feature or function in the story ("Sleeping Beauty," "The Little Mermaid," "Clever Hans"). In the economy of narrative, then, a myth speaks more efficiently than a novel (it can convey more ideas more concisely, because it is built upon an established body of knowledge about who the characters are), and it can convey more ideas, or ideas of greater complexity, than a folktale or fairy tale because its characters have more individualized depth, which can be encapsulated into the names themselves. The closest analogy for what myth accomplishes through its named actors, and how it does so, probably comes from contemporary fan fiction. The characters who populate fan fiction already possess well-developed personalities and histories that they carry forward into new narratives—Harry Potter, Hermione Granger, Ron Weasley, and others from J. K. Rowling's novels are popular cases, as are characters from the *Star Trek* oeuvre, from *Doctor Who*, and from the *Ender's Game* trilogy. So thoroughly versed in the characters' personalities and histories are the audiences of these fan narratives that, as the media scholar Henry Jenkins puts it, "a look, a raised eyebrow, the inflection of a line" is sufficient to evoke a character's total life experience.[50] By drawing actors from a pool of characters whose names are already associated with well-known histories and personalities, both myths and fan narratives are able to gesture towards a great deal more than they state; they can evoke ideas or themes that need not (and sometimes should not) be made explicit.

Double Characters and Double Names

No god shares a personal name with anybody else, nor does a hero who plays a major role in myths. "Theseus," "Heracles," "Perseus," "Bellerophon," and "Medea," for example, clearly denote only one particular person. But the situation is different with less prominent characters: we have more than one Leucippus, Atalanta, and Erigone, for example, and quite a few Agenors. In many cases, the shared name is transparently descriptive, and the stories about those who bear it reflect its meaning in different, but parallel, ways. Boys named "Leucippus" (White Horse) reflect a widespread Greek metaphor that compares young men on the brink of maturation to unruly horses. All three myths that are told about a boy named Leucippus articulate the danger of entering into sexual maturity in the "wrong" way.[51] Similarly, both characters named "Atalanta," whose name can be understood to mean either "Untiring Girl" or "Equal in Weight [to men]," are involved in physical pursuits otherwise restricted to males and prove to be their matches. In the case of both Leucippus and Atalanta, we can probably assume the independent generation of stories starring a character on whom narrators bestowed an appropriate name.[52] Other shared names are useful stop-gaps for characters who play relatively small roles in the myths of other people. Like the names found in fairy tales, they are usually straightforwardly descriptive. "Agenor" (Valiant, Heroic), for example, is never the star of a myth himself but rather the father, son or brother of more prominent characters. Occasionally, however, an author brings such a character into his or her own. "Creusa" (Princess) is a stop-gap name for the daughter of a king, including, for example, Creusa the daughter of King Creon of Corinth, whom Medea killed, and Creusa the daughter of King Erechtheus of Athens, who was mother of the Athenian dynastic hero Ion. Euripides, in his *Ion*, crafted that

Creusa into a woman of independent thought who acted in ways that threatened Ion's survival and rise to power. In a few other cases of double names, such as that of Ajax, we seem to deal with two genuinely separate characters who happen to share a name—a name whose etymology is obscure, perhaps because it is a survival from a pre-Greek language.

There are also names that send no clear message in and of themselves but that have come to be associated with a particular type of fate or experience. "Erigone" is a good example. The name "speaks" only insofar as the "-gone" syllable implies a noble birth; she is, like most of the characters in Greek myths, from the upper class. (The "eri-" means "early"—whatever we want to take that to mean.) Erigone's story, or at least its climax, always takes place in Athens, she is always a maiden who hangs herself, and her ghost always threatens to drive all Athenian maidens to do the same if she is not propitiated annually during the Anthesteria festival.

Two quite different stories of *why* Erigone hanged herself became attached to the name, however, each of which performed its own particular task. In one case, Erigone hanged herself in grief because her father, Icarius, had been murdered by other Athenian men. Icarius, an emissary of the god Dionysus, had introduced the men to the gift of wine and, never having been drunk before, the men concluded that Icarius had poisoned them and therefore attacked him. This story works to tie Erigone into the central concern of the Anthesteria as we know it in historical times, which was the opening of the new wine casks and more generally the celebration of Dionysus. We might guess that the story was created in order to pull the ritual in which Erigone's ghost was appeased, which probably had once stood independent from the Anthesteria, more firmly into the Anthesteria's orbit. (Icarius's story was probably always associated with the Anthesteria, in which case those who invented this myth about Erigone found him a handy figure upon whom to graft her.)

The second story about Erigone probably emerged only after the ritual meant to appease her had already been incorporated into the Anthesteria. It makes Erigone the daughter of Clytemnestra and Aegisthus, who wanted to see her half brother Orestes punished for her parents' murders. When an Athenian jury found Orestes not guilty, Erigone hanged herself in grief. This story, as well as another one that told about Orestes's arrival in Athens while local men were celebrating the Anthesteria, served to tie Athenian myths and rituals into the prestigious epic cycle in which Aegisthus, Clytemnestra, and Orestes already played starring roles.

The essence conveyed by the name "Erigone," then, was that of a girl who hanged herself and cursed Athenian maidens to do the same if she were not appeased; any story attached to her name, whatever else it might do, had to serve as an *aition* for an important Athenian ritual attached to Erigone and therefore had to include her suicide. But her name remained vague enough—malleable enough—that the stories attached to it could be molded to suit other purposes, as well: to bind together disparate parts or themes of a festival complex or to graft older Athenian traditions into a newer, and more glamorous, body of narratives.

Final Words

Ontologically, the Greek gods and heroes are an interesting lot. More fluid than even the most frequently presented characters of fiction, they nonetheless held on firmly to core identities through centuries of continual reinvention. Greater enough than humans to merit worship, they nonetheless were similar enough to humans in their failings to be credible. It was through myths that these productive tensions were held together. What would scarcely be convincing or memorable when stated as a formal credo played out extremely well as stories, and it was through those stories, therefore, that the Greeks were inculcated with a sense not only of the gods' and heroes' existence, but also of who their gods and heroes were and how they must be approached.

Personal names were an important part of this process. "Zeus! Whoever he may be! If it pleases him to be invoked by this name, then by this name I will call to him! Having considered all my options, I have nothing so good as the name of 'Zeus' to help me cast aside my burden!" cries the chorus of Aeschylus's *Agamemnon*, desperate to find a solution to their problems. As they continue with their plea, they briefly narrate a story that was surely familiar to everyone: the first, insolent ruler of the cosmos was overthrown by his son, and that son was, in turn, overthrown by his *own* son—Zeus. The chorus chooses not to mention the names of those first and second rulers, not because they were ill omened (the names had always been in widespread, common use), but rather so as to shine an even stronger spotlight on the glorious name of Zeus, which they immediately repeat again after they have finished narrating their succession story.[53] Zeus is a god so great and so varied that *only* his own name can capture all that he is, folding into a single word everything that poets and artists could ever tell us about him.

6

Metamorphoses

Over the past few years, I've learned that when my grandson asks me to tell him a myth, the myth I tell must include at least one of two things: an episode in which something or someone turns into something else (a metamorphosis) or a creature made up of parts from other creatures (a hybrid). If I really want to please him, the myth I tell must include *both* a metamorphosis *and* a hybrid. Having exhausted my supply of existing stories that meet these criteria (and silently justifying my actions on the basis of some of the principles that I've discussed elsewhere in this book), I've developed a repertoire of tales in which the Chimaera gives advice to Arachne, for instance, or young Pegasus takes flying lessons from Ceyx and Alcyone. Sooner or later, when my grandson reads other, more canon-bound narrations of Greek myths, I'll have to admit that the Chimaera as we traditionally know her wasn't the sort of character who would be helpful to anyone else (even a spider) and that the circumstances surrounding Ceyx's and Alcyone's transformation into seabirds probably left them in no mood to tutor a horse. But for the moment, the more metamorphoses and hybrids I can weave into my stories, the more attractive they are, and therefore I give my imagination free rein.

Tales of transformation, populated by strange creatures, appeal to most of us, whatever our age, and over the course of the centuries, humans have told a lot of them. In the Old Testament, Lot's wife

turned into a pillar of salt when she looked back at the burning city
of Sodom—a transformation tale with which the New Testament
Jesus admonished his apostles, lest they tarry on Judgment Day to
gaze at terrestrial spectacles. The Hindu god Prajapati lustfully
pursued his daughter; she fled from him in the form of a doe, but
Prajapati became a stag and raped her—a scandalous act that drove the
other gods to create Rudra, who hunted down Prajapati and thereby
earned the title "Lord of Animals." Prajapati's tale finds echoes in
Greek stories of goddesses turning themselves into mares to evade
lecherous gods, who then turned into stallions—which led, eventually, both to the birth of wonder horses and to the establishment of
new rituals to appease the angry mothers. We hear more distant
echoes in the stories that American Indians told of women metamorphosing into human-horse hybrids after falling in love with stallions. The horse-women gave birth to valuable ponies but became
outcasts from their tribes or were even killed—yet another variation
of the endless human thinking about what our relationship to animals could and should be. So, too, the world has known many stories about a girl who tries to rescue brothers who have been turned
into birds, sometimes by clothing them in human attire that she has
sewn herself. Racing against the clock, in some of these stories she
fails to sew a single sleeve on a single shirt, and the brother who dons
it carries a wing in place of an arm forevermore.[1]

We have Ovid to thank for the fact that in the Western world, our
appetite for metamorphosis has always been fed to a significant degree by Greek myths. Whatever his formal and ideological reasons
for taking metamorphosis as his theme, Ovid reveled in the opportunity to describe the fantastic, and the many artists and authors
whom he inspired—Bernini, Dante, Titian, Caravaggio, Rembrandt,
Moreau, Wharton, Updike, and Harryhausen (to name only a few)—
have reveled in that as well, arousing and then satisfying their audiences' appetites. As a result, Greek myths about metamorphoses and
hybrids have remained so widely familiar that they still can serve
as fodder for comic strips (a 2012 Bizarro Comic by Dan Piraro shows
a bald woman sitting across the table from a man dressed in bishop's
robe and mitre, with the caption "Ill-Fated Blind Date: St. Patrick
and Medusa").[2]

Some of the examples that I gave earlier of stories about metamorphoses and hybrids suggest that they offer more than just thrills
or amusement, however. Frequently, they have been adduced to explain how rituals, gods, animals or interesting features of the landscape came into existence (late antique writers identified a pillar of
halite near Mount Sodom as what remained of Lot's wife; similarly
the Weeping Rock on Mount Sipylus in Turkey was said to be the
transmogrified Niobe). The stories can also send messages about
how one should and shouldn't behave—don't look at what a god has
told you not to look at, don't have sex with your daughter—or with
stallions—and do keep your fingers nimble enough to finish your
needlework on time. The ease with which myths could be straitjack-
eted into explanatory or admonitory texts was one of the reasons, in
fact, that Ovid and the Greek myths he narrated were able to survive
the Christian purge of pagan detritus; one could transform almost
any myth into a moral lesson of which Jehovah would approve. In
the *Ovid Moralisé*, Callisto, the innocent victim of rape, became "a
hypocrite whose chastity was merely for show," and Myrrha, the
virgin daughter who secretly seduced her father, could be compared
to the Virgin Mary.[3]

Hybrids

In later sections of this chapter, I'll discuss some of the ways that
scholars have tried to understand Greek tales of metamorphosis—
why they were told, what they meant to the tellers and their listeners,
the "rules" by which they seemingly worked. At that point, I'll
leave behind the topic of hybrids, on which I'll focus for the next few
pages. The two are closely linked, however: both hybrids and
metamorphoses challenge the ontological boundaries of the world
and its creatures as we know them. Hybridity, moreover, is sometimes
the result of arrested metamorphosis, as in the case of the brother
who changes first into a swan and then back again into a human but
retains a swan's wing, in the American Indian tales of women who
turn partially (but only partially) into horses after falling in love with
stallions, or in one of several stories about the origin of Scylla,
whose upper half remained a beautiful girl but whose lower body

became a dreadful confusion of barking dogs after she waded (but only waist high) into a pool of poisoned water.[4] Whatever may be the particular roles played by such hybrids in the stories they inhabit, their very presence reminds us that there are more things in heaven and earth than we have yet encountered.

Or more precisely, they remind us that new things may continue to emerge in heaven and earth long after the formal creation of those spheres has come to an end. Implicitly, this is one of the points made by many other stories of metamorphosis, as well, even if they don't produce what we consider hybrids per se. This is most expansively so in Ovid's chain of tales borrowed from Greek sources. His epic starts with the self-assembly of a rudimentary physical cosmos out of raw, disordered matter, and then introduces an unnamed divinity who fashions the first plant and animal life. From there, Ovid rolls on through generations of humans that see the metamorphic emergence of swans, guinea hens, spiders, and other animals; the celestial emplacement of the Big and Little Bears and the Corona Borealis; the bursting forth of newly transmogrified youths and maidens into trees, flowers, and springs; and so on, until he finally reaches the catasterism of Julius Caesar—a modern metamorphosis that is meant to crown all the others. As seen through the lens of the *Metamorphoses*, then (and through the collective lens of the Greek authors who went before Ovid), the world has taken many centuries to become what it is and may still be a work in progress. It is also a place that has been created to a significant degree out of the raw material of human bodies and by the whim of the gods. Behind each man-turned-into-animal or girl-turned-into-plant lay divine anger, envy, pride or desire. It was Pan's desire that drove Syrinx's sister nymphs to turn her into river reeds, and in one version of the story it was Circe's jealousy that turned Scylla into a monster. Apollo pursued Daphne until she was desperate enough to prefer life as a tree; a spurned Leto changed peasants into frogs and a spurned Dionysus changed a king's daughters into bats. Callisto's double transformation— first into a bear and then into the Big Bear—was set in motion by a combination of Zeus's lust and Artemis' anger—and, in some stories, by Hera's anger as well. It was Venus who orchestrated Caesar's rise to the stars. The continuing lability of the world that Ovid and his Greek predecessors described, in short, was powered by gods' emotions. Each transformation was a memento of, and thereby evidence for, the gods' ongoing, and very personal, engagement with the world and its mortal inhabitants.

But to return to my main point, in spite of certain similarities and narrative overlaps between hybrids and metamorphoses, there are also differences. Most importantly, in Greek myths, hybrids are not usually the products of sudden metamorphosis but rather are conceived, born, and reared in more or less the normal biological way.[5] The sea goddess Ceto bore to her sea-god husband, Phorcys, both the Gorgons (women with snakes for hair and, according to some authors, the bodies of lions and the wings of eagles) and Echidna (who was half nymph and half snake). Echidna, in turn, "mingled in love" with Typhon (himself a hybrid with a hundred fiery snake heads) and bore to him the Chimaera and the two-headed dog Orthrus. Then, having been raped by Orthrus, Echidna gave birth to the Sphinx (woman from the breasts up, lion from the stomach down, and winged).[6] The bull-headed Minotaur was conceived during a sexual encounter that, although certainly odd, unmistakably mimicked the sort of thing that took place in pastures every day: Pasiphae, desiring the great white bull that Poseidon had given to her husband, crawled into a hollow wooden cow and awaited the bull's attention.[7] The centaurs were born from Centaurus, a man "bearing honor amongst neither mortals nor the laws of the gods," and a herd of horses with whom he mated. Centaurus himself was a child spawned by Ixion upon a cloud—but it was a cloud that Zeus had shaped to look like Hera.[8] Pegasus's birth was unusual—he sprang from his mother's neck after she had been decapitated—yet his conception, like that of so many other heroes and monsters in Greek myth, occurred when Medusa and Poseidon "lay down in a soft meadow amongst spring flowers."[9] Other monstrous creatures—the nine-headed Hydra, three-headed Cerberus, three-bodied (and three-headed) Geryon, the one-eyed Cyclopes—were similarly conceived during lovemaking between various gods—most typically sea gods or their descendants.[10]

The Greeks were insistent, in fact, that monsters were once somebody's babies. Their pedigrees could be announced like those of the heroes. Most famously, Polyphemus boasted to Odysseus that his father was Poseidon[11]—indeed, the Cyclops's paternity drives the rest of the *Odyssey*—and even within our scant fragments of Stesichorus's lost *Geryoneis*, Geryon manages to announce that he is the son of Chrysaor (Medusa's son by Poseidon) and Callirhoe (an ocean nymph). Just in case we missed hearing Geryon say it, Geryon's friend Menoetes mentions it, too, and the narrator mentions it a third time. Callirhoe herself pleads with Geryon not to meet Heracles in battle and opens her robe to display the breasts that once had suckled him—all three of him, I suppose, however odd a mental picture that may be.[12] In a fragment of Euripides's lost *Cretans*, Pasiphae complains about what it's like to nurse a Minotaur.[13] An Etruscan red-figure vase from the second half of the fourth century, showing a young Minotaur on the lap of an upper-class woman who looks disgruntled, evokes Pasiphae's complaint (see Figure 6.1). Yet another monstrous baby at the breast is conjured up by the Homeric *Hymn to Apollo*, which tells us that after Hera gave birth to Typhon—a dreadful creature "like unto neither gods nor humans"[14]—she gave him over to be nurtured by Python, the baneful supersnake. Hera herself nurtured the Hydra and the Nemean Lion, according to Hesiod. The verb that I translate here as "nurture"—*trepho*—is frequently used of nursing and rearing children, and the poets' insertion of these phrases immediately after they have described the monsters' births makes it clear that more than just metaphorical "nurturing" is meant.[15] Someone, be it Hera, Python or another extraordinary nursemaid, had to take these creatures in hand during those difficult years between infancy and adulthood.

Behind all of these creatures' monstrous features we glimpse a weird version of the idea that heredity counts, just as it does for humans: if your father was the Lord of Horses (Poseidon), you might end up as a winged horse (Pegasus); if your mother was a snake from the waist down (Echidna), you might have nine snaky heads (the Hydra) or a snake's head growing alongside those of a lion and a goat (the Chimaera). If your brother was a two-headed dog (Orthrus), you might be a three-headed dog (Cerberus). Behind the idea that heredity counts, we also glimpse a determination to bind these hybrids into that network of relationships that I discussed in Chapter 4. One

6.1 An upper-class woman (probably meant to be Pasiphae) with a baby Minotaur on her lap. Etruscan red-figure cup from the first half of the fourth century, now in the Cabinet des Médailles, Paris (detail). Inv. num. 1066. Photo credit: © Bibliothèque nationale de France/CNRS–Maison Archéologie & Ethnologie René Ginouvès.

way of being linked in was to be killed by a hero, but another way was to be born from the gods. Most hybrids were both.

No such genetic principle underlies myths of metamorphosis—narratively, it is the whim of a god that determines the end point of a change. It may *seem* as if a principle similar to heredity underlies many of them: after all, "Spider"-girl (Arachne) becomes a spider, "Wolf"-man (Lycaon) becomes a wolf, the youth named Narcissus becomes the narcissus flower and the nymph named Laurel (Daphne) becomes the laurel tree (*daphnē*). Doesn't this amount to a *nomen est omen* sort of cosmogonic thinking, a nominative determinism whose rules are just as inescapable as those of biological heredity? But a moment's thought suggests that most such stories developed "backwards." Someone, at some time, was asked where the spider had come from, with all of its distinctive talents and habits, and answered with a story involving a girl who shared the spider's talents and habits—and who gave the spider her name. It's not only metamorphic myths that work this way; it is, rather, a principle of aitiological nomenclature that runs through many types of Greek myths. Otherwise hazy characters with meaningful names hang off the branches of royal family trees to explain (or, rather, to lay claim to) a kingdom's geographic reach, for example. Achaeus, a son of the Athenian princess Creusa and her husband, Xuthus, furnishes an eponym for the Achaeans—thus tying the Athenian line firmly to the luster of Greek glory as Homer presented it—and then he disappears from view.

I will return to the issues raised by *nomina* that seem to be *omina* later in this chapter. But before we leave the topic of hybrids, we should remember that, as I noted in Chapter 4, many—perhaps most—of the monsters who terrorize Greek myths are not hybrids or teratomes at all. They are simply larger or stronger versions of the animals that populated Greek forests and fields: the Erythmanthian and Calydonian Boars, the Crommyonian Sow, the Mares of Diomedes, the Cretan and Marathonian Bulls, Python, the Nemean Lion, the Teumessian Vixen, and Sciron's gigantic turtle—who doesn't even look gigantic in some representations (see Figure 7.5). In contrast to some other cultures' myths, where hybrids proliferate, Greek myths kept them at bay. Genetically speaking, moreover, those that did exist tended to cluster on one branch of the divine family tree, which grew from the union of Ceto and Phorcys. This may express the ungovernable, unpredictable nature of the sea, an element with which the Greeks were never completely comfortable.[16] (In contrast, the main branch of the gods—culminating in Zeus, his siblings, and his children—is almost completely anthropomorphic, even if its members chose to disguise that fact on occasion by turning themselves into all manner of animals.)[17] When hybrids do enter the Greek mythic story world, they enter not as Dunwich Horrors, evoking existential revulsion as well as fear, but as variations on themes that were visible in everyday nature—the bird, the snake, the fish, the horse, the lion, the bull, and, just once, the goat—an odd detail in the Chimaera's makeup. In Chapter 4, I suggested that the story world of the Greeks is not a strongly secondary one, and even here, in its determination to contain the monstrous within certain bounds, it tethers itself firmly enough to the Primary World to preserve credibility. What was truly amazing was the fact that many creatures, plants, and minerals were created by divine fiat—and those were almost always creatures, plants, and minerals that were familiar from the everyday world.

But What Does It All *Mean?*

Is it really only divine whim that determines the end point of a metamorphosis? Scholars have made an industry out of decoding stories of transformation on the assumption that much more than that lay behind them. One of the most enduringly popular approaches focuses on determining what the animal, plant or mineral into which someone was changed "meant" to the culture concerned. Sometimes, little work on the part of the scholar seems to be needed; the answer already seems obvious from the story. Lycaon, whose name is built on the Greek word for "wolf," slaughters a child in order to test the omniscience of the gods: will they realize that the stew he is serving to them is full of human flesh? They do, and Lycaon, punitively transformed into the wolf whose name he has carried and whose outrageous alimentary habits he has adopted, snarls off into the woods.[18] Infanticide and cannibalism are wrong, the story tells us—but didn't we already know that? Is that really the reason that this story was told?[19] Similarly, the nymph Iynx, who used magic to seduce Zeus, was transformed by Hera into a bird called the *iynx*, whose body was used in love charms. Anthos, who was killed and partially eaten by horses, became a bird called the *anthos*, which had a habit of fleeing from horses.[20] Even when the protagonist's name does not proleptically signal his or her fate, the plot of the story often makes the connection between personal behavior and metamorphosis abundantly clear, or other clues seem to help us build a reassuringly logical network of associations. It could be said to "make sense" that Hera turned Io into a cow because Io was the priestess of Hera, who was particularly fond of cows. The fact that Io later became identified with Isis, to whom the cow was also sacred, rounds things off nicely.[21] Callisto, a nymph who had sworn to emulate Artemis's eternal virginity, was raped and impregnated by Zeus; Artemis punished her by turning her into a bear, a fate that can be said to "make sense" for any or all of several reasons: bears are creatures of the wild and thus fall prey to the goddess's arrows, for example, and/or Callisto became the mother of Arcas ("Bear"), the eponymous ancestor of the Arcadians.[22] The Lycian peasants who purposefully muddied the water that Leto and her infant twins wished to drink were turned into frogs, which "makes sense" (as Leto herself explained, in Ovid's narration of the story) because frogs are repulsive creatures who spend their lives wallowing in mud.[23] It's not only the Greeks and Romans who played these games. As one Jewish tradition has it, Lot's wife begrudged her husband's angelic visitors the salt that was a basic requisite of hospitality: ordered by her husband to provide it, she purposefully betrayed the angels' presence by borrowing extra salt from her neighbors.[24] And so, a quintessentially bad hostess found an appropriate end as the very stuff she should have been serving.

But there are problems with tying things up so neatly. First of all, some of the stories I just mentioned have variants in which the narrative logic that glues them together doesn't work so well. It's not always Hera who turns Io into a cow, in order to punish her; more often, it's Zeus himself, transforming the lover whom he is trying to hide from his wife into the very creature that would be likely to attract her attention.[25] It's not always Artemis who turns Callisto into a bear, either—sometimes it's Zeus or Hera.[26] We might still argue that cow-hood and bear-hood make sense insofar as these heroines become emblematic of the goddesses whom they first served and then offended or make sense in some other encoded way (the bear, which was understood in antiquity to be an especially maternal animal, could be taken to represent the mothers that all young dedicatees of Artemis must one day become, when they left her care—hence, the ritual called "playing the bear" that ancient girls performed in honor of Artemis at Brauron, for example),[27] but in championing these views, we'd still have to admit that *as part of a story*, the transformational logic we expect to see no longer works, and we'd also have to concede that some of our own analyses would have been far less obvious to many members of an ancient audience than they are to us (was mint, formerly the nymph Mintha, really understood by the ancients to be diametrically opposed to the cereal grains associated with Mintha's persecutor, Demeter, as Marcel Detienne suggests?).[28]

Another problem is that there are stories in which a name may foreshadow a transformation, but the behavior does not. Anyone could guess that a girl named Arachne would end up as a spider, and we might even guess that the story of how that happened would involve spinning or weaving, which are well-known occupations of spiders. But the element of hubris that motivates the story as Ovid tells it is not otherwise associated with spiders in any of our ancient texts.[29] Ovid's story of Arachne is different from the story of Iynx, then, in which the use of sex magic "logically" leads to the nymph's new form and function as the magical bird to which she gives her name. Other, more appropriate motivating behaviors (appropriate, that is, according to the ancient understanding of spider behavior) could also be used to explain Arachne's transformation, as we'll see, but it's Ovid's tale that remains well-known; it sticks in the mind and resurfaces over and over again in modern anthologies of ancient Greek myths. A big part of the reason for this, again, is Ovid's brilliant narration: we remember a story because it is intrinsically interesting, not because (or at least, not primarily because) it encodes information that makes sense in a strictly logical way according to the precepts of natural history, alimentary codes, astronomy, ritual practices or anything else. Things usually run exactly the other way, in fact; if the story is engaging, it is better able to send messages about natural history, alimentary codes, astronomy, ritual practices, and so on. Scholars of religion have had trouble accepting this in their dealings with myths—that is one reason that the myth-and-ritual approach that I looked at in Chapter 2 of this book took hold so strongly and for so long, and the structuralist and psychological approaches as well. Each offered a way of reading myths that made sense to twentieth- (or nineteenth-, or twenty-first-) century scholars. The assumptions behind these approaches are not completely wrong— each has the merit of revealing some of the ways in which myths affect or reflect the cognitive, emotional, and social worlds of their audiences—but they tend to ignore the hook embedded in the sheer pleasure of the story itself.

There are also cases in which the kernel of a good story takes off on its own, leaving behind some or all of the "logical" connections between the main characters and their transformations as it develops new vehicles in which to travel. I'll take the various stories about the origin of the nightingale (*aēdōn*) and the swallow (*chelidōn*) as a case study.[30] Each of these centers on a mother who has killed her child and who, as a result, is turned into a mournful bird—either as a punishment or out of the gods' pity. In the earliest such narration, in *Odyssey* 19, Penelope calls this mother Aedon (Nightingale), the daughter of Pandareus, and explains that Aedon eternally laments her child, Itylos, whom she slew while maddened.[31] This story "makes sense" because the song of the nightingale was perceived by the ancient Greeks, like many peoples, as having a mournful sound quite apart from its association with a lamenting mother.[32] But two early allusions to similar stories, from Hesiod and Sappho,[33] call the main character Chelidon (Swallow), the daughter of Pandion, and we presume that if we had the fuller stories behind these allusions, we'd learn that a swallow is what she was turned into. "Logically," this makes little sense, given that the song of the swallow was characterized by the Greeks as a twittering noise similar to the speech of barbarians[34]—far from the melodious, if mournful, sound associated with a lament. These stories have relinquished, in other words, any obvious connection between their main character's behavior and the behavior of the animal that she becomes. In a fragment from another Hesiodic work, we learn that *both* Aedon *and* Chelidon suffered eternally because of a crime they had colluded in committing. Aelian, the author who transmits the fragment to us, goes on to say that Aedon and Chelidon committed their crime during a feast held in Thrace.[35] Judging from what we hear about that feast in later sources, the crime was again infanticide.

We learn more about these two groups of stories in narrations from the fifth century onward. In the first group, a daughter of Pandareus, acting alone, kills her own son, whose name is Itys or Itylus. She turns into a nightingale who laments her slain child forever.

Three narrations of this story are set in Thebes;[36] other versions are set on the island of Dulichium or in Ephesus.[37] In the second group, two daughters of King Pandion of Athens, one married and one unmarried, collaborate in slaughtering the child of the married sister in order to avenge the fact that her husband, a Thracian king named Tereus, has raped the unmarried one. The sisters serve the dismembered child to his father in a stew. The sisters (and the husband) are turned into birds—a nightingale, a swallow, and either a hawk or a hoopoe—and the nightingale laments her slain child forever.[38]

The name of the main character and the bird into which she is transformed remain stable in the first group of stories as time goes by—she is always called Aedon, and she always becomes a mournful nightingale whose name she proleptically bears. Plot details do change, however: sometimes Aedon mistakenly kills her son thinking that he is the child of her sister-in-law, whose fecundity she envies;[39] sometimes she kills him because she thinks he has aided his father's adultery;[40] sometimes no reason is given other than "madness."[41] In contrast, by at least the fifth century, the names of the characters in the second story begin to vary. The role played by Aedon is often filled by Procne, daughter of King Pandion of Athens, and her sister is called Philomela rather than Chelidon.[42] Not only have we lost any direct aitiological connection between the women's names and the birds into which they are eventually transformed in these stories, but another "logical" connection disappears as well. Behind the name "Philomela," the Greeks (and the Romans) would have heard the words "lover of song" (*philo-mela*)—an apt name for a nightingale but not for the twittering swallow that Philomela would become.[43] The poor fit between name and fate is "fixed" in stories told by Sophocles and later authors, according to which Philomela's rapist cut out her tongue to prevent her from telling what she had suffered; she could make only the most guttural of sounds and was compelled to communicate instead through tapestries that she wove.[44] Ovid, a great fan of nominative determinism, conveniently sidesteps this problem by not telling us which girl turned into what bird—or even exactly what the birds were. Later narrators eventually "correct" the story by reversing the transformations: Philomela turns into the nightingale and Procne into the swallow. Some of these narrators also omit the episode of the tongue cutting, so that the nightingale can still sing melodiously.[45] But in those cases, we end up with the *aunt* of the slaughtered child becoming a mournful nightingale and his *mother* a twittering swallow, which upends the familial logic of earlier versions even as it attempts to restore ornithological propriety. One of the latest narrators of all, Eustathius, once again tries to impose sense by remodeling the early part of the story. Philomela becomes the wife of Tereus and Procne becomes the sister whom he rapes and whose tongue he cuts out. But Eustathius then reverts to the older stories at the end by having Procne turn into the melodious nightingale, in spite of her severed tongue, and Philomela into the twittering swallow.[46] And thus, we are back in the soup.

What are we to make of all this? How did the story of the bird who mourns for the child she slaughtered survive, even thrive, in spite of the fact that for centuries it didn't make much sense, aitiologically speaking and sometimes narratively speaking? Clearly, we need to try a different tack. As Wendy Doniger has pointed out, myths are mercenaries, serving the needs of whoever expends the effort to narrate them effectively.[47] In the myths that we have been looking at, what catches the imagination and remains in the mind— what makes these myths powerful mercenaries for anyone who cares to hire them—are two sensational elements: a mother kills her child and the mother is subsequently transmogrified into a bird. Once it has used these elements to hook us, the myth can expand itself to provoke thought on various issues (e.g., the debt a woman owes to her natal family versus the debt she owes to her marital family), can serve as an anchoring backstory for various ancestral or social groups (e.g., Athenian women, by Demosthenes's reckoning),[48] and can furnish various points of meditation: the nightingale story can be evoked by a lonely wife who fears for her son's safety (Homer's Penelope) and by a friendless woman to whom the infanticidal mother's fate looks better than what she herself is about to suffer (Aeschylus's Cassandra)—neither of whom adheres very closely to its original "logic." Formally speaking, on one level these are all still stories about the origin of the nightingale and the swallow, but the ease with which they slip free of certain moorings that seem essential to us tells us that transformations into animals in Greek myths are *not*, first and foremost, encoded lessons in etymology or natural history. It also tells us that the search for a single interpretative strategy that can be applied to all of them—or even a set of interpretative strategies—is fruitless.

My second case study will be Hecabe—the very poster child of interpretative difficulties for those who seek tidy correspondences between a character's backstory and the nature of the beast into which she is transmogrified.[49] We first get a full tale of her travails from Euripides, in his play of the same name: when Hecabe learns that King Polymestor has treacherously murdered her son, she kills his children and blinds the king himself. Polymestor then prophesies that Hecabe, who is about to set sail for Greece as part of the Trojan war booty, will be transformed into a dog with fiery eyes, run up the mast of the ship that bears her, leap overboard, and perish at a place along the Thracian coast that would thereafter be known as Cynossema—the Dog's Tomb.[50] Other stories have Hecabe leaping into the sea in grief as soon as Troy has fallen and then turning into a dog;[51] or being stoned to death by Polymestor's followers and simultaneously turning into a dog;[52] or being stoned to death by the Greeks for unspecified reasons and then turning into a dog;[53] or being stoned by Polymestor's followers, turning into a dog, and yet surviving to wander the Thracian wilds;[54] or turning into a *stone* dog while still in Troy;[55] or simply turning into a dog, for unspecified reasons, after her son Helenus has taken her safely to a new home.[56] The only consistent element amongst these remarkably varied stories is her transformation into a dog.[57]

This metamorphosis is likely to bedevil one, if one looks for consistent logic behind it. What does the dog *mean*? Exactly how does it reflect anything that Hecabe did, or was, in this variety of stories? Is there, perhaps, an inherent savagery in the ancient Greek view of the dog that resonates in Hecabe's deeds as we see them in Euripides's treatment of her story, for instance? This would seem to be hinted at in our earliest trace of Hecabe's transformation: an unattributed lyric fragment says it was the *Erinyes* who turned her into a howling dog with flashing eyes.[58] The Erinyes, after all (who were occasionally portrayed with dog-like features themselves), were goddesses bent on avenging wrongs, sometimes with dreadful ferocity. We could choose to understand this story to be telling us that, like the Erinyes, Hecabe did something that was dog-like in its savagery. Hecabe's declaration, in the final book of the *Iliad*, that she would like to sink her teeth into Achilles's liver,[59] might have laid the groundwork for such an association—or might have reflected that association, if the story of her metamorphosis into a dog was older than the *Iliad*. But still we must be cautious: we have no direct statement that Hecabe was turned into a dog *because* she was savage (and indeed, in some of the stories about her transformation, she does nothing savage at all). There is, moreover, no simple, one-to-one association between dogs and savagery in antiquity: dogs could also be portrayed as loyal friends, for example, or trustworthy guardians and, on the negative side (especially for women), as shameless as well as savage.[60]

Or perhaps (as at least one scholar suggested) Hecabe's transformation into a dog was inspired by the similarity of her name to that of the goddess Hecate, to whom dogs were sacred.[61] Temptingly, a fragment from another work by Euripides does seem to bring the two together, when someone proclaims (to Hecabe, scholars presume), "you will become a bitch, the delight of light-bearing Hecate."[62] This line was well enough known for Aristophanes to spoof it,[63] and Lycophron ran with its apparent connection between Hecate and Hecabe: in his story, Hecabe becomes part of the goddess's uncanny nocturnal kennel, charged with terrifying anyone who fails to worship her. In return, Lycophron goes on to say, Hecate compels Odysseus, who had thrown the first rock at Hecabe's stoning, to erect a cenotaph in her honor.[64] But explaining Hecabe's metamorphosis by reference to Hecate (that is, as a sort of one-off application of the *nomen est omen* principle) is a ticklish affair, for two reasons. First, the earliest possible attestation of the connection between Hecate and dogs comes from the very fragment of Euripides that is presumed to describe Hecabe; the argument becomes circular, in other words. Second, it's likely that Hecate's own connection to dogs originally sprang from her work as a birth goddess (to whom dogs were sacred in antiquity more generally), rather than any uncanniness that the dog and the goddess later came to share.[65] Of course, one might simply switch strategies and start anew from the association between dogs and birth, arguing that it was Hecabe's fame as a *mother* that led to her transformation into a dog (she did bear nineteen sons to Priam, after all, as well as an undisclosed number of daughters). A combination of the two aspects—savage and maternal—might be better still: the ancient Greeks, like us, used the simile "a bitch protecting her pups" to describe savage attacks on behalf of something one loved—the very sort of deeds that Euripides and some later authors described Hecabe as committing.[66]

But all of this is learnéd speculation—none of these suggestions is provided by the ancient stories themselves, and none provides the same satisfying click of a puzzle piece that we get, for example, from Lycaon's metamorphosis into a wolf following his cannibalistic feast or Iynx's transformation into a tool for love magic after seducing Zeus. This prompts two observations. The first is a reiteration of something I've already said several times in this book: myths were able to communicate ideas and emotions first and foremost because myths were entertaining, not because they were encoded with information that was intended, first and foremost, to be puzzled out by the audience members. Later in this chapter, I'll consider more closely what it was that myths of metamorphosis, as a group, were meant to communicate. The second observation concerns the rich diversity of potential meanings that we have been able to read into Hecabe's transformation, which spring forth from the diversity of associations that the dog had in antiquity. What sort of interpretative methodology can we use to approach such a situation that will enable us to appreciate, rather than try to eliminate, this diversity, at least in some cases?

Arachne and Her Brother

Like the dog, many animals, plants, and other metamorphic end points in Greek myths have spectrums of associations, rather than single, simple meanings. Even the wolf, as Richard Buxton has shown, could be admired for its community spirit, as well as feared as a ruthless predator.[67] Had Lycaon not tried to serve up his son to the gods in a stew—had he instead run off into the woods after some other transgression, such as trying to share the gods' food with his mortal tablemates (as Tantalus had, according to one story),[68] we might see a very different logic behind his metamorphosis: we'd probably say that he became a wolf because, like a wolf, he shared his food, but shared it with the wrong friends.

As a more extended case for investigation and for the testing of a particular methodological approach, I want to look at a myth that is unfamiliar to most people—one whose apparent meanings have not already been well burnished by scholars. It is a myth about Arachne that runs quite differently from the famous story that we inherit from Ovid. It comes to us from a scholiast to Nicander's *Theriaca*, a poetic treatise on dangerous animals:[69]

> Theophilus, of the School of Zenodotus,[70] relates that there once were two siblings in Attica: Phalanx, the man and the woman, named Arachne. While Phalanx learned the art of fighting in arms from Athena, Arachne learned the art of weaving. They came to be hated by the goddess, however, because they had sex with each other—and their fate was to be changed into creeping creatures that were eaten by their own children.

The scholiast's reason for mentioning Theophilus's story is Nicander's use, in his poem, of the word *phalangia* (the plural of *phalangion* and a cognate of Phalanx's name).[71] *Phalangia*, in contrast to *arachnai*, are spiders with venom strong enough to kill humans. What we have here, then, at least on the most obvious level, is an aitiology for two different families of spiders.

Transformation into a spider has a connection with the earlier pursuits of the sister: she was, after all, a weaver who had learned her skills from the very goddess of weaving herself. But what about Phalanx? Why did it "make sense" for him to turn into a spider? And what about the story's other sensational elements, the siblings' incest and the fact that they were doomed to be eaten by their own children? Do these plot twists somehow play into the metamorphic logic, or are they simply a spine-chilling transgression and its equally spine-chilling punishment?

To figure this out, we need to take a more thorough look at ancient ideas about spiders, but we also need a methodological tool that will help us make sense of the material we examine. For the tool,

I propose that we use the concept of *affordances*. The concept was invented in 1979 by the perceptual psychologist J. J. Gibson to designate a characteristic feature of an object, to which an individual (human or animal) can react in various ways, depending on the individual's own perceptions and capabilities. A stick, for example, may offer the affordances of straightness, length, and a tapering tip, but it is understood as "good to dig ants out of a hole with" only if the individual who picks it up possesses the fine motor skills necessary for the task and the cognitive sophistication to conceive of the possibility. A stick that is straight and long with a tapering tip might also be perceived as a weapon or a scepter, for example. Affordances *circumscribe* the potential meanings or uses of phenomena to which they are attached, but they do not *determine* those meanings and uses.[72]

Maurizio Bettini adapted the term "affordance" to the study of cultural phenomena and particularly to thinking about the ways in which human observers react to animals' characteristic appearances and habits. He suggested, for example, that the weasel's habit of carrying her pups in her mouth is an affordance that gave rise to the ancient belief that weasels give birth through their mouths and that the weasel's slim, tubular body is an affordance that led to her ancient reputation as a helper of women in labor—it was hoped that, like a weasel sliding through a hole, the baby might slip easily through the narrow space of the birth canal. Bettini emphasizes that neither characteristic of the weasel *compelled* ancient thought in a particular direction; rather, they *afforded* opportunities for thought that could lead in any of a number of directions, depending on the backgrounds of the observers—in another place or another context, the weasel's carrying of her pups in her mouth might be interpreted to mean that weasels ate their young. (Of course, there isn't necessarily any connection between the ancient associations of an affordance and its actual function within the life of the animal as we now perceive it from our lofty perch of twenty-first-century zoology.)[73]

"Affordance" is a more useful concept than "symbol" for articulating the ways in which myths and other cultural products—rituals and art, for instance—accumulate and convey ideas. A symbol usually has an essential and nearly static meaning (X symbolizes Y, or perhaps X can symbolize *both* Y and Z, but X usually can't move amongst symbolizing Y, Z, A, B, C, D, and so on). This essentialism is, in fact, crucial to the success of many of the symbols that we encounter: unless they can convey ideas clearly to a fairly wide range of observers, they fail in their task. Had the symbol of the lily not become associated almost exclusively with purity in Christian thought, for example, it could not have represented Mary across so many centuries and such a broad geographic span as it has.[74] An affordance, in contrast, because its meaning arises from interaction between the observer(s) and the thing in question, allows the development of *spectrums* of associations. Some stories draw on some of these, and others draw upon others. A particular spectrum might even include associations that seem to clash with each other—for instance, the dog can be associated with loyalty and shamelessness, savagery and maternal love. Some or all of these associations might be pondered by someone who watches a bitch protecting her pups and used by a skillful narrator to produce a subtly complex story about a dog.

But to get back to Arachne and Phalanx: what then, were the spider's most striking affordances in ancient eyes, and how can they help us to understand the way that Theophilus's story might have been received by ancient ears? I'll look at the three that are most often mentioned by ancient authors.[75]

Weaving webs. The affordance most often mentioned is the spider's ability to spin fiber and weave it into a web. The associations of this affordance vary quite a bit, however. It could indicate industriousness; spiders were almost as highly esteemed, in this respect, as were ants and bees.[76] Yet spiders' webs could also be used to signify neglect, in the sense that their presence indicated that an object or place had been abandoned by humans.[77] Sometimes, the spider's web was lauded as a work of delicacy, produced by an intelligent creature,[78] but at other times, it was viewed as a repetitively symmetrical product, created by dumb animal instinct rather than skill and art.[79] The ease with which a web could be destroyed suggested the transitory nature of artifice.[80] Finally, a spider's web could evoke entrapment and a predatory nature—the best-known case being Aeschylus's description of Clytemnestra capturing Agamemnon in a web-like net.[81]

Spiders and parricide. In the tale from Theophilus, Arachne and Phalanx are said to be "changed into creeping creatures that are eaten by their own children." This reflects an affordance of spiders that we first hear about from Aristotle, who says that young *phalangia* "when they grow to full size, very often surround their mother and eject and kill her; and not seldom they kill the male as well, if they can catch him." This information is repeated by several later authors, with Pliny adding the detail that the murderous spiderlings subsequently eat their parents' corpses. (There is, in fact, one species of Mediterranean spiders, *Stegodyphus lineatus* [Latreille, 1817], that eats its mother—it's possible that Aristotle, Pliny, and others observed young *Stegodyphi lineati* taking their meals.)[82]

Little needs to be said about the significance of this affordance—parricide can hardly be anything but negative—but it's worth noting that in ancient thought, parricide was often paired with incest, another transgression against the integrity of the family, and that cannibalism was also paired with incest, interfamilial murder or both to further mark their gravity. The tangled histories of the House of Atreus and the House of Laius furnish ready examples of these combinations. It is mythically "logical," in other words, for incestuous siblings such as Arachne and Phalanx to turn into creatures doomed to be killed by their progeny and then end up as the victims of cannibalism as well.

Spiders and priapism. Perhaps the most horrifying *phalangion* in Nicander's catalogue is the *rhōx* (also called the *rhax*). According to Nicander, its bite causes the victim's eyes to turn reddish and a shivering to settle upon his limbs; numbness overcomes his hips and knees. So far, this is not very different from the effects of a few other *phalangia* that ancient authors describe, but a further symptom is quite striking: "[The victim's] skin and genitals grow taut, and his penis projects, moistened with ooze." Several other authorities describe the same symptom, either echoing Nicander's phrases or using their own words; most of them extend this symptom to the family of *phalangia* as a whole.[83]

Working from ancient descriptions of the appearance and behavior of the *rhōx*, modern zoologists have identified it as a member of the genus *Latrodectus* (Walckenaer, 1805), still alive in Mediterranean countries today.[84] The bite of any member of the *Latrodectus* genus really does cause priapism and involuntary ejaculation if antivenin is not administered within a reasonable amount of time.[85] Thus, these ancient reports, incredible though they may seem, are probably based on something that ancient observers saw—that is, on an affordance of the *phalangion*. Nowadays, we know that the distressing symptoms that Nicander described are produced by neurotoxins that the spider injects into its victim, but in antiquity, not surprisingly, the symptoms were understood to mean that the spiders *themselves* were filled with an excessive lust with which they could infect others through their bite.[86]

These, then, were the three affordances of spiders that the ancient audience were likeliest to have had in mind when they encountered the story of Arachne and Phalanx for the first time: an ability to spin and weave, a habit of parricide that was sometimes followed by cannibalism, and a lustful nature. The associations of the second and third affordances are quite limited, which might lead to us reading this story straightforwardly as a cautionary tale in which sexual transgression within the family leads to other horrible abnormalities, but two things should encourage us to think further. First, the spider's most frequently mentioned affordance—the ability to spin and weave fibers—is still up for interpretation. Second, Phalanx is given a characteristic of his own that he shares neither with Arachne nor with the race of spiders: when the story opens, he is undergoing military training. The word *phalanx*, which means "battle array" as well as "poisonous spider," epitomizes this (the double connotation of the word probably helped to inspire the story, in fact).[87] Finally, both Arachne and Phalanx are pupils of Athena, within a story set in Athens, which suggests that what is at issue is not just the fact that Arachne and Phalanx failed to behave like proper humans, but also the fact that they failed to behave like proper citizens of their city, even when nurtured by its leading divinity. How did weaving, warfare, sexual misconduct and civic duty come together in the Athenian imagination?

Weaving frequently served as a metaphor (in Athens and elsewhere) for two institutions that underpinned a proper society: marriage and the coming together into civic groups of the families resulting from those marriages.[88] Particularly resonant for these representations was that fact that weaving began with fibers that could be viewed as opposing one another: some ran vertically (the warp) and some ran horizontally (the woof). And yet the proper combining of these fibers produced a textile that was strong, useful, and beautiful—and so it was also with marriage, which combined the "opposites" of male and female,[89] and with civic coalitions, which combined groups that might otherwise be at odds with one another.

The metaphors of "weaving a marriage" and "weaving a city" from disparate fibers are familiar from their extended use in Plato's *Statesman*, Aristophanes's *Lysistrata*, and other texts.[90] They were important as well at the Panathenaia, the main festival of the Athenian year, in which all members of the city, high and low, joined together to celebrate its accomplishments. A cluster of associated myths emphasized the festival's annual rearticulation of Athenian unity: Theseus was said to have founded the Panathenaia to celebrate the unification of the previously independent villages of Attica, for example.[91] The celebration culminated in the dedication of a new *peplos*, woven by girls and women from noble Athenian families, to Athena, Protector of the City (Athena Polias), at her main city temple on the Acropolis, in hopes of renewing her affection for the city that carried her name.

It was not only civic unity that the Panathenaia and its *peplos* celebrated, however; the preparation of the *peplos* brings us back to weaving as a metaphor for marriage and its extended significance as a task that every properly raised girl had to master before her wedding. For although the bulk of the work of weaving Athena's new *peplos* was done by older females, the ritually important inception of the project also involved young girls who were serving in another cult dedicated to Athena.[92] They were called Arrhephoroi, and their most important duty, performed during the night of a festival called the Arrhephoria, was to receive a mysterious package from the priestess of Athena on the Acropolis and carry it down a special staircase to a temple of Aphrodite. The priestess of Aphrodite gave them another mysterious package to carry back to the priestess of Athena. The myth associated with this journey told of how Aglaurus, Pandrosus, and Herse, daughters of Athens's first king, Cecrops, had once been charged by Athena with guarding a basket into which they were not allowed to look. They looked anyway and caught sight of

Athena's foster child, Erichthonius, who was part snake and part human—a natural-born hybrid. Maddened with fright at the sight, the girls jumped off the Acropolis to their deaths.[93]

Walter Burkert has noted that whereas the myth narrates a premature, improper introduction to motherhood and its concomitant sexuality, the ritual enacts a proper introduction, during which girls leave the realm of Athena, the virgin goddess, briefly visit the realm of Aphrodite, the goddess of sexuality, and then travel back again to Athena, whose duties also included receiving, at her temple on the Acropolis, each and every Athenian bride on the eve of her marriage.[94] All the while, these girls resist the temptation that the daughters of Cecrops did not: they do not peer into the mysterious boxes they have been told to protect. Burkert has also stressed the coherence of the two tasks with which the Arrhephoroi were charged: a girl's preparation for marriage properly comprised both an introduction to sexuality, in preparation for her role as a mother, and the mastery of spinning and weaving, a good wife's tasks par excellence. Other myths bring the two fields of activity together by associating the daughters of Cecrops not only with their flawed introduction to sexuality but also, and more successfully, with weaving and the care of textiles (traditional tasks that every well-brought-up virgin learned before marriage). Aglaurus and Pandrosus were said to have been the very first wool workers, and all three sisters were credited with weaving the first clothing for the people of Athens. Aglaurus also established the Plynteria and Kallynteria (festivals at which the statue of Athena and its clothing were cleansed).[95]

And Phalanx? If Arachne represents the failed virgin, then what does he represent? Our best clue comes straight from Theophilus's story itself: Athena was teaching him *hoplomacheia*, "fighting in arms," a type of war craft in which young Athenian men were trained.[96] One of the occasions on which young men's preparation for military service was highlighted was the Panathenaia, during which they competed in a variety of contests designed to display their military might, including a hoplite race—that is, a race amongst men dressed in full armor.[97] At the Panathenaia, in other words, young men exhibited their prowess in the skills that defined maturity as an Athenian male just as women exhibited their accomplishment in one of the skills that most centrally defined Athenian femininity.[98] Phalanx served as a (failed) representative of all Athenian youths and their potential just as Arachne served as a (failed) representative of all Athenian girls and their potential—and both Phalanx and Arachne failed not because of any lack of skill on their parts (they had been trained by Athena, after all) but because they could not channel their sexuality properly.

Theophilus's story of Arachne and Phalanx, then, explored some of the same ideas as were articulated in Athens's most important festival: weaving and military skills were the proper pursuits of young people, on which both strong marriages and strong cities could be built, but properly controlled sexuality was essential as well. If a strong city is built upon the union of diversified families and a strong family is built upon the union of diversified spouses, then the union of siblings, by definition, weakens the fabric of both. This leads to a final observation about the affordance of a spiderweb. Spiders, as the ancients already observed, are isolated creatures that share their webs only when they mate.[99] Indeed, our only ancient description of spiders sharing a web reads like a parody of marital unification: the female sits in the middle of her web, and the male sits on the periphery. She pulls on a strand to move him a bit closer, and then he pulls on a strand to bring her a bit closer. They repeat this until their hind parts finally meet, and it is in this awkward position that they clumsily engender the offspring that will eventually kill and consume them.[100] The spider's web, then, is very different from the cloth under which the new bride lay with her husband, which she had woven while still a virgin, and very different as well from the metaphorical textiles that Plato's Statesmen-Weavers produce: the spider's web is a clumsy marital bed from which only catastrophe can arise. Athena's erstwhile wards, Arachne and Phalanx, fail in their transitions to both sexual and civic maturity and doom themselves to lives as lonely creatures that lack any community at all.

If we have properly unpacked Theophilus's story of Arachne, then we have to assume that it had a lot of meaning for the ancient Athenians who were its original audience and also for later ancient readers, for whom the metaphors of weaving and marriage and weaving and the city-state continued to resonate. Why, then, did this story languish, ignored by everyone except the scholiast to Nicander? Why doesn't it show up in Ovid or anywhere else? Certainly, it was lurid enough to be attractive: what more could an audience want than incest, cannibalism, parricide, and metamorphosis?

A first, easy answer is that Ovid chose to narrate another story about Arachne—a story that he may have picked up from a Lydian tradition about the spider or may have made up himself. His enormous success as a narrator guaranteed that any other version would drift into the shadows. It is Ovid's Arachne whom Dante met in Purgatory, amongst the proud and Ovid's Arachne whom Velázquez and Rubens painted.[101] But this only pushes the question back a step: why didn't Ovid choose to narrate the Athenian story?

Programmatically and thematically, the story set in Lydia serves Ovid's purposes very well. Arachne gets in trouble for her skills as a weaver of textiles, an undertaking that already in antiquity was used metaphorically to represent the construction of texts—of stories. A storyteller is exactly what Ovid presents himself to be in the *Metamorphoses*: a meta-commentary on his own art seems to be embedded in his narration of the contest between Arachne and Minerva, then. The stories that Arachne and Minerva weave into their tapestries, moreover, gave Ovid ample opportunity to narrate numerous further myths of transformation. If myths are mercenaries, then Ovid's band of warriors beat out any army that may still have been fighting on behalf of Theophilus.

The Power of the Gods

So far, we have seen that Greek myths sometimes seem to have clear messages or at least make clear connections: Apollo's ardor causes Daphne to be turned into a *daphnē* tree; therefore, the *daphnē* becomes sacred to Apollo. Lycaon is willing to serve up human flesh as stew meat; therefore, he becomes a wolf—and therefore, dear listeners, be sure you don't serve human flesh. At other times, messages and connections seem to get lost in transmission as a great story is passed from narrator to narrator, each of whom crafts it to suit his or her own desires and purposes: Aedon becomes a tunefully lamenting *aēdōn*, and her sister Chelidon becomes a twittering *chelidōn;* but then the Athenians push Aedon aside in favor of someone named

Procne, and her sister takes the new name of Philomela—the tuneful one—but has her tongue severed. Then suddenly, it's the sister with a severed tongue who turns into the nightingale—a nonsensical transformation, zoologically speaking, yet in the meantime, the luridly attractive story has managed to do a lot of important work on behalf of its many narrators. Adopting the concept of affordances helps us to see that myths can send more complex messages than we have generally credited them with and to better understand a particular myth against the background of other myths, rituals, and social institutions with which it is in dialogue. Perhaps affordances would help us better understand what was going on with Hecabe, as well.

If anything is completely clear so far, it's that there is no standard key or even set of keys that's guaranteed to unlock the meanings of all metamorphic myths. The one unassailable observation that we circle back to over and over again, instead, is that whatever other aitiological, ideological or cautionary work was done by stories of transformation, one of their primary obligations was to be great *stories*—ripping good yarns about extraordinary events, about "wonders" (*thaumata*), as Richard Buxton has reminded us.[102] Indeed, as if to make sure we don't miss that point, characters in the narrations sometimes express wonder—or horror—at the events themselves. The most extended instances of this, before Ovid, come from Aeschylus's two descriptions of Io. In his *Suppliant Maidens*, the chorus describes the Egyptians who received her as "trembling at her strangeness, with pale fear at their hearts," as they beheld "a mixed-breed creature, half-cow, half-human—a monster to be marveled at." The verb "marveled at"—*ethamboun*—is a cognate of *thaumata*. The chorus of his *Prometheus Bound* declares that they have never seen something "so offensive to their eyes, so shameful and frightening, so chilling to the soul"—and this in spite of the fact that the chorus members themselves are ocean nymphs.[103]

With this point in mind, we should step back and ponder the sheer number of stories of metamorphosis that we inherit from Greek myths and, at the same time, the particularity of each. Already from Hesiod we hear about Actaeon, Battus, Lycaon, Callisto, Ceyx, and Alcyone, Atalanta, Io, and Hyacinthus—if we had more

than fragments of his *Catalogue of Women*, we would undoubtedly
hear about others. Our extant tragedies narrate or allude to twenty-
two metamorphoses; titles of lost tragedies promise quite a few more.
Other genres are less lush in their offerings, but nonetheless, we
glean some examples from lyric,[104] and the local historians and early
prose mythographers supply quite a few.[105] Then there is the huge
flowering of metamorphic narrations during the Hellenistic period,
when poets such as Nicander and Boeus assembled them from earlier sources, preserving for us some stories that we would not otherwise have. Finally, let us not forget visual representations: on vases,
we find Actaeon as a human with stag's horns (even in the Underworld!), Io as a cow with the face of a maiden, Niobe turning into
stone from the feet up, pirates turning into dolphins, and so on (see
Figures 6.2–6.4).[106]

6.2 Actaeon turns into a stag while his dogs devour him. Artemis and Zeus
look on; Lysa (Rabid Madness), who has a dog's head emerging from her own
head, urges Actaeon's dogs onward. Above Actaeon's head is the word
"Euaion," the name of a famous tragic actor. Attic red-figure bell krater by
the Lykaon Painter, dated to about 440 BCE (detail). Now in the Boston
Museum of Fine Arts, inv. num. 00.346. Henry Lillie Pierce Fund. Photograph © 2018 The Museum of Fine Arts, Boston.

6.3 Hermes prepares to kill Argus, who is guarding Io, here shown with the body of a cow but the face of a woman, to indicate her transformation. South Italian red-figure oinochoe by the Pisticci Painter, dated to between 445 and 430 BCE (detail). Now in the Boston Museum of Fine Arts, inv. num. 00.366. Henry Lillie Pierce Fund. Photograph © 2018 The Museum of Fine Arts, Boston.

6.4 Niobe, standing in a funeral *naiskos*, turning into stone from the feet upwards. Apulian red-figure loutrophoros by the Painter of Louvre MNB 1148, dated to third quarter of the fourth century (detail). Now in the J. Paul Getty Museum, inv. num. 82.AE.16. Digital image courtesy of the Getty's Open Content Program.

Amongst all of these materials, remarkably, seldom is there much room for confusion. Usually, each name is linked to only one story, or cluster of similar stories, and there is generally only one backstory, or cluster of similar backstories, for each animal, plant or mineral that started out as a human. It's unlikely that an ancient listener, hearing the name Io, would think of any metamorphosis other than that of a woman into a cow or, hearing about a hunter who was turned into a stag and then torn apart by his own dogs, would think of anyone other than Actaeon. Of course, there were some local stories that complicate this picture—the stories of Aedon and Chelidon seem to have coexisted alongside those of Procne and Philomela, each leading to transformations into a nightingale and a swallow. There were two different Scyllas—one turned into the monster with dogs below her waist and the other into a seabird.[107] In the overwhelming majority of cases, however, it must have been very clear which metamorphosis went with which name. This specificity is one of the reasons that Greek metamorphic myths survived through the centuries as allegories, metaphors, and significant allusions: each is so vividly distinct from the others that it can reliably convey a whole set of images and ideas through little more than a name and perhaps a telling detail. Vergil, in listing creatures that thwart the beekeeper's work, can refer to "the spider, cursed by Minerva," and expect us to know at least one of the stories of Arachne; Francis Bacon can describe traitorous servants as plotting to treat their master like Actaeon and expect us to know that the servants will tear that master apart, literally or figuratively.[108] It is one of the lures of modern works such as John Updike's *The Centaur*. Once we have realized who *Iris Osgood* really is, with her bovine eyes and milky arms, we are eager to see how her transformation into a cow will play out within the confines of the 1940s rural high school in which Updike's novel is set.[109]

Many metamorphosed characters, moreover, are tied into one of the great ancestral families of Greek myth: amongst other things, Actaeon's story is a story about the royal family of Thebes, and Io's story is about the royal family of Argos (and how one branch of it ended up in Egypt). This gives the characters, and their stories, a concrete link to the lives of their audiences: these are the great-grandfathers and great-grandmothers from whom their city (or

their neighbors' city) sprang and to whom noble families still trace
their lineage; these are the heroes and heroines who are worshipped
at local shrines. So persistent is this idea that even a royal maiden
transmogrified into a bear (Callisto) may nonetheless give birth to a
son (Arcas) who becomes the eponymous king of a land (Arcadia) and
the progenitor of a dynasty.[110] The story of the nightingale and the
swallow, once it had been firmly tied into the Athenian line of descent by its association with Procne and Philomela, daughters of the
primordial king Pandion, could be used by Demosthenes to exemplify the patriotic heroism of Athenian women: the sisters' infanticide was their own way of rebelling against a northern barbarian.[111]
Nicander, in his *Metamorphoses*, carefully ties each story to a locale:
it was in Calydon that the Meleagrides turned into guinea hens, in
Orchomenus that the daughters of Minyas became bats, on the far-
thest border of Thessaly that Aegypius and Neophron became vul-
tures. Sometimes one of his stories has aitiological implications for
a local cult: Leucippus turned from a girl into a boy on Crete, giving
rise to a new festival there in honor of Leto, who had worked the
trick.[112] In part, Nicander's focus on places bespeaks the same learnéd
love of obscure local histories that we see in Callimachus and other
Hellenistic poets, but the information had to be there for these poets to
use: they inherited older stories that had shaped local self-perceptions.

We are a long way, in other words, from the nameless swan brothers
and their sister whom I mentioned in the first section of this chapter
and the anonymous women who married stallions; Greek myths are
most often about people who are entrenched in the larger history
of a particular place. They are not "once upon a time, in a kingdom
far, far way." In fact, Greek myths more generally seem determined
to tell stories about specific individuals who lived in specific places.
This does not mean that the Greeks did not tell what we would call
fairy tales, in which the characters are usually given generic names.
It would be remarkable if they did not, given that fairy tales are
found in almost every culture. What it means, rather, is that myths
and fairy tales serve different purposes, even if they draw on a
shared pool of motifs such as the wicked stepmother and a pool of
plot themes such as the little man overcoming a giant or ogre through
cleverness. It is always horrifying to hear about a man being turned

into a predatory beast, but a man who is one of the ancestral kings of Arcadia turning into a predatory beast (Lycaon) is horrifying in a more resonant way.

It is also the particularity of these stories that keeps each of the marvels marvelous—that allows each to seize the imagination without sating the palate. Indeed, the lack of reliable "rules" or "logic" that govern metamorphoses enhances that particularity; the wonders offered by these stories cannot be circumscribed within any grammar of correspondences and therefore cannot become rote and predictable. They remain wondrous. But it is the sheer *number* of metamorphoses, cumulatively, that carries another kind of weight: as consumers of Greek myths, we are constantly reminded of something that I said earlier in this chapter: the gods can do almost anything they please. What we are accustomed to think of as reality remains fluid under their touch and is at the mercy of their emotions. In this sense, it becomes even clearer that the metamorphosis of humans into other creatures and things is just one, although an especially spectacular, type of a larger category of wondrous events that we hear about both in myths and in other types of narrative. Gods can enhance the beauty of an individual's true form, as Athena does for the wave-swept Odysseus before he meets Nausicaa on the Phaeacian shore.[113] They can cover great distances in the blink of an eye, as they do when darting on and off the Trojan battlefield, or send a winged golden ram to rescue their children from the sacrificial altar, as Nephele does in our earliest stories of the Golden Fleece.[114] They can work miraculous cures, as we hear from the Epidaurian *iamata*, even performing surgery while the patient is asleep.[115] They can fight alongside their worshippers against the barbarian Gauls, as Apollo and two "white maidens" (Artemis and Athena?) did in Delphi in 279 BCE, and as Demeter and Persephone did in a naval battle.[116] And of course, they can change their own forms as easily as we change clothing—not only in myths (in which they disguised themselves as humans as well as animals) but also in real life: St. Elmo's fire was understood as an epiphany of the Dioscuri; Asclepius appeared to the son of his worshipper Isyllus as a man gleaming in golden armor, but sometimes appeared to other worshippers as a snake. A priestess of Demeter named Alexandra asked Apollo, at his Didymean oracle, why the gods had recently manifested themselves so often in the forms of maidens, women, men, and children.[117]

Of course, manifestations such as those that Alexandra talks about were usually understood to have happened more recently than the mythic ones, perhaps in the generation of their audiences' parents or grandparents, perhaps even in the audiences' own. These wonders had the advantage, therefore, of temporal proximity and the credibility that comes with it, as well as the credibility that comes from a reasonable degree of experiential verisimilitude: "real-life" sources do not mention humans turning into plants and animals, but they do mention gods taking on human form (and occasionally snake form) to appear to their worshippers. Who is to say that the gods aren't lurking amongst right us now, disguised as sausage sellers, nursemaids, or the boa constrictor that's for sale in the local pet store? But the wonders described by myths had advantages as well. Most importantly, they included—indeed, they fervently embraced—the negative side of the gods' power and how it affected humans. Many mortals were transmogrified because of a god's anger or lust, and many of those who were transmogrified because of divine pity landed in their pitiable circumstances because of divine anger or lust—perhaps even the anger or lust of the very same god who later took pity. Myths, then, were a place where the Greeks could talk about an aspect of the gods' nature, and its potential to explode at any moment into mortal life that they did not care to confront in venues such as public inscriptions and prayers. So has it always been: narratives that stretch the imagination, narratives about the wondrous (whether they are strictly regarded as "fictional" or not), provide space to entertain all sorts of issues that are hard to address elsewhere. Indeed, the further they stretch the imagination, the safer they may seem, detached as they are from everyday experiences. As Victoria Nelson has observed, for example, representation of the supernatural in contemporary films predominantly takes the form of the grotesque and demonic, rather than the benign and angelic. Nelson attributes this to the secular, Aristotelian worldview that has held sway in the West for the past four centuries, which she suggests has repressed all religious thought outside of that prescribed by doctrine (which, in Western Judaism and Christianity tends to emphasize the benign aspects of divinity). The repressed thoughts—the negative side of the transcendent—bubble to the surface in media that can be neatly compartmentalized away from normal life.[118]

This is not exactly the case for antiquity, of course; practices and beliefs that we might describe as "demonic" in nature, or as directed against the demonic, were widely practiced—binding spells, amulets, monthly suppers left at the crossroads to avert bad luck. Yet the parallel holds insofar as almost all formal declarations about the gods in antiquity emphasized their benignity towards mortals. As Diogenes the Cynic said, if everyone who foundered and was lost at sea had been able to make dedications to the gods at Samothrace, they would have outnumbered by far the existing dedications, which had been thankfully set up by those who had survived the rigors of the waves.[119] Are those who suffer at the hands of the gods in any position to advertise the fact that they have suffered, and if they are, would they dare to do so? Myths were the proper places to explore the grimmer side of the mortal-divine relationship, whether it ended in metamorphosis or some other ill. These tales were closely tied to their audiences through ancestry, through the local landscape and through cultic aitiology, but they were conveniently kept at a distance through the perceived gap of time and through the very fact that audiences knew that fallible humans had had a hand in their creation. Who could be sure exactly how much of a tragedy, epicinician ode or other composition came from a poet's own imagination and how much had been inspired by the Muses (who in any case had boasted to Hesiod of being accomplished liars, when they chose to be)?

Many of these narratives—performed in the theater, danced at a victory celebration or sung from the rhapsode's dais—were delivered during festivals that were meant to honor the gods. The dark side of divine power was nonetheless power, and there is no question but that some myths of divine *thaumata* (metamorphic or not) were meant to remind listeners of the damage that the gods could do when they were not happy with their treatment at the hands of mortals. Here, we drift into the category of the aretalogy—a narrative meant to exalt a god's works. Typically, aretalogies focused on the good things that a god had done, but goodness always lies in the eyes of the beholder. We may sympathize with Dionysus's decision to turn the pirates who

have kidnapped him into dolphins, and we may therefore describe
that part of his Homeric *Hymn* as an aretalogy, but we may also sympathize with Metanira's outcries when she sees Demeter placing her
infant son in the hearth fire, in the Homeric *Hymn to Demeter*. What
are we to call the famine that follows this incident, signaling Demeter's rage?[120] That it establishes Demeter's absolute power over the
growth of grain is indisputable, but it surely brings no benefit to any
human. Or to take a real-life example, in the third century BCE., a
man on Delos set up an inscription praising Isis and Sarapis for
striking his opponents dumb in court—the lawsuit concerned his
right to establish a temple for the two gods in the agora. This was a
demonstration of the gods' powers, indeed, and we might understand
it to have been justified by their desire for a permanent home on the
island; but then, we don't know the other side of the story—or to
which gods the other side might have been praying.[121]

Transformation and Identity

Wonders, whether they happened in narratives or real life, changed
the lives of the mortals whom they touched. Those that involved
metamorphoses altered their victims' exterior forms. But did metamorphosis alter the essential self? It seems not: narrators could
present the person as being aware of what was happening during the
change and as reflecting on his or her new life in a new body after it
had happened. Ovid is the master of this. For his Callisto, "human
feelings remained, although she was now a bear; with constant moan-
ings she shows her grief and stretches up such hands as are left to her
to the heavens, and, though she cannot speak, still feels the ingrati-
tude of Jove." And his Actaeon "marvels to find himself so swift of
foot, and when he sees his features and his horns in a clear pool, tries
to say, 'O woe is me,' yet no words come."[122] We find authors earlier
than Ovid exploiting the possibilities as well: as Achilles tells Niobe's
story, Niobe "although being stone," still "broods over the sorrows the
gods gave her"; Euripides's Cadmus cries out, in mid-transition, that
his lower half has already become a serpent and Aeschylus's Io remembers the horrible moment when her "form and her wits were distorted."[123] Moreover, even as a cow, Io is able to carry on a detailed
conversation with Prometheus about what her future holds.[124] In

other cases, preservation of identity is poignantly suggested by the fact that the newly transmogrified mortals are compelled not only to continue doing whatever it was that led to their transformations in the first place but also to continue feeling the accompanying emotions: Phaethon's mourning sisters cry forever, even after they become poplar trees;[125] Alcyone and Aedon mourn for their lost loved ones even after they become birds;[126] Anthos flees in terror from horses, even after he has become a bird; Arachne spins and weaves forevermore.

One easy conclusion that can be drawn from this is that the Greeks understood humans to be dual in nature: there was the outer body, which might be changed, and then there was something else, representing the essential person, which remained stable. The *Odyssey*, describing the transformation of Odysseus's men into pigs, makes that stable element the mind (*nous*), but most narrators leave the details vague. Ovid occasionally also specifies that it is the mind (*mens*),[127] but then very late in his narrative, he seems to imply that it was the soul (*anima*) that survived transformation instead of, or as well as, the mind: he introduces Pythagoras, who claims that after the deaths of our current bodies, our souls will enter into new bodies, perhaps even those of animals or plants—metempsychosis.[128] From here, Pythagoras turns to discussing all sorts of transformations, including some that are not very different from those that Ovid has been narrating all along: Hyperborean men who grow feathers after bathing in a pool belonging to Minerva, hyenas that can change their gender as needed. Metamorphosis and metempsychosis are two ways in which a soul might experience different forms of embodiment—the first being a premature, and divinely imposed, version of the second.

Once having entered the Greek world with Pythagoras in the sixth century, the idea of metempsychosis never departed, persisting as a familiar alternative to the more traditional belief that the soul, after parting from the body at death, would spend eternity in the Under-world—in pleasure, in pain or simply in boredom as the corpse rotted away in the soil of the upper world. Under either scenario, the soul—implicitly the location of the self, eschatologically speaking—was separable from any body that it had inhabited or would inhabit in the future. From the concept of the separable soul there also grew

tales of extraordinary men who could temporarily send their souls
out of their bodies while they were still alive, to travel the world and
gather information before returning home: Abaris, Aristeas, Her-
motimus, Apollonius of Tyana and, earliest of all, Pythagoras himself.[129] From the concept of the separable soul, too, grew the Greek
fear of ghosts—the souls of those whom death had not been able to
restrain inside Hades's walls.[130] In other words, the duality of self that
is explored in stories of metamorphosis underlies other Greek ideas
as well.

Yet, although peoples other than the Greeks similarly understood
humans to be dual in nature, none of them developed myths of metamorphosis of the same type, or with the same vigor, as the Greeks
did. In spite of the deeply rooted Hindu belief in metempsychosis,
for example, the Hindus have no stories of humans changing into
other creatures or things, as far as I can discover. In many other cultures where stories of human metamorphosis do develop, the metamorphoses are only temporary, in contrast to Greek metamorphoses,
which are almost always permanent.[131] Temporary metamorphoses
can be reversed when a spell is broken, as in many fairy tales (the
swan brothers return to human form when they don the shirts their
sister has sewn; the Beast returns to human form when Beauty's tears
fall upon his prostrate form; the frog turns back into a prince when
the princess kisses him—or, as in the earlier version of the story,
when she throws him against a wall in frustration). Or temporary
metamorphoses might be deliberately undertaken by those who
have the ability to shape-shift back and forth of their own volition:
the Norse Berserker who shifts between man and bear, the Welsh
Selkie who shifts between seal and woman, the American Indian
skin-walker who shifts into whatever form he desires, the European
werewolf and his various relatives—the Chinese were-fox and were-
dog, the African were-hyena, and so on. The Greeks had notably few
stories about human shape-shifters: Periclymenus and Mestra are the
only two names that come down to us, each of whom were given their
special ability by an affectionate Poseidon, who himself was one of
the polymorphic gods of the sea.[132] The were-animal enters the
Greek imagination only as something that outsiders believe in: the
distant Scythians said that their neighbors, the Neuri, turned into

wolves and then back again; the Arcadians (paradigmatic primitives of the Greek world) claimed that boys undergoing rites of social maturation occasionally changed into wolves for nine years and then returned to human form if they had avoided eating human flesh.[133] In Greece, in other words, shape-shifting was a talent reserved almost exclusively for the gods—not only sea gods such as Thetis, Nereus and Proteus, who had a habit of changing from one form to another as rapidly as water runs between your fingers, but also Olympian gods such as Apollo, who changed form three times within fifty lines of his Homeric *Hymn* (into a dolphin, a star and a young man).[134]

All of this reemphasizes, by contrast, certain implications of mortal metamorphoses as we find them in the Greek world: not only are the changes almost always permanent (no tears, no kiss, no sisterly shirts will reverse them), but they also occur at a god's behest, rather than that of the individual who undergoes them. And they are presented as dire—descending either upon an unwilling human or upon one who is in such desperate straits that metamorphosis seems desirable.

This is not the case in every culture. In other places where stories of metamorphosis from human to animal are common, transformation is often presented as something to be celebrated, or at least as something that, at the time of the world's awakening, was normal. Particularly amongst African and American Indian peoples, myths tell of humans spontaneously metamorphosing into animals because it is simply the way things are: a woman who loved to swim became the first beaver, for example.[135] A Cherokee story tells of a man who began dwelling together with bears, living as they lived and growing thick fur. When he tried to return to his old life, with his human wife, he longed to be amongst bears again.[136] These same cultures also tell stories of humans marrying animals and producing animal children, of humans and animals adopting and raising one another's children, and of humans, as a species, developing from animals. There is an implicit assumption of what two scholars of Andean culture have dubbed "interpenetrability" amongst humans and animals, made possible by a core of sameness that underlies what are understood to be superficial differences.[137] The issue of whether the self is dual—of whether something such a soul or a mind "stays the same" even as the external body changes—is irrelevant, because the inner selves of humans and animals are not significantly different, even if they are clothed in different exteriors.

Many Greek metamorphoses seem to be aimed at tidying up the world, by moving a self that doesn't belong in the human realm out into a realm where it is more at home. Cannibalism, incest, infanticide and lesser transgressions such as rape and theft—all fairly common events in metamorphic backstories—must not be tolerated in our world, but in the natural world, the world of animals, they can be tolerated. Indeed, they might even be considered characteristic of animals, as the story of Arachne and Phalanx demonstrated: parricide, lust, and cannibalism are par for the course amongst spiders. What is bad behavior for a human, then, can be *naturalized* or *normalized* through metamorphosis[138]—a positive change for the world at large, which now has everything in its proper place, even if not for the transformed, who find themselves forever exiled from the communities into which they were born. This may, indeed, be the most significant loss that the self experiences during metamorphosis: the essential self remains Actaeon or Io, but he or she is no longer welcome amongst (and usually no longer recognized by) those whom he or she used to hold dear: Ovid's Io, to take an especially poignant case, finally has to write her name in the sand with her hoof, to make her family understand what has happened. The new community into which the transformed mortal must move, moreover, may be no community at all: Ovid's Callisto hides at the sight of other bears, forgetting what she has herself become, and flees from wolves, forgetting that her father (Lycaon) now runs with the pack.[139] Aeschylus's Io wanders the outer wastes of the world with only a gadfly for company. Procne, Philomela, and Tereus are doomed to chase one another through the sky in an endless loop.

The stark divide between human and animal communities that is implied by metamorphic myths surfaces in other Greek stories, as well—most importantly, in the story of the great Flood. In the Akkadian, Babylonian, Sumerian, and biblical tales of the Flood, the human in charge of building an ark (Atrahasis, Utnapishtim, Ziusudra, Noah) takes animals on board, thus carefully ensuring that their species will continue after the waters recede—and so also in a Hindu story of the Flood.[140] In all of these stories, in fact, where

enough text remains for us to hear the beginning of the tale, it is by
divine command that the animals are included. In the Greek story,
however (which may have been borrowed from the Near East and
adapted to Greek tastes), Deucalion and Pyrrha, having been fore-
warned of the storm by Deucalion's father, Prometheus, ride it out
alone in a *larnax*—a small chest usually used for storing household
goods and far too cramped to hold anyone other than Deucalion and
Pyrrha themselves. Upon drifting ashore at Mount Parnassus, the
couple is told by the goddess Themis how to re-create the human
race.[141] Not a single author talks about how the animals were regen-
erated after the Flood until we reach Ovid, who tells us that they
spontaneously burst forth from the postdiluvian soil without any help
from either gods or humans.[142] The Greeks, then, in contrast both
to their Mediterranean neighbors (from whom they inherited a
number of mythological themes) and to one of their Indo-European
neighbors, did not imagine humans and animals making common
cause against the gods' destructive rage. For Greeks who told the
story of the Flood, humans and animals were categorically different;
if humans had natural collaborators during this great disaster, they
were, rather, two of the more kindly gods (Prometheus and Themis).

Striking, too, is the lack of any Greek myth justifying the sacrifice of animals. The tale of how Prometheus performed the first sacrifice explains why the victim's meat was divided up between mortals
and immortals in the way that it was, but offers no justification for
the act itself.[143] Stories about specific sacrifices trace their origins to
bad behavior on the part of specific animals, thus placing the blame
firmly on the victims. The *aition* for the Buphonia (literally the
"Murder of a Cow") that was performed each year in Athens, for example, said that a cow had once wandered onto the Acropolis and
eaten the grain off of Zeus's altar. A pious bystander reacted angrily,
killing the animal. After a kangaroo court exonerated the cow's murderer, an oracle ordered the Athenians to repeat the act every year
thereafter.[144] Similarly, pigs deserved to be sacrificed to Demeter
because a herd of pigs that chanced to be in the vicinity when Persephone was dragged beneath the earth by Hades happened to be
swallowed up as well—guilt through association.[145] It is also animal
guilt that explains the *prohibition* of pig sacrifice in cults of Aphrodite:

she developed an aversion to the entire porcine race after a wild
boar killed her lover Adonis. (The same story could be used, however, to justify the sacrifice of pigs in a few of the goddess's cults—
once again, we see how flexible a mercenary myth could be).[146]

Quite different from these Greek stories is a Hindu myth about
the origin of sacrifice. In the beginning of time, there were five types
of animals deemed appropriate for sacrifice: the human, the horse,
the cow, the ram, and the goat.[147] The gods first sacrificed humans,
until their sacrificial qualities had left them. At that point, they
moved on to horses, until their sacrificial qualities had left them, too,
then to cows, and so on, until the elusive sacrificial quality finally
lodged itself in rice and barley—*et voilà*, vegetarianism. Once upon
a time, then, humans were not only *a* sacrificial animal but *the* sacrificial animal par excellence. When they escaped from this role, other
animals escaped with them. No Greek would ever imagine such a
thing—the few stories they told of human sacrifice associated it with
barbarians in distant lands such as Libya, with the maniacal rage of
an Achilles, or with an angry goddess who at the last moment changed
her mind, sending a deer to fill in for the virgin she had demanded.
It could never have been the norm, even at the beginning of time.

Animals were, at best, servants: Greek versions of the worldwide
topos of the abandoned child protected by a friendly animal (Telephus, Peleus and Neleus, Atalanta, Paris, and so on)[148] end the idyll
while the child is still an infant: herdsmen or hunters discover it being
nursed by a mare or doe or whatever other animal has adopted it and
take it home to be raised amongst humans. For the Greeks, there is
no Enkidu, Mowgli or Tarzan who grows to young adulthood in intimate acquaintance with the ways of the animals, learning their
skills and forming enduring bonds.[149] The few mythic figures who
obtain an animal talent do so without really interacting with the animal. Some seers obtain their prophetic abilities when snakes lick
their ears, for example, and others have honey dropped on their lips
by bees, but the recipients are asleep when these things happen.[150]
The healer-seer Polyidus observes one snake curing another and
adopts the technique for his own use, but the snake is not aware that
he is instructing Polyidus: there is none of the teacher-student relationship that normally accompanies the learning of a skill.[151] In con-

trast to many other cultures, there are no Greek heroes who are part animal—the closest we come is Heracles wearing a lion skin—and the Greeks knew of no paradisiacal time or place where humans and animals peacefully could live side by side.[152]

The dire tone of Greek myths about metamorphoses into animals, and the Greeks' fascination with such myths, then, may express both the perception of a greater ontological division between humans and animals than other cultures seem to have had and a greater anxiety about crossing it. This sharpens the formulation that I offered earlier about myths of metamorphosis: they were a place where the Greeks could talk about an aspect of the gods' nature, and its potential to explode at any moment into mortal life, that was central to their belief system but that they did not want to confront in other venues. The entertainment value that the myths offered heightened their usefulness as such not only because the audience could become more deeply immersed in, and thus more deeply engaged with, their subject matter but also because these myths were adamantly set in an earlier time. They were about ancestors: members of one's own group and yet distant, people like oneself and yet not oneself—models on which one might hope to have improved.

7

Heroes

It was Ovid who ensured that Greek stories of metamorphosis would survive down through the centuries, but no such patron saint of stories about heroes ever existed—nor does one seem to have been needed. From our earliest to our latest narrations of Greek myths, heroes are omnipresent. Perhaps this point seems facile: after all (one might say), didn't the plots of the *Iliad* and the *Odyssey* guarantee that heroes would be front and center at the dawn of Greek literature? And wasn't it simply the immense popularity of these two works, throughout antiquity and beyond, that guaranteed the renarration and elaboration of their protagonists' stories?

But some thinking about the types of characters that inhabit stories and a survey of Greek mythic narratives will show that matters are more complex than that. I'll start with the first. Stories can involve four types of characters, ontologically speaking: gods and other supernatural creatures (angels, demons, and so on), ordinary people (that is, humans who are more or less like us), animals (either real animals or the anthropomorphic animals of fables, who arguably might be put in the second category), and finally, heroes (whom I will define as *humans who either are born with or acquire status and abilities beyond that of other humans, which they retain after death and can use to benefit the living humans who worship them*).

Greek myths have very little to say about the second group, ordinary people. Once in a while, ordinary people play minor roles in a

220

myth: local people help to build Apollo's Delphic Oracle in the Homeric *Hymn to Apollo* and Cretan sailors then staff it; an old man in Hermes's Homeric *Hymn* tells Apollo where Hermes has hidden Apollo's cattle; Phaedra's nurse in Euripides's *Hippolytus* fatally intervenes in her mistress's affairs; the choristers in Greek tragedies, who are often identified as servants or other ordinary sorts of men or women, stand by to give advice that is usually ignored by the main characters—who come from the class of heroes.[1]

Greek myths have very little to say about the third group, either, in contrast to African and Native American myths, for example, in which animals are often the protagonists. In Greek myths, cattle are raided and a rabbit's pregnancy can serve as an omen, but as narrative agents, animals do almost nothing. Notable exceptions are the eagle who conveys Ganymede to Zeus's waiting arms and the eagle who consumes Prometheus's liver each day, Argus, the faithful dog who recognizes the disguised Odysseus, and the dolphin who rescues Arion.[2] Only the latter two might be said to act of their own volition; the eagles are merely tools serving Zeus's will. People sometimes *become* animals in myths, as we saw in Chapter 6, and we sometimes get brief, poignant glimpses into their new lives before they disappear into the underbrush, but stories of metamorphosis are more interested in exploring how human behavior or misadventure leads to transformation *into* an animal than in the animal qua animal. Other animals we meet in myths are abnormally large or fierce or swift, or are born hybrids—but almost any animal who is worth noticing in a myth is in one way or another connected with a god, a hero or both, either because it is the child of a god (Pegasus, Cerberus, the Lernaean Hydra), because it is the quarry of heroes (Cerberus, the Lernaean Hydra, the Nemean Lion), because it is a hero's steed (Pegasus, Xanthus, Balius) or, quite often, because of some combination of these reasons, as is the case with all of the examples I just gave. The few animals who are worthy of an individual name or a geographic tag are well knit into the mythic network of gods and heroes that I discussed in Chapter 4.

In other words, it was on the first and fourth groups of characters, the gods and the heroes, that myths focused in Greece. Before we can say more about that, however, we need to give more thought to the term "hero" itself. Provisionally, I defined heroes as *humans who either are born with or acquire status and abilities beyond that of other humans, which they retain after death and can use to benefit the living humans who worship them.* In Greece, this phrase covers a large and varied group of individuals. At one end of the spectrum would be someone such as Perseus, a son of Zeus who traveled to the end of the world, encountered strange creatures such as the Graeae and the Stygian nymphs, and, having been lent magical tools by the gods, managed to behead the Gorgon Medusa, the merest glimpse of whom would have meant death, had he not looked at her only indirectly, in the shining surface of his shield (as Athena seems to be instructing him to do on the bell krater shown in Figure 7.1). Perseus then went on to rescue a princess

7.1 Perseus gazes into a shield at the reflection of the head of Medusa, held aloft by Athena. Hermes, to the right, is barefoot because he has lent Perseus his winged sandals. The elaborate helmet worn by Perseus is presumably the one that Hades was said to have lent him. Apulian red-figure bell krater by the Tarporley Painter, dated to between 400 and 385 BCE (detail). Now in the Boston Museum of Fine Arts, inv. num. 1970.237. Gift of Robert E. Hecht, Jr. Photograph © 2018 The Museum of Fine Arts, Boston.

from a sea monster and to use Medusa's head to petrify the wicked
king who was trying to force Perseus's mother to marry him.[3]

Perseus's story is a fantastic adventure tale, set in exotic climes
populated by strange creatures; portions of the stories of Jason and
Odysseus share these characteristics as well, as do episodes in Heracles's career. Towards the other end of the narrative spectrum would
be heroes such as Thymoetes, the eponym of the Athenian deme
Thymoetidae. Thymoetes, who as a bastard had no right to inherit
his father's kingdom, killed his brother and seized the throne, thereby
also winning for himself the dubious honor of being the last of Theseus's descendants to rule Athens. He later lost his life in battle.
Although Thymoetes's life had some exciting moments, his story
lacks any of the fantastic details that made Perseus's story so narratively appealing. Nonetheless, Thymoetes was treated as a hero by
the Athenians—as a superhuman entity who could benefit their lives
if he were properly worshipped.[4] Even further towards the end of the
spectrum would be Iops, a Spartan hero who received worship at a
shrine outside the local marketplace but about whom we know only,
as Pausanias says, that he was born "in the time of Lelex or Myles."[5]
Iops's story doesn't seem to have much interested even the local folks
whom Pausanias interviewed. Also at the very end of the spectrum
would be Thoricus, the eponym of the Athenian deme Thoricus, who
received sacrifice twice a year according to inscriptions but who is
otherwise unknown.[6] Similarly, many of the *oikistai* (founding heroes)
of colonies lacked stories that were deemed worthy of passing down
by the poets and historians.

Somewhere in the middle of the spectrum would be heroes such
as Oedipus. Like Perseus, he killed a terrible monster, the Sphinx
(or rather, he drove the Sphinx to suicide when he solved her riddle),
but everything else that happened to Oedipus was completely possible within the everyday world of the audiences who heard his story,
even if highly unusual.[7] Ion belongs in the middle of the spectrum
as well: as the son of Apollo, his genetics should have predisposed
him to perform extraordinary deeds of bravery, like a Perseus or
Heracles, but his claims to fame ended up being those of a wise ruler
(he introduced synoecism to Athens, amongst other things) and a productive father (he sired four sons who became eponyms of Athenian

tribes and colonized Asia).[8] Menelaus belongs in the middle of the
spectrum, too. The son of a mortal man, Menelaus was a good warrior, but certainly not the best of those who fought at Troy. He won
immortality at the end of his life, but not because he had performed
any wondrous deeds himself; rather, it was granted to him because
he was the husband of Zeus's daughter Helen.[9]

All of these men, and many more, were called "heroes" by the
Greeks themselves, and modern scholars have followed suit: each of
them has an entry in the catalogue at the end of L. R. Farnell's *Greek
Hero Cults and Ideas of Immortality* (1921), and those who are Athenian also have entries in Emily Kearns's *The Heroes of Attica* (1989).
This forces us back onto the broad definition of heroes that I started
with, if we want to be inclusive, for there are no traits that all of the
men in this group share: not all kill monsters, not all fight battles,
not all are sons of gods, not all serve as kings, not all found cities or
establish dynasties.

This vagueness tells us something in itself: as a *class* of humans,
heroes were so important to the Greeks that the definitional boundaries were allowed to remain fluid; the Greeks preferred to be able
to add to the ranks, now and then, someone who would help them if
he received proper cult. The Delphic Oracle encouraged this practice: over and over, Apollo advised cities to establish cults to heroes
whom their citizens had not previously worshipped—heroes who the
citizens had not even known were heroes before Apollo told them so
in some cases.[10] Indeed, the category was so flexible that it may seem
to overflow, at one end of the spectrum, into that of ordinary humans.
After all, even ordinary humans, once they had died, were understood to have special powers in their new guise as disembodied
souls—as "ghosts"—that they could use to affect the living, for better
or for worse. The most salient distinction between heroes and ghosts
is that of time: ghosts fade away once no one amongst the living any
longer remembers the person they had been, whereas heroes remain
powerful down through many generations. Scope of worship is also
an important distinction: ghosts are primarily the concern of the
families they leave behind, helping or harming them as they deserve,
whereas heroes attract worshippers from a larger range: a clan, a city-
state or even many city-states.[11]

Modern attempts to divide heroes up into categories have largely foundered. For one thing, their basic premises have failed. It is hard to prove, in most cases, that a given hero belongs in whichever of seven categories Farnell placed him; few scholars would now agree with his proposal that Linus began as a god, for instance, simply because, like the infant Dionysus, he was torn into pieces.[12] Any such attempt at categorization, moreover, runs roughshod over the very inclusivity that I just emphasized. Although the Greeks probably would have conceded that some heroes, such as Heracles, were greater than others in terms of accomplishments, renown, and perhaps also postmortem power, no Greek author ever suggests that there was any *functional* or *ontological* difference amongst the heroes (indeed, not even the Neoplatonists of later antiquity, who had a penchant for precisely stratifying all the inhabitants of the cosmos, tried to subdivide heroes into smaller groups).

The class of heroes, in other words, exhibited variety within what was viewed as essential sameness. This inclusivity made the heroes, as a group, very useful to think with. Many heroes (such as Thymoetes) had lived lives that differed little from those of at least some men of the historical period, which implied that the difference between these heroes, while they were still alive, and the people who later paid them cult was no greater than that between, say, a king and a commoner. Those in the next tier up (the heroes who had fought in the Trojan War and their sons, for example) differed a little more from the average worshipper—they lived in a world where gods, and occasionally monsters, might still be encountered face-to-face—but these were chronologically amongst the youngest of the heroes and thus were closest in generational age to the audiences who listened to their stories, which helped to close the gap. Many of those heroes, moreover, shared adventures, ancestry or networks with older heroes and, by doing so, attached the heroes *as a group* to their audiences, implying that the distance between the ordinary man in the street and even Heracles himself was not impossibly vast. The Attic hero Antiochus, for example, who became one of the ten heroes after whom Cleisthenes named the tribal units of Athens in the late sixth century BCE, seems to have done nothing notable, himself, but Demosthenes and several later authors mention that he had been sired by Heracles upon an Athenian girl and that his own sons had spearheaded the return of the Heracleidae.[13] Antiochus ran in the right circles, in other words, and shone in the reflected light of his relatives. Perseus was the great-great-grandfather of Heracles, who in turn was the great-great-grandfather of Aristodemus, the ancestor of Spartan kings of the historical period.[14] Heracles was also the forefather of any number of other peoples with whose primordial princesses he had slept. Cumulatively, this suggested a continuity of descent that ran from Perseus, a remarkable slayer of monsters, all the way down through lesser heroes and finally to the man on the Spartan street. The father of *both* Perseus and Heracles was Zeus, which could be taken to hint, if one chose to read it that way, that ordinary Spartans weren't utterly different from the very gods themselves. Hesiod's myth of the generations intimates this, too, even as it insists on a grim evaluation of Hesiod's own fellow humans: by inserting the age of the heroes immediately before the Iron Age in which he himself lives, Hesiod implies that, although contemporary people are dreadfully immoral and overburdened with work, they are descendants of the gods.

In this chapter, I will focus on heroes who fall within that segment of the spectrum that runs between Perseus and Menelaus—that is to say, the heroes whose stories were fantastic enough, or in some other way striking and important enough, to become well-known both within and outside of the immediate geographic area where they were set (which typically was also the center of the hero's worship in cult). This is because I am writing a book on *myths*; heroes who had no myths, or whose myths are scarcely known to us, provide no grist for my mill, even if inscriptions or remarks by ancient authors assure us that they were paid cult. We don't want to forget these other heroes as we make our way through this chapter, however, precisely for the reason I have just sketched: as part of a larger group, they helped to bridge the divide between heroes and ordinary humans and thus helped to lend credibility to many of the other ideas that heroes' stories cumulatively conveyed. I will also focus mostly on *male* heroes, both because we have more stories about them than about females of that class and also because the nature of the female's stories is different enough to require separate treatment, which other scholars have provided.[15]

Gods versus Heroes

Greek myths are not populated by heroes alone, however. There are also gods. Which group takes pride of place? To answer this, I'll survey our mythic narratives chronologically, working through the main genres of literature from the Archaic and Classical periods, starting with epics.

In addition to the *Iliad*, the *Odyssey* and Hesiod's *Theogony*, we have the fragmentary remains or at least the titles and descriptions of quite a few other epics from the Archaic period: the *Little Iliad*, the *Returns*, and various other poems about the Trojan War and its aftermath; the *Thebaid* and the *Epigonoi*, both of which are about the heroes who fought around Thebes; and assorted poems about Heracles, Theseus, and Oedipus. We also have poems about the building and voyage of the *Argo*, a poem about the early rulers of Corinth, and some other poems about humans of an earlier age such as Phoroneus, the first inhabitant of Argos, who sprang from its very soil.

Although gods play significant roles in these stories, the focus in almost all of them is squarely on remarkable humans—on heroes. In contrast, for poems that focus squarely on the *gods* we have, in addition to Hesiod's *Theogony*, just the fragments of a few theogonies and narratives about the gods' early days that are attributed to Orpheus. Ancient authors tell us about some other poems that are now lost—the *Titanomacheia* and Epimenides's theogony, for instance—but not very many.[16]

Heroes continue to hold center stage in the myths narrated by poems that we collect under the terms "melic" or "lyric." Stesichorus, for example, focuses closely on heroes—most notably in his *Geryoneis*, which tells of the battle between Heracles and Geryon, and in his own version of the *Oresteia*.[17] Simonides gives us a song that was sung to the infant Perseus by his mother as they were swept over the waves in the chest that imprisoned them, and he also narrates the stories of Jason, Theseus, and other heroes.[18] Bacchylides's dithyrambs, when enough of them remains for us to identify their subjects, are always about heroes—Helen and Menelaus, Heracles, Theseus (twice), Io, Idas, Cassandra, and perhaps Meleager, Pasiphae, Achilles, and Orpheus.[19] Although Pindar was credited with returning the dithyramb to its Dionysiac roots, his contributions to the genre also concentrate on heroes, when we can identify a subject.[20] The poets also told stories of lesser-known, local heroes: Myrtis narrated the tale of Eunostus of Tanagra, and Corinna narrated that of Ogygus of Thebes, for instance.[21]

Two of the three remaining genres of Archaic and Classical poetry—epinician and tragedy—focus on heroes, as well (the third genre, comedy, uses both heroes and gods as characters, but outside of Aristophanes's *Frogs*, which stars Dionysus, most of its protagonists are ordinary people).[22] Of the tragedies that remain to us, only three might be said to take the problems of the gods as their central topics: the *Prometheus Bound*, the *Eumenides* and the *Bacchae* (and even these spend a great deal of time on human dilemmas). Twenty-eight of the twenty-nine other surviving tragedies focus on heroes (the remaining one, the *Persians*, focuses on an event in what was then recent history). These proportions seem to reflect the norm—of the more than 200 other tragedies that we know about through fragments or titles, there are only six that may have focused on gods.[23] I don't mean to minimize the important roles that gods play in tragedies, but I do want to stress the overwhelming interest that tragedies showed in humans of the heroic age.

The third remaining genre, epinician, was naturally drawn to stories of the heroes because their deeds, which typically required great strength, nimbleness, and endurance, mirrored the athletic feats performed by the victors whom epinicians celebrated. Heroes, moreover—like the athletes, but in contrast to gods—were human. Two of the three epinician poets whose works remain to us, Bacchylides and Simonides, follow this trend closely. Three of Bacchylides's five longer epinicians tell stories about heroes (Heracles and Meleager, the daughters of Proetus, the Trojan War). His story of Croesus, although historically based, is also told in the manner of a myth and gives Croesus the aura of a hero. The fifth epinician long enough to include a story is about the Telchines and their daughters, who are arguably gods.[24] Of other gods who play significant roles in these epinicians, we glimpse only Apollo, who plays an important part in the story of Croesus. Our fragments of Simonides's epinicians are frustratingly few and small, but he seems to have treated the stories of Castor and Polydeuces and of Heracles, at least.[25]

With the third epinician poet, Pindar, things get more complicated. Eight of his forty-six surviving epinicians take the affairs of the gods as their main narrative theme—*Pythian* 9, for example, includes a long dialogue between Chiron and Apollo concerning the latter's lust for the nymph Cyrene, and *Olympian* 7 is about the apportionment of the earth's lands amongst the gods and the birth of Athena.[26] In many other cases, however, stories about the gods are juxtaposed with stories about heroes to which they have little or no narrative connection. *Pythian* 8 squeezes the battle between the Olympians and the Titans in amongst stories of Amphiaraus and the descendants of Aeacus. *Nemean* 1 opens with the story of Zeus giving the island of Sicily to Persephone as a bridal gift before it moves on to describe the childhood of Heracles. Some of what we now consider well-known stories about the gods come down to us first through Pindar's glancing treatments (four lines of *Olympian* 7 tell us about Hephaestus splitting Zeus's head open with an axe to enable the birth of Athena, for example).[27] Suffice it here to say that, as a poet who struck some listeners as enigmatic already in antiquity, Pindar did things in his own way.

Many of the poets whom I have just mentioned are also credited with composing hymns and paeans, which are typically (although not exclusively) directed to the gods, but these poems usually concentrated on invoking, praising and entreating the gods, rather than on narrating their exploits—the hymns of Sappho and Alcaeus being characteristic in this respect and the seven longer Homeric *Hymns*[28] being the major exceptions.[29] Hymns and paeans of either type, moreover, are notably underrepresented in surviving literature for reasons that are hard to fathom. It's tempting to blame Christianity. We know that the Alexandrian scholars included two books of Pindar's paeans and hymns in their editions of his work but that centuries later, when Christian monks produced manuscript copies of Pindar, they included the epinicians but left out the hymns and

paeans. We might guess that the monks could justify preserving stories about pagan heroes more easily than praise of pagan gods.

But Christianity can't take all the blame for the paucity of hymns
and paeans. Had there been a lot of noteworthy hymns and paeans
by authors other than Pindar, we would expect a few of them to survive and also expect our ancient sources to mention more of
them—yet this is not the case. This brings us to a second tempting
assumption. Perhaps a lot of hymns and paeans are lost to us because
they simply were never recorded at all? We might hypothesize that
in some cases, this happened because the cults for which the hymns
and paeans had been composed considered them to be secret.
This would seem to be confirmed by the fact that we don't get any
hymns claiming to originate in a mystery cult until we reach the
Orphic Hymns of late antiquity. And yet logic dictates that this
can't be the whole explanation: we scarcely have any hymns or
paeans from Athens, a city that was otherwise obsessive about preserving its literature.

It's hard to avoid the conclusion that the reason few formal, polished narratives focusing on the gods survive is that there simply
weren't many. Stories about the gods must have circulated in other,
informal ways. We know that nursemaids and mothers told stories
about the gods to children.[30] We also know that local historians and,
in Athens at least, exegetes associated with cults recorded stories
about the gods.[31] We hear about women telling each other the story
of Demeter and Persephone at the time of the annual Thesmophoria;
other festivals to the gods must have prompted the exchange of tales,
too.[32] And finally, many stories about the gods were embedded within
compositions that focused on heroes. I've already noted that Pindar's
epinicians include quite a few of these, but there are plenty of other
examples. In *Iliad* 6, the hero Diomedes narrates the story about how
Dionysus punished the human king Lycurgus, just as he is about to
engage the hero Glaucus in combat. In *Iliad* 24, the hero Achilles
narrates the deeds of Artemis and Apollo to King Priam. The chorus
of Aeschylus's *Agamemnon* gives us a version of the divine succession
myth. The chorus of Euripides's *Helen* tells the story of how a goddess called "The Mother" searched for her missing daughter. In
Euripides's *Ion*, a conversation between Creusa and an old man pro-

vides the story of how Athena acquired her aegis while fighting in the Gigantomachy.[33] All of these instances, and many more like them, not only narrate divine stories but also—if we can assume that literary art is imitating life—confirm that informal, ad hoc narrations were a significant mode through which tales of the gods were transmitted. The visual arts narrated stories about the gods (as well as the heroes), too.

Greek Heroes and Their Neighbors

Nevertheless, when it came to *formal* narration of myths, myths that focused on heroes were far more popular in Greece than myths that focused on the gods—a rough estimate gives a three-to-one ratio. This may not strike us as particularly odd. After all, we might reason, people would have liked hearing about heroes more than gods because they could identify more closely with heroes. Moreover, an emphasis on heroes seems normal to most of us because, in the Western world, we have long grown up with Greek myths as our "default" myths: whatever characteristics they happen to possess have inevitably, implicitly, come to define what a myth is for us. Stories from the Old and New Testaments, which similarly permeate Western cultures, privilege exceptional humans as well. Jehovah commands, judges, and smites, but it's characters such as Eve, Abraham, Moses, David, Salome, and Jesus who stick in our minds. Some scholars have suggested that some of the Testaments' portrayals of notable humans, as we now have them, were influenced by Greek myths, in fact.[34] Perhaps this borrowing was motivated by the biblical authors' perception that their religion—which fought to establish itself within unwelcoming territory—needed the additional appeal that thrilling human narratives could provide.

Be that as it may, Greek myths and the two Testaments are actually the odd ones out. The narratives that we inherit from other ancient Mediterranean cultures are markedly more interested in gods than they are in heroes. From Mesopotamia, we have two versions of a theogony called the *Enuma Elish*; two versions of the *Anzu* (another epic about the gods' battle for cosmic supremacy);[35] yet another theogonic poem centered on the god Ninurta called the *Lugul-e* and its companion poem the *Angim,* which praises Ninurta;[36] the *Theogony of Dunnu;*[37] the *Descent of Ishtar* (or in its Sumerian version, the *Descent of Inanna);*[38] *Inanna and Enki;*[39] *Enki and Ninhursag;*[40] *Enki and Ninmah;*[41] *Nergal and Ereshkigal;*[42] and *Erra and Ishum*[43]—all of which concern the gods.

From Ugarit, we get the lengthy *Baal Cycle* and a number of shorter stories about the gods, such the tale of El's drunken feast and the hunt of the goddess Astarte. From Anatolia, we get the equally lengthy Hittite compositions known as the *Kumarbi Cycle,* three versions of *The Disappearance of Telipinu,* two versions of the *Story of Illuyanka,* the *Song of Hedammu,* the *Song of Ullikumi,* and numerous shorter divine tales such as *Telipinu and the Daughter of the Sea God,* the stories of the goddesses Inara and Kamrusepa, *The Disappearance of Hannahanna,* and others.[44] Egyptian myths, as has been often observed, are almost entirely about the gods.

The best-known Near Eastern hero story (both now and in antiquity) is the Mesopotamian *Epic of Gilgamesh,* which is preserved in several versions and languages. Gilgamesh is described, like many Greek heroes, as part human and part god, and like many Greek heroes, he defeats monsters.[45] His friend Enkidu, who accompanies him on his adventures, should probably also be described as a hero, given that he helps Gilgamesh defeat monsters. We also have two short stories about the adventures of Lugalbanda, the second king of Uruk and father of Gilgamesh. These constitute the latter half of a four-part tale of conflicts between the kings of Uruk and Arata that includes interaction between these kings and Inanna, Shamash, and other gods. In one of these stories, Lugalbanda gains the power of flying through the air at extraordinary speeds in return for his kindness to the chick of a lion-headed bird. Like his son, Gilgamesh, then, he has abilities beyond those of the ordinary human and therefore is similar to the hero as we know him in Greece.[46] In addition, there are three versions of a Mesopotamian Flood story with a hero who goes by different names, depending on the language in which the story is told,[47] and there is a story about Etana, a postdiluvian king who flies to heaven on the back of an eagle, seeking the means of siring a child.[48] There is a Sumerian story about the relationship between Inanna (called Ishtar in Akkadian)

and Dumuzi (Tammuz), the mortal lover whom Inanna uses to
ransom herself out of the Underworld. Later, Dumuzi is granted the
privilege of returning to life periodically—in some versions thanks
to the intervention of his faithful sister, Geshtinanna.[49]

Finally, the *res gestae* of two historical Mesopotamian kings began
to move them onto the spectrum of heroes, insofar as the kings interacted personally with gods and also because these kings' stories
attracted motifs that we find associated with heroes both in Greece
and in other cultures. The first figure is Sargon, who reigned from
2340 to 2284 BCE. According to an Assyrian tale of the seventh
century BCE, the infant Sargon, like Moses, was hidden in a basket
and cast into a river, whence he was rescued and raised by a humble
man to be a gardener. While still a gardener, he had an amorous encounter with Ishtar, which enabled him to become king.[50] In a Sumerian story, he cures the king of Kish of a urinary disease with
advice that he receives from Inanna in a dream (echoing the biblical
tale of Joseph and Pharaoh). This story also includes an adventure
similar to Bellerophon's, in which Sargon unknowingly delivers a
letter that instructs its recipient to kill him; again, Inanna saves him.[51]
In other parts of his biography, Sargon is portrayed as a strong warrior who leads campaigns against neighboring kingdoms and into
distant lands. The god Marduk is said to have eventually grown
angry with Sargon's excessive reach and plunged his kingdom into
famine.[52] The second figure is Naram-Sin, the grandson of Sargon,
who reigned from 2254 to 2218 BCE. Naram-Sin is said to have
joined forces with Erra, the god of war, to fight enemies backed by
the god Enlil. Eventually, Naram-Sin went too far by plundering
Ekur, Enlil's temple in Nippur. Enlil retaliated by plunging all of
Mesopotamia into plague, famine, and death until a delegation of
other gods intervened, decreeing that the city of Akkad alone should
be destroyed but that the rest of the country would be preserved.[53]

From Ugarit we get two hero tales. In one, King Danel prays to
the gods for a son. They duly give him Aqhat, who loses his life in a
fight with the goddess Anat. In the other Ugaritic tale, King Keret
similarly asks the gods for help in siring children and eventually finds
himself pitted against the angry goddess Athirat, whom he had failed
to thank after his sons were born.[54]

From Anatolia we have six Hittite stories, or fragments from stories, in which mortals who might qualify as heroes play prominent roles. One concerns a queen of Kanesh who bears thirty sons, abandons them to be reared by the gods and then bears thirty daughters. Another is about Appu, a man who seeks help from the Sun god in siring children. A third story, about the Sun god, a cow, and a fisherman, may be a continuation of Appu's tale. The fourth is about a hunter named Kessi, who neglects to honor the gods of the forest after he marries a beautiful woman; the fragments suggest that their anger manifests itself, at least initially, in bad dreams.[55] *The Song of Release* tells of the destruction of the town of Ebla by warriors overseen by the Storm god because the people of Ebla have refused to release hostages from the town of Ikinkalis. Although most of the interaction in our fragments of this poem takes place amongst the gods, there are also some encounters between gods and prominent humans.[56] Finally, in one version of the Hittite *Song of Illuyanka*,[57] the goddess Inara, wishing to help her brother the Storm god Teshub defeat the dragon Illuyanka, seduces a human named Hupasiya, and then, having gotten Illuyanka drunk, commands Hupasiya to tie him up, to make him an easy target for the Storm god, who finishes him off. Inara weds Hupasiya, but the marriage between goddess and mortal is predictably short-lived.[58]

From Middle Kingdom Egypt (2065–1650 BCE) we have two tales that share some traits with hero myths. One is the "Tale of Sinuhe," which tells of a courtier who flees from the prince he is serving, wanders the world, marries well and sires children, fights valiantly in a war, and then, growing old, goes home to die in peace. Sinuhe's wandering, his military glory, and his eventual return may remind us of some Greek heroes' stories. What is missing, however, is any encounter with "the marvelous"—with monsters or gods. The other is "The Tale of the Shipwrecked Sailor," which tells of a man who drifts to a mysterious island where he is befriended by a gigantic serpent. Certainly, we have the element of the marvelous here, but the story's protagonist remains unnamed—he is a sort of "everyman"—and (as Geraldine Pinch has observed) he fails to do anything that is particularly brave or strong.[59] We also have a tale about five divinities helping a human woman give birth to triplets who are the sons of

Ra and are destined to become kings (in which sense they are no different from all other Egyptian kings, who formally traced their paternity to Ra) and traces of another tale about a goddess trying to seduce a human herdsman. These two are closer, at least in plot, to some of the myths about heroes that we know from Greece.[60] From New Kingdom Egypt (1550–1069 BCE), we have the "Tale of the Two Brothers," in which, much as in myths about Hippolytus and Bellerophon, a man is falsely accused of raping a woman—in this case, his brother's wife. He is subsequently betrayed by his own wife, as are several Greek heroes in various circumstances. The problem with calling this story a *hero* myth is that the names of the two brothers, Inpu and Bata, are those of gods.[61] From Roman Egypt (31–311 CE), we get stories about magicians who have adventures. Several of these are about a magician named Setna who, like many heroes, journeys to the Underworld and sees the horrors of the souls in torment. Given its date, it is likely to have been influenced by Greek myths about several heroes' journeys to Hades.[62]

My survey has turned up approximately twenty-five ancient Near Eastern stories about heroes[63] and more than thirty about the gods, giving us a ratio of five-to-six to set beside the roughly three-to-one ratio that I calculated for Greek myths. My figures are approximate in the sense that some people might quibble with exactly where I drew the lines between hero stories and stories of average people in the Near Eastern material or where I drew the lines between what counted as a story about a god and a story about a hero in Greece. My survey is also approximate insofar as I may have missed a story or two from the Near East, in spite of my attempt to be complete. Nonetheless, my survey suggests that the Greeks preferred stories about heroes to stories about gods significantly more than did people in Near Eastern cultures. Most of the Near Eastern characters whom I have characterized as heroes, moreover, cluster together on one half of the spectrum that I sketched for Greek heroes in the first section of this chapter—the half that runs from Menelaus to Thymoetes and Iops. That is to say, many of the Near Eastern characters interacted with gods and were great warriors, but unlike Perseus or Heracles, for example (who sit at the other end of my spectrum), relatively few of them conquered any monsters or performed other superhuman feats. The heroes whom we meet in Near Eastern sources differ from Greek heroes in another way, as well: there are not enough of them in any single culture to form a strong and extensive network, as the Greek heroes do. Some of them are generationally linked in a short-term manner—Lugalbanda is the father of Gilgamesh, Sargon is the grandfather of Naram-Sin and Danel is the father of Aqhat, for instance—but they have no complex web of interrelationships with one another or with a larger cadre of heroes.

We might try to rationalize the relative dearth of hero myths that we find in the ancient Near East by positing that Near Eastern stories reflect what scribes were expected to record, and by hypothesizing that additional stories focusing on heroes circulated less formally, through channels that are now lost to us. But such a hypothesis only brings us to the question of why those scribes chose to focus on divine stories in the first place, in contrast to Greek poets. Or to put it otherwise, why did stories about heroes prove to be such an idiosyncratically attractive topic for the Greek poets and their audiences?[64]

The prominence of the Greek hero in myths is matched by the prominence of hero cults in Greece, which were established as early as the ninth century and were flourishing by the mid-Archaic period.[65] In contrast, there is almost a complete absence of anything like hero cults in Near Eastern cultures. Although many ancient Near Eastern peoples paid some type of cult to their dead ancestors at least in the years immediately after a death, there is no trace of cults in honor of specific, named individuals that endured through generations, after their immediate descendants were gone, and that spread throughout a wider group.[66] The distinction I am making is exemplified by the cult paid to the Ugaritic *rephaim*, a collective group of dead warriors and kings who were understood to serve Baal and Anat and to have some ties to the fertility of the harvest. Although they were imagined to have a leader, who was referred to as *rp'u* (the singular of *rephaim*), and to have anthropomorphic features insofar as they were imagined to feast and drink at the time that they were celebrated during rituals, the group of *rephaim* was just that—a *group*—without any individual names or individual personalities and stories as far as we can tell.[67]

The presence of hero cult in Greece cannot be used to explain the prominence of hero myths in Greece, however, for it is impossible to say whether the habit of paying cult to heroes is older than the flourishing of hero myths, the myths are older than the cults, or—as I think likely—the two developed concomitantly, nudged along by other things. One of the most important of these was probably the negotiation of Greek identity during the Dark Age and the early Archaic Age (approximately 900–700 BCE). The development of a shared pantheon of gods during this period and shared sanctuaries to those gods that drew worshippers from far and wide was one of the factors, as has often been pointed out, that helped to bind independent groups (Spartans, Thebans, Argives, and so on) into a collectivity that could understand itself, when it chose to, as being "Greeks together." But we can imagine that in response to this amalgamation of originally separate local divinities, each independent group would have clung all the more firmly to its own, separate traditions about exceptional men who had emerged from its local soil, and expanded upon those men's reputations as powerful entities by further developing both narratives about them and rituals performed in their honor.[68] In contrast, as Jan Assmann has argued,[69] ancient Near Eastern cultures that were ruled by a single individual, such as Mesopotamia and Egypt, had no room for a plurality of other humans who achieved divine or semi-divine status—this was reserved for royalty alone. This does not resolve the quandary completely, however; the Greeks wove many figures such as Theseus into the early parts of cities' king lists or embroidered the deeds of early historic kings until they looked like heroes. Other cultures could have found ways to embellish more of their kings or cultural leaders into heroes in the Greek sense as well—but few of them chose to do so. Once Israel had embarked upon monotheism, for example, it refused to grant superhuman power to even its most important founding figures.[70] Christianity, in contrast, embraced saints' cults early in its development. That is, while formally remaining just as monotheistic as Judaism, Christianity developed a penchant for honoring exceptional humans of the past who reputedly could help those who paid them cult—heroes, in a word. The popularity of Greek hero myths and hero cults may have had some influence here.

Another factor that may have contributed to the rise of the hero in Greece is the Greeks' perception that they were wanderers by nature—that they had come to the Greek mainland from somewhere else and that they would continue to move onwards, colonizing new lands.[71] With the exception of the Israelites (whose stories, as I noted earlier, also focused on exceptional humans), no other ancient Mediterranean culture chose to understand itself in this way; most peoples, in fact, firmly claimed that they had always been in the same place, from time immemorial. Groups that perceive themselves as relatively mobile may have a greater need to assert their attachment and entitlement to a place they currently inhabit. One way of doing that is to develop myths about ancestors who were connected to that place—heroes who were born there, who performed their great deeds there, or who died there. It's harder to make similar claims about one's gods. The Eleusinians could brag that their ancestors had *welcomed* Demeter during her search for Persephone and the Delians could claim that their island had been the *birthplace* of Apollo, for instance, but these and other gods were panhellenically at large to a much greater extent than any hero except Heracles ever was; because of this, ties to the gods could never feel as intimate and exclusive as could the ties to heroes.

In the end, one can only make conjectures about why the hero became so important in both narratives and cults in Greece. Perhaps it is more fruitful to *contextualize* the phenomenon of the hero by noting that other institutions and practices that highlight the potential of the human and the value of the individual were first manifested in Greece, amongst ancient Mediterranean cultures, as well. Athens developed the first democracy. It was in Greece that there first arose religious cults promising individual members an enhanced afterlife, separate from the crowd of other listless souls trapped in Hades (some inscriptions attesting to these ideas even call these privileged individuals "heroes"). Greek artists were the first to pursue anatomically and proportionally accurate portrayals of the human body, exalting its form. Hero myths, which suggested that there had once been exceptional human individuals who came close to the status of gods in their deeds, and hero cults, which suggested that those same individuals, after death, could come close to the gods in their power to affect mortal lives, fit well within this general trend of celebrating the human potential.

The Canonical Greek Hero

Over time, as Greek poets were hired to elaborate upon each hero's accomplishments and then carried those stories abroad to other cities, each hero's luster would have been burnished both by his wider fame and by his slow accrual of characteristics from other heroes' stories that similarly traveled throughout Greece. Inevitably, an informal, if unarticulated, canon of heroic traits developed. Few Greek heroes partook of all its elements, but collectively their stories presented the ideal hero as someone who (1) had a divine parent; (2) received help or advice from the gods; (3) relied upon help from a sibling or friend to accomplish at least some of his tasks; (4) used intellectual, as well as physical, skills to meet challenges; (5) was a good warrior; (6) founded cities; (7) established dynasties; (8) killed or conquered monsters; (9) journeyed to distant places, including Hades; and (10) remained active after his death.

Some of these traits will be discussed in detail later in this chapter, but here, before we finish comparing Greek heroes with heroes from other cultures, I want to touch on four of them that Greek heroes exhibit to a higher degree than do most heroes in other cultures:

(1) Relatively few heroes from other cultures have a divine parent. In the ancient Mediterranean, only Gilgamesh is an exception (if we leave aside the Egyptian habit of formally declaring that all pharaohs were the sons of Ra). Gilgamesh's mother was the goddess Ninsun, and his father was the mortal king Lugalbanda. The *Epic of Gilgamesh* tells us that this made Gilgamesh two-thirds divine, suggesting that at least in Mesopotamia, a divinity's genetic contribution to a child was understood to be twice as strong as a mortal's.[72]

If we go further afield geographically and chronologically, we find some other exceptions, such as the Norse hero Sigi, who was sired by Odin upon a mortal woman and who became the progenitor of the line that led to Sigurd, the greatest of Norse heroes.[73] Other exceptions are the five Pandava brothers of the *Mahabharata*, who were sired by five different gods upon the two human wives of King Pandu.[74] Of course, Jesus Christ is another example.

Having a divine parent more clearly marks a hero as someone who is situated between humans and gods. By his very existence, the hero implies that the two groups are not impossibly different. Divine parentage, and the divine siblings that come with it, also provide a narrative motivation for the many instances of divine help that heroes typically receive. In other words, in Greek myths, gods help the hero not only because he has demonstrated special abilities or traits that make him more deserving of help than other humans but also because he is as close to being one of them as any human ever can be. A black-figure lip cup dating to about 560 BCE that shows Athena excitedly tugging her half brother Heracles by the hand towards their father Zeus, eager for Heracles's apotheosis to be completed, is a touching expression of this familial feeling (see Figure 7.2).

This trope plays out in some other variations, too. The hero Pelops, for instance, was born of two mortal parents but became the lover of Poseidon, who later gave him a golden chariot and winged horses in order to ensure that Pelops would win a chariot race. Cadmus, Menelaus, and Peleus married goddesses, which guaranteed them places in an idyllic afterlife retreat. Having familial or romantic

7.2 Athena eagerly tugs her half brother Heracles towards their father, Zeus, following Heracles's apotheosis. Black-figure lip cup from Vulci by the Phrynos Painter, dated to about 540 BCE (detail). Now in the British Museum, inv. num. 1867.5-8.962. Photo © Trustees of the British Museum (CC BY-NC-SA 4.0).

connections to the gods, then, sets the hero apart not only genetically in some cases but more importantly socially—the hero runs with the right crowd. We see this in association with the heroes of some other cultures, too: Sargon is the favorite of Ishtar/Inanna, for example, and Odin helps several Norse heroes at crucial moments. The gods also helped Greek heroes who were not their relatives or lovers, Odysseus being the most notable example. In contrast, some heroes made careers without any apparent help from the gods at all (Meleager, for instance). As a rule, however, the Greek hero was distinguished from other humans by having close ties to the gods.

(2) Many Greek heroes kill or conquer monsters. Some, such as Heracles and Theseus, kill or conquer several.[75] From approximately the same time and place as our Greek examples, we can cite only Gilgamesh and his friend Enkidu, who kill Humbaba and the Bull of Heaven.[76] For additional examples of monster killers, we have to move forwards in time and further afield geographically (although my sample will stay largely within the Mediterranean and Europe, venturing no further east than India). The Avestan hero Thraetaona defeats the dragon Azi Dahaka.[77] Rustam, the main hero of the tenth-century Persian epic the *Shahnameh*, kills a dragon, as do several other characters in this lengthy poem, which scholars have shown to be indebted to Greek stories.[78] Rama, the semi-divine protagonist of the Indian *Ramayana*, dating perhaps to the fifth century CE, defeats Ravana, a demon who has kidnapped his wife, Sita.[79] In poems dating to the seventh century, the Irish hero Cuchulain kills a dog that had "the strength of 100 dogs," three monsters who manifested themselves as cats, twenty-seven sea wraiths, a great slimy worm, and a giant who emerged from the sea.[80] In a tale at least as old as its tenth- or eleventh-century manuscript, we hear about the Scandinavian hero Beowulf killing Grendel, Grendel's mother, and a dragon who simultaneously kills Beowulf himself.[81] In texts and representations as early as the eleventh century, the Norse hero Sigurd kills a dragon variously named Mimir or Fafnir.[82] Saint George and several other medieval knights also slay dragons, and several Arthurian knights pursue the Questing Beast (a hybrid animal made from parts of a snake, leopard, lion, and hart). King Arthur himself, according to early sources, defeats a cat monster, a divine boar, dog-headed

monsters, dragons, and giants.[83] European folktales and fairy tales take up the idea of monster killing, as well—there are many variations of the story in which a small man fools and subsequently kills a giant and some instances of dragon killing as well. These are not hero myths in the sense that our Greek examples are, however; the protagonist either is nameless ("a tailor," "the youngest brother," "the prince") or carries an all-purpose name such as Jack. He has no other history or connections to other characters in other stories.

I will discuss Greek monster killing in more detail later in this chapter; suffice it here to say that whatever else such episodes accomplished in myths, they made for thrilling narratives and also that, as far as our sources show, the Greeks told stories about monster killing in greater abundance than other ancient peoples did; probably, the Greek stories provided models for many such stories that were told in later centuries.

(3) Heroes from most cultures travel to distant places, but few of them, outside of Greece, journey to the realm of the dead and return. Gilgamesh travels through the Underworld on his way to visit Utnapishtim, from whom he hopes to learn the secret of immortality. Previously, he had sent his friend Enkidu to the Underworld to regain some lost possessions, but Enkidu could not return; the two friends have their last conversation either through a crack in the earth or during a dream (the text is unclear).[84] In the course of this conversation, Enkidu tells Gilgamesh what the Underworld is like. In the sixth book of *The Aeneid*, Vergil sends the Roman hero Aeneas to the Underworld to learn about the future of the kingdom he will found. Christ harrows Hell before ascending to Heaven, and late antique apocryphal works claim that various other biblical figures tour Hell (and sometimes) Heaven as well, bringing back reports of what kind of person ends up in either of these abodes and what sorts of treatment they receive.[85] The unnamed mother of the Finnish hero Lemminkäinen descends into Hell to recover the body of her son, which she then revives.[86]

The Greek heroes who visit the Underworld, like Gilgamesh, Enkidu, Aeneas, and Lemminkäinen's mother, have personal reasons for making the trip, which distinguishes them from the heroes of the apocryphal works, who, like Christ, act out of an interest in the

welfare of the entire human race; many of the latter, moreover, do
not make the journey of their own initiative but instead are snatched
away by God or an angel. The Greek heroes, then, fall into line with
most Mediterranean travelers to the Underworld in demonstrating
a pronounced determination to obtain or regain whatever it is that
they seek there for themselves—a lost wife in the case of Orpheus,
a new wife in the case of Pirithous (and therefore also his traveling
companion, Theseus), the dog of Hades in the case of Heracles, and
knowledge of what awaits him at home in the case of Odysseus. It is
the Christian travelers who stand apart.

If Greek hero myths are about pushing the boundaries between
human and divine, then the ability to visit the land of the dead certainly fits this model. The problem is that, of the four major heroes
who visit Hades—Heracles, Theseus, Orpheus, and Odysseus—one
(Theseus) cannot return without help from another one (Heracles),
and in doing so he must leave his friend Pirithous behind forever in
the land of the dead; a second hero (Orpheus) returns, having failed
in his quest and soon thereafter dies as an indirect result; and a third
(Odysseus) is never truly in the Underworld at all but rather lingers
on its border, calling the souls up to where he waits to interview
them. Only Heracles can be said to successfully journey to the Underworld and back with his goal accomplished, thereby truly conquering death—a feat that is echoed in the tale of his winning back
Alcestis's soul in a wrestling match against Death itself. Even Heracles needed help from the gods to complete this journey, as a number
of vases demonstrate by adding Athena, Hermes or both to the scene
of his victory over Cerberus (as we see on the black-figure hydria
from about 510 BCE that is shown in Figure 7.3, for example).

Not coincidentally, Heracles, the only hero to successfully return
from the Underworld, is also the only Greek hero to become a full-
fledged god, ascending to Olympus even as his mortal body burns
on a pyre. Most Greek myths about journeys to the Underworld underscore the idea that, although heroes are more resourceful and daring
than other humans, in the final result death wins out.

(4) In contrast to the lack of hero cults elsewhere, hero cults were
a distinctive characteristic of Greek religion—which brings us back,
again, to the point that heroes are defined by their relationship to

7.3 Heracles leads away a chained Cerberus while Athena and Hermes look on. Attic black-figure hydria by Painter S, dated to about 510 BCE (detail). Now in the Toledo Museum of Art (Toledo, Ohio). Purchased with funds from the Libbey Endowment, Gift of Edward Drummond Libbey, 1969.371. Photo credit: Richard Goodbody Inc.

death; they must eventually die if they are to become the powerful figures who could help their worshippers of later ages. This leads us to the next section of this chapter.

The Hero as Narrative Character

The time during which the heroes walked the earth amongst other living humans was understood by the historical Greeks to have preceded the time when they themselves were living. By the time that the heroes' stories were being told, therefore, the heroes were technically dead, but as recipients of cult, they were understood to wield significant power: they could protect cities at times of war, fend off plagues and perform various other sorts of feats. Part of the heroes' appeal lay exactly in their ambiguous nature, in fact: as godlike entities who had once been mortal, they could be assumed to have more empathy for humans than the gods would have, and as former mortals who now had godlike powers, they could put that empathy to work. Yet their ambiguous nature presented storytellers with an interesting dilemma: how do you juggle making a hero human enough that listeners will feel that he had once been one of us and demonstrating that he was extraordinary enough for listeners to accept the idea that he rose to a higher level after death?

It's a dilemma that brings us back to the broader question of how myths help to create and sustain beliefs, which I began to explore in Chapter 3. For another way of articulating the issue I just sketched is to say that, by straddling two categories that were otherwise mutually exclusive (mortals and immortals), heroes should have provoked a cognitive dissonance. This dissonance would have been amplified by the fact that whereas cult practice emphasized the heroes' superhuman status (after all, why make offerings to someone who wasn't more powerful than you?), myths emphasized the heroes' lives as *humans* and their very *human* deaths: there are almost no myths that talk about what a hero did *after* he ceased to be human and moved on to higher things.[87] Particularly when myths about heroes were performed in concert with their cults (that is, when stories about the *human* adventures of a hero were told in order to honor and please him in his now *more-than-human* manifestation)—and perhaps even more particularly when myths about heroes were performed in concert with the cult of a god (that is, in concert with myths that further emphasized, through contrast, the erstwhile mortality of heroes, most of whom had suffered at the hands of the gods while they were still alive)—myths about heroes had special work to do, if the ambiguous nature of the heroes was to be made not only credible but also fruitful.

Greek storytelling developed ways of doing this, but to think about them, we need to return briefly to two topics that were introduced in Chapter 5: plurimediality and accretive characters. I suggested that plurimedial portrayals of mythic characters laid the groundwork for belief in their existence by compelling each individual in the audience to develop his or her *own* conceptualization of a character, which led to strong cognitive and emotional bonds between that individual and the character. Each person had his or her own "Theseus," so to speak, made from pieces accrued from the different representations of Theseus to which he or she had been exposed since childhood. In a culture where these were not just "characters" in our usual sense of that word but entities whom most authorities— religious, political, poetic—said were real and able to affect the lives of humans for better or for worse, plurimediality made a significant contribution to the creation and sustenance of belief.

But plurimediality supports belief in the characters of myths in another way as well. In a plurimedial environment, as I noted in Chapter 5, it is impossible for audience members not to notice that varying—sometimes strikingly varying—portrayals of a character coexist. Under these circumstances, every story, however old and however popular, must be accepted as just a single report about a character who can never be fully known by the people who listen to his story. Such tolerance for varied opinions made it easier to continue developing new stories about a character.

Serials and Series

The topic of new stories brings us back to something else that I discussed, in Chapter 3. I noted there that narratologists have shown that telling a story *episodically* prompts people to engage with the story and its characters in between episodes, and I suggested that this also helps to sustain a belief that those characters exist and are poised to intervene in the lives of the audience—assuming, again, that authorities within the given culture support the idea that the characters exist.

I want to return now to the observation that there are two different types of episodic narration, each of which has its own characteristics. In episodic narration that constitutes a *serial*,[88] there is a chronologically determined sequence of episodes, which ideally are provided to an audience in a particular order. The modern examples that I used as illustrations in Chapter 3 included books such as George Eliot's *Middlemarch* and Charles Dickens's *The Old Curiosity Shop*, which were initially published in installments, and TV shows such as *Homeland* and *Downton Abbey*. As I also discussed there, some audiences will consume the episodes of a serial out of their proper order, but the awareness that there *is* an order—that there is a narrative arc that stretches across the episodes—nonetheless affects how the narrator crafts the story and therefore how the audience reacts to each episode. The longer arc more easily allows a narrator to portray characters undergoing changes—changes in status, in states of existence, or in moral and ethical outlooks. Traces of these ongoing changes are found in each episode, even if it is consumed independently of those that come before or after it.

Other episodic narratives are *series.* That is, there is no narrative arc that stretches across all of them. Instead, the episodes are constructed in such a way that the audience's attention focuses closely on one self-contained story and then on the next and then the next again after that. This makes it difficult to show significant development within a character. And in fact, significant development is usually undesirable in this sort of episodic narration: the coherence of a body of stories in a series typically relies on the continuing presence of one or two well-known characters, such as Sherlock Holmes and Dr. Watson. Were these characters to change significantly from one episode to another, some of that coherence would be lost. Many daily comic strips are series, too. In the course of the ten years during which Bill Watterson narrated the adventures of Calvin and Hobbes (1985–1995), neither boy nor tiger matured one whit.

Greek stories about heroes partake of *both* types of episodic narration—serial and series. Heroes' stories were virtually always delivered in the way that *series* are delivered: in discrete doses with little regard for whether the audience members had already heard formal narrations of chronologically earlier parts of the heroes' adventures, which were able to stand on their own or with only brief references to earlier events. Celebrants of Hippocleas's victory in the boys' double-course race at Delphi in 498 BCE heard Pindar's story about Perseus's trip to Hyperborea, for example, but not about the rest of Perseus's adventures.[89] Anyone present when a rhapsode recited what we now call *Odyssey* 12 would have heard about three of Odysseus's greatest adventures—his encounters with the Sirens, Scylla and Charybdis and the cattle of Helios—but that would still be only three out of many. Although tragedies sometimes offered "prequels" and "sequels" to their main plot through the mouths of gods and ghosts who appeared briefly at the beginning or end of the action,[90] each tragedy focused closely on just one episode, which tradition decreed must be dramatically contained within a single day. Thus, for example, those attending the Dionysia of 409 BCE would have heard Sophocles's story about Philoctetes's encounter with Neoptolemus (in the *Philoctetes*) but would have gotten only the briefest résumé of what happened to these two heroes next, when Heracles made an epiphany at the end of the play.

There were exceptions; there were occasions on which a hero's entire story was narrated, albeit succinctly. Some of them, interestingly, occurred when a character within a myth was narrating *another* myth (or at least that's how it looks from our perspective). In some of these cases, the internal narrator used the myth to try to persuade someone else of something: Diomedes told the whole story of Lycurgus in *Iliad* 6 when he wanted to impress upon Glaucus that the only opponent *he* would fear would be a god. And then Glaucus narrated the entire story of Bellerophon, at even greater length, because he wanted to impress Diomedes with his ancestral lineage. Phoenix told almost the whole story of Meleager in *Iliad* 9, when he wanted to convince Achilles to return to battle.[91] In some such cases (Lycurgus, Meleager), it was necessary to tell the full story in order to get the moral across (the audience needed to see the hero brought low at the end of his life). In other cases (Bellerophon), the full story enabled the narrator to squeeze in all the glory he could (although it must be said that this hero, too, was brought low at the end of his life).

Narrations such as these prove that people were familiar with heroes' complete biographies, and some of the cases also suggest that people could informally narrate those biographies themselves when they wanted to. Because of this—because at least the general outline and the high points of each hero's life were widely known—no single episode taken from a hero's career was ever completely disembedded from the longer tale of the hero's life.[92] Each was understood to be part of the longer narrative arc that necessarily stretches over every human life—audience members knew that every hero, like them, had been born a mortal and that every hero had experienced a mortal death, as they would. Or in other words, each episode implicitly participated in a *serial*, even if it was narrated in the manner of a *series*.

We should pause to take note of how much hero myths differed from divine myths in this regard. Gods escaped the chains of temporality almost completely. Gods were born (the Greek poets took particular delight in narrating their births and childhoods)[93] but they did not die, and very few other events in which they participated brought about any significant change—at least for them. Aphrodite's machinations led to the death of Hippolytus, Artemis's favorite acolyte, and in retaliation, Artemis contrived the death of Aphrodite's lover, Adonis, yet there is no indication that either of these human deaths had a lasting effect upon the two goddesses themselves.[94] The argument between Zeus and Poseidon over who would take Thetis's virginity led eventually to the Trojan War, in which every god took sides and sometimes even fought on the battlefield. But aside from a minor scratch here and there, it was the mortals who suffered, not the gods.[95] The lives of the gods truly ran as *series*, insofar as they continued forever, and few episodes within them had links to other episodes or carried lasting repercussions for the gods themselves. Trying to arrange a god's adventures along a timeline is nearly impossible. Even those of us well versed in Greek myths would struggle to say, for example, whether we should understand Aphrodite to have adopted the orphan daughters of Pandareus before or after she abducted Phaethon, the son of Eos and Cephalus. If we are determined to have an answer, the only way to construct one, notably, is from what we know about the *humans* involved—their adventures, familial lines, and relationships with one another. For the record, having performed these scholarly gymnastics with the help of the family trees appended to Timothy Gantz's *Early Greek Mythography*, I conclude that Aphrodite's adoption of the daughters of Pandareus preceded her abduction of Phaethon by one human generation. I base this on two points: (1) Pandareus was a companion of Tantalus, which makes him two generations older than Tantalus's grandson Pittheus; (2) Pittheus's grandson Theseus, according to the Athenian family tree, was two generations younger than Phaethon, whose mother was the goddess Eos and whose father was Cephalus, who was married to the Athenian princess Procris during the time he dallied with Eos and sired Phaethon. Thus, Phaethon was of the same generation as Pittheus and thereby younger than Pandareus's daughters by a generation.[96]

Yet not even the late antique mythographers tried to impose upon the gods such detailed chronologies as I have just compiled for the families of Pandareus and Phaethon. Once we are past the early days of cosmic warfare and Zeus has settled onto the throne, the gods' experiences are seldom perceived sequentially in the same way that humans' are, and any relationships that the gods have with one another—of love, of envy, of enmity—are fleetingly transitory, dwarfed by the unity of the gods as a whole. The scene in the Homeric *Hymn to Apollo* in which a group of the gods—Aphrodite, Artemis, and even Ares, amongst others—merrily dance together to the sound of Apollo's lyre is emblematic not only of their *dolce far niente* attitude but also of their cliquish solidarity.[97] They may squabble over such matters as whether Odysseus should be allowed to reach home, but neither the affairs of mortals nor their own affairs cause serious, enduring changes to their living conditions. One of the few exceptions to this rule brings us to a story that scholars have found odd for a number of other reasons: when Hades kidnapped Persephone, it changed Persephone's mode of existence forever. However hard her mother fought it, Persephone was compelled forevermore to spend part of her time in the Underworld. For Persephone, there *was* a narrative arc, and it *did* bend downward. (Although, strangely enough, it then bent up and down again every year. Was this truly an arc or rather just a particularly weird instance of the episodic nature of gods' existences?)

The implicit *serial* within which each hero's story was told—the sense that there was a beginning and an end, however many episodes lay between—reflects the greatest difference between mortals and immortals, then. It is not simply that mortals die and gods do not; more generally, mortals exist in a world where the passage of time inevitably brings significant change and immortals live in a world where it does not. In contrast to other heroes of *series*—say, Sherlock Holmes—Greek heroes are *meant* to die.[98] They *must* die, in fact, if they are to become the powerful entities who are worshipped in cult, and narratives must confirm that mortality by representing it. Heroic biographies take this even further: the disasters that befall heroes typically come at the end of a chain of events that slowly but surely concatenate over the course of many years that lie between. After killing the Hydra, Heracles dipped his arrows in its poison and later used one of them to kill Nessus, the centaur who was trying to rape his new bride. With his dying words, Nessus contrived to guarantee that, many years later, the bride herself would unwittingly murder Heracles with that very same poison.[99] Laius, in fear of an oracle that his own child would kill him, exposed his newborn son, Oedipus, who nonetheless grew up and, having received an oracle that he would murder his father, ran blindly into the very act of patricide that both he and Laius had sought to evade.[100] And so on. This was the stuff of tragedy, quite literally, and part of tragedy's brilliance was its ability to collapse all the freight of a heroic past that had been narrated as a *series* into a precise moment, a single episode in which its debts came due and the *serial* was clearly revealed as what it had really been all along.

As a genre, then, tragedy thrived on the tension that could be created between the series nature of Greek mythic narration (the fact that it focused on single adventures and circumscribed events) and the inevitable mortality of its protagonists (the fact that they lived within a narrative arc that had a beginning and an end). But to return to the topic of series narration more generally, when a character is presented in a series, the self-contained episodes between his or her implicit birth and death can be multiplied almost infinitely, as either need or desire demands. Who is to say how many opponents either Sherlock Holmes or Heracles defeated? And who will object if another is introduced, as long as the story is engagingly narrated? This flexibility enabled poets to graft new events into heroes' lives to suit the occasions for which their poems were commissioned (and so Pindar, in his third Olympian ode, could contrive to have Heracles travel to Hyperborea to fetch olive trees to beautify the Olympic precinct) and enabled local populations to pull famous heroes into their orbits (and so the people of Megalopolis could tell of how a maddened Orestes bit off his own finger while visiting their neighborhood, hoping to assuage local goddesses called the Crazy Ones).[101] But this flexibility also granted the heroes something similar to the eternity in which the gods existed: the golden mid-stages of their careers could be expanded indefinitely.

Multiplication could not be allowed to become rote, however; a hero who killed the same type of opponent in the same way too many times risked boring his audience. This brings us back to the Greeks' tolerance for—indeed, their apparent desire for—hearing different versions of a well-known story; such variation was yet another way of keeping a hero fresh, of lingering on a favorite tale without becoming sated. Poets might do this by offering new insights into heroes' morals and motivations: Euripides's Orestes is certainly different from that of Sophocles, who is again different from that of Aeschylus. Or rather, I should say, Euripides's *four* Orestai are different—not only from those of Aeschylus and Sophocles but also from one another: they range from a young hero off on a quest that restores his sister to home, in the *Iphigeneia in Tauris*, to a treacherous murderer in the *Andromache*. This is more than a matter of giving a hero a behavioral facelift just for the sake of variety or politics; each of these representations provided audiences with another opportunity to engage with the hero and the range of possible responses he could make to his circumstances. In contrast to characters such as Elizabeth II, whom I discussed in Chapter 5, there was little to constrain the narrative development of heroes.

Iteration

Some types of multiplication generate what Umberto Eco calls "iteration." Eco suggests that characters whose adventures are narrated serially—his prime examples are Superman, Hercule Poirot, Nero Wolfe, and Lieutenant Columbo—please their audiences by repetitively engaging in the same sorts of adventures and displaying the same behavioral (and sartorial) tics over and over again. Their predictability rewards loyal audiences with feelings of knowledge and intimacy, which in turn heightens the audience's desire to hear further stories about the character.[102]

Greek hero myths engage in iteration in two ways. First, certain heroes repeatedly perform certain types of tasks or apply certain types of skills to overcome challenges. Odysseus uses his cunning to outwit young Achilles on Scyros, Polyphemus in his cave and the suitors on Ithaca, amongst others. Heracles repeatedly conquers monstrous animals (the Hydra, the Erythmanthian Boar, Cerberus, and so on) and barbarians who engage in aberrant customs (Antaeus,

Busiris, Cycnus), and typically he wears the same lion-skin "outfit" to do it—a sartorial tic.

Second, Greek heroes *collectively* iterate certain behaviors. Although no one had as many notches in his club as Heracles did, Theseus and Odysseus each overcame several monsters, Perseus two, and Bellerophon, Cadmus, Oedipus, and some lesser-known, local heroes overcame one monster apiece. In doing so, they each contributed to an expectation that conquering monsters is something that heroes do, and thereby stoked audiences' appetite for hearing about it again. Artists also fueled this fire, as shown in Figures 7.1, 7.6, 7.7, and 7.9, and in metopes 2, 9, and 11 of Figure 7.4.

Eco also argues that iteration makes series ideal mechanisms for sending a simple message because the message is repeated over and over (whether the stories' narrators are conscious that they are doing so or not). What message, or messages, might we understand Greek hero myths to be sending? The most obvious answer is that there had once been a time when at least some humans were bigger, better and nearer in nature to the gods—the same message sent by the mythic genealogies that I discussed in the first section of this chapter.

But when we look more closely at other iterated features, we see something different. Frequently, these features emphasize the hero's *humanness* and thus his *distance* from the gods. The presence of one or more companions at his side as he performs his labors, for example—with Theseus, it's Pirithous; with Jason, it's the Argonauts, for instance—sets him firmly in the human realm. Gods form alliances to accomplish specific tasks—Hera, Hypnos, and Poseidon collude against Zeus in *Iliad* 14, for instance[103]—but these alliances are as shifting as the sands; the gods have nothing as enduring as friendship. The hero's frequent need to seek, and sometimes then interpret, information from a higher authority—an oracle, a *mantis*, or a god in disguise—is human as well. In contrast, I can think of only three or four instances in which gods seek information: Zeus attempts to learn from Prometheus upon which female he should not sire a son; Demeter attempts to learn what has become of Persephone; and in the Homeric *Hymn to Hermes*, Apollo attempts to learn, from an old man, where his stolen cattle have gone—an episode that I presume is meant to parody the many instances in which human heroes sought information from Apollo himself, a role of Apollo's that the poet of the *Hymn* later emphasizes, when he portrays Hermes and Apollo negotiating over which of them will control which kinds of prophetic knowledge.[104] Finally (a dubious case), Pindar presents us with an Apollo who dissembles, pretending not to know something so that he can ask Chiron (another famous prophet) about the identity and lineage of a lovely maiden whom he has glimpsed, and whether it is right for him to make love to her. Before answering, Chiron chides the god, asking how it is that someone who knows how many leaves the earth puts forth in spring, how many grains of sand lie in the sea and rivers, and all that will happen in its appointed time cannot discern for himself who the girl is and exactly what his lovemaking with her will bring about.[105]

More human yet are the labors in which heroes engage—and, in particular, the types of physical exertion required by those labors. Greek heroes are able to use a sword, spear or bow as well as any hero from another culture, but in many cases, the work they do evokes not that of a warrior or hunter (pursuits suitable for upper-class men in historical Greece) but rather that of a craftsman or even an agricultural worker. Homer tells us in detail about how Odysseus constructs the stake that he used to blind Polyphemus, the raft on which he leaves Calypso's island and his marital bed, using the tools and knowledge of a carpenter.[106] Heracles digs a ditch to clean manure out of stables; Heracles's traditional weapon, the club, points towards a humble station in life as well (Theseus often carries a club, too).[107] Jason and his Argonauts also have to dig a ditch, in order to launch the *Argo* on the journey that will win them glory, and later they have to carry the *Argo* on their shoulders across the Libyan desert.[108] Both Cadmus and Jason yoke animals, plow fields and plant things (even if the crops that spring up are unusual ones).[109] Odysseus knows how to plow, as well, as we learn from the episode in which he feigns madness by yoking an ox and a horse to a plow and sowing the seashore with salt.[110] At least half of the monsters that heroes overcome also pull them towards the human side of things, insofar as these monsters are simply bigger or more vicious versions of the same animals that the average person might encounter: the Marathonian Bull, the Crommyonian Sow, the Teumessian Vixen, the Nemean Lion, and so on. Half of the metopes from the Temple of Zeus at Olympia that show Heracles at his labors make this clear (metopes 1, 3, 4, 5, 7, and 8, as labeled in Figure 7.4), as do numerous vase paintings of the labors performed by Heracles and other heroes, such as Theseus.[111] One of the iterated messages in Greece, then, was that the heroes not only had to undertake remarkable tasks that other humans would not even attempt—killing Gorgons and Minotaurs, gathering Hesperian apples and Golden Fleeces—but also had to know how to do humbler, more ordinary tasks. Indeed, completing the ordinary tasks was often a perquisite for accomplishing the remarkable ones. Without the skills of a carpenter, Odysseus would not have escaped from Polyphemus's cave or from Calypso's island. Without the skills of a farmer, Cadmus and Jason would not have moved forwards in their careers. Without the sweat of the Argonauts, the *Argo* would not have been launched.

Perseus is furthest away from this model. He does nothing that mimics everyday labor, the monsters whom he kills are not found amongst the familiar fauna, and a large part of his adventures takes place in a realm that lies completely beyond the known world. But Perseus's foster father is a fisherman with the speaking name Dictys (Fishing Net), and it is in Dictys's house that Perseus grows to manhood—presumably being taught how to catch fish as well. It's tempting to shrug off this detail as a joke—a clever twist on the fact that Perseus and his mother, set adrift in a chest, were fished out of the sea by a net—but from early on, Dictys is given noble genealogies by ancient mythographers; he was regarded as more than just a clever play on words—and we have no way of knowing which idea appeared first and precipitated the other one, anyway: Perseus's rescue by a fisherman named Dictys or Perseus's rescue by means of a *dictys?*[112]

Some narrators emphasize the human side of heroes even further. The *Iliad* and the *Odyssey* recount their sweat and bodily pain, in battle and on seemingly endless journeys home. Their essential humanness is further accentuated in the *Iliad* and the *Odyssey* by the choices that the epics' protagonists make. Achilles, having come to terms with human mortality after losing his friend Patroclus, returns to battle in spite of the fact that he knows that this decision will lead to his own death. Odysseus refuses Calypso's offer of immortality in

7.4 Drawing of the metopes from the temple of Zeus at Olympia, as printed in *Olympia: Die Ergebnisse der von dem deutschen Reich veranstalteten Ausgrabung*, by Ernst Curtius and Friedrich Adler, vol. 3, plate 45 (Berlin, 1894–1897). The metopes, which date to between 470 and 457 BCE, show the twelve labors of Heracles.

order to return to a mortal life with a mortal wife in spite of having learned from Achilles's ghost that what awaits all mortals after death is a yawning emptiness.[113]

Tragedies show us heroes functioning in a world that is scarcely distinguishable from that of their Athenian audiences, populated by pedagogues, nurses, guards, and other ordinary people. Early in Euripides's *Alcestis*, a group of townspeople gather before the palace, gossiping about what will happen to their king and queen; a maid from the royal household brings them news of the events that will drive the rest of the play.[114] Euripides's *Medea* begins with a conversation between an old nurse and a pedagogue.[115] The action of Aeschylus's *Oresteia* is kicked off by a night watchman stationed on the palace roof, who complains about the "unrestful couch . . . drenched by dews" that he has occupied for many a year.[116] We first meet Euripides's Ion—the hero of his eponymous play—as he is cleaning the floor of a temple dedicated to his father, Apollo, and chasing away the birds that would soil it.[117] This is a pronouncedly humble start in life for a divinely sired child who would become king of Athens. Sophocles shows us the struggles of Philoctetes's life on Lemnos as he drags himself groaningly across the stage.[118]

And tragedy often dwells on the repercussions that heroes' actions have for the people who are close to them. In Euripides's *Heracles*, Heracles's first wife, Megara, her children, and Heracles's foster father await death at the hands of an enemy because Heracles has once again abandoned his family in order to dash off upon a labor.[119] In Sophocles's *Trachiniae*, Heracles's second wife, Deianira, describes her daily life as one of "nourishing fear upon fear" during his frequent absences and bemoans the fact that he scarcely knows his own children.[120] In Sophocles's *Ajax*, Tecmessa reminds the hero not only of the dire fate that will befall her and their child if he kills himself out of wounded pride but also of how harsh an old age his parents will endure if he does so.[121] I need scarcely mention the effect that Jason's choices have on his wife and children. However poorly they lived up to them, Greek heroes were shown to have human responsibilities—for wives, children, and parents—from which the gods were completely free.

We might expect that epinician odes, at least, would embroider the glorious side of the heroes' lives; after all, it was to the heroes that the young victors celebrated in epinicians were being compared. Bacchylides meets this expectation in two of his longer epinicians— his description of Heracles meeting the ghost of Meleager in the Underworld and that of Achilles and Ajax on the Trojan battlefield are colorful and rousing, for example.[122] In his dithyrambs, too, he paints vivid pictures of heroes' exploits, in Theseus's confrontation with Minos and visit to the undersea palace of his father, for instance, and in the description of Theseus's approach to Athens, ridding the Isthmus of monsters and villains as he goes—a popular topic for vase painters as well, as the images on the early fifth-century cup in Figure 7.5 show.

7.5 In the center of this image, Theseus upends Sciron, while Athena looks on and Sciron's turtle waits below. To the right, Theseus wrestles with Cercyon and at the far right is the back end of the Crommyonian Sow. Theseus's adventures on the Isthmus continue around the outside of the vase, and the image inside shows him fighting the Minotaur. Attic red-figure cup by Douris, dated to around 480 BCE (detail). Now in the British Museum, inv. num. 1843,1103.13 (BM E48). Photo © Trustees of the British Museum (CC BY-NC-SA 4.0).

But Pindar's treatments of the heroes are often clipped or focus attention away from their greatest deeds. *Pythian* 4 spends only seven lines (out of 299) on how Jason yokes Aeetes's fire-breathing bulls and forces them to plow straight furrows; we hear nothing of the teeth that Jason must plant in those furrows and his single-handed battle against the men that spring from them (a tale that the earlier, epic poet Eumelus had narrated). And although Pindar goes on to describe the serpent that Jason must confront in order to snatch the fleece, he truncates this climax of the story, giving it just a single line.[123] In other words, Pindar lingers longest on those of Jason's deeds that can most easily be aligned with labors familiar to his audience—even adding the quotidian detail that Jason used a goad to urge the bulls forwards.[124] *Olympian* 13 was composed for a Corinthian victor and therefore Pindar sensibly chose the Corinthian hero Bellerophon as his theme. Pindar lingers over Bellerophon's reaction to meeting Athena in a dream and then summarizes his three greatest deeds—slaying the Amazons, the Chimaera, and the Solymoi—in just four lines.[125] In *Pythian* 10, Pindar compresses the highpoint of Perseus's career into just three and a half of the seventy-two lines that constitute the poem: "he slew the Gorgon and, bearing her head adorned with locks of serpents, came to the islanders, bringing them stony death."[126]

It's not that Pindar is unimpressed by what the heroes do; on the contrary, he follows the lines about Perseus and the Gorgon with the comment, "but to me, no *marvel*, if the gods bring it about, ever seems beyond belief," and the lines about Bellerophon with the comment, "The gods' power easily brings into being *even what one would swear impossible and beyond hope*,"[127] phrases that firmly slide Perseus's and Bellerophon's accomplishments over to the divine side of the ledger. Yet Pindar chooses to emphasize the human nature of the heroes when he can. We can rationalize such choices by noting that they align well with Pindar's larger program of reminding athletes that they should not attempt to be something they are not, but it was the Greek conceptualization of the hero as suspended between mortal and immortal and yet essentially *human* that gave Pindar the leeway to do this. Bacchylides interrupts one of his most lavish descriptions of a hero's accomplishments with a similar comment. In the middle of his narration of Theseus's visit to the undersea palace of Amphitrite, the poet declares, "Nothing that the gods wish is beyond the belief of sane mortals."[128]

I suggested in the preceding section that treating heroes' stories as *series* enabled poets to extend the "golden mid-stages" of the heroes' careers, thus giving the heroes something similar to the eternity in which the gods existed, but that the implicitly *serial* treatment of heroes' stories emphasized the mortal arc of their lives, which always ended in death. I've now suggested, in addition, that the *iterative* potential of series narration could underscore either or both of these messages. The ways in which Greek hero myths were narrated, then, reflected and confirmed the heroes' suspension between the two otherwise mutually exclusive groups that they mediated. Yet the preference amongst Greek narrators was to locate heroes more firmly within everyday life and its challenges. Greek heroes as we meet them in narratives are unquestionably human.

Monsters and Gods

In the ancient Near East, there were quite a few stories about gods battling monsters. For instance, in the *Enuma Elish*, Marduk destroys an army of dreadful creatures that were called into existence by the primordial seawater goddess Tiamat—as well as destroying Tiamat herself, who is described as a dragon-like monster.[129] In the Hittite *Song of Illuyanka*, Teshub defeats the great sea serpent Illuyanka (whose name means "serpent") with the help of his daughter Inara.[130] In the Hittite *Song of Hedammu*, Tarhun and his sister Anzili battle the sea serpent Hedammu,[131] and in the *Song of Ullikummi*, Tarhun battles the rock monster Ullikummi.[132] Egyptian Ra battles the serpent Apophis every night to ensure that the sun will rise the next morning.[133] Yahweh battles the sea serpent Leviathan.[134]

All of these Near Eastern battles have cosmogonic significance. Not only do they determine which gods will be in charge of the cosmos, but they often also provide the raw material from which the physical cosmos is constructed or protect the physical order once it has been established: Marduk creates the physical world from Tiamat's corpse, for example, and Ra's repeated battle against Apophis ensures that the celestial order of things will continue, day by day.[135] It has also often been noted that most of the monsters who are defeated in these battles are snaky in form.[136] This strengthens the stories' cosmogonic messages, for in the ancient Mediterranean (as in many other parts of the world), the snake was viewed as a particularly dangerous creature, sometimes even an evil creature, that by its very nature was pitted against the forces of order.[137]

In Greek myths, in contrast, battles between gods and monsters are relatively rare, considering how many more myths in general survive from Greece compared with those that survive from the ancient Near East. I can name only five examples. (1) Cronus and his allies defeat a monster called Ophion—the name literally means "Snaky"—and Ophion's children, in order to establish Cronus's rule at an early stage of the cosmos' existence (thus, the story, like the Near Eastern stories, has cosmogonic implications). (2) Zeus defeats Typhon, who in most versions of this story is a direct threat to young Zeus's rule and who has one hundred snakes sprouting from his waist in place of legs (again, the snakes underscore the cosmogonic implications of this story).[138] (3) Apollo kills Python, a giant she-snake, in order to establish his Delphic Oracle (more on that shortly). (4) Hermes kills the herdsman Argus.[139] Argus is only a borderline monster, however; aside from the fact that he has extra eyes, there is nothing unusual about him. Some sources make him the son of Gaea, like some other monsters, but others give him human parents.

And finally, (5) all of the gods battle monsters called *gigantes* in the early days of the cosmos, in order to defend Zeus's right to rule the cosmos. We can't be certain what these *gigantes* were. The word is typically translated as "giants," but the only possible evidence that *gigantes* were particularly large is a passage from the tenth book of the *Odyssey* that says the Laestrygonians were more similar to *gigantes* than they were to humans.[140] Because the Laestrygonians themselves are described as large shortly afterward, we tend to assume that the *gigantes* were large, too, but Homer's comparison may have been meant to suggest, instead, that the Laestrygonians (and therefore also the *gigantes*) were non-anthropomorphic creatures of some sort. That would make them align nicely with three of the other foes whom Odysseus confronted in books 9 through 13: the Cyclopes (who had only one eye apiece), the Sirens (who were not described by Homer but who in texts and art from the later Archaic age are portrayed as part bird and part human), and Scylla (a maiden who had six dogs' heads springing from her waist). The earliest artistic representations show the *gigantes* as fully anthropomorphic—sometimes they even wear hoplites' armor—but beginning in about 380 BCE, visual representations show them with snakes for legs, as well, as we see in Figure 7.6. Poets seem to have described them with snaky legs, as well, by the late fourth century onwards, and certainly some (but not

7.6 Heracles, wielding his characteristic club, attacks a snaky-legged giant. To the left is the front portion of a two-headed griffin ridden by Dionysus. Attic red-figure wide-bellied lekythos dating to the first quarter of the fourth century (detail). Now in the Antikensammlung, Berlin, inv. num. V. I. 3375. Photo credit: bpk Bildagentur/Antikensammlung, Staatliche Museen, Berlin/Johannes Laurentius/Art Resource, NY.

all) of the *gigantes* have snaky legs when they make their most spectacular appearance, around 170 BCE, on the Great Altar from Pergamum.[141] Euripides offers us one more tantalizing bit of information: it was during the battle with the giants, he says, that Athena killed a Gorgon, whose head she mounted upon her breastplate.[142] Euripides may have invented this story (all of our other sources say that Athena received her Gorgon's head from Perseus), but even so, the detail must have more or less fit with what was generally known about the battle, and it therefore helps to confirm that the gods confronted creatures who were "monsters" in our usual sense of that word (that is, they did not look like normal human beings) and probably monsters with snaky aspects.

I kept the gods' battle against the *gigantes* until the end of my list of divine fights against monsters because it includes an important twist that sets it apart from almost all Near Eastern monster-killing stories. Already in Hesiod, we are told that the battle was won by the gods *with the help of Heracles*, who personally slew many *gigantes* and (as Euripides later says) "raised a victory cry alongside the gods." Artistic sources sometimes show Heracles fighting alongside the gods, too, as do the two images from vases included here (see Figures 7.6 and 7.7).[143] All of our textual sources insist that Heracles was still a living mortal when he participated in the battle; this gives us a singular Greek instance of gods needing human help to overcome monsters and a nearly singular instance within the ancient Mediterranean more broadly. The only comparable story concerns the help that Hupasiya gave Teshub to overcome Illuyanka, but Hupasiya's contribution was far smaller than Heracles's: rather than doing battle directly with Illuyanka himself, Hupasiya merely bound the sleeping serpent after the goddess Inara had enticed it to a feast and gotten it drunk. After the beast had been tied up, Teshub arrived and delivered the coup de grâce.[144]

More than a century of scholarship has established that Greek cosmogonic myths drew significantly on stories from other Mediterranean cultures. This, combined with the peculiarity of Heracles's fight against the *gigantes* and with the fact that two of the remaining four divine battles against monsters in Greece (Cronus against Ophion and Zeus against Typhon) had clear cosmogonic settings,

7.7 Heracles, wearing his lion skin and with his club lying nearby, joins the gods in their battle against the giants (detail of a larger scene). Attic red-figure amphora from between 410 and 400 BCE, attributed to the Suessula Painter (detail). Now in the Musée de Louvre, inv. num. S1677; MNB810. Photo credit: Chuzeville / Musée de Louvre / © RMN–Grand Palais / Art Resource NY.

raises the strong possibility that there was an earlier version of the Greek gods' battle against the *gigantes* in which Heracles did *not* appear, set at the dawn of the cosmos. This hunch is strengthened by the fact that the *gigantes* were children of Gaea and thus were both genealogically and conceptually parallel to the two other challengers of Zeus's rule, Typhon and the Titans, whom the gods overcame without human help. The snaky legs of the *gigantes* in at least later representations also align them with the Mediterranean cohort of cosmogonically threatening serpentine creatures.

If Heracles was stitched into what was once a gods-only cosmo-gonic battle, this would seem to betoken the rising prominence of heroes in Greece during the Archaic Age—and traces of similar stitchery can, in fact, be glimpsed elsewhere in Archaic sources. During his narration of divine generations, Hesiod pauses on the marriage of two primeval sea gods, Phorcys and Ceto, from whom springs a family of monstrous creatures, many of whom have snaky attributes. Ceto bears the three Graeae, Medusa and the two other Gorgons, Echidna, and the snake that guards the apple tree that grows at the ends of the earth. Medusa and Echidna, in turn, have monstrous children and grandchildren of their own: Geryon and his dog Orthrus, Cerberus, the Lernaean Hydra, the Chimaera, the Sphinx, and the Nemean Lion.[145]

Five times in the sixty-seven-line section treating Phorcys and Ce-to's dreadful offspring, Hesiod pauses to interject comments about how a particular monster eventually fell at the hands of a human hero. Perseus cut off Medusa's head. Geryon, Orthrus, the Hydra, and the Nemean Lion were killed by Heracles. The Chimaera was slain by Bellerophon.[146] These insertions preemptively remind us, before we reach Hesiod's narration of the battle between Zeus and Typhon near the end of the *Theogony* (820–880), that humans will be the ones to finish the fight against monsters that Zeus began. The fact that Typhon is named by Hesiod as the father of three of the monsters (Orthrus, Cerberus, and the Hydra) underscores the point: Zeus may have imprisoned a progenitor of monsters, but it was left to Zeus's mortal descendants to complete the larger task. In Homer, too, monsters are mentioned almost always in connection with human heroes who defeat them: we are told that Bellerophon defeats the Chimaera, that Heracles overcomes Cerberus, that Meleager and his companions kill the Calydonian Boar and that Odysseus overcomes several monsters, or at least (in the case of Scylla) minimizes their impact. In contrast, we hear only once—and even then briefly, within a metaphor—about Zeus's defeat of Typhon.[147]

Even the story of Typhon itself was adapted to bring mortals to the fore as the Archaic period rolled on. Most later authors who refer to this story draw on Hesiod's version, stating that Zeus hurled Ty-phon into Tartarus (or some other underground realm), where he lay forevermore, but the Homeric *Hymn to Apollo*, which probably dates to the early sixth century,[148] gives it a full treatment with a different spin. To begin with, the *Hymn* says that Typhon was not born from Gaea, a powerful goddess who had existed from the very beginning of time (thus disagreeing with Hesiod), but rather from Hera, a younger, Olympian goddess who was Zeus's wife and his equal, generationally speaking.[149] This change already moves Typhon out of the most cosmogonically active stage of the universe's development and into a period when the world and the gods' roles within it had already been settled. Hera's motivation for bearing Typhon can, in fact, be understood as a bid not to *claim* the cosmos but rather to *re-claim* a right within it that she and other females had previously held exclusively. For, feeling insulted by Zeus's parthenogenic production of Athena and ashamed of her own botched attempt at single parenthood (which produced the disabled god Hephaestus), Hera beat the earth with her hands and begged a group of older gods, many of whom had been displaced by the younger generation (Gaea, Ouranos, the imprisoned Titans and Tartarus), to send her a son who would be stronger than Zeus. Hera duly became pregnant with Typhon without any help from Zeus, but after her first glimpse of an infant who "looked like neither gods nor mortals," she handed him over to Python to be reared.[150]

In spite of having told us that Hera prayed for a son stronger than *Zeus*, the *Hymn* makes no subsequent mention of any fight between Zeus and Typhon.[151] Instead, it tells us that it was *mortals* for whom "dreadful and problematic Typhon" was an "affliction" (*pēma*). Indeed, it tells us this twice—once at the beginning of Typhon's story and once at the end.[152] These comments strengthen the analogy between Typhon and Python, the latter of whom the poet similarly describes, three times, as a monster who was an affliction (*pēma*) or evil (*kakon*) for mortals and their herds.[153] By extension, the comments also strengthen the analogy between the two monsters' conquerors: Zeus and Apollo. But in which direction were those analogies supposed to work? Certainly, by drawing a parallel between Typhon and Python, the author of the *Hymn* can be taken to imply that Apollo's monster killing was one of the final acts of tidying up the cosmos, but at the same time, by making Typhon a problem for *humans* (like Python), the poet further shifts Typhon out of an early stage of cosmic history and into a later stage when not only had the universe and the family of gods settled into their final forms (indeed, at least two of the younger gods, Hephaestus and Athena, were born *before* Typhon was created, according to the *Hymn*, which contradicts Hesiod's timeline) but the human race had also appeared on the horizon. Neither Typhon nor Python is presented as a *cosmogonic* threat, in other words, but both, instead, are emphatically monsters who fall into line with those I mentioned earlier, who were killed by human heroes in order to protect human interests—the Nemean Lion, whom Hesiod called a "bane (*pēma*) to humans"; the Sphinx, whom Hesiod called the "deadly destruction of the Cadmeians" and whom Aeschylus described as eating humans raw; the Chimaera, whom Homer called an "evil to many people"; Scylla, whom Homer called a "bane (*pēma*) for mortals"; the Erymanthian Boar, who harmed the people of Psophis; and so on. The tendency to explicitly connect monsters to the harm they do to humans only grows stronger as time goes on, in fact—in Euripides's *Heracles*, even the Cerynitian Deer is described as a marauder of country folk.[154]

Remarkably, not only does the poet of the Homeric *Hymn* recraft Typhon into a monster who threatens humans and their flocks (and probably either creates or recrafts Python into such a monster, too, although we have no earlier version of this story with which to compare the *Hymn*), but he also recrafts Apollo into someone who is similar to a human hero. Our first indication of this comes immediately before the poet begins to tell us about Apollo's search for a place to build his Oracle. Briefly, the poet considers treating another topic, instead: one of the many courtships of Apollo. But which one? he asks himself. In listing his top choices, the poet makes one thing curiously clear: in all of the cases, it was with a *mortal man* that Apollo competed for a woman's love.[155]

Having aired the theme of Apollo's love life before us for eight lines, the poet rejects it and decides instead to describe the foundation of the Delphic Oracle. He begins with a lengthy list of the places that Apollo considered as locations—Iolchus, Euboea famed for shipping, the Lelantine Plain, grassy Teumessus, and so on, each of which is invoked with just one or two words. But then he pauses for four entire lines on the future site of the city of Thebes, which at the time of Apollo's quest, the poet says, was "cloaked in vegetation, for no mortal yet dwelt in holy Thebes, and there were not yet any paths or roads crossing the wheat-bearing Theban plain, but it was occupied by wild growth."[156] This is an interesting place for the poet to linger. Thebes was reputed to be one of the oldest cities in Greece, and the myth of its foundation was well known by the time that our *Hymn* was composed. Cadmus, wandering through Greece in search of his kidnapped sister, was told (by the Delphic Oracle, no less) to give up on finding her and instead to follow a cow until it lay down and then to establish a city on that spot. Having followed the cow, and having built the city of Thebes, Cadmus asked some friends to fetch water with which he could perform a sacrifice. When those friends approached a nearby spring, they were killed by a gigantic snake that guarded it. Cadmus killed the snake, made his sacrifice and became Thebes's first king.[157]

The Delphic foundation myth that we get in the *Hymn to Apollo* mirrors the Theban one; in each case, a giant snake, lurking at a nearby spring, must be killed before a foundational act can be completed by an individual who has journeyed from afar in order to perform it. If I am correct that the *Hymn*'s extended meditation on the site where Thebes will soon be established would have evoked that city's well-known foundation myth, then the poet of the *Hymn* is prompting us to have Cadmus in our minds when listening to the tale of Apollo's monster killing that he is soon to narrate. Again, Apollo's cohort—the individuals to whom we are invited to compare him—is human.[158]

Once at the site of Delphi, Apollo lays the foundations of his temple with his own hands—unusually amongst the gods, he is a do-it-yourselfer. Upon Apollo's foundations, the famous (human) heroes Agamedes and Trophonius lay a stone floor, and then "tribes of humans" erect the walls of the temple, setting the blocks in place.[159] This is a collective effort, in other words, with the god working, if not necessarily alongside humans, then at least on a common project. This story marks a contrast with what scholars think was an equally early, or perhaps even earlier, story, according to which the first temple in which the Oracle was housed had been built out of laurel branches by Apollo alone, the second by birds and bees out of wax and feathers, the third by the gods Athena and Hephaestus out of bronze and the fourth, finally, by Agamedes, Trophonius, and other humans. In our *Hymn*, the three "magical" or "divine" temples are omitted altogether, and the god collaborates with humans on the first and only structure that houses his Oracle. It also marks a contrast with what was the canonical myth of Apollo's arrival at Delphi (a myth embraced by the personnel of the Oracle itself), according to which he took over its functions, peaceably or not, from earlier, female owners.[160] In short, the poet of the *Hymn* made a very conscious decision to present Apollo as he did.

Finally, Apollo turns his mind to staffing his new Oracle. Spotting a ship full of Cretan sailors out at sea, he pulls it into Delphi's harbor. Personally leading the sailors up the hill to the Oracle, he shows them around, describing all its features. Subsequently, he explains to them that they will be able to feed themselves and their families—thus satisfying a very mortal need—from the sacrifices of animals that worshippers will bring. Here, as in his eagerness to help build that Oracle, Apollo is a god who is notably willing to rub elbows with humans—not in disguise, as did the grief-stricken Demeter in Eleusis, nor in disguise, under duress and with shame, as did Aphrodite on a Trojan hillside in her Homeric *Hymn*, but of his own free choice and more or less in his own form.

The Homeric *Hymn to Apollo* turns Typhon, a great cosmogonic monster, into a threat to humans rather than gods and shows us one of the younger gods, Apollo, filling the role that a human hero would fill when he defeats Python, another monster that is markedly presented as a threat to humans. Apollo himself is made out to be a very human god, similar to a hero such as Cadmus. In three early Archaic compositions, then (the *Hymn to Apollo*, Hesiod's brief but pointed interjections about monster-killing heroes in the *Theogony* and Hesiod's mention of Heracles's participation in the gods' battle against the *gigantes*), we encounter subtle but clear transitions away from the pattern of divine, cosmogonic monster killing that we find in Near Eastern myths and in Hesiod's own story of Zeus killing Typhon, towards monster killing that brings human heroes, and human concerns, to the forefront. The introduction of heroes into what had previously been exclusively divine territory suggests that the Greek hero as we later know him was still a relatively new phenomenon at the time that those compositions were created and that storytellers had a free hand in how they developed him.

Monsters and Heroes

Hesiod's scattered catalogue of heroic monster killing is just the tip of what is already a large iceberg by the end of the Archaic period, at latest. To give only a partial list, Heracles killed the Nemean Lion, the Lernaean Hydra, the Stymphalian Birds, Geryon, Geryon's dog Orthrus, and a Trojan sea monster, and he overcame (without killing them) the Erythmanthian Boar, the Cerynitian Deer, the Cretan Bull, the Mares of Diomedes, and Cerberus. Theseus conquered the Crommyonian Sow, the Bull of Marathon (who was formerly known as the Cretan Bull), and the Minotaur. Bellerophon killed the Chimaera. Perseus decapitated Medusa and killed a sea monster off the coast of Joppa. Oedipus drove the Sphinx to her death. Amphitryon killed the Teumessian Vixen—or some say that Oedipus killed her. Cadmus and Jason killed dragons. Odysseus outsmarted a Cyclops, evaded the Sirens, and at least stood his ground against Scylla.

These were exciting stories, even if some authors chose to narrate them rather tersely. But who, exactly, were these monsters and how did their identities add to the excitement? As I also discussed in Chapter 4, Greek monsters were well woven into the network of relationships not only because they were the victims of heroes (and occasionally of gods) but also because many monsters were the children of gods. In Chapter 6, I discussed how vividly, and sometimes even tenderly, the births and childhoods of these monsters could be narrated: dreadful though they might seem to the mortals whose lives and herds they threatened, many of these monsters were the objects of a god's affection, or at least the product of a god's loins.

This lends important nuances to what became the Greek pattern of *heroes* killing monsters within situations that were set well after the universe has reached its finished form. If Hesiod's discussion of the race of Phorcys and Ceto proleptically implied that the heroes were destined to clear up the bits of monster killing that Zeus had left unfinished after his victory over Typhon, then the heroes could be understood as nearly the equals of the gods in this one particular talent, at least. But we could also understand Hesiod's treatment—and particularly his choice of narrating the monsters' *deaths* at the hands of the heroes immediately after his description of the monsters' *ancestries and births*—to imply that, by killing the monsters, the heroes *intruded* upon the divine realm. However dim and elemental Phorcys and Ceto may seem in contrast to the anthropomorphic Olympians, they are gods, and their children are gods just as fully as are, for instance, the river children of the equally dim and elemental Tethys and Oceanus, whom Hesiod lists immediately after he finishes listing the descendants of Phorcys and Ceto. Some of Hesiod's monsters, moreover, are said to be lovely in ways that evoke the loveliness of anthropomorphic goddesses or human women. The Graeae are described as "having beautiful cheeks"; one of them, Pemphredo, is also called "fair-robed" and her sister Enyo has "robes dyed with saffron." Ceto, who is the progenitor of all these monsters, is described as having beautiful cheeks, as well, and even Echidna, who eats raw flesh in a cave beneath the earth, is a "quick-eyed nymph, with beautiful cheeks" (or at least her upper half is—her bottom half is a terrible snake).[161] Some of these monsters "mingle in love" with one another just as other gods do. Indeed, one of them mingles in love with a god who has nothing monstrous about him at all: Medusa is bedded by Poseidon in a soft meadow amongst spring flowers. There is no indication here that Medusa is anything but a snaky-haired Gorgon when Poseidon makes love to her; Hesiod's insertion of the scene in the middle of his discussion of the Gorgons and his general discussion of monsters underscores this.[162]

We could choose to explain away these things as confused "holdovers" from a time when there were alternative traditions about such creatures (was Medusa always ugly?)[163] or as attempts to raise a frisson (let's imagine what it would be like to have sex with a snaky-haired woman!) or simply as a formulaically poetic way of denoting sexual intercourse and formulaically poetic ways of describing important females, for example, but whatever the origins of these traditions, what the audiences heard when the *Theogony* was performed was that the monsters whom the heroes killed were divine and not altogether dissimilar from other divinities.

Greek myths nuance heroic battles with monsters in another way, too. Most heroes receive divine help in conquering monsters. Athena is their most constant companion, followed by Hermes. Already in the *Odyssey*, Heracles reports that Athena and Hermes helped him fetch Cerberus from Hades, as shown in Figure 7.3, for example. Athena is often Heracles's helper in other adventures, as well, and Helios lends Heracles the cup in which he crosses the ocean each day in order that Heracles might get to where he needs to be (see several of the metopes shown in Figure 7.4 and the scene in Figure 4.1).[164] In the Hesiodic *Shield*, Perseus is described as wearing the helmet of invisibility that Hades had lent him to combat Medusa. Perseus received two other important divine gifts that would help him in his quest, as well—Hermes's winged sandals and a special bag in which to hold Medusa's decapitated head—and Athena and Hermes are frequently recorded as helping Perseus in other ways.[165] (Figure 7.1 shows Perseus wearing the sandals while Hermes stands nearby, notably barefooted, and Athena carefully holding Medusa's head out of Perseus's direct line of sight.) Bellerophon received a bridle with which he could capture Pegasus, as well as advice about how to do it, from Athena—although in a fragment of Hesiod's *Catalogue*, it seems to have been Poseidon, Pegasus's father, who gave the bridle to Bellerophon, who was also his son (accentuating the odd situation of one brother riding another into battle against the Chimaera).[166] Theseus was helped by his father's wife, Amphitrite, when Minos sent him to the bottom of the sea to retrieve a ring, according to Bacchylides's seventeenth ode. A crown that was given to him by either Amphitrite or Ariadne, the latter of whom perhaps had received it from Dionysus, lit Theseus's way through the Labyrinth. We see Theseus's underwater visit to Amphitrite in Figure 7.8, with Athena standing by (probably, she is there because Theseus is the ancestral hero of Athens, her special city). Sometimes Athena also shows up next to Theseus in artistic representations of his victory over the Minotaur and other monsters—or over humans who behave monstrously, as on the vase shown in Figure 7.5.[167] Already in the *Odyssey*, Jason is described as the special favorite of Hera,[168] and he is often

7.8 Theseus visiting his stepmother, Amphitrite, under the sea; Athena mediates the encounter. A small triton supports Theseus while dolphins swim around him. Interior of an Attic red-figure cup, signed by Euphronios (the potter) and attributed to Onesimos (the painter). Dated to between 500 and 490 BCE (detail). Now in the Musée de Louvre inv. num. G104. Photo credit: Stéphane Maréchalle / Musée de Louvre / © RMN–Grand Palais / Art Resource NY.

portrayed as being helped by Aphrodite and Athena. On the column krater shown in Figure 7.9, Athena expresses delight, or perhaps even surprise, as Jason takes the Fleece away from the serpent who guards it.[169] We get an alternative story on an Athenian kylix from about 480 BCE, attributed to Douris, which shows Athena standing by while the dragon guarding the Fleece apparently disgorges Jason after swallowing him.[170] Are we to understand Athena as having

7.9 Jason snatches the Golden Fleece away from the dragon that guards it, while Athena and an unidentified man look on. The prow of the *Argo*, with its speaking figurehead, is to the far right. Attic red-figure column krater by the Orchard Painter, dating to between 470 and 460 BCE (detail). Now in the Metropolitan Museum of Art, New York. Purchased through the Harris Brisbane Dick Fund, inv. num. 1944.11.7. Photo credit: © The Metropolitan Museum of Art/Art Resource, NY.

caused the dragon to do this, and thus as rescuing a hero who had been swallowed alive?

Even this partial list of the divine help given to Greek heroes who set out to conquer monsters establishes it as a standard theme. Such alliances confirm that the Greek hero is special, of course—that he is a sort of junior partner of the gods. It is the hero, however, who does most of the grunt work: the physical fighting against the monster when necessary, the slogging across barren countrysides to find the monster in the first place, the plowing, the digging of ditches and other mundane labors[171] that enable him to complete the task. Typically, what the god contributes to these partnerships is a new technology or strategic insight, while staying away from anything that raises a sweat—the castanets or rattles that Athena gives to Heracles to ward off the Stymphalian Birds, the winged sandals given to Perscus and the magic bridle that Bellerophon receives from either Athena or Poseidon, for example.[172] The basic identity of the hero as *human*, then, is emphasized even as he is being set apart from other humans; he is elevated by the fact that he receives divine help to complete the task, but he does the heavy lifting. An amusing variation that underscores this point is the portrayal of Heracles holding up the sky on one of the metopes from the early fifth-century Temple of Zeus at Olympia: Heracles is bent over with strain, while in back of him, out of his sight, his sister Athena is casually carrying the bulk of the weight on one upraised hand (see metope 10 in Figure 7.4). We could choose to understand these incidents of divine help as merely metaphorical—just as some scholars choose to understand the Homeric formulation of a god breathing strength or courage into a warrior as metaphorical. But even if poetic statements of the gods' help were meant metaphorically (which I doubt), the expression of this idea through the vivid *presence* of gods, especially in artistic representations, insistently emphasizes this element in the hero's story.

We once again see the Greek hero, then, being pulled in different directions. Monster killing, by the very nature of its victims, required heroes to intrude upon the gods' world, but by the very nature of what was required to kill a monster and to accomplish some of their other labors, the heroes were once more confirmed as human beings who depended upon the gods. The fact that the heroes killed monsters on behalf of other mortals, whose lives and livelihoods the monsters threatened, emphasizes the human orientation of the heroes' deeds, too. Monsters and monster killing, then, mark a point of uneasy balance between heroes and gods, a juncture between human and divine through which heroes must negotiate a passage.

As we meet them in Greek myths, moreover, monsters are representatives not of a general chaos that had once, long ago, been inflicted on a nascent cosmos, but rather of the chaos that gods might always inflict upon mortals and against which mortals had to be continuously on guard. In the daily world of historical Greece, people did not expect to encounter new Hydras or Chimaeras or Gorgons, but they did fear the ever-present demonic forces that might bring illness, sterility, famine, and other evils. Many of these forces were personified into characters: Ephialtes (The Guy Who Leaps on You), who brought nightmares, for instance, and Mormo (The Frightening Woman), a bogey who attacked children. A few of them even became woven into the network of gods and heroes. Lamia, for example, whose name means something such as "The Gobbler," was both the generic term for a demon who killed infants and pregnant women and the name of a woman whom, according to myths, Zeus had once seduced and Hera had subsequently persecuted, driving Lamia into a maddened state in which she killed her children.[173] According to Stesichorus, Lamia's father was Poseidon and Scylla was her daughter.[174] In other words, Lamia became well entrenched within the mythic web of relationships. All of these demonic forces, whether or not they received formal narrative development, were combatted not only by gods to whom one might pray and pay cult, as in other ancient Mediterranean countries (thus, for instance, to combat Lamia and other demons who thwarted successful motherhood, one might pray to Artemis or Hera), but also, and most pronouncedly by *Heracles*, the greatest heroic conqueror of monsters in myths and the greatest protection from evil in daily life. His common cult title, "Alexikakos" (Averter of Evils), attests to this; the declaration that "Heracles Alexikakos dwells here!" was engraved above many a house door throughout Greek-speaking parts of the Mediterranean. Amulets against illness that survive from later antiquity frequently feature Heracles's image. He is invoked for help in a fragment of the Getty Hexameters that I discussed in Chapter 3 in a context that equates his victory over the Hydra with his ability to ward off all of the ills that Hexameters promise to avert.[175]

The End of Monsters—and of Heroes

It seems that by the time that the Trojan War took place, there were no more monsters left to kill, other than those that Odysseus claimed to have encountered while traveling through the outer limits of the world. The other monsters mentioned in the *Iliad* and the *Odyssey* had been dispatched by earlier generations of heroes by the time that the action of those poems took place: the Calydonian Boar had been conquered by Meleager and his friends, who predated the heroes of

the *Iliad* by a generation,[176] and the Chimaera had been killed by Bellerophon, who predated them by two generations.[177] When the shade
of Heracles met Odysseus in the Underworld, his labors were long
past; his quest to bring Cerberus to the upper world was just a
memory.[178] By the time of the war, those who would be called heroes
had nothing left to kill except one another, and the war provided excellent opportunities for them to display their skills in doing so.

Which brings me to the final topic in this chapter. According to
a story that we can put together with bits of information from the
scholia to the *Iliad* and Proclus's summary of the lost epic *Cypria*,
there came a time when Gaea felt burdened by the flourishing human
population. She demanded a solution, and Zeus and Themis decided
to goad humans (or, more specifically, the heroes) into killing each
other off. The result was the Theban War. Yet the resulting drop in
population proved to be insufficient, and so Gaea complained again.
Zeus was on the verge of using thunderbolts and floods to thin out
the ranks of humanity, but the god Momus (Blame) suggested that
he try another war, which, Momus explained, could easily be instigated if Zeus did two things: sire a beautiful daughter upon Leda and
give the goddess Thetis to a mortal in marriage.[179] Thus began the
Trojan War, which, according to a fragment of Hesiod's *Catalogue*,
enabled Zeus not only to decrease the population of humans in general but more specifically to destroy the race of *hemitheoi*—the "half
gods" or heroes.[180]

Walter Burkert may be right that the kernel of this story was borrowed from a line in the *Erra and Ishum*, a Mesopotamian tale that
dates back at least to the eighth century BCE. In it, Erra, the god of
war, is urged by his seven weapons to begin a new conflict. Erra subsequently claims that his reason for instigating the war was that
humans no longer respected him, but the weapons themselves provide two other reasons: first, that they themselves had become rusty
with disuse, and second, that humans had become too noisy for the
Anunnaki (a group of gods associated with the earth) to endure—a
reason that approximates Gaea's complaint.[181]

Mesopotamian influence of some kind does seem to lurk behind
the Greek idea of gods making a decision to destroy a significant portion of humanity, for we have not only the weapons' speech from

the *Erra and Ishum* but also several versions of a Mesopotamian story whereby the older gods complain that there are too many humans and plot to wipe them out—first by famine; then by drought and famine; then by plague; then by plague, drought, and famine all at the same time; and then finally by a flood. Each time, however, the god Ea (Enki) saves humanity by warning a human confederate (variously called Atrahasis or Utnapishtim or Ziusudra) and providing him with a plan to survive (much as Noah receives such a plan from Yahweh in the book of Genesis). Therefore, the human race is able to regenerate itself each time that the gods try to destroy it.[182] Scholars presume that these Mesopotamian stories were known by Greek poets and that they helped to inspire the Greek version of the Flood story. Thus, even if Burkert is right that the *Erra and Ishum* specifically spurred the Greek poets to craft a story whereby the human race was diminished by *war*, the poets are likely to have done so while having other choices in front of them—other ways by which gods could thin the ranks of humanity and bring the age of heroes to an end. We should look more closely, therefore, at the differences between the tale of Erra and the tale of Troy and what they may tell us about the Greek hero.

The *Erra and Ishum* focuses closely on Erra's decision to go to war, the attempts of his fellow god Ishum to moderate Erra's ferocity, and the capitulation to Erra's decision by Marduk, the king of the gods, who must ceremoniously leave his throne before the chaos of war can be unleashed. Of the war itself and its effect on humans, we hear almost nothing in this poem. In contrast, the *Iliad* emphasizes the individual talents and quirks of the warriors, their personal involvements with one another, their moments of glory on the battlefield, their losses, and their homecomings, successful or not. The same can be said of many of the other epics narrating the Trojan War, which we now possess only in fragments. Many of these works, as I commented earlier, gave the poets opportunities to focus on the human condition more generally—the inevitability of death, the personal choices that could ruin or save one's companions, the physical and emotional strains of war and its effects on the families of those who fought. The first lines of the *Iliad* and the *Odyssey* epitomize this:

Sing, Goddess, Achilles' rage,
Black and murderous, that cost the Greeks
Incalculable pain, pitched countless souls
Of heroes into Hades' dark,
And left their bodies to rot as feasts
For dogs and birds, as Zeus' will was done.
Begin with the clash between Agamemnon—
The Greek warlord—and godlike Achilles.

Speak, Memory, of the cunning hero,
The wanderer, blown off course time and again
After he plundered Troy's sacred heights.
Speak of all the cities he saw, the minds he grasped.
The suffering deep in his heart at sea
As he struggled to survive and bring his men home.
But he could not save them, hard as he tried—
The fools—destroyed by their own recklessness
When they ate the oxen of Hyperion the Sun,
And that god snuffed out their day of return.[183]

In each case, there are gods at work—what happened in the *Iliad* unfolds according to the will of Zeus, and in the *Odyssey*, Hyperion, and also Poseidon, wreak a terrible vengeance upon humans who offend them. Nonetheless, it is Achilles (and to a lesser degree, Agamemnon) who is responsible for the pains and deaths of the Greeks, it is human bodies that rot and are consumed by scavengers, and it is Odysseus who, in a very human way that no god ever shared, has to learn to understand how the minds of other people work and use that knowledge to save himself.

In choosing to end the age of heroes with a war, then, the poets who were responsible for the evolution of this story once again underscored the centrality of the hero—the remarkable human—within the mythic network that they were creating. There are plenty of gods on the Trojan stage as well, but their actions are significant primarily apropos the humans. As deviously enchanting as Hera's deception of Zeus may be in *Iliad* 14—and as much as it "shows divinity in a naturalistic, cosmic setting which is not otherwise a feature of

Homeric anthropomorphism," as Burkert suggests[184]—the scene makes sense within the poem as a whole only insofar as Zeus's post-coital slumber provides an opportunity for Ajax to knock Hector to the ground with a huge rock, which enables the Greeks to trounce the Trojans. Hera's machinations, divinely charming though they may be, underscore the fascination that a *human* conflict could exert over the gods. However much those gods pursued their selfish aims in Greek myths, the myths, which were narrated by humans for human audiences, returned time after time to the ramifications that those divine pursuits had on the humans of earlier generations—the heroes.

Epilogue

GREEK MYTHS—precisely as they were created by the ancient poetic narratives that we still admire today for their beauty and force—were central elements in the formation of the Greeks' belief in their gods and heroes. Understanding this should alter not only the way in which we study the myths themselves but also the way in which we reconstruct and understand Greek religion more generally. The study of rituals (that is, what one "does" in religion, as opposed to what one "thinks" or "feels") should no longer dominate the field as it did in the twentieth century; we must begin to give appropriate weight to the important work that the myths themselves did and strive to understand it better.

To do so, we need to approach these myths not only with the tools of philology, literary criticism, and cultural studies that we have always used, but also with the tools that narratologists, folklorists, sociologists, psychologists, and cognitive scientists have developed to understand how modern narratives—as found in novels, films, television shows, and other cultural forms—affect audience members' cognition, emotions, ethics, and beliefs. Recently, the ability to tell stories has itself been identified as one of humanity's most important evolutionary advantages: stories enable us to imagine situations that we have not experienced and to play through the ways in which we might react if confronted by those situations ourselves one day.

As such, stories are a particularly important means of creating and sustaining *religious* beliefs—beliefs in entities that we cannot access through ordinary means. The Greek gods and heroes are excellent figures against which to test this idea because we possess a rich trove of narratives—of myths, that is—about them. Most of these myths are about what happened when gods and mortals interacted. As such, they served not only to expand and intensify ideas of who the gods and heroes were but also to limn the possible effects that the divine world could have upon the mortal world. Myths did this more memorably, and therefore more effectively, than any set of doctrines or dogmas ever could.

In borrowing tools from scholars of modern narratives to better understand how Greek myths did these things, I selected those that engage with aspects of human cognition and emotion that are unlikely to vary from time to time or place to place. Thus, for example, the tendency to continue pondering an intriguing experience after it is over would seem to be intrinsic to humans (and, indeed, perhaps also to other higher primates). Therefore, I assumed that what narratologists had concluded about the effects of modern episodic narration—that it causes an audience to think about the story's characters in between episodes and to bond with them more deeply than they would if the story had been narrated in one fell swoop—would also be true for episodic narration in antiquity.

I also chose to use, with one exception, methodologies that focus primarily on those cultural forms that Dorothy Noyes, in her model as I presented it in Chapter 1, includes in her first category: forms that are deliberately sought out by, and retain the focused attention of, their audiences. Noyes characterizes these forms as having maximal internal coherence, maximal salience, and maximal indexical connections to their audience, and as being produced with the assumption that they will be evaluated for their potency of effect and skillful execution. Given that the Greek myths that come down to us are the highly polished products of professional poets, which were intended to be performed by experienced choruses or actors, they match these criteria closely. Therefore I assumed, as I looked for methodologies to borrow, that by and large, what makes first-category forms successful in our own time and place would have worked in Greece, as well, mutatis mutandis. My one exception was the use I made of what folklorists have discovered about the techniques that people use when telling memorates, a narrative form that I suspect belongs in Noyes's fourth category (that is, unsought experiences that nonetheless demand focused attention). As I briefly showed, however, successful authors of modern *literary* tales about the supernatural (which belong in Noyes's first category) often choose to adopt the narrative techniques used in memorates. Therefore, it did not seem to me to be a stretch to look for those techniques within ancient literary tales about the gods and heroes, as well.

Other than the two guidelines I have just sketched, I set no limits for myself as I borrowed my methodological tools. For the past ten years or so I have read widely in fields that seemed likely to produce results, picked out approaches that seemed useful and then tested them against ancient materials. I clove to no particular school of theory, but was sometimes surprised and delighted to discover that different scholars whose work I liked—scholars who were, sometimes, from very different fields—had a tendency to know and admire one another. This gave me confidence that the cumulative approach I was slowly building was not just the product of my own perceptions.

As I step back now from my work, I know that I leave some issues open. One is the question of to what degree it makes a difference for a narrator to be aware of the cognitive and emotional effects that his or her narrative will have. Or in other words: do the techniques that I have discussed in this book work better when there is a driver at the wheel?

I suspect that the answer to this depends on the technique. Joshua Landy's formative fictions, which I discussed in Chapter 3, would work even if an individual narrator weren't conscious that he or she was wielding this tool (long-standing modes of narration that had been noticed to have desirable effects could be adopted by new narrators who knew that they were successful but did not know, or care, why). Yet, as in Landy's case of Jean Eugène Robert-Houdin, for instance, a narrator who aims for a specific effect and knows that certain techniques will achieve it is likelier to have a higher degree of success. Tanya Luhrmann's Vineyard Christians are another excellent example of this. That said, however, narrators do not always purposefully aim for all the effects they end up achieving. William Peter Blatty did not set out to make more Americans believe in demons when he wrote *The Exorcist*, yet the book and the movie that followed it accomplished just that, at least temporarily.

Greek narrators of the archaic or classical period did not set out to induce *belief*. Their job was to tell engaging stories, which often carried institutional or personal agendas, as well. Sometimes, the agenda was to attract people to a *particular* cult of a *particular* god or hero—but the poets were not evangelizing the very existence of those gods and heroes. If they consciously wielded the tools that I have described as being conducive to belief, then, they did so primarily with other goals in mind.

Other phenomena that I discussed, such as parasocial relationships (Chapter 3) and plurimediality and accretive characters (Chapter 5), are by their very nature impossible to wield deliberately; they develop under circumstances that cannot be controlled by a single individual or group of individuals. In still other cases, such as that of constructing a story world (Chapter 4), I have argued that there is a difference between modern narrators and ancient narrators. Modern narrators who set out to create a story world typically do so from scratch, and therefore must make deliberate, calculated choices; ancient narrators, in contrast, reacted to and helped to develop a story world that was already well established by the time it began to leave a record for us to consider. In either case, certain effects of a well-wrought story world will work (for instance, crossovers and hyperseriality), but the perceived connection between that story world and the real, "historical" world will be different.

The other major issue that I leave open is that of specific application. Each time that I introduced a technique or phenomenon, I gave enough examples of how it worked in ancient narratives, I hope, to persuade my readers that I was on to something, but I have by not exhausted the possible texts against which my proposals can be tested and weighed. I look forward to seeing other scholars try their hands.

In Chapters 6 and 7, I explored two subjects that I suggest are distinctively characteristic of Greek myths, metamorphosis and heroes, and used them as opportunities to extend some of the methodological arguments I made earlier in the book. In Chapter 6, I suggested that the primary purpose of narrating stories about marvelous creatures and events was to sustain belief in the gods and heroes. I also noted that ancient Greek narratives of the marvelous, like those of some other cultures, including our own, provide an opportunity to articulate the negative side of divinity, which is avoided in more formal liturgical contexts such as prayers. In Chapter 7, I returned to the topic of episodic narration that I introduced in Chapter 3 and proposed that myths about heroes partook of two different kinds of episodic narration, the series and the serial. This had the effect of sharpening the inherent contradiction of the Greek hero. Like a god, the hero could be suspended in time and his adventures could be multiplied infinitely, unfolding like the separate episodes of a series. But like other mortals, the hero lived a life that was known to have a beginning and an inevitable end, as in a serial. This hero was peculiarly *Greek* in this and other ways that I discussed that set his myths (and, correspondingly, his cult) apart from almost anything we find in the Near Eastern cultures whose myths otherwise influenced those of Greece so significantly.

Whatever else I have accomplished in this book, I hope that I have stimulated further conversations about how religious beliefs not only in ancient Greece but also in other cultures are created and sustained by the consumption of engaging narratives. Until now, the two groups of people who have the best potential to shed light on this topic—the social scientists and psychologists who have studied the construction of belief, on the one hand, and the humanists who have studied the particular ways in which narratives affect audiences, on the other hand—have interacted with one another very little. There has been almost no interaction, moreover, between that second group and the scholars who study religions. Here I have tried to integrate ideas from each of these fields. Whether or not my readers agree with my particular conclusions, I hope that I have motivated them to try to do the same.

Notes

1 THE STORY OF MYTH

1. Burkert 1979: 23.
2. Csapo 2005: 9. Csapo draws on Bascom 1965.
3. Lincoln 1999: xii.
4. Mills 1990: 28–29.
5. I take some of my observations about Sleeping Beauty from Tatar 2002: 95–104.
6. The rape interpretation that I offer here draws on comments made by *Maleficent* star Angelina Jolie, as quoted in Holmes 2014. The quotation is taken from Shapiro 2014 (and was widely reposted on the web).
7. It is only in Walt Disney's 1959 animated movie version (*Sleeping Beauty*) and the 2014 reworking of it (*Maleficent*) that all of the characters are given personal names. Some earlier versions bestowed a personal name on the main character—e.g., Giambattista Basile's *Sole, lune e Talia* (1934), in which she is named Talia.
8. *Od.* 12.69–72.
9. I borrow the term from social and cultural anthropologists, who use it as a concise way of referring to a variety of nonhuman entities whose presence is not always detectable.
10. As stated, for instance, in a conversation between George Lucas and Bill Moyers (Moyers & Company 1999).
11. *Od.* 4.214; *Od.* 19.502.
12. Pl. *R.* 377a3–d6.
13. For more on this large topic, see Morgan 2000; Buxton 1999b; P. Murray 1999; Rowe 1999.
14. Most famously, probably, Pi. *O.* 1.28–29.
15. Further, see Fowler 2016; Calame 2015: 23–62; Csapo 2005: 10–30; Lincoln 1999: 51–75; Most 1999; Graf 1993: 9–34.
16. Claude Calame has several times fought the battle against looking for an absolute description of myth: most recently, Calame 2015: 17–19 and 403–414, but also, for example, the "Avant-Propos II" of the second edition of his *Mythe et histoire dans l'Antiquité grecque* (Calame 2011b). See also the review of recent books on Greek myths by Philippe Matthey (2016), which summarizes the state of the question.
17. See Graf and Johnston 2013: 66–93; Johnston 1999: 161–199.

18. I have chosen to limit myself to these periods because the ways in which myths were narrated changed significantly after approximately 300 BCE. Most importantly for my purposes, there was far less creative reshaping of myths by authors, as N. J. Lowe has observed (2000: 97–99).

19. Burkert 1979: 23–24.

20. Hansen 2017 takes as its quest the side-by-side assembling of a great many stories from a wide variety of these genres, which are divided up and discussed according to their topics (for example, '"Kings and Princesses"). Precisely as such, the book demonstrates my point nicely. See also Buxton 1994, esp. 40–44.

21. E.g., Pl. *R.* 2.381d1–e6 and *Lg.* 10.887c5–e1.

22. *Od.* 23.301–341. Odysseus, not surprisingly, seems to have done the lion's share of the talking, although Atwood 2005 begins to make up for this.

23. I say "almost" because recent observations suggest that some of the higher primates can engage in sustained periods of what we would call make-believe, carrying around a log as if it were a baby, for example (Jolly 1999: 290–292).

24. In my formulation here, I rely particularly on Harari 2015: 31–37; Sjöblom 2011; and Boyd 2009, esp. 1–16 and 191–196.

25. Cf. O'Flaherty 1988: 27–28.

26. D.S. 5.4.7.

27. Noyes 2016: 127–178.

28. Noyes 2016: 141–148 for the basic description of the categories; for the quotation, 141.

29. I borrow the image from the literary critic Alessandro Portelli (1997).

30. I am thinking here of the fact that King Demetrius of Macedon had a mistress named Lamia—a name she shared with a monster who was reputed to steal and eat infants and to seduce men, and sometimes to eat them, too (on the monster, see Johnston 1999: 173–179). The relationship was parodied by Alciphron in his "Letter from Lamia to Demetrius" (4.16) and mentioned by several other ancient authors, e.g., Plut. *Dem.* 27; Ath. 101e, 128b, 253a and (most interestingly) 577d–f.

31. Noyes 2016: 144.

32. The only extant example is A. *Pers.*, but we know that Phrynichus wrote a *Sack of Miletus* (notably, it met with public disapproval). Phrynichus also wrote a *Phoenician Women*, set at the court of Xerxes. There was probably a tragedy treating the near death of Croesus on the pyre, and there are fragments of a few more historical plays, as well. See Edith Hall (1996: 7–10), who rightly points out that although the Greeks distinguished between what we would call a "mythic" age and a "historical age," they felt that certain events (such as the battle of Salamis) were of a highly significant nature that raised their importance near to those of the mythic age. Events connected with the Persian Wars, she notes, were particularly likely to be included in that category.

33. *Od.* 19.570–575; A. *Ag.* 611–612.

34. Pi. *O.* 1.23–89 and *P.* 9. Cf. Medea's appearance as a surprisingly Pythia-like figure in *P.* 4, and see O'Higgins 1997.

35. Bacch. 17. There is debate about how much of this story was new at the time that Bacchylides narrated it. We have no earlier textual evidence for Theseus jumping into the sea. A vase painting showing Theseus amongst undersea divinities (the Onesimos cup—see Figure 7.8 and further at Gantz 1993: 263–264) dates to between 490 and 500 BCE, which has encouraged some scholars (e.g., Maehler 1997: 170) to date the ode to the early 490s and make the entire leap into the sea Bacchylides's invention, on the assumption that artists are likelier to illustrate an existing story than to create a new one. Other scholars argue, on the basis of possible political allusions in the poem, that Bacchylides's ode dates to the 470s (e.g., Fearn 2007: 242–244), which would make Onesimos's painting, and probably also some now-lost textual narration of the story, earlier than Bacchylides's treatment. Even when accepting the later date, however, most scholars agree that the detail of Theseus retrieving Minos's ring was Bacchylides's own invention. See Pavlou 2012 for a recent discussion, with summary and references to previous discussions.

36. Cf. N. J. Lowe (2000: x–xi), who notes that the "Classical" plot (i.e., that endorsed by Aristotle, as found in epic and tragedy) became the "classical plot" (i.e., the one still used frequently in storytelling today, even if, at times, through media that Aristotle never dreamt of).

37. Hufford 1982. Or as the classicist and folklorist Andrew Lang put it nearly a century earlier than Hufford, modern people have been habituated to hastily offer "a very mixed theory in which rats, indigestion, dreams, and of late, hypnotism, are mingled much at random," in order to dismiss those who claim they have experienced something outside of the ordinary (Lang 1894; the quotation is taken from chapter 6, "Cock Lane and Common-Sense").

38. Calame 2015: 493–503.

39. Schaeffer 1999: 327–335. See also an interview with Schaeffer about his book by Alexandre Prstojevic (2017) in *Vox-Poetica*.

40. "Hogwarts Extreme puts you in the world of Harry Potter. From the Common Room to Diagon Alley: interact and role-play. Win the Quidditch World Cup, engage in the wizard economy, take classes, and more! Your Hogwarts letter has arrived. Enroll now. The Sorting Hat awaits" (HEXRPG, LLC 2017).

41. Let us not forget, either, that even historians used such techniques: Thucydides (1.22) tells us that telling a true story sometimes requires the narrator to provide details and dialogue that would otherwise be missing, if the story is to be convincing.

42. Landy 2012.

43. Luhrmann 2012.

44. E.g., Giles 2010.

45. E.g., Saler 2012.

46. Tolkien 1947.

47. Bettini 2013.

48. Scheid and Svenbro 1996.

2 RITUAL'S HANDMAID

1. E.g., Harrison (1924) 1963: ix, as cited by Csapo 2005: 157. See also Harrison (1912) 1927, e.g., 16, 327.

2. He was also a minister of the Free Church of Scotland, which had once defrocked him on charges of heresy: Beidelman and Segal 2005.

3. Later published as *Lectures on the Religion of the Semites* (1889).

4. W. Smith 1889: 18, as quoted in Segal 1998: 2.

5. First published in two volumes in 1890, then in three in 1900, and finally in twelve in 1911–1915.

6. Frazer 1921: appendix 13 (quotation from 404); cf. Csapo 2005: 57–67. Interestingly, in spite of Frazer's declared intention to simply provide parallels to demonstrate the diffusion of this myth, he seems to have taken great relish in narrating each of the stories in vivid detail. Something deep in his soul seems to have cried out for a well-told tale.

7. See R. Parker 2007 for an excellent analysis of Murray's work on this topic and its entanglements with that of Harrison. I take the quotations from Parker (95), who cites Murray 1925: 72–78.

8. On the glamour of Harrison, see Beard 2002, esp. 37–84.

9. This was first used as a term, as far as I can tell, at Harrison (1912) 1927: 225.

10. Harrison (1912) 1927: 1–74; cf. Csapo 1995: 146–149.

11. Frazer 1901 (*non vidi*). Frazer is cited by Harrison (1912) 1927: 18.

12. Harrison (1912) 1927: 18.

13. E.g., Furley and Bremer 2001: 1.65–75; Perlman 1995.

14. Murray (1912) 1927.

15. Harrison and Verrall 1890: iii; cf. page xxxiii.

16. Harrison (1912) 1927: 16, 330; cf. Harrison 1921: 27.

17. Harrison (1912) 1927: 16 (shifting, manifold); Harrison and Verrall 1890: xxxiii (unsatisfactory, absurd).

18. On Nietzsche and Harrison, see further Csapo 1995: 145–146; Peacock 1991: 170–171. A crucial passage is Harrison (1912) 1927: viii.

19. The phrase is taken from the title of the fifth chapter of Harrison (1903) 1922: 163.

20. This is the general course taken in Harrison (1903) 1922 and to a great extent also in Harrison (1912) 1927.

21. Harrison (1925) 1965: 344.

22. Harrison moved in the same social circle as the Stokers, sharing the stage with Mrs. Stoker one evening for an amateur production of *The Tale of Troy* (Beard 2002: 39–40).

23. Ackerman 1991: 11–12, 15; and, on Murray, Lowe 2007.

24. Kripal 2010: 36–91; Ackerman 1991: 12.

25. Magliocco 2004: 40–43; Hutton 1999: 122–127.

26. Beard 2002: 135–136.

27. Harrison (1924) 1963: xviii.

28. Harrison (1924) 1963: 144. Or yet again: "[The Greeks] could not tolerate the Gorgon form of the Earth-Mother. It was the mission of the Greek artist and the Greek poet to cleanse religion from fear" (71).

29. The heyday of the approach lay between 1890, when the first edition of *The Golden Bough* appeared, and 1912, when Harrison's *Themis* appeared. In 1921, Harrison published her short (forty-one pages) *Epilegomena to the Study of Greek Religion*, in which she touched on the issue of myth and ritual again in passing, but she focused there primarily on applying the comparative approach and the Durkheimian concept of collective group emotion to interpreting ancient Greek religion. In 1913, *Greek Divination: A Study of Its Methods and Principles* was published by W. R. Halliday—formally a student of Gilbert Murray and L. R. Farnell at Oxford but closely mentored by Harrison as well, as he makes clear in the preface to this book. Halliday embraced ideas that were dear to the Cambridge Ritualists' hearts, most notably that there was an inner core of primitivity in Greek religion, that Greek religion could therefore be elucidated through cross-cultural comparisons to contemporary primitive religions and that the figure of the sacred king was central to Greek religious thought and social practice (more at Johnston 2008: 18–19). One of the few acknowledgments of the book's appearance was an anonymous review in a 1913 issue of the *Journal of Hellenic Studies*, which praises Halliday for using "comparative spectacles" and knowledge of "primitive cultures" to understand the Greeks and for looking for the "pre-Olympian element" in Greek religion. In other words, the reviewer valued Halliday's work precisely because it had taken up the Ritualists' banner. Another figure who was to loom very large in the study of Greek religion, the Swede Martin P. Nilsson, wrote on the historical origins of Greek myths early in his career (in the course of which he rejected the comparative approach as outdated: Nilsson 1932: 10–11) and in the maturity of his career, placed ritual so firmly at the center of ancient Greek religion, and myths so firmly at its margins, as to perform what now seems like an impossible feat: he managed to write his two-volume, 1,573-page *Geschichte der griechischen Religion* almost without mentioning myths at all (Nilsson [1950] 1961 and [1941] 1967).

30. On Hooke, see also Harrelson 2005: 6380–6381; Segal 1998a: 5–7; Segal 1998b: 83–84 (editor's introduction to the reprinted introduction of Hooke's book). *Myth and Ritual* was the first of what became a trilogy of edited volumes on the topic: see also Hooke 1958, 1935.

31. Hooke 1933b. Hooke eschewed, however, any specific connection with Frazer and his ideas, particularly the idea that a myth might be invented independently by different cultures: Segal 1998a: 6–7.

32. Hyman 1955; further in Segal 1998b: 231 (the editor's introduction to Hyman's reprinted article); Weston (1920) 1993; Murray 1914. Fascinating information about the development of Hyman's adherence to the ritualist approach can be found throughout Franklin 2016—a biography of Hyman's wife, the novelist Shirley Jackson (who was herself deeply interested in the ritualist approach); see especially 338–341 but also 179–180 and 292–296.

33. Kluckhohn 1942: 68.

34. Leach 1954: 13. Further on anthropologists' acceptance of the approach at Versnel 1993: 37–41.

35. Fontenrose 1959: 3.

36. Fontenrose 1959: 461.

37. Hyman 1960: 127.

38. Fontenrose 1961: 125.

39. Fontenrose 1961: 124.

40. Fontenrose 1966: 59.

41. Kirk 1974: 68.

42. Kirk 1974: 229–230.

43. Kirk 1974: 231.

44. Kirk 1974: 234.

45. Kirk 1974: 241.

46. Kirk 1974: 252, 246–247.

47. Kirk 1974: 235.

48. Better than Pindar had, for example, when narrating the story of Neoptolemus in Delphi at *N.* 7 and *Pa.* 6.

49. Particularly important in this regard is Burkert (1966) 2001.

50. See, e.g., Burkert 1979, especially 26–29 and 56–58.

51. On Burkert, see also Csapo 2005: 161–180; Versnel 1993: 51–60.

52. I think here particularly of Burkert 1983: 1–82 (first published in German in 1972); and Burkert 1979: 35–58.

53. Gernet 1981; Brelich 1969; Jeanmarie 1939; Lorenz 1963.

54. Graf 2003.

55. Burkert 1983: 130–134, 168–179; Burkert 1979: 123–142.

56. Burkert (1966) 2001: 50 (emphasis added).

57. E.g., Graf 2000; Leitao 1995; Bremmer 1978.

58. Propp (1928) 1958. Burkert also draws on Dundes 1964.

59. Burkert 1979: 6–18.

60. Burkert 1979: 23 (emphasis added).

61. Heracles, for example, may have begun as one instance of a broader type that scholars call the "master of animals"—this may be the "original" reason that he fights with and defeats the Nemean Lion and numerous other beasts—but when he was subsequently drafted into being the ancestor of the Dorian kings, his victory over a lion (which was considered the most valiant and noble of animals), and his habit of wearing that lion's skin gained a new resonance (Burkert 1979: 78–98).

62. Versnel 1993: 15–89.

63. Versnel 1993: 15–88; the quotation is from 87.

64. See particularly Lévi-Strauss 1958: 233–236; cf. Csapo 2005: 219–237.

65. Vernant 1974: 177–194 (=Vernant 1980: 55–77).

66. Detienne 1979: 7.

67. Detienne 1979: 5–6. In setting this Straussian course, he was also reacting to something that Geoffrey Kirk had said a few years previously. Kirk had claimed that Greek myths as we knew them were defective, because they represented reworkings—sometimes many times over—of whatever the "original" myth had been. In other words, Kirk, like many earlier scholars, ardently desired to find the "real" myth buried beneath narrative elaboration, even if he was less sanguine than they had been about succeeding.

68. A colloquium organized by Richard Buxton at the University of Bristol in 1996 marked a culmination; many of the scholars who participated argued

that, for the particular author, genre, or period they had chosen to treat, there simply was no easy way of dividing Greek "mythic" thinking from Greek "rationality" and therefore no way of defining what a Greek myth was (published as Buxton 1998a). See also Calame 1995; Graf 1995.

69. E.g., Johnston 2002; Graf 1997; Dowden 1989. See also Bremmer 2005.

70. Calame 2003: 27.

71. See also Calame 1991.

72. See particularly Calame 2003: 29: "Only by abstraction, by bracketing of the ritual situations in which they are represented, by exclusion of the poetic forms that are the medium of their communication, is one able to constitute a myth of Oedipus or a legend of the Atreidae." See also Calame 2009, the translation of a French book published in 2000. The French version has recently been revised and expanded as Calame 2015. Where possible, I refer in this book to the 2009 English translation, referring to the 2015 French revision only when it presents new material.

73. Johnston 2002.

74. Lloyd-Jones 1985.

75. Bacch. 16.

76. Pi. *Pa.* 8, Aristonous's paean to Apollo (Käppel 1992: no. 42), Athenaeus's paean to Apollo (Käppel 1992: 387–391), and *HHAp.* 514–419. Generally on paeans, see Furley and Bremer 2001: 1.76–102; Rutherford 2001.

77. Pi. *Pa.* 12.

78. As in *HHHerm.* and Alcaeus's *Hymn to Hermes*. The Homeric *Hymn to Demeter* is a notable exception to this rule, providing as it apparently does the *aitia* for several rituals performed during the Mysteries and / or the Thesmophoria.

79. Nilsson (1941) 1967: 548.

80. Furley and Bremer 2001: 1.99–102.

81. Rutherford 2001: 312–315.

82. Bacch. 5; Pi. *O.* 2 and *O.* 3; *HHAp.* 207–215.

83. Looms: E. *Ion* 190–200. Symposia: this is the setting of Call. *Aet.* frs. 43 and 178 (and see Harder's commentary ad loc.).

84. Isoc. *Paneg.* 4.27–31.

85. There is debate as to whether we can trust Euripides to be transmitting correct aitiologies or even correct information about the rituals. See L. Parker's comments on the *aitia* in the *Iphigenia in Tauris* (Parker 2016: 346–347), and also Seaford 2009 and Scullion 1999. My opinion is that the audiences of Euripides's tragedies would have been used to hearing more than one *aition* for a given ritual and would not have been shocked by Euripides's presenting a different one from those they already knew. See also Christine Hamilton (2017), who fruitfully adopts a similar approach. In any case, for my immediate purposes, the answers to these questions do not matter much; the point is that *aitia* were transmitted by Euripides and other tragedians.

86. Hellanicus: *FGrH* 4F*38; Androtion: *FGrH* 324F16.

87. Call. *Aet.* fr. 43b–c Harder.

3 NARRATING MYTHS

1. O'Flaherty 1988: 26 (this scholar now uses the name "Doniger"). On "mythological zombies," see 26 and more generally chaps. 2 and 3.

2. The neologism *historiola* was coined by scholars of folklore, from whom it was adopted by scholars of ancient magic: Maas 1942: 37, 37n22; Heim 1892–1893: 495 with notes.

3. Further on mythic names, see Johnston 2013 and Chapter 5 of the present book.

4. Taken from P. British Museum 10059 [37]; Borghouts 1978: 24–25, no. 34, slightly modified.

5. I adopt the term "paradigm" from Frankfurter 2001; cf. Frankfurter 2009.

6. Pócs 2009: 29, from a Romanian example that is still in use today.

7. A large number of European *historiolae* from a range of periods can be found in the essays contained in Roper 2009 and 2004a.

8. For example, the spell including the *historiola* involving Isis and Nephthys, cited in note 4, further specifies that the milk must be that of a woman who has borne a male child (as Isis bore Horus) and that the milk must be mixed with resin from an acacia, dough made of barley, and other materials, over which the *historiola* itself has been recited. Once completed, the mixture must be applied with a leaf of the ricinus plant. Another *historiola* from Borghouts's collection, to be used against headache, specifies that it must be recited "over the buds of a Unique Bush. To be twisted leftwise, to be soaked in mucus, and the bud of the *snb*-plants laced to it. To be fitted with 7 knots and to be applied to a man's throat" (Borghouts 1978: 30–31, no. 43). A third example, to protect a house against snakes, other reptiles, and spirits of the dead, specifies that the words must be spoken over garlic that has been ground and pulverized with beer; the house must be sprinkled with this mixture in the night, before daybreak (Borghouts 1978: 82–83, no. 121). *PGM* VI.1–47, a divinatory spell that uses laurel, tells about how Apollo first discovered the divinatory properties of the plant; it also specifies the date, moon phase, and time of day when the spell is to be spoken. Further on felicity conditions, see Roper 2004b: 2.

9. Excerpted from *PGM* IV.94–153, a love spell in a fourth-century CE Greco-Egyptian magical papyrus.

10. Excerpted from Davies 2004: 98, from a manuscript belonging to a French bonesetter, dating to about 1900.

11. I find it impossible to come up with a really satisfying alternative to the word "realm"; most of the words we might be tempted to substitute, such as "sphere," evoke place at least as strongly as does "realm." "Mythic *mode*," perhaps?

12. There are a few exceptions, although most of these cannot be called completely "Greek" and are substantially later in date than the period on which I am focusing in this book. In addition to the Getty Hexameters that I will discuss in this section, they include the Philinna Papyrus (P. Berol. 7504 plus P. Amherst II col. ii (A), which dates to the first century BCE and narrates a *historiola* of Egyptian origin in the Greek language (Ritner 1998; cf. Faraone

2001, 1995); and a few *historiolae* found in the late antique Greek magical papyri, which were found in Egypt. These owe a great deal to Egyptian models and are almost always populated by Egyptian gods—except for *PGM* VI.1–47, a divinatory spell that tells of how Apollo first tasted the divinatory laurel.

13. The tablet from Himera that shares three lines with col. II Side A (Bernabé 2013: 82, F) is dated to the early fifth century, and two other tablets from Selinus itself (Bernabé 2013: 82, G and H) that share phrases with the Getty text are dated to the fifth century as well. Janko 2013 posits that the Getty tablet copies an earlier archetype and suggests that at least some of the material may be as early as the late sixth century.

14. A fuller, although differently oriented, version of my arguments here can be found in Johnston 2013. See also Caliva 2016; Waller 2015.

15. Translation from Faraone and Obbink 2013: 12, slightly altered.

16. Johnston 2013: 133–138.

17. Some examples are Gold Tablets 3, 5, 26a and 26b G&J; Ov. *Met.* 1.111; Verg. *G.* 1.132; Lucian *True History* 2.3, 2.13, 2.26; Hippocr. *De morbis mulierum* 1.120 and Dioscorides *De Materia Medica* 5.99. See further at Johnston 2013: 139–144; cf. Graf 1980.

18. Lakoff and Johnson 1980; the example "Love is a journey" is first introduced on 44.

19. Richard Janko (2013: 34) suggests that it means a tomb or chthonic shrine (i.e., a place like those where *defixiones* were deposited). It may also be poetic language for some kind of carved vessel or box into which the inscription should be placed.

20. Nor would it have worked well, in this case, for a festival, ritual or sacred place to have more than one *aition*, as with, for instance, the origin of the Delphic Oracle (Johnston 2008: 38–60). The myths of the Proetides, which were associated with the festival of the Agriania or Agrionia and with offerings of hair at the tomb of the maiden Iphinoë, offer another example. According to some of them the girls offended Hera and according to others they offended Dionysus; in some stories they were cured by Melampus, and in others they were cured by waters sacred to Artemis. Even if Ken Dowden (1989: 71–96) is correct to stress that an "initiatory" pattern underlies all of these myths, the fact remains that there was apparently no problem, in the opinion of the Greeks, with changing the story considerably. See also Fowler 2013: 169–178; Johnston 1999: 66–70; Gantz 1993: 311; Seaford 1988.

21. Calame 2009: 98–99.

22. Calame 2011b; Calame 2009: esp. 53–93, 98–99, 116–118; Calame 2003: 29–34, 86. Specifically on melic poetry: Calame 2009: 98–99.

23. Johnston 1995; Braswell 1988: 359–361. It's not clear whether Damophilus's plea for return was granted; if it was, it may have been granted before Pindar's performance, which then would have been an elaborately staged opportunity for Arcesilas to demonstrate his generosity—a different purpose but pragmatic nonetheless.

24. *Il.* 24.599–627.

25. It is possible to imagine that, if we are correct in assuming that the story of Demeter and Persephone was narrated or performed at the Eleusinian mys-

teries, and if the episode in which Demeter drinks a *kykeon* or in which Iambe makes her laugh were narrated / performed at the same moment as the initiates experienced their own version of such an event, the myth may have been understood to (further) empower the ritual action. But this depends on a great deal of speculation, and in any case, the other instances in which we can imagine something like this happening are very few in number and are all (so far as I can see) associated with mystery cults, which may have developed the use of myths in new directions for their own purposes.

26. Calame 2011a; Calame 2011b; Calame 2009: 63.

27. Bacch. 17. It's worth noting that there are also instances in which we witness the failure of a narrative that was intended to effect change. In *Iliad* 9.529–655, Phoenix tells a myth about Meleager in order to persuade Achilles to return to battle, but Achilles continues to sulk in his tent.

28. Antiphanes fr. 189. I thank Heinz-Günther Nesselrath for pointing me towards this passage.

29. On the *Erechtheus*, see Calame 2011a. On *Pythian* 4, see Calame 2003: 35–66; Felson 1999; cf. Felson 2004b.

30. Krummen 1990: 33–95.

31. On *deixis* in general, see *Arethusa* 37, no. 2 (2004), a special issue edited by Nancy Felson, and particularly for the purposes of *deixis* that I emphasize them here, the articles by Athanassaki, Calame, Felson, and Martin.

32. Athanassaki 2004: 330.

33. Calame 2011a.

34. Calame 2003: 2, 68–74; Greimas 1983.

35. Pi. *I.* 4.12 (Pillars of Heracles in the west), 52 (Antaeus's home in the west) and cf. *zophos* in line 18, a word meaning "dark" but cognate with *zephyros*, "west."

36. Calame 2003: 43–66; cf. Athanassaki 2004; Felson 2004b, 1999; Martin 2004.

37. Pi. *N.* 5.46; and cf. Pi. *P.* 9.91.

38. Calame (2009: 116–117 and cf. 98) does suggest that, in the case of epinicians, the pragmatic force of mythic narratives was so powerful as to make them into performative utterances: that is, as the myth within an epinician was narrated, the audience began to perceive the victor differently, which simultaneously changed his status within the community at that very moment. This stretches the concept of "performative utterance" further than I am comfortable with, however.

39. Landy 2012. Of course, we might consider a work of fiction to be both "formative" and "informative" (*pace* Landy, who thinks that fiction can never be truly informative in the sense of changing minds in more than the simplest ways).

40. Brakke 1999.

41. Cf. the example offered by William Doty (2000: 51–52) of the use made of proverbs by the Lele, a Bantu people of East Zaire: adult males who have learned thousands of traditional proverbs during their initiation period as youths view the entire universe through the proverbs' cumulative lens.

42. Landy 2012: 10.

43. Barkun 2013: 29–33; Kripal 2011: 2; Partridge 2004: chap. 6, esp. 119, 124–138. Or as Graham Harvey (2000) says, "Fantasy does not necessarily misdirect people away from consciousness raising, it need not be an opiate, but can be the much-needed catalyst for change." Cf. also Clark 2003.

44. Cf., too, the remarks of E. M. Forster: "People in a novel can be understood completely by the reader, if the novelist wishes, their inner as well as their outer life can be exposed. And this is why they seem more definite than characters in history, or even our friends" (Forster [1927] 1985: 57, as cited by Eder, Jannidis, and Schneider 2010: 53). Cf. Hoorn and Konijn 2003: 253–255.

45. As Wendy Doniger [O'Flaherty] (1988: 27–28) notes.

46. Cuneo 2001: 27–28, 127. Cf. Christopher Partridge (2004: 119–141), who demonstrates that popular culture (films, television shows, novels) is a "key sacralizing factor" that plays a highly influential role in shaping spiritual and religious beliefs, "contributing to a sense of what the real world is all about" (119).

47. Cf. Arist. *Poetics* 9 (1451a37–1451a38) and 24–25 (1460a12–1461b25); Phelan 2017: 32–36.

48. Luhrmann 2012.

49. Luhrmann 2012: 189–226; the quotation is from 221. For the study, see 202–215.

50. Luhrmann 2012: 48, 74–86.

51. Biblical metaphors of God as a lion include Hosea 5.14 and Rev. 5.5. On Evangelical fiction reading, see Luhrmann 2013c; and Luhrmann 2012: 83, 73–74, 129–131; cf. Luhrmann 2013a, 2013b.

52. Luhrmann 2012: 39, 52, 94.

53. MRI studies have shown that personal prayers to God (as opposed to formalized, rote-memorized prayers such as the Lord's Prayer) activate the same regions of the brain as does social interaction. In other words, cognitively, God is experienced as a social relationship. Luhrmann 2012: xvi and additional information in her note 10; see also Schjoedt et al. (2009), who show that whereas informal, personal prayer to God stimulates the social areas of the brain, formal prayers and expressing wishes that Santa will bring you something, do not.

54. For a general introduction to PSI and PSR, see Giles 2010, 2002. The term was introduced by Horton and Wohl 1956. On the differences between PSI and PSR, see Schmid and Klimmt 2011; Giles 2002. What researchers call PSI might sail less formally under a variety of other names. In a piece in the *New York Times Magazine* (November 22, 2013), JoAnn Klimkiewicz describes how she and her sister, fresh from reading Rhoda Byrne's self-help manual *The Secret*, "secreted" the supermodel Christy Turlington right into their lives.

55. On PSI with fictional characters, see, for example (in addition to Schmid and Klimmt 2011; Giles 2010, 2002), Mittell 2015: 124–149; Eder, Jannidis, and Schneider 2010; Reicher 2010; Schmid and Klimmt 2010; Hoorn and Konijn 2003.

56. The anecdotes about the reception of Little Nell's death are mentioned by many treatments of Dickens and of seriality; see, for example, Gardner 2012: 56–57; Walsh 2007: 148–169. More generally on audience reaction to serials, see Mittell 2015: especially 118–163; Gardner 2012: 29–60; Nussbaum 2012. The

anecdote about Daniel O'Connell is taken from an article published in the *Irish Times* on January 7, 2012 (https://www.irishtimes.com/opinion/an-irishman-s-diary-1.950636). And then there is Dickens camp, held for a week each summer at the University of California at Santa Cruz, where adults dress up as their favorite characters: Lepore 2011. Similarly, when Sidney Smith, author of a long-running daily comic strip called "The Gumps," killed off a beloved character named Mary Gold in 1929, the collective grief amongst readers brought an avalanche of letters to newspapers that carried the strip, demanding that Mary somehow be revived. Like Dickens, Smith refused to relent (Gardner 2012: 53–55).

57. Letters to Holmes: Rule 1989. When the BBC's interpretation of Holmes's death was aired as "The Reichenbach Fall" on January 15, 2012, it met with a similar (even if much more self-consciously constructed) response and generated an enormous number of memes (of which "I Believe in Sherlock," perhaps orchestrated by the BBC itself, was the most prominent), discussions on social networks and articles in traditional print media. Not surprisingly, given that any twenty-first-century audience could feel secure that Holmes would eventually return, many of these focused more on the question of *how* Holmes's apparent death would be explained away than on lamenting the death itself.

58. Gunn 2013; cf. Arngrim 2010: 130–134 (a memoir by the actress who played Nellie Oleson on *Little House on the Prairie*, which includes descriptions of viewers accosting her for what "she" did to Laura Ingalls). Further on PSI with unpleasant characters, see Mittell 2015: 142–163, with 364n2; Hoorn and Konijn 2003.

59. Giles 2010: 454.

60. As I was writing the first version of this chapter, I was struck by a review, posted on December 16, 2013, of the third-season finale of *Homeland*, in which the television critic Willa Paskin says, "I am more surprised than anyone about what happened while watching the season finale of *Homeland*, 'The Star.' I cried. Three times" (Paskin 2013).

61. Luhrmann (2012) and Schjoedt et al. (2009) certainly treat the topic but without ever mentioning the terms PSI and PSR. Similarly, John Caughey (1984) discusses social relationships in the realms of what he calls fantasy and hallucinations or delusions but never mentions PSI and PSR.

62. Verity Platt (2010) has convincingly made the argument that we must similarly erase the distinction between viewing portraits of the gods and heroes *as art* and *as sacred objects* during antiquity.

63. The *iamata* and the confession *stelai* provide the best-known examples, but we might also think of various other reports of encounters with gods, such as that by the *nympholeptos* Archedamus (*IG* I^3 976–980) or the story of Phidippides's encounter with Pan, which was said to have prompted the Athenians to establish new cult to the god (Hdt. 6.105–106; I return to the incident later in this chapter).

64. Of course, very few people actively, consciously, and consistently hold any religious belief, all of the time. Nor do the majority of people who follow politics, who campaign to protect the environment or who engage in any

number of other things to which they are sincerely committed think about them actively, consciously, and consistently, all the time. As Paul Veyne has noted, the mind changes its programs of truth as it changes its interests; whether you "believe" in something can only be measured by whether you are committed to what you are doing or saying at the moment that you are doing or saying it. (Veyne 1983: 86–87, drawing on the work of Paul Pruyser). Cf. Partridge 2004: 125, discussing TV viewers: "Some people will receive what is communicated uncritically, others will reject the message and yet others will enter into a relationship of negotiation. Some viewers of a news report, for example, or even a television series such as *The X-Files*, may uncritically accept everything communicated. Others will accept parts of what is presented as an accurate representation of reality and reject other elements as distortion or simply fiction. Yet others will reject everything presented. Such decoding, of course, is influenced to a large extent by prior commitments, and plausibility structures."

65. On the seriality of *The Old Curiosity Shop* and *Middlemarch* and their similarities to serial television—and on the allures and frustrations of serial storytelling more generally—see O'Sullivan 2013.

66. Mittell 2015: 124–149; Schmid and Klimmt 2011: 254; Giles 2002; Murray Smith 1995. Cf. O'Sullivan 2013.

67. Cf. O'Flaherty 1988: 49.

68. On episodic serials, see, e.g., O'Sullivan 2013; Mittell 2010: 228–242.

69. In Euripides's version of Antigone's story, Haemon and Antigone marry (hypothesis to Sophocles's *Antigone* and the scholia to line 1350). Ion of Chios (fr. 1 Page) had Antigone and Ismene burned to death inside of Hera's temple by their nephew Laodamas. Cf. Johnston 2006; Gantz 1993: 519–522. Euripides's *Electra* presented a heroine who had been married off to a peasant; Sophocles's lost *Aletes* had her married off to Pylades.

70. O'Sullivan 2013. I will discuss series and episodic serials in more detail in Chapter 7.

71. Jason Mittell (2015: 165–166) discusses the experiential differences between what he calls "ideal" and "competent" viewers.

72. Hitchcock, as quoted in Chatman 1978: 60. I take the citation from Mittell 2015: 177. Cf. also Bordwell 1985: 57–61.

73. Bacch. 17; Pi. *P.* 4.

74. And even epics are themselves only a smaller section of a larger story—a couple of weeks out of the Trojan War, for example. Had we Homer's sources, we would probably discover that he was playing the same games as Pindar and the tragedians.

75. Hes. *Th.* 1011–1018.

76. Phelan 2017: x, 5.

77. Hänninen 2017; Bennett 1999.

78. I should also note that "ghost story" is a term into which both literary authors and scholars collapse a wider range of stories about the supernatural—not just those explicitly involving ghosts.

79. Wooffitt 1992: 114–152.

80. Bennett uses capital letters to indicate that her informants raised the volume of their voices.

81. Bennett 1999: 61–62.

82. Hänninen 2017: 131.

83. Hänninen (2017: 128) adds, "For readers or listeners, it is more plausible to hear or read extraordinary, uncanny and marvelous events taking place in a distant tale world than in everyday reality. When supernatural experiences take place in everyday reality, it may leave the readers or listeners perplexed. When that happens, narrators need to express that they realize the distinction between the ordinary realm of everyday life and the supernatural realm and locate themselves in the ordinary realm of rationality by the end of the story at latest."

84. The quotation is from James's preface to his collection *More Ghost Stories of an Antiquary*, first published in 1911. He made similar remarks in his introduction to Collins 1924. These and similar short essays by James on the writing of ghost stories are gathered by Darryl Jones at the end of his edition of James's work (James 2011). The present quotation is from page 406 of that edition. Some of Joseph Sheridan Le Fanu's work, which preceded James by several decades, began to introduce elements that fit the X/Y model (e.g., "Green Tea," 1872). At about the same time as James, E. F. Benson, Algernon Blackwood, and Arthur Machen often used the X/Y model in their ghost stories, too, as did Sir Arthur Conan Doyle in his supernatural fiction (which has recently been collected in Doyle 2017). Later works that notably use the X/Y format include F. Scott Fitzgerald's "A Short Trip Home" (1927), Daphne Du Maurier's "The Blue Lenses" (1959), Peter Straub's *Ghost Story* (1979), many of Stephen King's novels, and Joyce Carol Oates's *The Accursed*, for instance. Authors such as James were reacting to the Gothic horror story in its purest form, which tended to be, if not supernatural all the way through, certainly not a portrait of everyday life—e.g., Horace Walpole's *The Castle of Otranto: A Gothic Story* (1764) or Matthew Lewis's *The Monk* (1796).

85. Bennett 1999: 16.

86. Bennett 1999: 115.

87. M. R. James, "Canon Alberic's Scrapbook," first published in *Ghost Stories of an Antiquary* (1904)=James 2011: 3–13; the quotation is from page 13.

88. I use the word "diegetic" here not as Plato does in *R.* 3 (392d3) to mean simply a narrative, but rather as scholars of narrative do, to refer to the world within which a story, or series of related stories, unfolds. "Non-diegetic" comprises external elements that might be used to enhance the story, such as the background music in a film.

89. Cf. Hänninen (2017: 128–129), who develops the work of Cohn 1978. Cohn envisioned a sliding scale that ran from "consonance" to "dissonance" in the relationship between what the Narrating I and the Experiencing I reported. Hänninen notes that when people report their supernatural experiences, those whose two I's are consonant typically are still processing their experience; they are unsure what happened, what it meant and whether it is worth telling. Conversely, those whose reports are dissonant are more confident in the accuracy of what they are telling.

90. I paraphrase a statement from Bennett 1999: 38. By "traditions of disbelief," she refers to the post-Enlightenment assumption, widely held in the

Western world (and increasingly outside of the Western world), that religious or supernatural experiences can be explained away with reference to something such as (as Andrew Lang long ago put it) "rats, indigestion, dreams and of late, hypnotism" (Lang 1894: 173, quoted in Bennett 1999: 32). "At the last ditch," Bennett continues, "rationalists fall back on the argument that, even if none of their arguments will fit the case now, given time and the advance of scientific knowledge, a 'rational' cause *will eventually be found*." On "traditions of disbelief," see also the seminal piece by David Hufford (1982).

91. Bennett 1999: 3 (emphasis added); cf. Hänninen 2017: 127–128.

92. I take the term from William Hansen (2017: 24), who cites Labov and Waletsky 1967: see esp. 32, 34.

93. Hdt. 6.105–106.

94. Healed people would dedicate ex-voto inscriptions that narrated their stories in a formalized first- or third-person voice; some of these were collected by the priests and inscribed on the *stelai*, which were erected in the sanctuary during the second half of the fourth century BCE. Pausanius mentioned that there were six such large *stelai* when he visited in the second century CE; we have found two of these and fragments of two more (Paus. 2.27.3). For the Greek texts and a translation, see Edelstein and Edelstein 1945: testimony 423; and cf. discussion in LiDonnici 1995. I cite individual *iamata* from the *stelai* by the numbers that the Edelsteins use.

95. There is also a long healing inscription from Epidaurus, dated to about 160 CE, in which the patient, a man from Mylasa in Asia Minor, tells us that Asclepius called him to Epidaurus (presumably in a dream): "During the sea voyage, when in Aigina, he told me not to be so angry" (*IG* IV^2 1, 126 = Edelstein and Edelstein 1945: testimony 425, the Edelsteins' translation). Here we may be getting a less-mediated, personal voice, i.e., something closer to a memorate.

96. *Iamata* nos. 27 (abdominal abscess), 30 (arrow in lung), and 14 (kidney stone).

97. The word I am translating as "it seemed" is ἐδόκει. The phrase is found in testimonies nos. 2, 3, 4, 6, 7, 8, 9, 17, 18, 21, 23, 24, 27, 28, 29, 30, 31, 32, 34, 35, 37, 38, 39, 40, 41, 42. The phrase clearly became formulaic but nonetheless would have functioned to remind the audience of the distance between narrator and the events being narrated.

98. Hes. *Th.* 22–34.

99. *Th.* 26–28, trans. Most, slightly modified.

100. See West 1966: 158–164; and, more recently, with more nuancing of the Hesiodic experience against Near Eastern *comparanda*, López-Ruiz 2010: 48–83.

101. West 1966: 160–161.

102. López-Ruiz 2010: 54.

103. Joshua Katz and Katharina Volk (2000; followed by Carolina López-Ruiz 2010: 77–78) have persuasively argued that in "mere bellies" we are meant to hear an allusion to *engastrimythoi*, "belly-talkers," who claimed to have spirits in their stomachs and who therefore could offer a cheap, easy-to-access local version of the prestigious form of prophecy offered by the Delphic Pythia.

I think this is correct, but it does not contradict (indeed, it enhances) the contrast that Hesiod's Muses are drawing between shepherds and themselves.

104. The expression has Near Eastern precedents, as López-Ruiz (2010: 56–73), amongst others, has argued, which helps us understand how Hesiod is using it to subtly underscore the divine source of his information, but nonetheless, as an interjection, the expression plays the dialectical role that I describe here.

105. Hesiod's quotation of the Muses' claim that they can lie persuasively when they want to but also tell the truth is interesting in this respect, as well, since it introduces ambiguity on yet another level: even if we decide to believe that Hesiod really did meet the Muses and received their gift, we can't be sure that the gift itself is not riddled with misleading statements. This means that, at least initially, attentive listeners will weigh every word that Hesiod sings, hoping to catch the Muses out at their game. Notably, the seventy lines or so that immediately follow Hesiod's remark about the oak and rock are a treatise on the nature of the Muses themselves—their parentage, their birth, their names, their central role in the creation not only of poets but also of kings, or in other words, topics on which we would least doubt the Muses' honesty. Will attentive listeners have let down their guard by the time we get to the creation of the cosmos itself?

106. The *Hymn to Hermes* also includes encounters between a mortal and the gods: an old man, who sees Hermes stealing Apollo's cattle, is told by Hermes not to admit that he knows anything but later reports what he has seen to Apollo (lines 87–93 and 187–211). In contrast to humans in the other episodes that I am discussing here, the old man expresses no alarm or even surprise during either encounter and suffers no ills. This fits the ludic nature of this *Hymn*, which humorously showcases the young god's craftiness. The typical awe and terror associated with divine encounters in the other *Hymns* would strike a wrong note in this atmosphere. Notably, other myths about this old man give him a name—Battus ("The Babbler")—and end with him being turned to stone by Hermes: Ant. Lib. 23, citing a number of earlier treatments, including Hesiod's *Catalogue* fr. 256 MW.

107. *HHDem.* 98–295.

108. *HHAp.* 388–447.

109. *HHAph.* 75–184.

110. *HH* 7.1–53.

111. *HHDem.* 235

112. Buxton 2009: 29–37, his translation.

113. *Od.* 3.371–373, trans. Buxton 2009: 29.

114. Buxton 2009: 43.

115. This terseness was first noted by Allen 1908. The Chimaera: *Il.* 6.179–183 and 16.326–329; Cerberus, *Il.* 8.368, cf. *Od.* 11.623, where Cerberus is called simply a dog; Typhon: *Il.* 2.782–783.

116. I am also attracted by the suggestion of Marianne Govers Hopman (2012: 24–25) that Odysseus emphasizes the monstrousness of Scylla because it is an episode in which he feels that he failed to win the day.

117. Scylla: *Od.* 12.85–99 (fifteen lines); and Typhon: *Th.* 823–835 (twelve lines).

118. I think particularly of the passages that immediately precede the episodes with Polyphemus and Circe (*Od.* 9.62–233 and 10.133–188), each of which shows us the workaday world of Odysseus and his men.

119. *Od.* 12.235–245.

120. *Od.* 12.245–250.

121. *Od.* 12.251–260.

122. *Od.* 13.1–6.

123. Although in *I.* 4.49–51, to flatter Melissus, a victor who was small in stature, Pindar does claim that Heracles was small in stature as well.

124. Bacch. 17.117–178, 3.54–59. I am counting Croesus as a hero here, although he was a historical figure, because Bacchylides's treatment of his story, and particularly the interventions of Zeus and Apollo, align him with the heroes treated elsewhere by Bacchylides, such as Theseus and Heracles.

125. Pi. *O.* 13.83, *P.* 2.49–51, *P.* 10.48–50, *P.* 3.11–12.

126. For example, Pi. *O.* 7.47, *I.* 4.52, *I.* 8.59.

127. Pi. *O.* 1.28–36.

128. "It is proper for a man to speak well of the gods, for less is the blame. Son of Tantalus, of you shall I say, contrary to my predecessors, that when your father invited the gods to his most orderly feast and to his friendly Sipylos, giving them a banquet in return for theirs, then it was that the Lord of the Splendid Trident seized you, his mind overcome with desire, and with golden steeds conveyed you to the highest home of widely honored Zeus" (Pi. *O.* 1.35–42, translation William Race).

129. Pi. *O.* 1.24–25: "[The victor's] glory shines in the settlement of fine men founded by Lydian Pelops, with *whom* the mighty holder of the earth Poseidon fell in love."

130. E. *Hercl.* 844–866; E. *Alc.* 1578–1612; S. *OC* 1586–1666.

131. E. *Hipp.* 1173–1254.

132. E. *Hipp.* 1173, 887–898.

133. E. *Hipp.* 1185–1198.

134. E. *Hipp.* 1201–1243.

135. Hippolytus is named already in the (sixth-century?) epic *Naupactica* as someone whom Asclepius brought back to life, which typically is said to have happened after his chariot wreck (fr. 10, West). Plutarch, in his *Theseus* (28.2) says, "Theseus did, indeed, marry Phaedra, but this was after the death of Antiope, and he had a son by Antiope, Hippolytus, or, as Pindar says, Demophon. As for the calamities which befell Phaedra and the son of Theseus by Antiope, since there is no conflict here between historians and tragic poets, we must suppose that they happened as represented by the poets uniformly" (trans. Bernadotte Perrin). Cf. Gantz 1993: 285–288.

136. Bacch. 16.

137. Outside of Athens, tragedies could be (re)performed at the festivals of other gods—but the subject matter had just as little to do with those gods, most of the time, as it did with Dionysus: Scullion 2002.

4 THE GREEK MYTHIC STORY WORLD

1. Lewis 1947; cf. remarks made in the essays collected in Lewis 1966.

2. Coleridge 1817: chap. 14.

3. Tolkien 1947: 60.

4. Saler 2012: 28.

5. M. Wolf 2012: 25.

6. Kalidah: a vicious beast that has the body of a bear, a head like a tiger and claws sharp enough to tear a lion in two, first featured in *The Wonderful Wizard of Oz* (1900) and appearing in other Oz books thereafter. Mangaboos: an underground race of people made of vegetable material, introduced in *Dorothy and the Wizard in Oz* (1908).

7. M. Wolf 2012: 33.

8. Fourteen books about Oz were written by L. Frank Baum between 1900 and 1920; after his death, his publishing house, Reilley and Lee, commissioned twenty-six more. In addition, Baum published eleven books that many people consider as canonically belonging to the "Oz World," and others published an additional six books and two short stories. A complete and accurate list, so far as I can establish, is to be found at http://oz.wikia.com/wiki/List_of_Oz_books. Potentially more complete, but also more confusing, is the information at http://en.wikipedia.org/wiki/List_of_Oz_books. Vidal 1977a and 1977b are helpful and insightful.

9. First printed on the end papers of Faulkner 1946.

10. Mittell 2015: 261–291; M. Wolf 2012: 153–197. Other examples are *The Languages of Tolkien's Middle-Earth: A Complete Guide to All Fourteen of the Languages That Tolkien Invented* (Noel 1980); *Stephen King's "The Dark Tower": The Complete Concordance, Revised and Updated* (Furth 2012); and (just published as I write this) *Flora of Middle-Earth: Plants of J. R. R. Tolkien's Legendarium* (Judd and Judd 2017).

11. And then there are Herodotus's gigantic, gold-digging Indian ants—which he assumes are real (Hdt. 3.102–105). Herodotus also mentions that some people believe that each year, a single man turns into a wolf for a few days and then turns back again. But these shape-shifting people are the Neuri—living far away from Greece, beyond even the distant Scythians, and he reports that it's only the Scythians and Greeks who have lived amongst the Scythians who believe that the Neuri actually can do such a thing (Herodotus certainly doesn't believe it: Hdt. 4.105). Should we call these tales myths and add the ants and the werewolves to our bestiary? By a criterion that I used for my heuristic definition of myth in Chapter 1 and that I will explore more later in this chapter, we should not: they have no place in the complex web of relationships amongst heroes and gods.

12. Epimenid. frr. 27–29, Bernabé; cf. Plut. *Dinner of the Seven Wise Men* 157d.

13. *Il.* 6.171–183, trans. Lombardo, slightly modified; cf. *Il.* 16.328–329, where the Chimaera is described simply as "raging" and "an evil for many people."

14. *O.* 13.90. *HHAp.* 368 calls her merely "ill-named." Hes. fr. 43a MW 84 calls her "fire-breathing," although it's possible that another adjective was

squeezed into the six syllables that are missing from the line. Hesiod takes fuller advantage of the possibilities at *Th.* 319–322: "she breathes forth invincible fire, is terrible, swift and mighty with three heads: a fierce-eyed lion's, a she-goat's, and a snake's—a mighty dragon's—breathing forth the terrible strength of burning fire." On textual problems in the lines that immediately follow these (323–324), continuing the description in a contradictory way, see West 1966: ad loc. Most editors regard these two lines as interpolation from *Il.* 6.181–182.

15. S. *Tr.* 573–574; A. *Ag.* 1234; E. *Med.* 1359.

16. See my comments in Chapter 3 on Odysseus's narration of the episode with Scylla and Charybdis.

17. Hes. *Th.* 820–868.

18. It is possible that one reason that ancient authors could get away with restrained descriptions of the monstrous is that art portrayed many of these creatures fairly frequently and with gusto. We know this not only from the representations that remain to us but also from ancient reactions to those representations that are embedded in literature: e.g., E. *Ion* 184–218 and Paus. 2.27.2, which tells us that the throne on which sat the large statue of Asclepius in Epidaurus was decorated with scenes of Bellerophon fighting the Chimaera and Perseus beheading Medusa.

19. Cf. my discussion of memorates in the final section of Chapter 3, where I make the same point but with reference to how myths work to establish credibility more generally.

20. Gaiman (1996) 2001: 214.

21. Heracles in the Hesperides: attested as early as Pherecyd. *FGrH* 3 F 16 and 17. See further Fowler 2013: 291–299 and Gantz 1993: 410–413. The visit, in all its narrative variations, is well attested in art from the early sixth century on. The vase shown in Figure 4.1 is especially interesting because the painter has managed to combine so many elements from what are different parts of the story of Heracles's labors as we best know it: Atlas holding up the sky, one of the Hesperides (so labeled), the tree with apples guarded by the snake and Heracles in what appears to be the cup he borrowed from Helios (which is more typically associated with the Labor to obtain the cattle of Geryon, although Pherecyd. *FGrH* 3 F 18 has him use it for both Labors: Fowler 2013: 294–299). Hermes and Athena have been added on either side, ready to aid Heracles. Perseus in the Hesperides: Hesiod places the Gorgons in the same place as the Hesperides, "beyond glorious Ocean, towards the edge of Night" (*Th.* 270–271) and Perseus's visit to their garden is attested by a red-figure hydria from Paestum now in Lisbon, dated to 340–330 BCE, showing the hero with three nymphs, a dragon and an apple tree (*RVP* 258, 1022 = *LIMC* Hesperides 62). See further Gantz 1993: 305–306.

22. Pi. *P.* 10.29–30—a poem that gives us our earliest attestation of Perseus in Hyperborea. Heracles: Pi. *O.* 3.16–33 and perhaps also in Pherecydes, although in association with his quest for the apples of the Hesperides: Fowler 2013: 295–297. Further on Hyperborea in the early Greek tradition, see Fowler 2013: 132–133, 606–607.

23. Hawes 2017a appeared too late for me to make full use of it, but I would single out as particularly relevant to this discussion Hawes's own contribution to the volume and that of Clarke.

24. In using the word "network," I don't mean formally to invoke "network theory," although some of the implications of the subdivision known as "social network theory" certainly might be applied to my material.

25. *HHAp.* 353–354, 368; *Il.* 6.179–182; Hes. *Th.* 304–325.

26. Gantz 1993: xxxix; Hes. *Th.* 280–283; *Il.* 6.179–182.

27. Hellanic. *FGrH* 4F51; Musae. fr. 100 Bernabé; Pherecyd. *FGrH* 3F88 and Gantz 1993: 467–468; *Il.* 14.321–322, *Il.* 12.292 with scholia = IIes. *Cat* fr. 140; Bacch. fr. 10 SM; Pherecyd. *FGrH* 3F89; Hes. *Cat.* frs. 141 and 145; Bacch. 26; Sapph. 206 LP and Gantz 1993: 260–268. See also Gantz 1993: 811.

28. *Od.* 11.630–631; Paus. 9.31.5 and 10.28.3 (citing early works now lost); Hes. fr. 280 and Gantz 1993: 291–295; Hellanic. *FGrH* 4F168a; Alcm. 21 *PMG*; Stesich. fr. 191 *PMG*; Bacch. 5; Hes. *Cat.* fr. 25 MW; *Od.* 11.601–627. Note that there is also a tradition of *Theseus* meeting Meleager's ghost in the Underworld, according to Hes. fr. 280 MW.

29. Pherecyd. *FGrH* 3 F 88 and 22; Pherecyd. *FGrH* 3 F 112 and 31; Pi. *P.* 4.220–242; Call. fr. 233 Pf. But the story is much earlier—see Gantz 1993: 255–266; Ibyc. 291 *PMG* and Lyc. 174 and 798.

30. First told fully at Apollod. 3.14.4, but Reed 1996 traces the story of Adonis's death to the late fifth / early fourth century author Antimachus of Colophon and artistic representations suggest this part of the story is earlier, too: Gantz 1993: 102–103 and 729–731 and cf. Reed 1995. See also E. *Hipp.* 1420–1422, Theocr. 3.46–48, Sapph. 140 LP, Apollod. 3.14.4 and Hyg. *astr.* 2.7.3.

31. *Il.* 14.153–360; *HHHerm.*

32. Pi. *O.* 13.63–92; Hes. *Cat.* fr. 124 and 126; Gantz 1993: 199 and 811.

33. Ov. *Met.* 6.148–149.

34. Lyc. 143, 174 and 798.

35. Hes. *Cat.* frs. 190 and 191; Bacch. 5; E. *Hipp.* 1416–1422.

36. Graf and Johnston 2013: 66–93.

37. Gantz 1993: 248–245; Kearns 1989: 117–124; but see also Fowler 2013: 470–472 for a different view.

38. Medea: our first mention of her involvement in Theseus's story is Call. *Hec.* frr. 232 and 233 Pf. Vases from the mid-fifth century seem to show her attempting to poison him (details at Gantz 1993: 255–256, and see also Sourvinou-Inwood 1979). Heracles: earliest evidence is a shield band relief from Olympia dated to about 560 BCE, showing figures labeled "Theseus" and "Pirithous" sitting on a chair, while a third figure approaches with a drawn sword; this figure's name has been worn away (inv. B 2198). See discussion at Fowler 2013: 487–488 and Gantz 1993: 292. Theseus's attempt to kidnap Helen seems to be alluded to at *Il.* 3.143–144, where Theseus's mother is Helen's servant and a scholium A to *Il.* 3.242 says the story was told in the epic cycle.

39. Graf and Johnston 2013: 167; Graf 1987.

40. Apollod. 1.9.16; Apollod. 1.82–83, probably derived from Euripides's lost *Meleager.*

41. Cf. Eco 1990: 198.

42. *Od.* 19.394–398 says that Hermes taught Autolycus thievery and the art of making slippery oaths in return for generous sacrifices. Pherecydes (*FGrH* 3 F 120) says that Hermes was Autolycus's father.

43. M. Wolf 2012: 205–12.

44. On crossovers, see, for example, Mittell 2015: 267–270; Mittell 2010: 28, 46.

45. Amongst the earliest of our own era were the *Houseboat* books by John Kendrick Bangs (1895 and 1897), which posited gatherings of the ghosts of famous men and women, real and fictional, in a houseboat sailing down the Styx (Sherlock Holmes was a central figure in the second volume, *The Pursuit of the Houseboat*).

46. Paus. 1.28.7.

47. Or perhaps by Euripides in his *Phoenissae*, depending on how you judge some controversial lines; on both matters, Gantz 1993: 295–297; Kearns 1989: 208–209.

48. Johnston 1999: 219–220 with notes.

49. Notably including one in which a girl passes through the wardrobe in a spare room of her aunt's house and enters another world: "The Aunt and Amabel" (included in Nesbit 1912; original pagination is not available to me).

50. Th. 1.3.

51. Johnston 1999: 279–287; Lardinois 1992.

52. Calame 2003: 68.

53. Pi. *P.* 9.26–65.

54. Pherecyd. *FGrH* 3 F 22; A. *Eu.* 727–728; E. *Ion* 985–1010.

55. In a letter to Robert E. Howard, dated August 14, 1930, as cited at http://www.hplovecraft.com/creation/necron/letters.aspx.

56. Further on the topic that follows, see the excellent treatments at Fowler 2016, 2011.

57. Cf. Fowler 2016: 201–203.

58. Th. 1.8.4, 1.9.4. Thucydides subsequently stresses that a good historian should not accept every detail that comes down through tradition even in connection with relatively recent events such as the Athenian tyrannicide, and all the more so when it comes to the sorts of earlier events that are favored by poets and some prose writers. Such narrators, he charges, are more interested in catching the public's attention than in discovering the truth, and their subject matter, in any case, has been "lost in the unreliable streams of mythology." Yet he puts what he himself has said about Troy and Minos into a different category (1.21).

59. This principle permeates Eliade's work: e.g., Eliade 1963, 1959, 1954. See also Rennie 1996: 77–225.

60. Green 1997: 30; see also 14–15.

61. Parian Chronicle: *FGrH* 239. See Oxford fr. entries 1, 3, 10–12, 17, 40, and Paros fr. entries 8 and 10; Lindian Chronicle = *IG* XII, 1 Lindos II.2 = *SEG* 39.727. Generally on the Lindian Chronicle, see Higbie 2003.

62. D. 60.6–8, 60.28 (the *Funeral Oration*). Cf. Th. 2.29.3.

63. Pl. *Phdr.* 229b4–c3.

64. Paus. 1.39.1, 2.35.11, 8.2.1–4; generally on the question of which myths Pausanias held to be true, see Pirenne-Delforge 2008. Some of the monuments that our ancient sources describe provide tantalizing glimpses of myths that we no longer have in any full narrative form: Philochorus, most enticingly, tells

us of a tomb in the Delphic precinct on which was inscribed "Dionysus, son of Semele" (*FGrH* 328 7).

65. Further on Asclepius's cures, see the section "Ancient Narrations of Remarkable Incidents" in Chapter 3. For an overview of Amphiaraus, see Johnston 2008: 90–95. Pan: Hdt. 6.105–106. Apollo: Cic. *Div.* 1.37, D.S. 22.9, *SIG* 398, Pomp. Trog. 24.8, Paus. 10.23–24, 1.4, and cf. Call. *H.* 4.171–184.

66. The description of Athena bringing rain is at *IG* XII, 1 Lindos II.2. D 1–59. On manifestations of the gods, see Henrichs 2010; Graf 2004; Bravo 2003; Versnel 1987.

5 CHARACTERS

1. In my summary here, I am most indebted to Maria Reicher (2010), who provides a good bibliography of earlier treatments, and to a lesser extent to Eco 2009. In contrast, see, for example, Richardson 2010.

2. Reicher's (2010) maximal character is in some ways similar to Eco's "fluctuating character," which had been introduced the previous year in an Estonian journal (Eco 2009). I find Reicher's articulation of the relationship between maximal and submaximal characters more compelling than that between Eco's fluctuating and what, I presume, he would call non-fluctuating characters, because of Reicher's emphasis on the functions served by submaximal characters.

3. Reicher (2010: 129–130) suggests that there are also cases in which a character has become so diversely represented as to produce *two* maximal characters, between whom there are few overlaps and each of whom has its own submaximal characters. (For an example, she offers Marlowe's Faust as a maximal character and Goethe's Faust as a separate maximal character, each of which has spawned submaximal Fausts.)

4. See Rule 1989.

5. This is similar to what the social psychologist Robert Cialdini (2016) calls "pre-suasion," although he is interested in how individuals' actions and choices (particularly purchasing choices) may be affected by front-loading particular opinions.

6. *Th.* 1.22, trans. Radice.

7. I am reminded of E. M. Forster's remarks about people in novels, as I cited them in Chapter 3, note 44. I am also reminded of an anecdote told by Alexandre Dumas and repeated by Umberto Eco (2009: 83). When, in 1860, Dumas joined a group of tourists visiting the Chateau d'If, where his hero Edmond Dantès, the Count of Monte Cristo, had languished, he was surprised to hear the guides speaking of Dantès and other characters in the novel as if they had been real, and completely ignoring a real, historical figure who actually *had* been imprisoned there. Dumas comments in his *Memoirs*, "It is the privilege of novelists to create characters who kill those of the historians, the reason is that historians only evoke mere ghosts, while novelists create persons in flesh and bones."

8. *Il.* 24.334–335.

9. *Il.* 5.370; Hes. *Th.* 188–192.

10. An actor portraying Elizabeth II parachuted out of a helicopter at the opening ceremonies of the 2008 London Olympics—alongside an actor portraying James Bond—with the enthusiastic support of the real Elizabeth, who played herself in scenes leading up to the point when "she" climbed into the helicopter. This stunt presented an Elizabeth who was far outside of her usual portrayals but it was greeted enthusiastically—perhaps because her accompaniment by James Bond clearly marked it as fictionalizing.

11. As is the case with mythic characters, most of these treatments are careful to plant their roots within some trait or episode that is already part of the canon—that is, a trait or episode that has already been mentioned by Doyle himself: Holmes's intention to retire into beekeeping, his admiration for Irene Adler or his obsession with Moriarty, for example.

12. The neologism "plurimediality" and its cognates are used in different ways by different scholars, as are the terms "transmedial" and "intermedial," which sometimes seem to be regarded as synonyms for "plurimedial." I adopt "plurimedial" (and my initial example here) from Denson 2011. Generally, see also Mittell 2015: 292–318; Ryan 2012; Eder, Jannidis, and Schneider 2010: 17–20, 28–30; Richardson 2010; W. Wolf 2007, 2005; and Jenkins 2006: 95–134. Mittell (2015: 310–318) notes that *transmediality* most often refers to a phenomenon that has been orchestrated by the creator of the "mother-ship" representation—that is, the relationship between different representations is purposefully built to be one between what is perceived as a "main narrative" and "spin-offs" (e.g., *Star Wars* movies on the one hand and *Star Wars* action figures on the other hand). In cases of plurimediality, in contrast, as I will stress, there are no orchestrators other than the individual consumers' minds, and it is usually harder to pinpoint anything that is clearly a "mother-ship" narrative. Henry Jenkins talks about "balanced transmedia" as a form of transmediality that is similar to plurimediality but argues that it is seldom realized.

13. Cf. Denson 2011.

14. Denson 2011.

15. As Denson (2011) has made especially clear, "original" portrayals have no particular authority as a character becomes plurimedial. To return to Holmes as an example, his calabash pipe was never mentioned by Doyle, who described him using only a clay pipe, a briarwood pipe and a cherrywood pipe; the calabash was introduced by the actor William Gillette, who portrayed Holmes on the stage in the early 1900s.

16. Plu. *Thes.* 36.4; cf. Ar. fr. 594 Edmonds and Pherecr. fr. 49.

17. Cf. Plu. *Thes.* 36.4, and see Kearns 1989: 120–124, 168–169. It is likely that Theseus had formal cult sites in at least four other Attic locations, as well (Philoc. *FGrH* 328 F 18).

18. Pi. *O.* 3; Bacch. 17. On whether Bacchylides was the first to tell this story, see note 35 in Chapter 1.

19. Pi. *O.* 1.24–89.

20. Hes. frs. 37.10–15, 131a and b, 132–133 MW; Acus. *FGrH* 2F28; Pherecyd. *FGrH* 3F114, Bacch. 11.53–58, 92–95. See also Fowler 2013: 169–178; Gantz 1993: 311; Dowden 1989: 71–96; Seaford 1988.

21. Pi. *I.* 4.35–38.

22. Hdt. 2.44.

23. Plu. *Thes.* 1, Kilvert's translation.

24. Stesich. frs. 192–193. Cf. Pi. *O.* 1.34–35.

25. On "diegetic," see Chapter 3, note 88.

26. Lycaon: already glimpsed in Hes. frs. 161–168 and Pherecyd. *FGrH* 3F156; fuller story at Eratosth. *Cat.* 8. See also Fowler 2013: 104–109, and Gantz 1993: 728. Croesus: Hdt. 1.46–51.

27. Poseidon in Ethiopia: *Od.* 1.25–30. Polyphemus calling to his father: *Od.* 9.526–535.

28. Zeus needs Prometheus's advice: A. *Pr.* 167–195, 907–917, 944–953, and cf. Pi. *I.* 8.26a–45a, which puts Themis, traditionally an oracular goddess, in Prometheus's role.

29. Persephone lured by flower: *HHDem.* 15–18. Hecate hears her: *HHDem.* 22–25, 54–58. Helios tells who kidnapped Persephone: *HHDem.* 74–81. None of the gods heard her cry: *HHDem.* 22–23. Zeus spares himself the sound: *HHDem.* 27–29. Persephone eats something: *HHDem.* 371–374, 405–413.

30. Eileithyia in a cloud: *HHAp.* 97–101. Telphousa tricks Apollo: 254–274, 375–381.

31. *HHHerm.* 190–200.

32. Demeter distracted by grief: implied by the story that Pindar rejects at *O.* 1.27, fully told first by Lyc. 152–155, and cf. Ov. *Met.* 6.403–411. Children of Helios forget fire: Pi. *O.* 7.39–48. Eos forgets to ask for youth: *HHAphr.* 218–238.

33. *Il.* 16.431–461.

34. *Il.* 5.330–352, 392–404, 439–442, 846–863.

35. Hermes uses special sandals: e.g., *Il.* 24.339–345, which is repeated at *Od.* 5.43–49 (and note that Athena has similar sandals at *Od.* 1.96–98). Hermes's sandals are more specifically described as winged in Hes. *Shield* 220. Hermes is represented as wearing winged sandals already on vases dated between 550 and 520 BCE (for example, Musée du Louvre, F 19 and F 30). See also Figures 7.2 and 7.3, in the latter of which Perseus, rather than Hermes, wears the winged sandals because Hermes has lent them to him. Note, however, that in Figure 6.3, Hermes's feet are bare, and in Figure 4.1, Hermes wears ordinary sandals. Iris uses special sandals, too, on occasion, although she is usually described and represented as being winged herself: discussion at Gantz 1993: 17–18.

36. Hades owns a cap of invisibility and Athena borrows it: *Il.* 5.844–845.

37. Athena shakes her aegis: *Il.* 2.450–452; and see Gantz 1993: 84–85. Hermes uses special shoes: *HHHerm.* 75–86. Hermes throws them into the Alpheus: *HHHerm.* 138–140. Hermes slips through the latch-hole: *HHHerm.* 145–147.

38. Boyer 2001: 87–90, drawing on Barrett 1996.

39. "Officially" includes what canonical texts say, but it also includes ideas that become canonical in other ways. The Bible never describes Satan as having horns on his head, yet artists' renditions show him that way in stained-glass windows and other church art from the medieval period onward; by now, therefore, the horns approach canonicity.

40. Boyer 2001: 87–88, drawing on Barrett 1996.

41. Boyer 2001: 59.

42. E. *Ba.* 1388–1392.

43. Pi. *P.* 3.27–29. Another example comes from one of the myths that Plato invents. When Poseidon creates a precinct for his lover Clito, we are told that "he adorned the island at the center with his own hand—*in the way that gods easily do*—causing two fountains to flow . . ." (Pl. *Cri.* 113e2–6). This is typical of Plato's myths, in which the gods are omnipotent as well as morally unimpeachable.

44. Reicher 2010: 130. Reicher uses "vague" here in the sense that analytical philosophers do, to mean something whose limits cannot be reliably defined, the classic example being a cloud made up of water molecules. She is responding to scholars who have argued that each instantiation of a character is an ontologically separate entity: thus, the Julius Caesar we see in Shakespeare's *Julius Caesar* is a separate character from the Caesar of Shakespeare's *Antony and Cleopatra*, for example.

45. As is well explored in Pirenne-Delforge and Pironti 2016.

46. See further Henrichs 1994, 1991.

47. Pi. *P.* 4; cf. O'Higgins 1997.

48. Barthes 1972: 110.

49. Notably, when Disney takes on a fairy tale whose main characters are nameless and turns it into a ninety-minute feature film, it bestows personal names upon those characters, as one step of giving them enough depth to carry the lengthier action. The Little Mermaid becomes Ariel, Beauty (of Beauty and the Beast) becomes Belle (which, for the average American, has no association with the word "beauty" and is just another moniker), the Snow Queen becomes Elsa, the Prince in Sleeping Beauty becomes Prince Philip, Cinderella's evil stepmother becomes Lady Tremaine and the wicked fairy of Sleeping Beauty becomes Maleficent—who becomes so well developed as a character, in fact, as to have merited a live-action, megabudget backstory (*Maleficent*) fifty-five years later (Holmes 2014).

50. Jenkins 1992: 99.

51. See Leitao 1995.

52. Cf. Philippe Borgeaud's study of the names of early mythic inhabitants of Athens and Crete (2004: 46–64) and Marianne Govers Hopman's different approach to mythic names belonging to more than one individual (2012).

53. A. *Ag.* 160–176.

6　METAMORPHOSES

1. Gen. 19:26 and Ev. Luc. 17:32; *Aitareya Brahmana* 3.33–34, as taken from O'Flaherty 1988: 86–87; ponies: e.g., Boas 1917: 53 and Dorsey 1904: 294–295, 295n. Dorsey collected a number of other Pawnee stories about people turning into animals, sometimes after having sex with an animal.

2. Piraro 2012.

3. *Ovide Moralisé* 2.1365–1819, 10.3478–3795; see also Dimmick 2002: 264–287.

4. See Hopman 2012.

5. In addition to snaky-haired Medusa and bedogged Scylla, as examples of transformational hybridity I can offer only Salmacis, who starts out as a woman but ends up as a hermaphrodite (Ov. *Met.* 4.285–388).

6. Hes. *Th.* 270–336.

7. First mentioned, apparently, in the fragments of Bacch. 26; see Gantz 1993: 260–261.

8. Pi. *P.* 2.42–43; see also Gantz 1993: 718–721.

9. Hes. *Th.* 278–279.

10. Hydra, Cerberus and Geryon: Hes. *Th.* 288–289, 306–318. Callirhoe as ocean nymph: *Th.* 351, 979. Cyclops: *Od.* 1.71–72.

11. Polyphemus: *Od.* 9.528–535.

12. Stesich. *Ger.* frr. 10–13. Another case is Scylla; at *Od.* 12.124–126, Circe advises Odysseus that when he sails past Scylla, he should call out to Crataeis, the mother of Scylla, asking her to hold back her daughter.

13. POxy 2461 = fr. 81 Aus.

14. *HHAp.* 351; Hes. *Th.* 824–828.

15. Hes. *Th.* 313–315, 328–329.

16. Hes. *Th.* 270–336; cf. Gantz 1993: 19–25.

17. Cf. West 1966: ad loc.

18. We get the whole story from Eratosthenes (*Catastr.* 8), who cites Hesiod as a source (= fr. 163 MW).

19. One reason that the story was told was that it could be used to explain a cult established near Mount Lykaos in Arcadia (see Pl. *R.* 565d; Paus. 8.38.7; Pliny *HN* 8.81 and discussion in Buxton 1987 and Burkert 1983: 83–10). From an early time, however (apparently already Hes. frr. 161–168; see Fowler 2013: 104–109 and Gantz 1993: 728), the story was well known outside of Arcadia, suggesting that its appeal was not due only to the fact that it explained the existence of a local cult.

20. Iynx: Call. fr. 685 (= schol. Theocr. 2.17); cf. schol. Pi. *N.* 4.56a and Forbes-Irving 1990: 243–244. Anthos: Ant. Lib. 7, citing Boeos.

21. Io turned into cow by Hera: A. *Supp.* 299. Io as priestess of Hera: Hes. fr. 124 MW and later sources including A. *Suppl.* 291–293. Io equated with Isis: first with certainty Call. *Epig.* 57 but perhaps also Hdt. 1.1. Cf. also Fowler 2013: 235–248; Gantz 1993: 198–203; Forbes-Irving 1990: 212–215; Seaford 1980.

22. Artemis transforming Callisto and Callisto as mother of Arcas: Eratosth. *Cat.* 1, citing Hes.; Amphis fr. 47. See also Fowler 2013: 107–108.

23. Lycian herdsmen muddying water: Ant. Lib. 35, crediting Nicander and Menecrates the Xanthian (*FrGH* 769F2); Ov. *Met.* 6.339–381.

24. Midrash Aggadah [Buber] Gen. 19:26.

25. Zeus turning Io into a cow: Apollod. 2.1.3–4, probably drawing on Hesiod; see Gantz 1993: 199–201; Fowler 2013: 235–248.

26. Zeus turning Callisto into bear: Apollod. 3.8.2. Hera turning Callisto into a bear: Call. fr. 632 Pf. and later sources, including Ov. *Met.* 2. 476–488 and *Fast.* 2.177–178. Cf. Fowler 2013: 107–108.

27. On playing the bear, with full ancient sources and citations to earlier scholarship, see Faraone 2003.

28. Our sources for Mintha are late but numerous enough that it is hard to imagine that the story was not popular from an early time: Oppian *H.* 3.486; schol. Nic. *Alex.* 375; Photius s.v. *Mintha*; Strabo 8.3.14. Ov. *Met.* 10.728 hints at it. See also Detienne 1977: 72–98.

29. Ov. *Met.* 6.1–145.

30. Discussions of the stories to be analyzed in this section can be found at Fowler 2013: 365–366; Levaniouk 2008; Johnston 1994; Gantz 1993: 239–241; Forbes-Irving 1990: 248–249; and Burkert 1983: 201–207.

31. *Od.* 19.518.

32. See, e.g., Parth. 11, quoting Apollonius Rhodius (nightingales mourn Adonis).

33. Hes. *Op.* 568; Sapph. 135 LP, cf. 136 LP.

34. Swallow's song as barbarian: *LSJ* s.v. *chelidōn*.

35. Hes. fr. 312 MW = Ael. *VH* 12.20.

36. *Od.* 19.518–523; Pherecr. fr. 124 = schol. *Od.* 19.518; Paus. 9.5.9.

37. Helladius *ap.* Phot. *Bibl.* 531; Ant. Lib. 11.

38. A. *Suppl.* 58–65 and *Ag.* 1144–1145; S. fr. 585; Th. 2.29; Ov. *Met.* 6.424–676; Apollod. 3.14.8; Paus. 1.5.4, 1.41.8.

39. Ant. Lib. 11.

40. Helladius *ap.* Phot. *Bibl.* 531.

41. E.g., *Od.* 19.518–523.

42. S. fr. 585; Th. 2.29; Ov. *Met.* 6.424–676; Apollod. 3.14.8; Paus. 1.5.4, 1.41.8.

43. This meaning cannot be correct ("Philomela" would more accurately mean "lover of sheep") but it would have been heard nonetheless.

44. The cutting of the tongue appears first in Sophocles but is developed most elaborately, and most famously, in Ovid.

45. Hyg. *Fab.* 45; Serv. *Ec.* 6.78 (both of whom omit the tongue cutting); *Myth. Vat.* I 4 and II 261 (who retain it).

46. Eust. *Od.* 1875.15–27 and *Od.* 19.518.

47. Doniger 1996: 119.

48. D. 60.30.

49. The meaning of Hecabe's transformation has been treated by Franco 2014: 109–116, Buxton 2009: 58; Burnett 1994; Forbes-Irving 1990: 207–210.

50. E. *Hec.* 1259–1273.

51. Nic. fr. 62 = schol. E. *Hec.* 3.

52. Lyc. 333.

53. Lyc. 1174–1188.

54. Ov. *Met.* 13.565–575.

55. Q. S. 14.347.

56. Apollod. *Ep.* 5.23.

57. Some but not all of them manage to connect Hecabe's transformation, or at least her burial, with the Cynossema on the Chersonese—but that may well have been Euripides's innovation. (Notably, moreover, there were plenty of other Cynossemata in antiquity that didn't manage to attract such a myth.)

58. *PMG* 965.

59. *Il.* 24.212–213.

60. See also Franco 2014 for the full range of associations.

61. E.g., Burnett 1994.

62. E. fr. 968 Nauck.

63. Ar. fr. 567 Edmonds: "*I* will become a nasty-tempered bitch, the *agalma* of light-bearing Hecate."

64. Lyc. 1174–1188.

65. Johnston 1999: 203–215.

66. E.g., *Od.* 20.17–18; Semon. fr. 7 West lines 32–36. I thank Tom Hawkins for pointing this out. See also Franco (2014: 108), who understands the trope as a more strongly negative one than I do, and Burnett (1994), who argues that the canine transformation is Euripides's own development on Hecabe's previously existing reputation as a mother.

67. Buxton 1987.

68. Pi. *O.* 1.61–64.

69. Nic. *Ther.* 12a.

70. Theophilus can be dated to the Hellenistic period—probably the late fourth and early third centuries. For more on this, see Johnston 2009.

71. As we learn both from Nicander and from other ancient writers, the term *phalangion* could designate any member of a whole family of venomous spiders. In some discussions, ancient authorities distinguish between *phalangia* and non-venomous spiders, to which they apply the term *arachnai*, but other authorities understand both *phalangia* and non-venomous spiders to be subgroups of a more inclusive family, to all of which the term *arachnai* can be applied. Further on methods of categorization, see Bevis 1988: 34–35; Scarborough 1979.

72. Gibson 1979. The example of the stick is mine.

73. Bettini 2013: 123–230.

74. Of course, the original meaning of *symbolon* relies on this restricted one-to-one relationship; see Struck 2004: 78–84. The essentialism of symbols was developed by Neoplatonists; subsequently, during the Middle Ages and the Renaissance, a greater range of potential meaning might be admitted to a given symbol, but in any particular instance, its meaning was set by the artist or author. Works such as Vincenzo Cartari's *Le imagini degli dei antichi* (ca. 1400) were handbooks intended to aid in the assignment of proper meaning (cf. Graf 2008: 153–157).

75. Except where noted, for the rest of this discussion, I subsume both *arachnai* and *phalangia* under the word "spider."

76. E.g., Hes. *Op.* 777; Arist. *HA* 622b23; Ael. *NA* 1.21; further at Bevis 1988: 39.

77. Although this could have a negative valence (Odysseus's marital bed is said to be covered with webs after his twenty years of absence), it could also be positive (Bacchylides describes peace as a time when shields are covered with webs). Bacch. fr. 4.69–70; *Od.* 16.35. See also Hes. *Op.* 475; E. fr. 369 Nauck; Pherecr. fr. 142; S. fr. 264; Theoc. 16.96; Philostr. *Imag.* 2.28.2; further at Bevis 1988: 40.

78. *Od.* 8.280; Arist. *HA* 623a8; *AP* 9.372; Plut. *Mor. De soll. an.* 966e–f; Philostr. *Im.* 2.28.1; Plin. *HN* 11.79–82; cf. Paus. 6.26.7. "A spider-like thread" (*arachnaios mitos*) proverbially meant a "very fine thread," e.g., *AP* 6.39.3.

79. Arist. *Ph.* 199a20–22; Ael. *VH* 1.2 and *NA* 1.21 (but cf. *NA* 6.57, which is more nuanced); Pliny *HN* 11.80.2; Sen. *Epist.* 121.23. Cf. Feeney 1991: 193–194. Arist. *HA* 622b28–623b1 distinguishes amongst different types of spiders, some of which spin webs that are sloppy and crude and others of which spin webs that are clever and polished. Plut. *De soll. an.* 966e–f lauds the fineness of the thread and regularity of the weaving but notes that there is no warp—i.e., he confirms its simplicity even as he admires it. Pliny, on the other hand, mentions both warp and a woof (*tela* and *subtemina*) at *HN* 11.80. Further at Bevis 1988: 39.

80. E.g., Pl. Com. fr. 22 line 2 Kock; many other citations, mostly from later antiquity, are offered at Bevis 1988: 39–40. Cf. Plut. *De Is. et Os.* 358f, where the spider's web is compared to hasty, poorly developed thoughts.

81. A. *Ag.* 1492 and 1516, *Suppl.* 887; Xen. *Mem.* 3.11.6; *AP* 9.372; Philostr. *Im.* 2.28.3–4.

82. Arist. *HA* 555b10–15, 555a23–26 (where he uses *arachnai*, not *phalangia*); cf. Antig. *Mir.* 87 and schol. Nic. *Ther.* 715a; Plin. *HN* 11.85. In the fuller version of this discussion at Johnston 2009, I include a discussion of spider cannibalism based on modern arachnological data. (I thank the arachnologist Daniel Gloor for his help with information concerning real, as opposed to mythic, spiders.)

83. E.g., Pliny *HN* 24.61–63; Ael. *NA* 17.11; schol. Nic. *Ther.* 721–724; Paul. Aeg. *Epitomae medicae libri septem* 5.6t1; [Ps.] Dioscorides *De iis* 4; Philum. *Ven.* 15.6; Aët. 13.20; Eutecnius Soph. *Paraph. Nic. Ther.* 59.

84. E.g., Scarborough 1979: 7–8. Species are found throughout the world; the American variety is the black widow (*Latrodectus mactans* [Fabricius, 1775]).

85. Scarborough 1979: 8n70; websites for physicians mention it, e.g., http://precordialthump.medbrains.net/2008/12/06/problems-in-toxicology-003/and http://medbrains.net/tag/toxicology/.

86. Further at Johnston 2009; Von Staden 1993: 36–37; Scarborough 1979: 3–6; Gow and Scholfield 1953: 18.

87. The basic meaning of *phalang-* is "beam" or "plank" (IE *bhelg-*); from this, it comes to refer to a number of things that are long and relatively slender. Most notably, the word *phalanx* can also mean a finger or toe bone. The application of the words *phalanx* and *phalangion* to spiders is established by the Classical period (e.g., Ar. *Ra.* 1314, Pl. *Euthd.* 290a and Xen. *Mem.* 3.11.6), but it is unclear why; perhaps it is because their legs, which have two joints, look like fingers (this is especially so in the *Latrodectus* genus, in which the legs tend to be longer and more slender than in other genuses). Ovid appreciates this similarity: *Met.* 6.143 (cf. Ar. *Ra.* 1314; Ov. *Am.* 1.14.7; *AP* 9.372).

88. The significance of weaving within Athenian society has been well studied by several scholars, most importantly by Scheid and Svenbro 1996. I will not repeat the details of their analyses here but will instead summarize those of their conclusions that will be of the greatest significance for the present discussion.

89. The fact that words for the warp have masculine connotations and words for the woof have feminine connotations adds strength to the metaphor: Scheid and Svenbro 1996: 13.

90. Further on all of this at Johnston 2009 and Scheid and Svenbro 1996.

91. Further examples at Johnston 2009.

92. Reviews of the issues and evidence in Barber 1992 and Burkert (1966) 2001.

93. Our main source is Paus. 1.27.3; further at Goff 2004: 198–205; Kearns 1989: 21–27; and Burkert (1966) 2001.

94. Barbara Goff (2004: 198–205) offers an attractive interpretation that downplays the secrecy of the myth and ritual; her differing conclusions do not affect my argument here.

95. Phot., Hsch. and Sud. s.v. *protonion*; Phot. s.v. *Plynteria*; and Hsch. s.v. *Kallynteria* and *Plynteria*.

96. Pl. *Lg.* 833d–e; cf. *La.* 181e–182a, *Grg.* 456d. See also Kyle 1992: 87–88; Wheeler 1982.

97. Kyle 1992: 88–89.

98. Further on the complementarity of the roles at Johnston 2009.

99. According to I. Agnarsson, director of the Zoology Museum at the University of Puerto Rico, only twenty to twenty-five species of spiders (out of about 39,000) are "quasi-social"; most of these are tropical. See Agnarsson Lab 2017.

100. Arist. *HA* 542a12–17. If Plutarch's opinion that a spider's webs were all woof and no warp was shared, then this, too, would have signaled failure on the spider's part to weave opposites into a single whole (see note 79 above).

101. *Purg.* 12.43–45.

102. Buxton 2009.

103. A. *Supp.* 565–570, *Pr.* 687–692. Cf. also, for example, *Il.* 2.308–320. Buxton (2009: 29) comments on passages in which characters express their astonishment at a *god's* transformation, e.g., *Od.* 3.371–373.

104. E.g., Corinna sang of the daughters of Minyas (fr. 665) and Bacchylides of Io and Niobe (19 and fr. 20D).

105. E.g., Pherecydes told of Aedon (*FrGH* 3F124) and the Hyades (fr. 90); Acusilaus told of Io and Actaeon (*FGrH* 2F26, 27, 33); Menecrates told of Leto turning peasants into frogs (*FGrH* 769F2); several authors told of Niobe (see Fowler 2013: 366); and Deilochus told of how Cleite's tears turned into a spring named after her (*FGrH* 471F6).

106. The vase showing pirates turning into dolphins recently was returned to Italy by the Toledo Museum of Art (Toledo 1982: 134); its current whereabouts have not been disclosed. It is Etruscan and has been dated to 510–500 BCE. It is attributed to the Painter of Vatican 238. The vase showing a horned Actaeon in the Underworld is Toledo 1994: 19, *RVAp. Supp.* 2, p. 508 18/41a1, attributed to the Darius painter and dated to 340–330 BCE.

107. For a study of the two Scyllas that aims at showing that they developed from a single collocation of ideas, see Hopman 2012.

108. Verg. *G.* 4.246–247; Bacon, *The Wisedome of the Ancients* (1619) (STC 1130), X.

109. Updike 1963: chap. 1.

110. The earliest source for Callisto as the mother of Arcas is Charon of Lampsacus *FGrH* 262F12, but the story probably goes back to Hesiod; a fuller story is at Paus. 8.3.6–7. See also Fowler 2013: 105–108; Gantz 1993: 725–729.

111. D. 60.30.

112. Ant. Lib. 17.

113. *Od.* 6.229–231.

114. The story seems to be as old as Hesiod and Pherecydes. See Hes. fr. 68 MW; Pherecyd. *FGrH* 3F98, 99 and cf. discussions at Fowler 2013: 195–201 and Gantz 1993: 176–180. A complete version of the story appears at Apollod. 1.80–83.

115. For an overview of Asclepius at Epidaurus and similar healing shrines, see Johnston 2008: 90–95; for specific instances, see the section of Chapter 3 entitled "Ancient Narrations of Remarkable Incidents."

116. Apollo: Cic. *Div.* 1.37; D.S. 22.9; *SIG* 398; Pomp. Trog. 24.8; Paus. 1.4.4 and 10.23.4–6; and cf. Call. *H.* 4.171–184; Demeter and Persephone: Plut. *Tim.* 8.

117. St. Elmo's fire: *HH* 27; Alc. fr. 34; Isyllus's *Paean to Apollo and Asclepius = IG* IV² 128; and see Furley and Bremer 2001: 1.227–239, 2.180–192. Demeter: Rehm and Harder 1958: no. 496. See also Henrichs 2010; Bravo 2003; Graf 2003; Versnel 1987.

118. Nelson 2001. The specific reference is to page viii, but the topic is one of the foci of the book as a whole.

119. D.L. 59.

120. *HHDem.* 243–249, 305–313.

121. *IG* XI.4 1299; see also Engelmann 1975.

122. Ov. *Met.* 2.484–488, 3.200–201; Miller's translations, slightly altered.

123. *Il.* 24.617; A. *Pr.* 673–674; E. fr. 930 Nauck.

124. A. *Pr.* 673–674.

125. E. *Hipp.* 732.

126. E. *IT* 1089–1092.

127. E.g., Callisto at Ov. *Met.* 2.485; Actaeon at Ov. *Met.* 3.203.

128. Ov. *Met.* 15.158. At 167, he calls it the *spiritus* instead; at 172 and 175, he again uses *anima*.

129. Bremmer 1983: 24–53.

130. Johnston 1999.

131. Io and Odysseus's men are rare exceptions, as is, in later times, the hero of Lucian's *Ass* and Apuleius's *Golden Ass*. Tiresias has a similar experience, given that he is turned from a man into a woman and then back again in some versions of his story: Hes. fr. 275 MW and see Gantz 1993: 529–530.

132. Mestra's full story is at Ov. *Met.* 8.738–878. Mestra as lover of Poseidon: Hes. fr. 43a MW; as shape-shifter: Palaeph. 23, Lyc. 1391–1396; see also Gantz 1993: 68–69. Periclymenus: Hes. frs. 33a and 35 MW; see also Gantz 1993: 184–185.

133. Hdt. 4.105; Pl. *R.* 565d; Paus. 8.38.7; Plin. *NH* 8.81. Discussion at Buxton 1987 and Burkert 1983: 83–10.

134. *HHAp.* 400–450.

135. Kemmerer 2011: 43, citing Erdoes and Ortiz 1984: 392.

136. Kemmerer 2011: 43, citing Brown 1979: 22.

137. Valladolis and Apfell-Marglin 2001: 639–670; cf. Kemmerer 2011: 43–44.

138. I thank my former student Karen Ravelli for discussing this idea with me.

139. Ov. *Met.* 2.485–494.

140. *Atrahasis* Tablet III; *Epic of Gilgamesh* Tablet XI; Gen. 6–9. The Hindu myth of the Flood, the hero of which is Manu, is from the *Matsya Purana* 1.11–34, 2.1–19 (well narrated in translation by Doniger 2004: 181–185).

141. For a complete account, we must go to Apollod. 1.7.2, but it is clear that the basic story was around already in the Archaic period. We get fragments of it from Hellanicus (*FGrH* 4F117a) and Pindar (*O.* 9.44–53). Andron fr. 8 and Epicharmus fr. 113 each explicitly mention the *larnax*. Later, Ov. *Met.* 1.319 calls the craft a *parva ratis*, "tiny boat." See also Mark Smith 2014; Fowler 2013: 113–121; and Bremmer 2008.

142. Ov. *Met.* 1.416–421.

143. Hes. *Th.* 535–564.

144. For complete citations and discussion of the ancient sources for the Buphonia and its myth, see Burkert 1983: 136–143 (although his tendency to export conclusions about the Buphonia to the rest of Greek sacrifice are overdone). The myth seems to be at least as old as the late fifth century.

145. Clem. Al. *Protr.* 2.17; schol. Lucian 275–276 (Rabe).

146. See Pirenne-Delforge 1994: 388–393.

147. From the *Shatapatha Brahmana*, as cited in O'Flaherty 1988: 84.

148. Telephus: Apollod. 2.7.4; S. fr. 89; Ael. *VH* 12.42; Hyg. *Fab.* 252. Peleus and Neleus: schol. *Il.* 10.334; Eust. ad *Od.* 11.253, p. 1681; Ael. *VH* 12.42. Atalanta: Apollod. 3.9.2 and Ael. *VH* 13.1. Paris: Ael. *VH* 12.42.

149. Cf., too, the story of the Iranian hero Zal as told in the *Shahnameh*. Zal is abandoned at birth and raised to adulthood by a bird. When he is a young man, they part, but the bird later saves the life of Zal's wife, Rudaba, when she is giving birth to the hero Rustam.

150. E.g., Pi. *O.* 6.44–47; Anticlides *FGrH* 140F17, POxy 56.3830.

151. Apollod. 3.3.1–2.

152. In Vergil's fourth *Eclogue*, we come close—but the paradise is a paradise by virtue of the lions *staying away* from the flocks and the serpents *dying*.

7 HEROES

1. Ovid, in his *Metamorphoses*—and in many cases, probably, Ovid's Hellenistic sources—showed a greater interest in ordinary people than did poets who narrated myths during the Archaic and Classical periods. For example, Baucis and Philemon, who are a poor, elderly Phrygian couple, become the stars of one of Ovid's myths (*Met.* 8.620–724) and his Arachne is set apart from other women only by her extraordinary skill at weaving (*Met.* 6.5–145). Ascabulus, who is turned into a gecko by Demeter, begins as an ordinary boy, remarkable only for his bad manners (*Met.* 5.446, cf. Ant. Lib. 24, which follows Nic. *Ther.* 484).

2. Ganymede: the earliest story makes it a whirlwind that carries the boy away (*HHAphr.* 202–217); the eagle first appears in the fourth-century-BCE poet Leochares, as cited by Pliny *HN* 34.79, after which it becomes a common

element in the story: Gantz 1993: 559–560. Prometheus: Hes. *Th.* 523–525. Argus: *Od.* 17.290–327. Arion: Hdt. 1.23–24.

3. At least parts of the story are found already in Hes. *Th.* 280–281 and fr. 135 MW of his *Catalogue*. Full discussions at Fowler 2013: 248–259 and Gantz 1993: 399–311.

4. Thymoetes: Hellanic. *FGrH* 4F*38; Diod. Ath. *FGrH* 372F28; Paus. 2.18.9; Demon *FGrH* 327F1; Nic. Dam. *FGrH* 90F48. See also Kearns 1989: 170.

5. Paus. 3.12.5.

6. Thoricus: Hsch. s.v.; Lupu 2005: 115–149 (number 1 = *SEG* xxxiii 147); Kearns 1989: 169.

7. Sphinx: first attested in Corinna fr. 672 and A. *Th.* 773 but alluded to, perhaps, at Hes. *Th.* 326–327. Further at Gantz 1993: 490–506.

8. Hes. fr. 10a.20–24 MW; E. *Ion*; Hdt. 8.44. Further at Gantz 1993: 244–245 and Kearns 1989: 108–110, 174–175.

9. Menelaus's afterlife: *Od.* 4.561–569. Generally on Menelaus: Gantz 1993: 564–547, 572–664.

10. I give a list of these oracles at the end of Johnston 2005.

11. During the Hellenistic period, however, the designation and status of "hero" began to be applied to some amongst the recently dead—particularly rulers and other prominent people. See most recently Jones 2010.

12. Farnell 1921: 23–30.

13. D. 60.31; Apollod. 1.8.3; Paus. 1.5.2, 2.4.3; D.S. 4.37; cf. Kearns 1989: 80–91, 149.

14. Hdt. 6.52, 7.204, 8.131.

15. On this, see Lyons 1997; Larson 1995; Dowden 1989.

16. I do not include the Homeric *Hymns* in my category of epics. Although they share meter and diction with epic poems, their function as hymns was clear already in antiquity. Discussion of the problems—but ultimate necessity—of distinguishing hymns from epics in Clay 1989: 3–16.

17. *Geryoneis* = frs. S7–87 as in David Campbell's Loeb edition, which uses the order also found in the *S.L.G. Oresteia* = frs. 210–219 of the Loeb. Stesichorus apparently had some interest in the early days of the gods as well; he described Typhon as the son of Hera, who bore him to spite Zeus (fr. 239). On his invention of the hymn: Clem. Al. *Strom.* 1.16.78.5 (ii Stählin).

18. Perseus: fr. 543 *PMG*; Jason: frs. 544–548 *PMG*; Theseus: fr. 550 *PMG*.

19. Helen and Menelaus: Bacch. 15, Heracles: 16, Theseus: 17 and 18, Io: 19, Idas: 20, Cassandra: 23, Meleager: 25, Pasiphae: 26, Achilles: 27, Orpheus: 28.

20. Pi. dithyrambs 1 and 4 (Perseus), 2 (Heracles) = frs. 70a–d.

21. Myrtis: fr. 716 *PMG*; Corinna: fr. 671 *PMG*.

22. There were some other comedies that starred Dionysus, the god of theater, as well: Dover 1997: 39.

23. The titles of lost tragedies suggest a few more that may have focused on gods: from Aeschylus, the *Prometheus Unbound*, the *Nurses of Dionysus*, the *Daughters of Phorcys*, and the *Daughters of Helios*; and from Sophocles, the *Inachus* and the *Muses*.

24. Heracles and the ghost of Meleager: 5, the daughters of Proetus: 11, the Trojan War: 13, Croesus's story: 3, the Telchines and their daughters: 1.

25. Castor and Polydeuces: frs. 509 and 510; Heracles: 509.

26. The others are Pi. *P.* 2 (Ixion's pursuit of Hera and Zeus's punishment of him), *P.* 3 (the conception and birth of Asclepius, in which Apollo plays a large role), *P.* 5 (Apollo as founder of Cyrene, as healer and as prophet), *P.* 7 (Apollo's foundation of Delphi), *P.* 12 (Athena's invention of the *aulos*) and *I.* 8 (Zeus's seduction of Aegina and Zeus and Poseidon's quarrel over Thetis).

27. *P. O.* 7.35–38 and fr. 34 SM; earlier vases seem to refer to Hephaestus's role as well: Gantz 1993: 51–52, 78. In a few cases, these stories come down to us *only* through those glancing treatments: without Pindar, we would know nothing of how and why Helios received the island of Rhodes as his special realm (*P. O.* 7.54–76), for example.

28. In these Homeric *Hymns*, indeed, the gods themselves are often portrayed much as heroes would be: we hear of them battling a giant serpent, stealing cattle and, in the case of female divinities, disguising themselves to serve as the nursemaid or lover of heroic humans. It is possible that, in the Homeric *Hymns'* role as *prooimia* for the performance of episodes taken from epics, they not only borrowed meter and diction from epics but also leaned towards selecting stories of the gods that were typologically similar to those found in epics.

29. Alc. fr. 307. See also Men. Rh. (iii.340), who mentions "genealogical" hymns by Alcaeus and other poets, describing the birth of various gods.

30. E.g., Pl. *R.* 2.381d1–e6, *Lg.* 10.887c5–e1.

31. For instance, Timotheus (an Eleusinian exegete) narrated a cult myth for the mysteries of the Mother: Paus. 7.17.10–12 and Arn. 5.5–7 with comments at Burkert 1987: 73; the Parian Chronicle (=*FGrH* 239) included a history of divine and human deeds stretching from the early days of the gods down to 299 BCE, including, for instance, entry no. 3, which notes the dispute between Poseidon and Ares that led to the foundation of the court at the Areopagus, and entry no. 12, Demeter's invention of seed corn. See also Jacoby's introductory comments to the fragments of the local historian Philochorus of Athens (*FGrH* 328)=IIIB vol. 1. 226; Jacoby argues that Philochorus treated the myths of the gods systematically.

32. This is implied by a number of ancient sources that claim that the women explain their actions at the Thesmophoria with reference to the story (e.g., D.S. 5.4.7 and Apollod. I.5.1) and by Call. *Hymn* 6.1–6 (his hymn to Demeter), where women on their way to the Thesmophoria begin to tell the story of Demeter and Persephone and then switch to the story of Demeter and Erysichthon, lest the first story sadden Demeter.

33. *Il.* 6.130–141, 24.602–609; A. *Ag.* 160–176; E. *Hel.* 1301–1366 and *Ion* 985–988.

34. E.g., Darshan 2013a, which includes a sketch of recent controversy over the topic at 517–518, and cf. Darshan 2013b; Schüle 2009. Bruce Louden (2011: 10–15) describes the relationship between Greek myths and the Old Testament as "dialogic," emphasizing that influence went both ways. Brian Doak (2012) argues that a group of figures in the Old Testament who are associated with giants share features both with the giants of Greek myth and with Greek heroes, and that both the Israelite and Greek traditions draw on a "pan-Mediterranean style of religious thought regarding heroic warriors and

their fate and meaning after death," which he suggests was anchored in Canaan (esp. 195–199).

35. *Enuma Elish* = Dalley 1989: 228–277; *Anzu* = Dalley 1989: 203–227.

36. *Lugul-e* and the *Angim: ETCSL* at http://etcsl.orinst.ox.ac.uk/cgi-bin /etcsl.cgi?text=t.1.6.2# and http://etcsl.orinst.ox.ac.uk/cgi-bin/etcsl.cgi?text=t.1 .6.1#.

37. *Theogony of Dunnu* = Dalley 1989: 278–281.

38. *Descent of Ishtar (Inanna)* = Dalley 1989: 154–162 and http://etcsl.orinst .ox.ac.uk/section1/tr141.htm.

39. *Inanna and Enki* = Farber 1997.

40. *Enki and Ninhursag* = *ETCSL:* http://etcsl.orinst.ox.ac.uk/cgi-bin/etcsl .cgi?text=t.1.1.1#.

41. *Enki and Ninmah* = Klein 1997.

42. *Nergal and Ereshkigal* = Dalley 1989: 163–181.

43. *Erra and Ishum* = Dalley 1989: 282–316.

44. *Kumarbi Cycle* = *CTH* 344; *The Disappearance of Telipinu* = *CTH* 324; *Story of Illuyanka* = *CTH* 321; *Song of Hedammu* = *CTH* 428; *Telipinu and the Daughter of the Sea God* = *CTH* 322; *Inara* = *CTH* 366; *Kamrusepa* = *CTH* 457.1; *The Disappearance of Hannahanna* = *CTH* 334.

45. *Epic of Gilgamesh* Tablet I, i and ii.

46. *Lugalbanda in the Wilderness* and *The Return of Lugalbanda* = Vanstiphout 2003: 97–166. The two other poems, *Enmerkar and Ensuhgirana* and *Enmerkar and the Lord of Aratta,* are at Vanstiphout 2003: 23–96. See also the relevant *ETCSL* translations: http://etcsl.orinst.ox.ac.uk/cgi-bin/etcsl.cgi?text=t.1.8.2.1# (and t.1.8.2.2#, t.1.8.2.3#, t.1.8.2.4#).

47. Dalley 1989: 1–38.

48. Dalley 1989: 189–202.

49. Dalley 1989: 154–162; and *ETCSL:* http://etcsl.orinst.ox.ac.uk/section1 /tr141.htm.

50. "The Birth Legend of Sargon": Westenholz 1997: 39–49, esp. 41 and cf. 35.

51. "The Sargon Legend," segment B: *ETCSL:* http://etcsl.orinst.ox.ac.uk /section2/tr214.htm.

52. The *Res Gestae Sargonis:* Westenholz 1997: 57–139; with *The Chronicle of Early Kings,* Tablet A, lines 20–23, as at Glassner and Foster 2004: 270–271.

53. "Erra and Naram-Sin": Westenholz 1997: 189–201; "The Curse of Agade": *ETCSL:* http://etcsl.orinst.ox.ac.uk/cgi-bin/etcsl.cgi?text=t.2.1.5#.

54. "The Kirta Epic" and "The Aqhatu Legend": Pardee 1997. Mark S. Smith (2014: 154) has suggested that it was in the interest of the Ugaritic monarchy to recall important kings and warriors of the past, to whom they paid cult under the collective name *rephaim* (more on this shortly), but in terms of full-blown storytelling, we have only the tales of the warriors Danel and Aquat and of King Keret.

55. *CTH* 7.1, 360, 363, 361. All four stories are found in Hoffner 1990: 62–68.

56. *CTH* 789; López-Ruiz 2018: sec. 4.2.

57. *CTH* 321; Hoffner 1990: 11–12.

58. Brian Doak (2012: 187) has conjectured that there was once a larger corpus of Ugaritic heroic epic, which does not survive, describing the exploits of the *rp'um* (=*rephaim*, warrior ancestors from the distant past).

59. "The Tale of Sinuhe" and "The Tale of the Shipwrecked Sailor" can be found at Parkinson 1997: 21–53 and 89–101. See also Pinch 2002: 86.

60. Birth of triplets: "The Tale of King Cheops' Court": Parkinson 1997: 102–127. "The Tale of the Herdsman": Parkinson 1997: 287–288. See also Pinch 2002: 16–17.

61. "The Tale of Two Brothers" can be found in Maspero and El-Shamy 2004: 1–16. "Inpu" is a variant of "Anubis" and Bata was the city god of Saka; he was sometimes understood as a manifestation of Seth.

62. Pinch 2002: 43–44.

63. I am not counting the Egyptian "Tale of Sinuhe," "Tale of the Ship-wrecked Sailor," or "Tale of the Two Brothers," for the reasons given earlier, or the tale of Setna because of its late date and likely indebtedness to Greek myths. I have otherwise erred on the side of generosity in what I am counting as a hero myth from the Near East. For example, I count all four stories about the conflicts between the kings of Uruk and Arata, although only the two about Lugalbanda include significant aspects of the marvelous. To reflect the popularity of stories about Gilgamesh, and the varying ways in which they circulated, I have counted the *Epic of Gilgamesh* as one story and two Sumerian stories that independently circulated about Gilgamesh (*The Envoys of Akka* and *The Great Bull Is Lying Down*) as two more (thus, I count "Gilgamesh" as three). Similarly, I count each story about Sargon and Naram-Sin separately.

64. My arguments here about the relative abundance of hero myths in Greece and the relative paucity of them in cultures of the ancient Near East is not meant to refute the convincing arguments that many scholars have made for the influence of Near Eastern narratives upon the Homeric epics or other early Greek myths. See, for example (to take only three notable recent works), Louden 2011, 2006; López-Ruiz 2010. Louden's emphasis on the dialogic nature of interaction between Greek myths and Near Eastern myths is especially important to remember; influence traveled both ways (Louden 2011: 10–15). The decades-long dedication to this topic of Walter Burkert and M. L. West was extraordinarily important and a list of their relevant publications would be too long to include here; I will mention only West 1999 and Burkert 1992.

65. Gunnel Ekroth (2015) provides an excellent overview and up-to-date bibliography for this large topic. Ekroth (2002) and many of her other articles are also foundational resources.

66. Doak (2012: 164) notes a recently discovered eighth-century stele from Sam'al (part of the Hittite empire) with an Aramaic inscription that implies the notions that "the dead live on in specific locales (i.e., at the monument), periodic feasting at the tomb and the designation of monuments only for certain, important individuals."

67. Mark Smith (2014) discusses this group particularly in his fifth and twelfth chapters; see 145 for a summary description of them. The word *rephaim* enters the Hebrew Bible as a term for "giant," i.e., threatening outsider, as discussed in M. Smith 2014: 314–232 and Doak 2012.

68. Cf. Antonnacio 1994: 409–410.

69. See, for example, Assmann 2009.

70. Cf. Doak 2012: 198.

71. I thank Irad Malkin for this suggestion.

72. Dalley 1989: 51 = tablet I, ii. I am not counting the three Egyptian kings who were sons of Ra in the story mentioned earlier because the formal attribution of a king's paternity to Ra was a standard practice in Egypt.

73. *Volsungsaga*, chap. 1. Other sources, such as Snorri Sturluson's *Edda*, made Odin the father of descendants who became the first kings of Scandinavian countries. Some of these figures were originally thought of as gods themselves, but Snorri, good Christian that he was, euhemerized them: for example, Yngvi (= Frey), from whom the kings of Sweden are descended; Veggdegg, who ruled over East Saxony; Beldegg (= Balder), who ruled over Westphalia; Skjöldr, from whom the kings of Denmark descend. Other figures, such as Frodi, a descendant of Skjöldr, are more clearly mortal kings who in many cases have at least a foot in historical reality. Some of their stories include extraordinary elements—for instance, the fifth book of the *Gesta Danorum* tells us that a wicked woman turned herself into a sea cow and gored King Frodi to death. The Danes concealed his death by embalming his corpse and carrying it around in a cart for three years.

74. *Mahabharata* I (*Adi Parva*), part 6 (*Adivansavatarana Parva*). But Hinduism primarily works to create an ontological category that falls between gods and humans in a different way, positing that each of the gods has numerous avatars, or incarnations, some of which are human. Thus Rama, a prince who is the protagonist of the *Ramayana*, is an avatar of Vishnu, for instance, and his friend Hanuman is an avatar of Shiva. Even if we decide to count such human avatars amongst the heroes, there are more narratives about the Hindu gods and their affairs than about the heroes. The two closest things that India has to heroic epic—the *Mahabharata* and the *Ramayana*—weigh in at a combined 140,000 verses or so, but the eighteen major *Puranas* and eighteen minor *Puranas*, which take myths about the creation of the cosmos and the affairs of the gods as their main foci, come in at about 400,000. And, as in Greek narratives, tales about the gods are also embedded in stories that are mainly about heroes, most notably the *Mahabharata*.

75. For a more complete list, see later in this chapter.

76. *Epic of Gilgamesh*, Tablets III–VI.

77. Calvert Watkins (1995: 297–518) gives a detailed analysis of Indo-European poetic formulae for slaying dragons, with many examples of dragon slayers along the way. Almost all of them who are not Greek are divine rather than human. On Thraetoana, see 313–320.

78. *Shahnama* 1.5.1.

79. *Ramayana*, Book 6 (the *Yuddha Kanda*), chap. 108.

80. Gregory 1902: 9–10, 69–70, 75–81.

81. *Beowulf*, lines 766–823, 1492–1650, 2712–3182.

82. E.g., *Volsungsaga*, chap. 18.

83. Cat: This story is told in the document now called the *Prose Merlin*; an easily accessible text is at the University of Rochester's database *The Camelot*

Project: http://d.lib.rochester.edu/teams/text/conlee-prose-merlin-defeat-of-lucius-and-arthur-and-the-devil-cat. Boar: for an overview of the several boars against whom Arthur and his knights fight, with links to texts, consult the Rochester database at http://d.lib.rochester.edu/camelot/theme/boar. Further Arthurian foes, with links to texts, can be found in this database as well.

84. *Epic of Gilgamesh,* Tablets X–XII.

85. Christ's harrowing of Hell is first attested in the *Gospel of Nicodemus,* from the fourth century CE. Other late antique journeys to Hell include the *Apocalypse of Peter* (perhaps second century CE) and *Apocalypse of Paul* (perhaps third century CE). See Frankfurter 2000; Himmelfarb 1983.

86. *Kalevala,* Song 15.

87. Leucothea's rescue of Odysseus at *Od.* 5.333–375 is a rare exception. Although one might emphasize the fact that at the time that she rescues him, she is no longer human but rather a god (-thea), Homer stresses the fact that she used to be Ino, the daughter of Cadmus, which would have inevitably evoked the tragic tale of her life and its violent end. Historians and cult documents such as the Asclepian *iamata* sometimes tersely describe a hero's intervention in human life after he has risen to superhuman status, but full-blown narratives that were developed with the intention of entertaining an audience focus closely on the hero's mortal life—and on his very mortal death.

88. In using "series" and "serial," I am adopting the system used by Mittell (2015) and most other scholars who work on contemporary media.

89. Pi. *P.* 10.31–48.

90. E.g., the ghost of Polydorus at the beginning of E. *Hec.,* Athena at the end of E. *IT* and Heracles at the end of S. *Ph.*

91. *Il.* 6.130–141, 145–211; *Il.* 9.527–605.

92. Ancient narrators occasionally chose to weave stories that were complete in and of themselves into a longer, known timeline. For example, when Heracles enters the action of Euripides's *Alcestis,* the chorus asks him what he's doing in the city of Pherae. He explains that he is just stopping by on his way to Thrace, where he must capture the mares of Diomedes (thus completing Labor eight in his series of twelve). If, as some scholars suspect, it was Euripides who invented the idea of Heracles wrestling with Death to save Alcestis, then Heracles's reference to the mares anchors this new episode within his established story.

93. E.g., in Homeric *Hymns* 3 (Apollo), 4 (Hermes), 19 (Pan), 28 (Athena).

94. E. *Hipp.* 10–59, 1416–1422. It is not clear whether Aphrodite's involvement in the death of Hippolytus was an innovation of Sophocles's or not; Artemis's involvement certainly seems to be his invention: Gantz 1993: 287–288. See also Reed 1996, 1995.

95. E.g., *Il.* 5.330–352, 392–404, 439–442, 846–863.

96. Gantz 1993: charts 12, 17.

97. *HHAp.* 186–206.

98. Nothing underscores the nature of Holmes as a character in a series better than the fact that Doyle was compelled by fans to resurrect his hero.

99. As told, e.g., at S. *Tr.* 555–581, 1141–1172.

100. As told, e.g., at S. *OT* 717–833, 998–1085, 1110–1176.

101. Paus. 8.34.

102. Eco 1985, 1972. Eco himself did not admire the use of iteration very much; he thought it was a cheaply easy way of hooking audience members.

103. *Il.* 14.153–377.

104. *HHHerm.* 190–210.

105. Pi. *P.* 9.30–50.

106. *Od.* 9.318–330, 5.234–262, 23.187–204.

107. Cleaning manure from Augeas's stables implied at Pi. *O.* 10.28 (where the word for Heracles's labor is *latrion*, which denotes particularly menial work) and is illustrated on one of the metopes from the fifth-century Temple of Zeus at Olympia: see metope 12 in Figure 7.4. Scholiasts on the *Iliad* tell us that the tale of Heracles cleaning the stables was more fully narrated by Callimachus in his *Aitia* (schol. *Il.* A 2.629, 11.700); the use of the diverted rivers, for which Heracles had to dig ditches, is fully described at D.S. 4.13.3 and Apollod. 2.5.5.

108. Digging ditch to launch the *Argo*: A.R. 1.367–393; carrying the *Argo* across the Libyan desert: first at Pi. *P.* 4.25–27.

109. Cadmus plowing a field and sowing dragon's teeth: as early as Pherecyd. *FGrH* 3F22. The same fragment tells us that half of these dragon's teeth went to Aeetes in Colchis, where Jason later plowed the ground with fire-breathing bulls (Pherecyd. *FGrH* 3F30, 31, 112; Pi. *P.* 4.233–238) and planted the teeth (Eumelus fr. 21 West). Discussion at Fowler 2013: 225–226, 360.

110. Odysseus plowing the seashore: Hyg. *Fab.* 95 and Apollod. *Epit.* 3.7.

111. See, for example, Figure 7.5, from an Athenian cup dating to about 480 BCE, which shows a tortoise that ate human flesh as being no larger than a normal tortoise; at the right edge of the image, we see the hindquarters of the Crommyonian Sow, which similarly look to be normal in size. Another portion of this vase shows the Marathonian Bull, which is of normal size as well.

112. Fowler 2013: 250–251.

113. *Il.* 19.418–424; *Od.* 5.204–224, 11.488–503.

114. E. *Alc.* 77–212.

115. E. *Med.* 1–88.

116. A. *Ag.* 1–20.

117. E. *Ion* 102–184.

118. S. *Phil.* 254–316.

119. E. *HF* 1–86.

120. S. *Tr.* 28–35.

121. S. *Aj.* 492–525.

122. Bacch. 5, 13, 17, 18.

123. Pi. *P.* 4.232–238, 250; Eumelus fr. 21 West.

124. Pi. *P.* 4.235–236.

125. The dream: Pi. *O.* 13.63–82; the deeds: 97–100.

126. Pi. *P.* 10.46–48.

127. Perseus: Pi. *P.* 10.49–50. Bellerophon: Pi. *O.* 13.83–84. The two translations are by William H. Race. Emphasis added.

128. Bacch. 17.117–118 (trans. David A. Campbell).

129. Dalley 1989: 237–255, Tablets I–IV.

130. *CTH* 321 = Hoffner 1990: 10–13.

131. *Song of Hedammu* = *CTH* 428; Hoffner 1990: 48–51.

132. *Song of Ullikummi* = *CTH* 345; Hoffner 1990: 52–57.

133. See Assmann 1995: 49–57.

134. Ps. 74; Is. 27.1.

135. Ritner 1997: 32; *Enuma Elish*, Tablets IV and V; Dalley 1989: 254–257.

136. Apophis, Illuyanka, Hedammu, Leviathan.

137. Watkins (1995) has demonstrated the similar popularity of the god-fighting-dragon topos in Indo-European poetry.

138. Ophion: Pherecydes of Syros *FGrH*, 7B4; cf. A.R. 1.503–506. Discussion at Gantz 1993: 739–741.

139. Argus: Hes. fr. 126 MW.

140. *Od.* 10.118.

141. Further discussion of the appearances of the *gigantes* at Gantz 1993: 445–454; the mention that the *neoteroi* (poets of the fourth century and later) showed them with snaky legs comes from schol. *Od.* 7.59.

142. E. *Ion* 989–996.

143. Hes. frs. 43a65 MW and 195.28–29 MW and cf. *Th.* 954; E. *HF* 177–180; discussion at Gantz 1993: 445–454.

144. Cf. Burkert (1979: 8–9), who suggests that Hupasiya's story seems to have started out as a kind of novella of its own, which eventually became loosely attached to the story of Illuyanka.

145. Hes. *Th.* 270–336.

146. Perseus: Hes. *Th.* 280–281; Heracles: Hes. *Th.* 289–294, 313–318, 332; Bellerophon: Hes. *Th.* 325.

147. Bellerophon: *Il.* 6.183; Heracles: *Il.* 8.362–369, *Od.* 11.620–626. Zeus and Typhon: *Il.* 2.780.

148. For a résumé and analysis of the controversy about whether our present *Hymn to Apollo* is actually two hymns joined together and on the date of the *Hymn* or at least the "Pythian" portion of it, see the comments in West 2003: 9–12. West tentatively suggests that the *Hymn* was performed at the first Pythian games in 586 BCE.

149. *HHAp.* 305–354. Stesichorus also made Hera the mother of Typhon, but we know nothing else about his treatment: fr. 239, taken from the *Et. Gen.* see *Typhōea*.

150. Most scholars consider this excursus to be an interpolation into an earlier version of the *Hymn*, but that doesn't let us off the hook as far as understanding the role it played in the *Hymn* as we now have it. Part of the reason that it exists, I suggest, is that it neatly balances out another story about Hera that was told earlier in the *Hymn*, concerning the birth of Apollo. In that story, Hera persecutes Apollo's pregnant mother, preventing her from giving birth for a long time (*HHAp.* 88–125).

151. Andrew Miller (1986: 88) suggests that this is because any description of the fight between Zeus and Typhon would inevitably put Apollo's defeat of Python in the shade. But whatever the motivation, the elision of the battle has the effect of muting Typhon's power.

152. *HHAp.* 306, 352. Like most recent editors of the *Hymns*, for line 352, I accept the reading of all the manuscripts except M, which substitutes *theoisin* for *brotoisin*, making Typhon an affliction to the *gods* instead of *mortals*.

153. Python as an affliction for mortals: *HHAp.* 302–304, 355–356, 364–366.

154. Sphinx: Hes. *Th.* 326, A. *Th.* 541, cf. 777; Chimaera: *Il.* 16.328; Scylla: *Od.* 12.125; Boar: Hecat. *FGrH* 1F6; later descriptions: e.g., Apollod. 2.77–80 and Hyg. *Fab.* 30 (the Hydra); D.S. 4.42.1 (the Trojan sea monster); Cerynitian Deer: E. *HF* 375.

155. *HHAp.* 207–215. Moreover, as an audience familiar with these stories would have known, in each case, Apollo lost the woman to that mortal man.

156. *HHAp.* 216–228 (translation by Martin West).

157. For the myth and our textual evidence, Gantz 1993: 467–473. Gantz concludes that the tale was known by the seventh century, if not earlier, although the full story does not appear until Pherecydes in the fifth century (*FGrH* 3F22). Further discussion at Fowler 2013: 351–352.

158. Jessica Lamont has suggested to me that the allusion to the foundation of Thebes additionally was meant as a "tacit nod" to the Ismenion in that city, a nearby oracle with which the Delphic Oracle probably understood itself to be in competition. By describing Thebes as not yet even founded, the *Hymn* thus emphatically asserts the priority of Delphi. I find this suggestion persuasive.

159. *HHAp.* 294–300 and cf. 254–255, where Apollo lays the foundations of a temple near Telphousa, which he subsequently abandons when Telphousa deceptively sends him away. Later, Apollo returns to bury Telphousa under stones and then builds himself an altar on top: *HHAp.* 382–385. He is not a god who worries about getting his hands dirty.

160. Earlier temples of Apollo: Pi. *Pa.* 8; and see discussion at Furley and Bremer 2001: 93–95. Of the earlier (female) owners, we first hear from A. *Eum.* 1–8 and Pi. fr. 55. See the important discussion at Sourvinou-Inwood 1987. See also Graf 2008: 30; Furley and Bremer 2001: 95–97; Clay 1989: 61–62.

161. Graeae: Hes. *Th.* 270–273; Ceto: Hes. *Th.* 238; Echidna: Hes. *Th.* 297–298. Medusa is called fair-cheeked at Pi. *P.* 12.16.

162. Chrysaor and Callirhoe: Hes. *Th.* 288; Echidna and Typhon: Hes. *Th.* 306–307; Ceto and Phorcys: Hes. *Th.* 333; Medusa and Poseidon: Hes. *Th.* 277–278.

163. According to Ovid, Medusa was originally beautiful and was punished by Athena for her alleged enjoyment of Poseidon's rape; Athena turned her into the monster we now know her as (*Met.* 4.790–803; cf. Apollod. 2.4.3).

164. *Od.* 11.625–626. The metopes on the Temple of Zeus at Olympia, built during the second quarter of the fifth century BCE, show Athena supporting Heracles in his labors (Figure 7.4). Athena is frequently shown in other artistic representations of Heracles's labors, too (e.g., Figure 7.3); these are discussed in Gantz's treatment of each labor (1993: 381–416). Helios: Pisander fr. 5 *PEG* and discussion at Fowler 2013: 294–295, 298 and Gantz 1993: 404–405.

165. Hes. *Shield* 216–237; Pherecyd. *FGrH* 3F11; Pi. *P.* 10.45; for artistic representations of the gods helping Perseus and other textual references, see Gantz 1993: 304–307.

166. Pi. *O.* 13.65–87; Hes. fr. 43a MW.

167. Bacch. 17; and see Gantz 1993: 263–264 on artistic representations of the undersea scene. The tradition concerning the crown is confused but may

be as early as Epimenid. fr. 3; see Gantz 1993: 264–266 for discussion and 266–268 on artistic representations of Athena, and see also Fowler 2013: 472–473.

168. *Od.* 12.72.

169. Aphrodite: Pi. *P.* 4.216–217; Athena: our earliest attestation is Apollonius of Rhodes (e.g., 1.526–527 etc.).

170. Vat. 16545 = Beazley Archive 205162; see also Gantz 1993: 359–360.

171. Plowing: note 109 above; ditch digging: notes 107 and 108 above.

172. Castanets: Apollod. 2.5.6. On sandals and bridle, see notes 165 and 166 above.

173. D.S. 20.41, 3–5; Duris *FGrH* 76F17; Phot. and *Suid.*, s.v. "Lamia," and schol. Ar. *Pax* 758; cf. Apostol. ap. Leutsch *Paroim. Gr.* 2.497–498 and schol. Aristid. p. 41 Dindorf. For further discussion, see Johnston 1999: 161–183.

174. Stesich. fr. 220.

175. Getty Hexameters fr. i, Side B, lines 45 and 46: "O son of Zeus, and whoever . . . Forceful . . . with your bow . . . and of the Hydra, many-."

176. *Il.* 9.543–605. Meleager was the half brother of Tydeus, Diomedes's father.

177. *Il.* 6.197–211. Glaucus himself describes the lineage; he is the grandson of Bellerophon.

178. *Od.* 11.602–626.

179. *Cypr.* fr. 1 West with schol. A *Il.* 1.5–6; cf. Hes. *Op.* 156–165, which says that Zeus decided to destroy the race of heroes (*hemitheoi*) with two wars—the one at Thebes and the one at Troy. Further at Gantz 1993: 567–569.

180. Hes. fr. 204 MW lines 98–101.

181. Burkert 1992: 100–113. *Erra and Ishum* = Dalley 1989: 288. See also the recent analysis of George 2013.

182. For these stories, see Dalley 1989: 1–38.

183. *Il.* 1.1–7 and *Od.* 1.1–9, both translations by Stanley Lombardo, slightly altered.

184. Burkert 1992: 92.

References

Ackerman, Robert. 1991. "The Cambridge Group: Origins and Composition." In *The Cambridge Ritualists Reconsidered: Proceedings of the First Oldfather Conference, Held on the Campus of the University of Illinois at Urbana-Champaign, April 27–30, 1989*, edited by William M. Calder III, 1–19. Atlanta.

Agnarsson Lab. 2017. "Social Spiders." http://theridiidae.com/Social-Spiders.html.

Allen, T. W. 1908. "The Epic Cycle." *CQ* 2: 64–74, 81–88.

Antonaccio, Carla. 1994. *An Archaeology of Ancestors: Tomb Cult and Hero Cult in Ancient Greece*. Lanham, MD.

Arngrim, Alison. 2010. *Confessions of a Prairie Bitch: How I Survived Nellie Oleson and Learned to Love Being Hated*. New York.

Assmann, Jan. 2009. "Der Mythos des Göttkonigs im Alten Ägypten." In *Menschen-Heros-Gott: Weltenwürfe und Lebensmodelle im Mythos der Vormoderne*, edited by Christine Schmitz and Anja Bettenworth, 11–26. Stuttgart.

———. 1995. *Egyptian Solar Religion in the New Kingdom: Re, Amun and the Crisis of Polytheism*. London. German original published in 1983.

Athanassaki, Lucia. 2004. "Deixis, Performance and Poetics in Pindar's *First Olympian Ode*." *Arethusa* 37, no. 2: 317–341.

Atwood, Margaret. 2005. *The Penelopiad*. Edinburgh.

Barber, Elizabeth J. Wayland. 1992. "The Peplos of Athens." In Neils 1992a, 103–118.

Barkun, Michael. 2013 *A Culture of Conspiracy: Apocalyptic Visions in Contemporary America*. 2nd ed. Berkeley, CA.

Barrett, J. L. 1996. "Anthropomorphism, Intentional Agents and Conceptualizing God." PhD diss., Cornell University.

Barthes, Roland. 1972. *Mythologies*. London. (= Barthes, Roland. 1957. *Mythologies*. Paris.)

Bascom, William. 1965. "The Forms of Folklore: Prose Narratives." *Journal of American Folklore* 78: 3–20.

Beard, Mary. 2002. *The Invention of Jane Harrison*. Cambridge, MA.

Beidelman, T. O., and Robert A. Segal. 2005. "W. Robertson Smith." In *Encyclopedia of Religion*, edited by Lindsay Jones, 8451–8453. Detroit.

Bennett, Gillian. 1999. *Alas Poor Ghost: Traditions of Belief in Story and Discourse*. 2nd expanded ed. Logan, UT.

Bernabé, Alberto. 2013. "The *Ephesia Grammata*: Genesis of a Magical Formula." In Faraone and Obbink 2013, 71–96.

Bettini, Maurizio. 2013. *Women and Weasels: Mythologies of Birth in Ancient Greece and Rome.* Chicago. (=Bettini, Maurizio. 1998. *Nascere: Storie di donne, donnole, madri ed eroi.* Torino.)

Bevis, I. C. 1988. *Insects and Other Invertebrates in Classical Antiquity.* Exeter, UK.

Black, Jeremy, Graham Cunningham, Jarle Ebeling, Esther Flückiger-Hawker, Eleanor Robson, Jon Taylor, and Gábor Zólyomi, eds. 1998–2006. *The Electronic Text Corpus of Sumerian Literature.* Oxford. http://etcsl.orinst.ox.ac.uk/.

Boas, Franz. 1917. *Folk-Tales of Salishan and Sahaptin Tribes.* Lancaster, PA.

Bordwell, David. 1985. *Narration in the Fiction Film.* Madison, WI.

Borgeaud, Philippe. 2004. *Exercises de mythologie.* Geneva.

Borghouts, J. F., trans. 1978. *Ancient Egyptian Magical Texts.* Leiden.

Boyd, Brian. 2009. *On the Origin of Stories.* Cambridge, MA.

Boyer, Pascal. 2001. *Religion Explained: The Evolutionary Origins of Religious Thought.* New York.

Brakke, David. 1999. "Parables and Plain Speech in the Fourth Gospel and the Apocryphon of James." *Journal of Early Christian Studies* 7: 187–218.

Braswell, Bruce. 1988. *A Commentary on the Fourth Pythian Ode of Pindar.* Berlin.

Bravo, Jorge. 2003. "Heroic Epiphanies: Narrative, Visual, and Cultic Contexts." *Illinois Classical Studies* 29: 63–84.

Brelich, Angelo. 1969. *Paides e Parthenoi.* Rome.

Bremmer, Jan. 2008. "Near Eastern and Native Traditions in Apollodorus' Account of the Flood." In *Greek Religion and Culture, the Bible and the Ancient Near East,* edited by Jan Bremmer, 101–116. Leiden.

———. 2005. "Myth and Ritual in Ancient Greece: Observations on a Difficult Relationship." In *Griechische Mythologie und frühes Christentum,* edited by Raban von Haehling, 21–43. Darmstadt.

———. 1983. *The Early Greek Concept of the Soul.* Princeton, NJ.

———. 1978. "Heroes, Rituals and the Trojan War." *Studi storico-religiosi* 2: 5–38.

Brisson, Luc. 1982. *Platon, les mots et les mythes.* Paris.

Brown, Dee. 1979. *Folktales of the Native American: Retold for Our Times.* New York.

Burkert, Walter. 1992. *The Orientalizing Revolution.* Cambridge, MA. (=Burkert, Walter. 1984. *Die orientalisierende Epoche in der griechischen Religion und Literatur.* Heidelberg.)

———. 1987. *Ancient Mystery Cults.* Cambridge, MA.

———. 1983. *Homo Necans: The Anthropology of Ancient Greek Sacrificial Ritual and Myth.* Berkeley, CA. (=Burkert, Walter. 1972. *Homo Necans.* Berlin.)

———. 1979. *Structure and History in Greek Mythology and Ritual.* Berkeley, CA.

———. (1966) 2001. "Kekropidensage und Arrhephoria: Vom Initiationsritus zum Panathenäenfest." Translated by Peter Bing as "The Legend of Kekrops' Daughters and the Arrhephoria: From Initiation Ritual to Panathenaic Festival," in Burkert, *Savage Energies: Lessons of Myth and Ritual in Ancient Greece,* translated by Peter Bing, 37–63. Chicago. Citations refer to the 2001 translation.

Burnett, Anne Pippin. 1994. "Hekabe the Dog." *Arethusa* 27: 151–164.

Buxton, Richard G. A. 2009. *Forms of Astonishment: Greek Myths of Metamorphosis.* Oxford.

———, ed. 1999a. *From Myth to Reason? Studies in the Development of Greek Thought.* Oxford.

———. 1999b. Introduction to Buxton 1999a, 1–24.

———. 1994. *Imaginary Greece.* Cambridge.

———. 1987. "Wolves and Werewolves in Greek Thought." In *Interpretations of Greek Mythology,* edited by Jan Bremmer, 60–79. London.

Calame, Claude. 2015. *Qu'est-ce que la mythologie grecque?* Paris.

———. 2011a. "Myth and Performance on the Athenian Stage: Praxithea, Erechtheus, Their Daughters and the Etiology of Autochthony." *Classical Philology* 106, no. 1: 1–19.

———. 2011b. *Mythe et histoire dans l'Antiquité grecque: La création symbolique d'une colonie.* 2nd ed. Paris.

———. 2009. *Greek Mythology: Poetics, Pragmatics and Fiction.* Cambridge. (= Calame, Claude. 2000. *Poétiques des Mythes dans la Grèce Antique.* Paris.)

———. 2006. "La fabrication historiographique d'un passé héroïque et classique: *Archaia* et *palaia* chez Hérodote." *Ktèma* 31: 39–49.

———. 2004. "Deictic Ambiguity and Auto-Referentiality: Some Examples from Greek Poetics." *Arethusa* 37, no. 2: 415–443.

———. 2003. *Myth and History in Ancient Greece: The Symbolic Creation of a Colony.* Princeton, NJ. (= Calame, Claude. 1996. *Mythe et histoire dans l'Antiquité grecque: La création symbolique d'une colonie.* Lausanne.)

———. 1995. "Mythe et mythologie: Taxonomies indigenes et categories occidentales." In *Presenze classiche nelle letterature: Occidental il mito dall'età antica all'età moderna e contemporanea,* edited by Margherita Rossi Cittidini, 57–76. Perugia, Italy.

———. 1991. "Mythe et rite en Grèce: Des categories indigenes?" *Kernos* 4: 179–204.

———. 1990. *Thésée et l'imaginaire athénien.* Lausanne.

Caliva, Kathryn. 2016. "Speech Acts and Embedded Narrative Structure in the Getty Hexameters." *Archiv für Religiongeschichte* 17: 139–164.

Caughey, John L. 1984. *Imaginary Social Worlds.* Lincoln, NE.

Chatman, Seymour. 1978. *Story and Discourse: Narrative Structure in Fiction and Film.* Ithaca, NY.

Cialdini, Robert. 2016. *Pre-suasion: A Revolutionary Way to Influence and Persuade.* New York.

Clark, Lynn Schofield. 2003. *From Angels to Aliens: Teenagers, the Media, and the Supernatural.* New York.

Clarke, Katherine. 2017. "Walking through History: Unlocking the Mythical Past." In Hawes 2017a, 14–31.

Clay, Jenny Strauss. 1989. *The Politics of Olympus.* Princeton, NJ.

Cohn, Dorrit. 1978. *Transparent Minds: Narrative Modes for Presenting Consciousness in Fiction.* Princeton, NJ.

Coleridge, Samuel Taylor. 1817. *Biographia Literaria.* London.

Collins, V. H., ed. 1924. *Ghosts and Marvels.* Oxford.

Csapo, Eric. 2005. *Theories of Mythology.* Malden, MA.

Cuneo, Michael W. 2001. *American Exorcism: Expelling Demons in the Land of Plenty.* New York.

Dalley, Stephanie, ed., trans., and comm. 1989. *Myths from Mesopotamia: Creation, the Flood, Gilgamesh, and Others.* Oxford.

Darshan, Guy. 2013a. "The Biblical Account of the Post-Diluvian Generation (Gen. 9:20–10:32) in the Light of Greek Genealogical Literature." *Vetus Testamentum* 63: 515–535.

———. 2013b. "The Reinterment of Saul and Jonathan's Bones (II Sam. 21,12–14) in Light of Ancient Greek Hero-Cult Stories." *Zeitschrift für die alttestamentliche Wissenschaft* 125, no. 4: 2–6.

Davies, Owen. 2004. "French Charmers and Their Healing Charms." In Roper 2004a, 91–112.

Denson, Shane. 2011. "Marvel Comics' Frankenstein: A Case Study in the Media of Serial Figures." *Amerikastudien* 56, no. 4: 531–553.

Detienne, Marcel. 1986. *The Creation of Mythology.* Chicago. (=Detienne, Marcel. 1981. *L'invention de la mythologie.* Paris.)

———. 1979. *Dionysus Slain.* Baltimore. (=Detienne, Marcel. 1977. *Dionysus mis à mort.* Paris.)

———. 1977. *The Gardens of Adonis.* Princeton, NJ. (=Detienne, Marcel. 1972. *Les jardins d'Adonis.* Paris.)

Dimmick, Jeremy. 2002. "Ovid in the Middle Ages: Authority and Poetry." In *The Cambridge Companion to Ovid,* edited by Philip Hardie, 264–287. Cambridge.

Doak, Brian R. 2012. *The Last of the Rephaim: Conquest and Cataclysm in the Heroic Ages of Ancient Israel.* Boston.

Doniger, Wendy, ed., trans., and comm. 2004. *Hindu Myths: A Sourcebook.* New York.

———. 1996. "Minimyths and Maximyths and Political Points of View." In *Myths and Method,* edited by Laurie Patton and Wendy Doniger, 109–127. Charlottesville, VA.

Dorsey, George A. 1904. *Traditions of the Skidi Pawnee.* London.

Doty, William G. (1986) 2000. *Mythography: The Study of Myths and Rituals.* Tuscaloosa, AL. Citations refer to the 2000 edition.

Dover, Kenneth, ed., trans., and comm. 1997. *Aristophanes. Frogs.* Oxford.

Dowden, Ken. 1989. *Death and the Maiden: Girls' Initiation Rites in Greek Mythology.* London.

Doyle, Arthur Conan. 2017. *Gothic Tales.* Edited by Darryl Jones. Oxford.

Dundes, Alan. 1964. *The Morphology of North American Indian Folktales.* Helsinki.

Eco, Umberto. 2009. "On the Ontology of Fictional Characters: A Semiotic Approach." *Sign Systems Studies* 37, nos. 1–2: 82–97.

———. 1990. *Travels in Hyperreality.* San Diego.

———. 1985. "Innovation and Repetition: Between Modern and Post-Modern Aesthetics." *Daedalus* 114, no. 4: 161–184.

———. 1972. "The Myth of Superman." *Diacritics* 2, no. 1: 14–22.

Edelstein, Emma J., and Ludwig Edelstein. 1945. *Asclepius: Collection and Interpretation of the Testimonies.* Baltimore.

Eder, Jens, Fotis Jannidis, and Ralf Schneider. 2010. "Characters in Fictional Worlds: An Introduction." In *Revisionen 3: Characters in Fictional Worlds: Understanding Imaginary Beings in Literature, Film and Other Media*, edited by Jens Eder, Fotis Jannidis, and Ralf Schneider, 3–64. Berlin.

Ekroth, Gunnel. 2015. "Heroes: Living or Dead." In *The Oxford Handbook of Ancient Greek Religion*, edited by Esther Eidinow and Julia Kindt, 383–396. Oxford.

———. 2002. *The Sacrificial Rituals of Greek Hero-Cults in the Archaic to the Hellenistic Periods.* Liège.

Eliade, Mircea. 1963. *Myth and Reality.* San Francisco.

———. 1959. *The Sacred and the Profane: The Nature of Religion.* San Diego.

———. 1954. *The Myth of the Eternal Return.* New York. French original published in 1949.

Engelmann, Helmut. 1975. *The Delian Aretalogy of Sarapis.* Leiden.

Erdoes, Richard, and Alfonso Ortiz, eds. 1984. *American Indian Myths and Legends.* New York.

Faraone, Christopher. 2003. "Playing the Bear and the Fawn for Artemis: Female Initiation or Substitute Sacrifice?" In *Initiation in Ancient Greek Rituals and Narratives: New Critical Perspectives*, edited by David Dodd and Christopher Faraone, 43–67. London.

———. 2001. "Handbook or Anthology? The Collection of Greek and Egyptian Incantations in Late Hellenistic Egypt." *Archiv für Religionsgeschichte* 2: 195–214.

———. 1995. "The Mystodokos and the Dark-Eyed Maidens: Multicultural Influences on a Late-Hellenistic Incantation." In *Ancient Magic and Ritual Power*, edited by Marvin Meyer and Paul Mirecki, 297–333. Leiden.

Faraone, Christopher, and Dirk Obbink, eds. 2013. *The Getty Hexameters: Poetry, Magic, and Mystery in Ancient Selinous.* Oxford.

Farber, Gertrude, ed., trans., and comm. 1997. "Inna and Enki." In Hallo and Lawson 1997, 522–526.

Farnell, L. R. 1921. *Greek Hero Cults and Ideas of Immortality.* Oxford.

Faulkner, William. 1946. *The Portable Faulkner.* Edited by Malcolm Cowley. New York.

Fearn, D. 2007. *Bacchylides: Politics, Performance, Poetic Tradition.* Oxford.

Feeney, Denis. 1991. *The Gods in Epic: Poets and Critics of the Classical Tradition.* Oxford.

Felson, Nancy. 2004a. Introduction to *Arethusa* 37, no. 2: 253–266.

———. 2004b. "The Poetic Effects of Deixis in Pindar's *Ninth Pythian* Ode." *Arethusa* 37, no. 2: 365–389.

———. 1999. "Vicarious Transport: Fictive Deixis in Pindar's *Pythian* Four." *Harvard Studies in Classical Philology* 99: 1–31.

Fontenrose, Joseph. 1966. *The Ritual Theory of Myth.* Berkeley, CA.

———. 1961. "Some Observations on Hyman's Review of *Python*." *Carleton Miscellany* 2: 122–125.

———. 1959. *Python: A Study of Delphic Myth and its Origins.* Berkeley, CA.

Forbes-Irving, P. M. C. 1990. *Metamorphosis in Greek Myths.* Oxford.

Forster, E. M. (1927) 1985. *Aspects of the Novel*. San Diego. Citations refer to the 1985 edition.

Fowler, Robert. 2016. "History." In *The Oxford Handbook of Ancient Greek Religion*, edited by Esther Eidinow and Julia Kindt, 195–209. Oxford.

———. 2013. *Early Greek Mythography*. Vol. 2, *Commentary*. Oxford.

———. 2011. "*Mythos* and *Logos*." *Journal of Hellenic Studies* 131: 45–66.

———. 2000. *Early Greek Mythography*. Vol. 1, *Text and Introduction*. Oxford.

Franco, Cristiana. 2014. *Shameless: The Canine and the Feminine in Ancient Greece*. Berkeley, CA.

Frankfurter, David T. M. 2009. "The Laments of Horus in Coptic: Myth, Folklore, and Syncretism in Late Antique Egypt." In *Antike Mythen: Medien, Transformationen und Konstruktionen*, edited by Ueli Dill and Christine Walde, 229–247. Berlin.

———. 2001. "Narrating Power: The Theory and Practice of the Magical *Historiola* in Ritual Spells." In *Ancient Magic and Ritual Power*, edited by Marvin Meyer and Paul Mirecki, 457–476. Leiden.

———. 2000. "Early Christian Apocalypticism: Literature and Social World." In *The Encyclopedia of Apocalypticism*, vol. 1, *The Origins of Apocalypticism in Judaism and Christianity*, edited by John J. Collins, 415–456. New York.

Franklin, Ruth. 2016. *Shirley Jackson: A Rather Haunted Life*. New York.

Frazer, James G., ed., trans., and comm. 1921. *Apollodorus: The Library; With an English Translation*. Cambridge, MA.

———. 1901. "On Some Ceremonies of the Central Australian Tribes." Paper read before the Australian Association for the Advancement of Science. Melbourne.

———. (1890) 1911–1915. *The Golden Bough: A Study in Magic and Religion*. 3rd expanded ed. London.

Furley, William, and Jan Maarten Bremer, eds., trans., and comms. 2001. *Greek Hymns: Selected Cult Songs from the Archaic to the Hellenistic Period*. 2 vols. Tübingen.

Furth, Robin. 2012. *Stephen King's "The Dark Tower": The Complete Concordance, Revised and Updated*. New York.

Gaiman, Neil. (1996) 2001. *Neverwhere*. New York. Citations refer to the 2001 edition.

Gantz, Timothy. 1993. *Early Greek Myth: A Guide to Literary and Artistic Sources*. Baltimore.

Gardner, Jared. 2012. *Projections: Comics and the History of Twenty-First Century-Storytelling*. Stanford, CA.

Geertz, Armin, and Jeppe Sinding Jensen, eds. 2011. *Religious Narrative, Cognition and Culture: Image and Word in the Mind of Narrative*. Sheffield, UK.

George, A. R. 2013. "The Poem of Erra and Ishum: A Babylonian Poet's View of War." In *Warfare and Poetry in the Middle East*, edited by Hugh Kennedy, 39–71. London.

Gernet, Louis. 1981. *The Anthropology of Ancient Greece*. Baltimore. (= Gernet, Louis. 1968. *Anthropologie de la Grèce antique*. Paris.)

Gibson, J. J. 1979. *The Ecological Approach to Visual Perception*. Boston.

Giles, David. 2010. "Parasocial Relationships." In *Revisionen 3: Characters in Fictional Worlds: Understanding Imaginary Beings in Literature, Film, and Other Media*, edited by Jens Eder, Fotis Jannidis, and Ralf Schneider, 442–448. Berlin.

———. 2002. "Parasocial Interaction: A Review of the Literature and a Model for Future Research." *Media Psychology* 4, no. 3: 279–305.

Glassner, Jean-Jacques. 2004. *Mesopotamian Chronicles*. Edited and translated by Benjamin R. Foster. Atlanta. French original published in 1993.

Goff, Barbara. 2004. *Citizen Bacchae*. Berkeley, CA.

Gow, A. S. F., and A. F. Scholfield, eds. and trans. 1953. *Nicander: The Poems and Poetical Fragments*. Cambridge.

Graf, Fritz. 2008. *Apollo*. London.

———. 2004. "Trick or Treat? On Collective Epiphanies in Antiquity." *Illinois Classical Studies* 29: 111–130.

———. 2003. "Initiation: A Concept with a Troubled History." In *Initiation in Ancient Greek Rituals and Narratives*, edited by David B. Dodd and Christopher A. Faraone, 3–24. London.

———. 2000. "The Locrian Maidens." In *Oxford Readings in Greek Religion*, edited by R. G. A. Buxton, 250–270. Oxford. German original published in 1978.

———. 1997. "Medea, the Enchantress from Afar: Remarks on a Well-Known Myth." In *Medea: Essays on Medea in Myth, Literature, Philosophy and Art*, edited by James J. Clauss and Sarah Iles Johnston, 21–43. Princeton, NJ.

———. 1995. "Il mito tra menzogna e 'Urwahrheit.'" In *Presenze classiche nelle letterature occidental: Il mito dall'età antica all'età moderna e contemporanea*, edited by Margherita Rossi Cittidini, 43–56. Perugia.

———. 1993. *Greek Mythology: An Introduction*. Baltimore. (= Graf, Fritz. 1987. *Greichische Mythologie*. Zurich.)

———. 1987. "Orpheus, a Poet among Men." In *Interpretations of Greek Mythology*, edited by Jan Bremmer, 80–106. London.

———. 1980. "Milch, Hönig und Wein: Zum Verstandnis der Libation im griechischen Ritual." In *Perennitas: Studi in onore di Angelo Brelich*, 209–221. Rome.

Graf, Fritz, and Sarah Iles Johnston. 2013. *Ritual Texts for the Afterlife: Orpheus and the Bacchic Gold Tablets*. 2nd ed. London.

Green, Peter. 1997. Introduction to *The Argonautica*, by Apollonios Rhodios, 1–41. Berkeley, CA.

Gregory, Lady Augusta. 1902. *Cuchulain of Muirthemne*. London.

Greimas, A. J. 1983. *Structural Semantics: An Attempt at a Method*. Lincoln, NE. (= Greimas, A. J. 1966. *Sémantique structural; recherché de method*. Paris.)

Gunn, Anna. 2013. "I Have a Character Issue." *New York Times*, August 23.

Hall, Edith, ed., trans., and comm. 1996. Aeschylus. *Persians*. Warminster, UK.

Halliday W. R. 1913. *Greek Divination: A Study of Its Methods and Principles*. London.

Hallo, William K., and Lawson Younger Jr., eds. 1997. *The Context of Scripture*. Vol 1. Leiden.

Hamilton, Christine R. E. 2017. "The Function of the *Deus ex Machina* in Euripidean Drama." PhD diss., The Ohio State University.

Hänninen, Kiri. 2017. "Narrating Supernatural Experiences." In *Narrating Religion*, edited by Sarah Iles Johnston, 125–140. New York.

Hansen, William. 2017. *The Book of Greek and Roman Folktales, Legends and Myths*. Princeton, NJ.

Harari, Yuval. 2015. *Sapiens: A Brief History of Humankind*. New York.

Harrelson, Walter. 2005. "Myth and Ritual School." In *Encyclopedia of Religion*, edited by Lindsay Jones, 6380–6383. Detroit.

Harrison, Jane Ellen. (1928) 1976. *The Myths of Greece and Rome*. London. Citations refer to the 1976 edition.

———. (1925) 1965. "Reminiscences of a Student Life." *Arion* 4, no. 2: 312–346. Citations refer to the 1965 edition.

———. (1924) 1963. *Mythology*. New York. Citations refer to the 1963 edition.

———. 1921. *Epilegomena to the Study of Greek Religion*. Cambridge.

———. (1912) 1927. *Themis: A Study of the Social Origins of Greek Religion*. 2nd ed. Cambridge. Citations refer to the 1927 edition.

———. (1903) 1922. *Prolegomena to the Study of Greek Religion*. 3rd ed. Cambridge. Citations refer to the 1922 edition.

Harrison, Jane Ellen, and Margaret de G. Verrall. 1890. *Mythology and Monuments of Ancient Athens*. London.

Harvey, Graham. 2000. "Fantasy in the Study of Religions: Paganism as Observed and Enhanced by Terry Pratchett." *Discus: The Journal of the British Association for the Study of Religions* 6. http://www.basr.ac.uk/diskus/diskus1-6/harvey-6.txt.

Hawes, Greta, ed. 2017a. *Myths on the Map: The Storied Landscapes of Ancient Greece*. Oxford.

———. 2017b. "Of Myths and Maps." In Hawes 2017a, 1–13.

Heim, Ricardus. 1892–1893. "Incantamenta magica Graeca Latina." In *Jahrbücher für classische Philologie*, suppl. 19. Leipzig.

Henrichs, Albert. 2010. "What Is a Greek God?" In *The Gods of Ancient Greece: Identities and Transformations*, edited by Jan Bremmer and Andrew Erskine, 19–39. Edinburgh.

———. 1994. "Anonymity and Polarity: Unknown Gods and Nameless Altars at the Areopagus." *Illinois Classical Studies* 19: 27–58.

———. 1991. "Namenlosigkeit und Euphemismus: Zur Ambivalenz der chthonischen Mächte im attischen Drama." In *Fragmenta Dramatica: Beiträge zur Interpretation der griechischen Tragikerfragmenta und ihrer Wirkungsgeschichte*, edited by Heinz Hofmann and Annette Harder, 161–201. Göttingen.

Herman, David, Manfred Jahn, and Marie-Laure Ryan, eds. 2005. *The Routledge Encyclopedia of Narrative Theory*. London.

HEXRPG, LLC. 2017. "Hogwarts Extreme: The Interactive Hogwarts Experience." http://hexrpg.com.

Higbie, Carolyn. 2003. *The Lindian Chronicle and the Greek Creation of Their Past*. Oxford.

Himmelfarb, Martha. 1983. *Tours of Hell: An Apocalyptic Form in Jewish and Christian Literature*. Philadelphia.

Hoffner, Harry A., Jr. 1990. *Hittite Myths.* Atlanta.

Holmes, Sally. 2014. "Angelina Jolie Says Violent *Maleficent* Scene Was a Metaphor for Rape." *Elle*, June 12. http://www.elle.com/culture/celebrities/news/a15426/angelina-jolie-maleficent-scene-metaphor-for-rape.

Hooke, S. H., ed. 1958. *Myth, Ritual and Kingship.* Oxford.

———. 1938. *The Origins of Early Semitic Ritual.* London.

———, ed. 1935. *Labyrinth: Further Studies in the Relation between Myth and Ritual.* London.

———, ed. 1933a. *Myth and Ritual.* London.

———. 1933b. "The Myth and Ritual Pattern of the Ancient East." In Hooke 1933a, 1–14.

Hoorn, Johan F., and Elly A. Konijn. 2003. "Perceiving and Experiencing Fictional Characters: An Integrative Account." *Japanese Psychological Research* 45, no. 4: 250–268.

Hopman, Marianne Govers. 2012. *Scylla: Myth, Metaphor, Paradox.* Cambridge.

Horton, Donald, and Richard R. Wohl. 1956. "Mass Communication and Parasocial Interaction: Observations on Intimacy at a Distance." *Psychiatry* 19, no. 3: 185–206.

Hufford, David. 1982. "Traditions of Disbelief." *New York Folklore* 8: 47–55.

Hutton, Ronald. 1999. *The Triumph of the Moon: A History of Modern Pagan Witchcraft.* Oxford.

Hyman, Stanley. 1960. Review of *Python* by Joseph Fontenrose. *Carleton Miscellany* 1: 124–127.

———. 1955. "The Ritual View of Myth and the Mythic." *Journal of American Folklore* 68: 462–472.

James, M. R. 2011. *Collected Ghost Stories.* Edited by Darryl Jones. Oxford.

Janko, Richard. 2013. "The Hexametric Incantations against Witchcraft in the Getty Museum: From Archetype to Exemplar." In Faraone and Obbink 2013, 29–53.

Jeanmaire, Henri. 1939. *Couroi et Courètes: Essai sur l'éducation spartiate et sur les rites d'adolescence dans l'antiquité hellénique.* Lille.

Jenkins, Henry. 2006. *Convergence Culture: Where Old and New Media Collide.* New York.

———. 1992. *Textual Poachers: Television Fans and Participatory Culture.* London.

Johnston, Sarah Iles. 2014. "Goddesses with Torches in the Getty Hexameters and Alcman fr. 94." *Zeitschrift für Papyrologie und Epigraphik* 191: 32–35.

———. 2013. "Myth in the Getty Hexameters." In Faraone and Obbink 2013, 121–156.

———. 2009. "A New Web for Arachne." In *Antike Mythen: Medien, Transformationen und Konstruktionen*, edited by Ueli Dill and Christine Walde, 1–11. Berlin.

———. 2008. *Ancient Greek Divination.* Malden, MA.

———. 2006. "Antigone's *Other* Choice." *Helios* 33S: 179–186.

———. 2005. "Delphi and the Dead." In *Mantike: Studies in Ancient Divination*, edited by Sarah Iles Johnston and Peter T. Struck, 283–306. Leiden.

———. 2002. "Myth, Cult and Poet: The Homeric *Hymn to Hermes* and Its Performative Context." *Classical Philology* 97: 109–232.

———. 1999. *Restless Dead: Encounters between the Living and the Dead in Ancient Greece.* Berkeley, CA.

———. 1995. "The Song of the *Iynx:* Magic and Rhetoric in *Pythian* 4." *Transactions of the American Philological Association* 125: 177–206.

———. 1994. "Penelope and the Erinyes: *Odyssey* 20.61–82." *Helios* 21: 137–159.

Jolly, Alison. 1999. *Lucy's Legacy: Sex and Intelligence in Human Evolution.* Cambridge, MA.

Jones, Christopher. 2010. *New Heroes in Antiquity: From Achilles to Antinoos.* Cambridge, MA.

Judd, Walter S., and Graham A. Judd. 2017. *Flora of Middle-Earth: Plants of J. R. R. Tolkien's Legendarium.* Oxford.

Käppel, Lutz. 1992. *Paian: Studien zur Geschichte einer Gattung.* Vol. 37 of *Untersuchungen zur antiken Literarur und Geschichte.* Berlin.

Katz, Joshua, and Katharina Volk. 2000. "'Mere Bellies'? A New Look at *Theogony* 26–28." *Journal of Hellenic Studies* 120: 122–131.

Kearns, Emily. 1989. *The Heroes of Attica.* London.

Kemmerer, Lisa. 2011. *Animals and World Religions.* Oxford.

Kirk, Geoffrey S. 1974. *The Nature of Greek Myths.* Harmondsworth, UK.

———. 1970. *Myth: Its Meaning and Functions in Ancient and Other Cultures.* Berkeley, CA.

Klein, Jacob, ed., trans., and comm. 1997. "Enki and Ninmah." In Hallo and Lawson 1997, 516–518.

Klimkiewicz, JoAnn. 2013. "Desperately Seeking Christy." *New York Times Magazine,* November 22.

Kluckhohn, Clyde. 1942. "Myths and Rituals: A General Theory." *Harvard Theological Review* 35: 45–79.

Kripal, Jeffrey. 2011. *Mutants and Mystics: Science Fiction, Superhero Comics, and the Paranormal.* Chicago.

Krummen, Eveline. 1990. *Pursos humnon: Festliche und mytbisch-rituelle Tradition als Voraussetzungen einer Pindarinterpretation (Isthmie 4, Pythie 5, Olympie 1 und 3).* Berlin.

Kyle, Donald G. 1992. "The Panatheniac Games: Sacred and Civil Athletics." In Neils 1992a, 77–102.

Labov, William, and Joshua Waletsky. 1967. "Oral Versions of Personal Experience." *Journal of Narrative and Life History* 7: 3–38.

Lakoff, George, and Mark Johnson. 1980. *Metaphors We Live By.* Chicago.

Landy, Joshua. 2012. *How to Do Things with Fictions.* Oxford.

Lang, Andrew. 1894. *Cock Lane and Common-Sense.* London.

Lardinois, André. 1992. "Greek Myths for Athenian Rituals: Religion and Politics in Aeschylus' *Eumenides* and Sophocles' *Oedipus Coloneus*." *Greek, Roman, and Byzantine Studies* 33, no. 4: 313–327.

Laroche, Emmanuel. 1971. *Catalogue des textes hittites.* Paris. This resource is now available online and is regularly updated: http://www.hethport.uni -wuerzburg.de/CTH/.

Larson, Jennifer. 1995. *Greek Heroine Cults.* Madison, WI.

Leach, Edmund. 1954. *The Political Systems of Highland Burma.* London.

Leitao, David D. 1995. "The Perils of Leukippos: Initiatory Transvestism and Male Gender Ideology in the Ekdusia of Phaistos." *Classical Antiquity* 14: 130–163.

Lepore, Jill. 2011. "Dickens in Eden: Summer Vacation with 'Great Expectations.'" *New Yorker*, August 29.

Levaniouk, Olga. 2008. "Penelope and the Pandareids." *Phoenix* 62: 5–38.

Lévi-Strauss, Claude. 1958. *Anthropologie structural*. Paris. (= Lévi-Strauss, Claude. 1972. *Structural Anthropology*. London.)

Lewis, C. S. 1966. *Of Other Worlds: Essays and Stories*. New York.

———. 1947. "On Stories." In *Essays Presented to Charles Williams*, edited by C. S. Lewis, 90–105. Oxford. Reprinted in Lewis 1966, 3–21.

LiDonnici, Lynn R. 1995. *The Epidaurian Miracle Inscriptions*. Atlanta.

Lincoln, Bruce. 1999. *Theorizing Myth: Narrative, Ideology and Scholarship*. Chicago.

Lloyd-Jones, Hugh. 1985. "Pindar and the Afterlife." In *Pindare: Entretiens sur l'antiquité classique*, vol. 31, 245–284. Geneva.

López-Ruiz, Carolina. 2018. *Gods, Heroes and Monsters: A Sourcebook of Greek, Roman and Near Eastern Myths in Translation*. 2nd ed. New York.

———. 2010. *When the Gods Were Born: Greek Cosmogonies and the Near East*. Cambridge, MA.

Lorenz, Konrad. 1963. *Das sogenannte Böse: Zur Naturgeschichte der Aggression*. Vienna: G. Borotha-Schoeler. Translated as *On Aggresion* by Marjorie Kerr Wilson. New York: Harcourt, Brace & World, 1966.

Louden, Bruce. 2011. *Homer's "Odyssey" and the Near East*. Cambridge.

———. 2006. *The "Iliad": Structure, Myth and Meaning*. Baltimore.

Lowe, N. J. 2007. "Gilbert Murray and Psychic Research." In *Gilbert Murray Reassessed: Hellenism, Theatre, and International Politics*, edited by Christopher Stray, 349–370. Oxford.

———. 2000. *The Classical Plot and the Invention of Western Narrative*. Cambridge.

Luhrmann, Tanya. 2013a. "Belief Is the Least Part of Faith." *New York Times*, June 30.

———. 2013b. "Conjuring Up Our Own Gods." *New York Times*, October 14.

———. 2013c. "C. S. Lewis, Evangelical Rock Star." *New York Times*, June 25.

———. 2012. *When God Talks Back: Understanding the American Evangelical Relationship with God*. New York.

Lupu, Eran. 2005. *Greek Sacred Law: A Collection of New Documents*. Leiden.

Lyons, Deborah. 1997. *Gender and Immortality: Heroines in Ancient Greek Myth and Cult*. Princeton, NJ.

Maas, Paul. 1942. "The Philinna Papyrus." *Journal of Hellenic Studies* 62: 33–38.

Maehler, Herwig. 1997. *Die Leider des Bakchylides*. Vol. 2. Leiden.

Magliocco, Sabina. 2004. *Witching Culture: Folklore and Neopaganism in America*. Philadelphia.

Martin, Richard. 2004. "Home Is the Hero: Deixis and Semantics in Pindar *Pythian* 8." *Arethusa* 37, no. 2: 343–363.

Maspero, Gaston, trans., and Hasan El-Shamy, ed. 2004. *Popular Stories of Ancient Egypt*. Oxford.

Matthey, Philippe. 2016. "Étudier les mythes en context francophone: À propos de quatre ouvrages récents." *Kernos* 29: 1–15.

Miller, Andrew. 1986. *From Delos to Delphi: A Literary Study of the Homeric Hymn to Apollo.* Leiden.

Mills, Mary. 1990. *Human Agents of Cosmic Power in Hellenistic Judaism and the Synoptic Tradition.* Sheffield, UK.

Mittell, Jason. 2015. *Complex TV: The Poetics of Contemporary Television Story-telling.* New York.

———. 2010. *Television and American Culture.* New York.

Morgan, Kathryn. 2000. *Myth and Philosophy from the Presocratics to Plato.* Cambridge.

Most, Glenn W. 1999. "From Logos to Muthos." In Buxton 1999a, 25–49.

Moyers & Company. 1999. "The Mythology of 'Star Wars' with George Lucas." June 18. http://billmoyers.com/content/mythology-of-star-wars-george-lucas/.

Murray, Gilbert. 1925. *Five Stages of Greek Religion.* Oxford.

———. 1914. *Hamlet and Orestes: A Study in Traditional Types.* Oxford.

———. (1912) 1927. "An Excursus on the Ritual Forms Preserved in Greek Tragedy." In Harrison (1912) 1927, 341–363.

Murray, Penelope. 1999. "What Is a *Muthos* for Plato?" In Buxton 1999a, 251–262.

Neils, Jennifer, ed. 1992a. *Goddess and Polis: The Panathenaic Festival in Ancient Athens.* Princeton, NJ.

———. 1992b. "The Panathenia: An Introduction." In Neils 1992a, 13–28.

Nelson, Victoria. 2001. *The Secret Life of Puppets.* Cambridge, MA.

Nesbit, Edith. 1912. *The Magic World.* Kent, UK.

Nilsson, Martin P. (1950) 1961. *Geschichte der griechischen Religion.* Vol. 2. 2nd ed. Munich.

———. (1941) 1967. *Geschichte der griechischen Religion.* Vol. 1. 3rd ed. Munich. Citations refer to the 1967 edition.

———. 1932. *The Mycenaean Origin of Greek Mythology.* Berkeley, CA.

Noel, Ruth. 1980. *The Languages of Tolkien's Middle-Earth: A Complete Guide to All Fourteen of the Languages That Tolkien Invented.* New York.

Noyes, Dorothy. 2016. *Humble Theory.* Bloomington, IN.

Nussbaum, Emily. 2012. "Tune in Next Week: The Curious Staying Power of the Cliffhanger." *New Yorker,* July 30.

O'Flaherty, Wendy Doniger. 1988. *Other People's Myths: The Cave of Echoes.* Chicago.

O'Higgins, Dolores. 1997. "Medea as Muse: Pindar's *Pythian* 4." In *Medea: Essays on Medea in Myth, Literature, Philosophy and Art,* edited by James J. Clauss and Sarah Iles Johnston, 103–126. Princeton, NJ.

O'Sullivan, Sean. 2013. "Serials and Satisfaction." *Romanticism and Victorianism on the Net* 63. http://ravonjournal.org/.

Pardee, Dennis, ed. and trans. 1997. "The Kirta Epic and the Aqhat Legend." In Hallo and Lawson 1997, 331–355.

Parker, L. P. E., ed. 2016. *Iphigenia in Tauris,* by Euripides. Oxford.

Parker, Robert. 2007. "Gilbert Murray and Greek Religion." In *Gilbert Murray Reassessed: Hellenism, Theatre, and International Politics*, edited by Christopher Stray, 81–102. Oxford.

Parkinson, Richard, ed., trans., and comm. 1997. *The Tale of Sinuhe and Other Ancient Egyptian Poems, 1940–1640 BCE*. Oxford.

Partridge, Chrisopher. 2004. *The Re-enchantment of the West*. Vol. 1. London.

Paskin, Willa. 2013. Review of the season finale of *Homeland*. *Slate*, December 15. http://www.slate.com/articles/arts/television/2013/12/homeland_recap_the_star_season_3_finale_reviewed.html.

Pavlou, Maria. 2012. "Bacchylides 17: Singing and Usurping the Paean." *Greek, Roman, and Byzantine Studies* 52: 510–539.

Peacock, Sandra J. 1991. "An Awful Warmth about Her Heart: The Personal in Jane Harrison's Ideas on Religion." In *The Cambridge Ritualists Reconsidered*, edited by William M. Calder III, 167–184. Atlanta.

Perlman, Paula J. 1995. "Invocatio and Imprecatio: The Hymn to the Greatest Kouros from Palaikastro and the Oath in Ancient Crete." *Journal of Hellenic Studies* 115: 161–167.

Phelan, James. 2017. *Somebody Telling Somebody Else: A Rhetorical Poetics of Narrative*. Columbus, OH.

Pinch, Geraldine. 2002. *Egyptian Mythology: A Guide to the Gods, Goddesses and Traditions of Ancient Egypt*. Oxford.

Piraro, Dan. 2012. "Ill-Fated Blind Date: St. Patrick and Medusa." Bizarro, March 16. http://bizarro.com/comics/march-16-2012/.

Pirenne-Delforge, Vinciane. 2008. *Retour à la source: Pausanias et la religion greque. Kernos*, suppl. 20. Liège.

———. 1994. *L'Aphrodite grecque: Contribution à l'étude de ses cultes et de sa personalité dans le panthéon archaïque et classique*. Liège.

Pirenne-Delforge, Vinciane, and Gabriella Pironti. 2016. *L'Héra de Zeus: Ennemie intime, épouse définitive*. Paris.

Platt, Verity. 2010. "Art History in the Temple." *Arethusa* 43, no. 2: 197–213.

Pócs, Eva. 2009. "Miracles and Impossibilities in Magic Folk Poetry." In Roper 2009, 27–53.

Portelli, Alessandro. 1997. "On the Lower Frequencies: Sound and Meaning in *Native Son*." In *Critical Essays on Richard Wright's "Native Son*," edited by Kenneth Kinnamon, 213–230. New York.

Propp, Vladimir. (1928) 1958. *Morphology of the Folktale*. Bloomington, IN. Citations refer to the 1958 edition.

Prstojevic, Alexandre. 2017. "Pourquoi la fiction? Entretien avec Jean-Marie Schaeffer, directeur de recherches au CNRS, auteur de *Pourquoi la fiction?* (Seuil, 1999)." *Vox-Poetica*. http://www.vox-poetica.org/entretiens/intSchaeffer.html.

Raglan, Lord. (1936) 2003. *The Hero: A Study in Tradition, Myth and Drama*. Mineola, NY. Citations refer to the 2003 edition.

Reed, Joseph D. 1996. "Antimachus on Adonis?" *Hermes* 124: 381–383.

———. 1995. "The Sexuality of Adonis." *Classical Antiquity* 14, no. 2: 317–347.

Rehm, Albert, and Richard Harder. 1958. *Didyma II: Die Inschriften*. Berlin.

Reicher, Maria. 2010. "The Ontology of Fictional Characters." In *Revisionen 3: Characters in Fictional Worlds: Understanding Imaginary Beings in Literature, Film, and Other Media*, edited by Jens Eder, Fotis Jannidis, and Ralf Schneider, 111–133. Berlin.

Rennie, Bryan S. 1996. *Reconstructing Eliade: Making Sense of Religion*. Albany, NY.

Richardson, Brian. 2010. "Transtextual Characters." In *Revisionen 3: Characters in Fictional Worlds: Understanding Imaginary Beings in Literature, Film, and Other Media*, edited by Jens Eder, Fotis Jannidis, and Ralf Schneider, 527–541. Berlin.

Ritner, Robert K. 1998. "The Wives of Horus and the Philinna Papyrus (*PGM* XX)." In *Egyptian Religion: The Last Thousand Years; Studies Dedicated to the Memory of Jan Quaegebeur*, edited by Willy Clarysse, Antoon Schoors, and Harco Willems, 1027–1041. Leuven.

———, ed. and trans. 1997. "The Apophis Battle." In Hallo and Lawson 1997, 32.

Roper, Jonathan, ed. 2009. *Charms, Charmers and Charming: International Research on Verbal Magic*. New York.

———, ed. 2004a. *Charms and Charming in Europe*. New York.

———. 2004b. Introduction to Roper 2004a, 1–6.

Rowe, Christopher. 1999. "Myth, History and Dialectic in Plato's *Republic* and *Timaeus-Critias*." In Buxton 1999a, 263–78.

Rule, Sheila. 1989. "Sherlock Holmes's Mail: Not Too Mysterious." *New York Times*, November 5. http://www.nytimes.com/1989/11/05/world/sherlock-holmes-s-mail-not-too-mysterious.html.

Rutherford, Ian. 2001. *Pindar's "Paeans": A Reading of the Fragments with a Survey of the Genre*. Oxford.

Ryan, Marie-Laure. 2012. "Narration in Various Media." In *The Living Handbook of Narratology*. Hamburg. http://wikis.sub.uni-hamburg.de/lhn/index.php/Narration_in_Various_Media.

Saler, Michael. 2012. *As If: Modern Enchantment and the Literary Prehistory of Virtual Reality*. Oxford.

Scarborough, John. 1979. "Nicander's *Toxicology* II: Spiders, Scorpions, Insects and Myriapods." *Pharmacy in History* 21, no. 1: 3–34.

Schaeffer, Jean-Marie. 2010. *Why Fiction?* Lincoln, NE. (= Schaeffer, Jean-Marie. 1999. *Pourquoi la fiction?* Paris.)

Scheid, John, and Jesper Svenbro. 1996. *The Craft of Zeus*. Cambridge, MA. (= Scheid, John, and Jesper Svenbro. 1994. *Le métier du Zeus: Mythe du tissage et du tissu dans le monde gréco-romaine*. Paris.)

Schjoedt, Uffe, Hans Stødkilde-Jørgensen, Armin W. Geertz, and Andreas Roepstorff. 2009. "Highly Religious Participants Recruit Areas of Social Cognition in Personal Prayer." *Scan* 4: 199–207.

Schmid, Hannah, and Christoph Klimmt. 2011. "A Magically Nice Guy: Parasocial Relationships with Harry Potter across Different Cultures." *International Communication Gazette* 73, no. 3: 252–269.

———. 2010. "Goodbye Harry? Audience Reactions to the Ends of Parasocial Relationships: The Case of Harry Potter." Paper presented at the annual meeting of the International Communication Association, Suntec Singapore International Convention & Exhibition Centre, Suntec City, Singapore, June 22. http://www.allacademic.com/meta/p404037_index.html.

Schüle, Andreas. 2009. "The Divine-Human Marriages (Genesis 6:1–4) and the Greek Framing of the Primeval History." *Theologische Zeitschrift* 65, no. 2: 116–128.

Scullion, Scott. 2002. "'Nothing to Do with Dionysus': Tragedy Misconceived as Ritual." *Classical Quarterly* 52, no. 1: 102–137.

———. 1999. "Tradition and Invention in Euripidean Aitiology." *Illinois Classical Studies* 24–25: 217–233.

Seaford, Richard. 2009. "Aitiologies of Cult in Euripides: A Response to Scott Scullion." In *The Play of Texts and Fragments: Essays in Honor of Martin Cropp*, edited by J. R. C. Cousland and James R. Hume, 219–234. Leiden.

———. 1988. "The Eleventh Ode of Bacchylides: Hera, Artemis and the Absence of Dionysus." *Journal of Hellenic Studies* 108: 118–136.

———. 1980. "Black Zeus in Sophocles' *Inachos*." *Classical Quarterly* 30: 23–29.

Segal, Robert. 1998a. Introduction to Segal 1998b, 1–14.

———. ed. 1998b. *The Myth and Ritual Theory: An Anthology.* Oxford.

Shapiro, Jordan. 2014. "Why Disney's 'Maleficent' Matters." *Forbes*, June 5.

Sjöblom, Thomas. 2011. "Pumping Intuitions: Religious Narratives and Emotional Communication." In Geertz and Jensen 2011, 163–175.

Smith, Mark S. 2014. *Poetic Heroes: Literary Commemorations of Warriors and Warrior Culture in the Early Biblical World.* Grand Rapids, MI.

Smith, Murray. 1995. *Engaging Characters: Fiction, Emotion, and the Cinema.* New York.

Smith, R. Scott. 2014. "Bundling Myth, Bungling Myth: The Flood Myth in Ancient and Modern Handbooks of Myth." *Archiv für Religionsgeschichte* 16: 239–258.

Smith, William Robertson. 1889. *Lectures on the Religion of the Semites.* Edinburgh.

Sourvinou-Inwood, Christiane. 1987. "Myth as History: The Previous Owners of the Delphic Oracle." In *Interpretations of Greek Mythology*, edited by Jan Bremmer, 215–241. London.

———. 1979. *Theseus as Son and Stepson: A Tentative Illustration of Greek Mythological Identity.* London.

Struck, Peter. 2004. *Birth of the Symbol.* Princeton, NJ.

Tatar, Mary, ed. 2002. *The Annotated Classic Fairy Tales.* New York.

Tolkien, J. R. R. 1947. "On Fairy-Stories." In *Essays Presented to Charles Williams*, edited by C. S. Lewis, 38–39. Oxford.

Updike, John. 1963. *The Centaur.* New York.

Valladolis, Julio, and Frederique Apffel-Marglin. 2001. "Andean Cosmovision and the Nurturing of Biodiversity." In *Indigenous Traditions and Ecology: The Interbeing of Cosmology and Community*, edited by John A. Grim, 639–670. Cambridge, MA.

Vanstiphout, Herman. 2003. *Epics of Sumerian Kings: The Matter of Aratta.* Atlanta.

Vernant, Jean-Pierre. 1974. *Mythe & société en Grèce ancienne.* Paris. (= Vernant, Jean-Pierre. 1980. *Myth and Society in Ancient Greece.* Baltimore.)

Versnel, Hendrik S. 1993. *Transition and Reversal in Myth and Ritual.* Leiden.

———. 1987. "What Did Ancient Man See When He Saw a God? Some Reflections of Greco-Roman Epiphany." In *Effigies Dei: Essays on the History of Religions,* edited by Dirk van der Plas, 42–55. Leiden.

Veyne, Paul. 1983. *Did the Greeks Believe in Their Myths? An Essay on the Constitutive Imagination.* Chicago. (= Veyne, Paul. 1979. *Les Grecs ont-ils cru à leurs mythes?* Paris.)

Vidal, Gore. 1977a. "On Rereading the Oz Books." *New York Review of Books* 24, no. 16.

———. 1977b. "The Wizard of the 'Wizard.'" *New York Review of Books* 24, no. 15.

Von Staden, Heinrich. 1993. "Spiderwoman and the Chaste Tree: The Semantics of Matter." *Configurations* 1, no. 1: 23–56.

Waller, J. D. 2015. "Echo and Historiola: Theorizing Narrative Incantation." *Archiv für Religiongeschichte* 16: 263–280.

Walsh, Richard. 2007. *The Rhetoric of Fictionality: Narrative Theory and the Idea of Fiction.* Columbus, OH.

Watkins, Calvert. 2001. *How to Kill a Dragon.* Oxford.

West, M. L., ed. and trans. 2003. *Homeric Hymns. Homeric Apocrypha. Lives of Homer.* Cambridge, MA.

———. 1999. *The East Face of Helicon: West Asiatic Elements in Greek Poetry and Myth.* Oxford.

———, ed. and comm. 1966. *Hesiod. Theogony.* Oxford.

Westenholz, Joan Goodnick, ed., trans., and comm. 1997. *Legends of the Kings of Akkade: The Texts.* Winona Lake, IN.

Weston, Jesse. (1920) 1993. *From Ritual to Romance.* Princeton, NJ. Citations refer to the 1993 edition.

Wheeler, E. L. 1982. "Hoplomachia and Greek Dances in Arms." *Greek, Roman, and Byzantine Studies* 23: 223–233.

Wolf, Mark J. P. 2012. *Building Imaginary Worlds: The Theory and History of Subcreation.* London.

Wolf, Werner. 2007. "Description as a Transmedial Mode of Representation: General Features and Possibilities of Realization in Painting, Fiction and Music." In *Description in Literature and Other Media,* edited by Werner Wolf and Walter Bernhart, 1–90. Amsterdam.

———. 2005. "Intermediality." In Herman, Jahn, and Ryan, 252–256.

Wooffitt, Robin. 1992. *Telling Tales of the Unexpected: The Organization of Factual Discourse.* Hemel Hempstead, UK.

Acknowledgments

THIS BOOK HAS benefited from the insights and critiques of my colleagues, friends, and relatives.

I am lucky enough to teach at a university where there is a large and engaging group of faculty and graduate students working on ancient Mediterranean religions and myths. They have served as test audiences for my ideas and helped me learn more about the myths of ancient cultures other than Greece. I particularly thank Michael Beshay, Michael Biggerstaff, David Brakke, Katie Caliva, Hanne Eisenfeld, Julia Nelson Hawkins, Tom Hawkins, Warren Huard, Anthony Kaldellis, Matt Maynard, Tina Sessa, Michael Swartz, Jimmy Wolfe, and Marcus Ziemann. My greatest debts, however, are owed to Carolina López-Ruiz, who for many years now has been teaching me about the intercultural transmission of myths within the ancient Mediterranean world, and Tim McNiven, who, as he has so many other times in the past, helped me better understand the artistic representations of Greek myths and their relationships to literary texts.

Other Ohio State colleagues made vital contributions to my work, as well. I am grateful to Dorry Noyes and Jim Phelan, whose research gave me useful models to think with and who talked me through some of those models' more challenging aspects. Team-teaching a seminar on narrative with Jim in Autumn 2016 was a wonderful experience. Merrill Kaplan welcomed me as an auditor into her course on Scandinavian myths, which gave me a wider comparative outlook.

I am also indebted to scholars outside of my home university. Kathryn Morgan has for almost thirty years been my ideal go-to person when I want to talk about Greek myths and many other kinds of entrancing narratives, even if we must usually do it at a distance.

A semester of fellowship at the Lichtenberg-Kolleg at the Universität Göttingen in 2012 introduced me to Regina Bendix, Jason Mittell, and Annette Zgoll, all of whom opened my eyes to new ways of approaching myths. The Lichtenberg-Kolleg also reintroduced me, happily, to Antoine Cavigneaux, who shared some ancient Near Eastern myths that were new, at least to me. Heinz-Günther Nesselrath, one of my hosts in Göttingen, helped me with some of the literary sources. I thank Jeff Kripal, Tanya Luhrmann, and Mike Murphy for conversations we've had both inside and outside of colloquia at the Center for Theory and Research at Esalen. I also thank Toni Bierl, Philippe Borgeaud, Jack Emmert, David T. M. Frankfurter, Jessica Lamont, David Leitao and John Furman, Sabina Magliocco, Elaine Pagels, Joy Reed, and Antonia Syson. I am grateful to my hosts and audiences at the University of Crete, Université de Gèneve, Columbia University, the University of California–Los Angeles, the University of Washington, the University of Minnesota, Wright State University, San Francisco State University, the University of California–San Diego, Yale University, the Midwestern Consortium on Ancient Religions, and the Universität Basel for their questions and comments following presentations in which I tried out early versions of my ideas.

The referees who read my manuscript for Harvard University Press pushed me to think differently about some issues and thereby made this book better than it would have been. Katie Caliva excellently served as research assistant throughout the final year of the book's development.

Some of what is in this book springs from discussions not with my academic colleagues, however, but with my friends and family (not that these groups are mutually exclusive, of course). It was conversations with my brothers, Bob and James Iles, my brothers-in-law Wayne Johnson and Eric Rudolph, and my son Tristan Johnston that helped me appreciate more fully the similarities between ancient myths and contemporary television shows. Kelly Allan, Alice Conklin, Barbara Haeger, and Geoffrey Parker, with whom I have watched many a movie and Netflix episode, helped me think through some of the arguments that I make in Chapters 3 and 5. My son Pelham conceptualized a way of visually presenting an idea that I introduce in Chapter 4 and created the charts that do so. My son-in-law Daniel Gloor, an arachnologist, taught me a lot about spiders, which in turn helped me understand poor Arachne a little better. My niece Rebecca Graf helped me during an early stage of Chapter 3's development. My grandchildren, to whom this book is dedicated, have been, and continue to be, audiences that compel me to think more carefully about how stories are told.

There are also those who are no longer amongst the living but whose presence I continued to feel as I finished this book—somewhat like the heroes of Chapter 7, I suppose. As I worked, I often thought of Walter Burkert and Martin West, each of whom contributed so much to the study of Greek myths within a broader Mediterranean context, and each of whom was always generous with help to a younger scholar. I was amused to realize, upon finishing my manuscript, that Walter was invoked on both the first page of the first chapter and the final page of the final chapter, bookending everything else I said.

I will never be able to sufficiently express my gratitude for the early and continuous support of my interest in myths by my late parents, Robert and Phyllis Iles. Before I could read for myself, my mother gamely met my repeated requests to read aloud Nathanial Hawthorne's version of the story of Pandora, which was included in an anthology of children's stories that we owned. As I grew older, my father steered me away from books about Greek myths that he thought dumbed them down. I longed for a brightly colored copy of *D'Aulaires' Book of Greek Myths*, but (rightly) judging it to be feeble, he instead put into my hands Padraic Colum's *The Children's Homer* and *The Golden Fleece and the Heroes Who Lived before Achilles*, with Willy Pogány's marvelous line drawings. Later, he gave me Isaac Asimov's *Words from the Myths* and, later still, W. H. D. Rouse's *Gods, Heroes and Men of Ancient Greece*. All of these would probably seem terribly out-of-date and unglamorous now, to generations lucky enough to have been reared on Usborne's eye-catching and excellently narrated series of books of Greek myths, but for me, the books my father gave me were wonderful. My parents' willingness to occasionally contradict my teachers was important as well. For career day in third grade, I did a project in which I stated that I planned to become a mythologist. The teacher told me that there were no such things as mythologists and made me do the project over (the second time, I chose "mother," which the teacher accepted). My parents, however, told me to ignore what she had said about mythologists and encouraged me to pursue both careers. (Are you reading this, Mrs. Harmon? I'm two for two.)

Finally, my husband, Fritz Graf (who is colleague, friend, and relative all rolled into one), was an indispensable sounding board during the years when this book was developing. I don't know what I would have done without him.

Earlier versions of some discussions in this book have appeared in print elsewhere. Portions of Chapters 3 and 5 were included in "Narrating Myths: Story and Belief in Ancient Greece," in *Arethusa* 48, no. 2 (2015): 173–217, © 2015 by Johns Hopkins University Press. An earlier version of Chapter 4 appeared as "The Greek Mythic Storyworld," in *Arethusa* 48, no. 3 (2015): 283–311, © 2015 by Johns Hopkins University Press. A longer version of the section on Arachne in Chapter 6 was published as "A New Web for Arachne," in *Antike Mythen: Medien, Transformationen und Konstructionen*, ed. Ueli Dil and Christine Walde (Berlin, 2009), 1–22.

Index of Names and Terms

Index Locorum

Note: Passages are indexed according to where they appear in the notes, and also, in many cases, where they appear, are discussed, or are alluded to in the text.

HEBREW BIBLE, NEW TESTAMENT, AND APOCRYPHA